NORTH CHINA VILLAGES

BOOKS BY SIDNEY D. GAMBLE

PEKING: A SOCIAL SURVEY (*New York: George H. Doran, 1921*)

HOW CHINESE FAMILIES LIVE IN PEIPING (*New York: Funk and Wagnalls, 1933*)

TING HSIEN: A NORTH CHINA RURAL COMMUNITY (*New York: Institute of Pacific Relations, 1954*)

SIDNEY D. GAMBLE

David

North China Villages

SOCIAL, POLITICAL, AND ECONOMIC

ACTIVITIES BEFORE 1933

UNIVERSITY OF CALIFORNIA PRESS

Berkeley and Los Angeles   1963

University of California Press
Berkeley and Los Angeles, California

Cambridge University Press
London, England

© 1963 by The Regents of the University of California
Library of Congress Catalog Card Number: 63–21616
Printed in the United States of America

TO

C.L.C.

A.B.H.

P.G.C.

D.B.G.

C.L.G.

E.T.H.

PREFACE

CH'ING-MIAO HUI—"Green Crop Association"—was a term that kept coming up again and again in connection with our social research work in the area around Peiping. It was recognized as a term related to the agricultural side of village life, and we became more and more intrigued with the notion of discovering just what sort of organization the association was, how it operated, and what was its function in the life of the village. The village origin and connections of one of our Chinese colleagues made it possible for him to approach the leaders of a village and from them learn how their village was managed and something of its historical development. Further, it was possible for him to see the account books of the village and learn the story of its economic life, where and how it got its money, and how it handled expenditures. That village is Village I in our detailed studies of eleven sample villages.

The wealth of social, political, and economic material available in that one village suggested that similar studies of other villages would be very rewarding. For help with such a research program we turned to one of Peiping's universities whose Department of Sociology had recently completed a study of a nearby town and was becoming interested in the problems of the countryside. We worked out with them the details of a coöperative survey of village life. The field work, which ended in 1933, was largely done by university students under the direction of a Chinese professor who held an American doctoral degree in sociology. It was agreed that the data collected by the survey was to be published in two reports under different authorship, one in Chinese, the other in English. The Chinese report and a considerable amount of unanalyzed field material were lost when the Japanese invaded Peking in 1937.

At first it was planned that the study should include only villages around Peiping, but, as the students who were natives of Shantung, Honan, and Shansi told what they knew about villages in those provinces, it became evident that a much larger area should be included. With the basic patterns established through intensive studies of sample villages, the latter part of the work became extensive in order to discover how individual villages varied from those patterns. Besides the first group of villages studied in Hopei, about a hundred villages were visited in more than thirty hsien in Shansi and a smaller number in Honan and Shantung.

The material collected soon showed that there was constant variation from village to village and often wide dissimilarities among the villages of different provinces. In fact, no two of the villages we studied were alike. They varied in the number of resident families, the amount of land they controlled, their political organization, the stage of their political development, the amount of individual family participation, the qualifications and terms of their officers, the services provided for their residents and the amounts of money collected to finance those services, the bases for their assessments, their educational activities, and their religious procedures. We are confident that the material available to us provides sufficient information to give a basic picture of social, political, and economic activities in the villages of North China before 1933.

Our report is made in three sections:

First: Chapter i is a general summary of our findings and their relationship to the political and historical events of the period.

Second: Chapters ii through vii describe and discuss various phases of village life and organization—the village itself, village associations, village leaders, village activities, and village finances reported by the villages we contacted and by various studies of special topics.

Third: Chapters viii through xviii give detailed stories of eleven sample villages.

Because much of the material is treated in more than one section, there is necessarily some repetition, but this seems to be unavoidable.

It was the term *ch'ing-miao hui* that first attracted us to our village study, so we were specially interested in gathering information on the crop-watching activities of the villages and what they did when crops were stolen. If our report seems to stress those activities, it is because we found a large amount of interesting material on them that has not been treated elsewhere. Then, too, they may have been special features of the village activities in the Peiping area where most of our survey work was done. If Shansi had been the principal center of our study, we undoubtedly would have had much more to say about the theatrical plays that were given in some villages as often as once a month.

All of our material describes what is now a bygone period in North China's history, but, as history and as a description of factors in the life of the villages during the period from the late 1800's to the early 1930's, we feel that it depicts the large amount and wide variety of democratic activity that went on at the village level. We hope that it will help in the understanding of the China of those days and of the life of some of China's "farmers of forty centuries."

It also is hoped that this study will provide information useful to those who are interested in the problems of village improvement, especially the details of how the villages were organized and how the villagers coöperated in their traditional ways to promote culture, education, self-protection, etc. The story of how they financed their activities is probably unique, for that side of village life has been given little if any consideration by other investigators.

The change in the name of the chief city of North China from Pei Ching ("Northern Capital") to Peiping ("Northern Peace") by the Nationalist government in 1928 has given us a minor problem in nomenclature. In general, we have used Peiping, since that was the city's name when we were making our study, but in referring to dates and events before 1928 we have used Peking, the English equivalent of Pei Ching.

For obvious reasons family names have been changed, our sample villages have been lettered rather than named, and other village references give only the name of the hsien where the village was located.

In discussing village finances we have used the terms "assessment" and "levy" rather than "taxes." The latter term has been used only when an official governmental organization was involved.

We are fully conscious of the fact that there is a considerable possibility of error in any Chinese statistics. For most villagers "several tens" would describe a large number with sufficient accuracy. In the registering of land for taxes or assessments there were often considerable omissions. One village increased the total registration on its books by almost 50 per cent when it agreed to record the land on a one-for-two basis. Another village attempted to increase its registration by using village bullies and by requiring a farmer to have a harvesting permit for all his land before he could cut his crop. In that case there was no resulting increase. A Chinese friend who served for a time as a magistrate in a Shantung hsien said that an accurate survey increased the land registration by nearly 50 per cent —about one third had been "black land," i.e., unregistered. We have taken the land figures as we found them in the village books.

In gathering population statistics we have depended upon the coöperation of the head of the village both in explaining the purpose of our study and in getting reasonably complete and accurate totals. Where comparisons have been possible, we have found that our figures have been quite consistent.

The principal statistics in our studies of population, landownership, education, village leadership, cost of village activities, village finance, and so on are discussed in the text. The complete figures are given in tabular form at the end of the book.

All dollar signs are for Chinese silver dollars, yuan. For the year 1933 the exchange rate between Chinese and American dollars averaged 3.84 Chinese dollars for one American dollar. The monthly averages ranged from 5.06 in January to 3.00 in December. (Cf. [Republic of China] National Tariff Commission. *The Shanghai Market Prices Report* [Shanghai, Oct.–Dec., 1933], p. 47.)

We must express our great appreciation of the work of our Chinese colleagues who gathered, organized, and translated our material. We should be glad to name them, except that present conditions seem to indicate that they should remain anonymous. Others who are versed in Chinese terms, Chinese gods and their attributes, and general Chinese historical material have been most generous with their help and have clarified many items for us. To them we give our thanks. We are especially appreciative of the invaluable help of Mr. Hung-chun Chang.

Permission from the Harvard-Yenching Foundation to include among our sample villages the story of Village I (previously published in the *Harvard-Yenching Journal*), from the Institute of Pacific Relations to use pertinent material from our volume *Ting Hsien: A North China Rural Community*, from the University of Washington Press to quote from K. C. Hsiao's *Rural China*, and from John Lossing Buck to use data from his *Chinese Farm Economy* is gratefully acknowledged.

We are also grateful for the help that Miss Gertrude Shafer, Mrs. Mary K. Seabury, Miss Mary C. McMahon, and Mrs. Miriam de Longpré have given with the typing of the manuscript and for the careful editorial work of Dr. Elizabeth K. Bauer.

SIDNEY D. GAMBLE

New York, N. Y.
March, 1963

CONTENTS

ILLUSTRATIONS
(follow page 144)

FIGURES

I: A SUMMARY

In North China before 1933, the land was dotted with thousands and even tens of thousands of villages. Although they lay fairly close together, they were separate and distinct communities. There were only a few instances where two or more villages united for political or economic reasons. No two villages were alike in the sample groups we studied in Hopei, Shansi, Shantung, and Honan. They differed in size, in the number of families living within their boundaries, in the number of clans and name groups, in the amount of land they controlled, in the number and organization of their leadership groups, in the qualifications demanded of their leaders, in their political development, in their finances, in the amounts and methods of levying and collecting their assessments, and in their religious activity. These differences and the distinct individuality of each village are the outstanding features of our study and will be constantly evident as we describe our findings in detail.

VILLAGE AUTONOMY

The upper governmental organizations—*ch'ü* (hsien subdivision), *hsien* (county), *chou* (provincial subdistrict), *fu* (provincial district), provincial, and national—were, until 1911, part of an imperial form of government that was largely directed from above. After 1911, the republic followed very closely the earlier imperial organization. At the village level, however, the activities that most closely affected the people were controlled locally by the leaders and officers of the villages.

Our study tended to confirm an earlier impression that, under the empire and generally during the early years of the republic, the North China villages tried, as far as possible, to handle their own problems and affairs, and usually they were allowed to do so. The hsien magistrates normally were not permitted to serve in their native provinces and so were unacquainted with local customs. Ordinarily, they expected to be transferred to a new area every few years. The average term of a magistrate in a Honan hsien, for the years 1875–1897, was only 0.9 of a year. In a Hunan hsien the average was 1.5 years for the period from 1875 through 1901.[1] In a Hopei hsien it was 1.1 years for the period from 1901 through 1928.[2]

The magistrates' main interests were collecting taxes, trying civil and criminal cases, and keeping the peace so that no one would file a complaint against them with the higher authorities. Consequently, they paid but little attention to routine village affairs. Since the magistrates were interested in producing unofficial income from their area, dealings with them were usually expensive for the persons or the villages involved.

During the later years of the period covered by our study, which ended in 1933, there were definite indications that the higher governmental organizations were giving increased attention and direction to the villages under them and exerting more control over village affairs. New ideas concerning village life and organization were coming into the country from abroad, and, because of the general conservatism of the rural population, the only way to get the villages to adopt them was by orders from above. Toward the end of our study, some of the hsien governments had promulgated regulations and issued orders for their villages to the point where, because of official pressure from the government and trouble with the military and in some areas with bandits, the position of village head was a very unhappy one. The officials complained to him if their orders were not carried out; the villagers complained when they had to furnish the money required. Our investigators commented on the fact that, instead of being sought after, the office was being avoided and refused.

CHANGES IN VILLAGE ORGANIZATION

The form of village organization and its activities varied considerably from province to province and from village to village, and there were distinct changes in both organization and activities that came at different rates and times during the more than thirty years covered by our study. There was, however, an over-all pattern of organizational change and development to which the villages conformed more or less closely. This usually was divided into three distinct stages.

First stage.—In the first stage most of the villages had one or more informal groups of leaders who were in charge of various village activities, such as watching and protecting the crops growing in the fields, maintaining the temples and renting temple lands, and giving plays to honor the gods and entertain the villagers. The groups raised the money needed for their activities by assessing the village families, sometimes according to the amount of land they owned or operated, sometimes according to the number of persons in the family and the number of animals they owned, sometimes on a purely arbitrary basis.

In some villages all the family heads shared in the control of local activities and served in rotation for a definite term, usually a year. In others the administration was less democratic, and only family heads who met certain property and other qualifications could hold office. In still others the control was quite autocratic, being in the hands of a small, self-perpetuating group of leaders. In some villages all the members of the leadership group, in annual rotation, handled the finances and other affairs. In other villages a small inner group or executive committee of the self-perpetuating group rotated the responsibility among themselves and called the whole group together only when an unusual or especially difficult problem had to be faced.

The political relations of the village and the hsien, or the district government of the hsien, were carried on through the *ti-pao* ("local man," "local political agent," or "local constable"), who was a resident of the village appointed by the hsien magistrate. Messages and orders from the upper governments were sent to the ti-pao and communicated by him to the village. He was put to some expense to entertain the messengers from the hsien, and he looked to the village families to reimburse him. Because of his position he was able to obtain, sometimes practically by blackmail, gifts and donations in considerable amounts from the village families. Naturally, the wealthier the family, the larger was the donation expected at harvest-time and New Year's.

Second stage.—In the second stage of village development, which began in the Peiping area about 1900 and in Shansi in 1917, the position of "local man" generally was discontinued. By order of the hsien government, his place was taken by a village head and one or more assistant heads who were appointed by the village leaders rather than the magistrate.[3] The number of the assistant heads was usually one for every hundred families in the village.

The village head and his assistants were most often chosen from among their own number by the village leaders in charge of crop-watching, who were more closely related to the general life of the village than were the groups in charge of the temples, the plays, or the granary and therefore had a somewhat higher political status.

The power and authority of the village head varied with the personality and prestige of the man holding that office. Sometimes he had almost autocratic power. Usually he and the group of leaders who appointed him worked well together in handling village affairs.

Sometimes he was a figurehead and village administration and finance was completely in the hands of an informal, self-perpetuating group of leaders.

Once appointed, the village head generally served an indefinite term, in some cases for twenty-five years or more. But if he became too autocratic or increased the village expenditures unduly, he could be forced out of office, either by public opinion or by a lawsuit before a magistrate.

In many villages, especially in the Peiping area, the group of leaders that included the village head and assistant heads gradually took over more and more of the activities that earlier had been handled by other village groups. Some that they could not take over they suppressed.

Third stage.—The third stage started on June 5, 1929, when the Nationalist government promulgated a Hsien Organization Act which was to apply to the entire country. The act required that a village, to be recognized as a *hsiang*, or official village, should have a minimum of a hundred families. Those with less than that number were to unite to reach the minimum. The law spelled out in detail how the villages were to be organized, what officers and committees they were to have, and how these were to be elected.

The electorate was to consist of all adults who had lived in the village for a year or had maintained a residence there for two years. Elections were to be supervised by an officer of the hsien government.

By 1933 many villages had adopted the new type of organization and already had held several elections. Since, however, some villages elected the same officers year after year, the officials in some hsien were attempting to insist that a village officer could not serve for more than three years in succession. In other villages, elections had not been held and probably would not be until the old village head retired.

Some villages were still in the first stage of development. Officially they were in the second stage, with a head and an assistant head, but those officers were figureheads, and political and financial power was retained by the informal, self-appointed group of village leaders.

EFFECT OF NATIONAL DEVELOPMENTS
ON VILLAGE LIFE

The forty years from 1893 to 1933 brought many political and economic changes to China as a whole and thus to the provinces included in our investigations: Hopei, Shansi, Shantung, and Honan.

It has not been possible to determine minutely how much our villages were affected. Some changes directly involved many of the villages; others had very little, if any, impact.

Military events.—The outstanding military events of the period were the war with Japan in 1895; the Boxer uprising in 1900, with the resulting foreign expedition to relieve the siege of Peking and the occupation of a considerable part of North China by foreign troops; the revolution of 1911; the civil wars of the 1920's; the Nationalists' capture of Peking in 1928; and finally the fighting between Chiang Kai-shek and Feng Yü-hsiang in 1930. Levies were made on many villages for money and for forage, grain, food, and carts for the various Chinese armies. Sometimes when an army took over an area, an assessment was collected from the villages for "saving" them. A large part of the village expenditure in the Peiping area went to the military forces.

In Shansi the demands of the military were so heavy that the theatrical performances given annually by the villages had to be discontinued for lack of funds.

By 1933 only a few villages were operating granaries from which grain might be lent to needy farmers. Interest for the loan of grain might be as much as 30 per cent. Profits from granaries were used for village school expenses or for public works such as the repair of temples and bridges. Most of the granaries had been given up because the military forces had either requisitioned the grain or forced the sale of it by their demands for money.

Educational reform.—The arrival of new ideas was less dramatic, but certainly accounted for much of the change in the villages. New-style, nonclassical schools were opened in some villages as early as 1894. At first privately supported, they were later taken over by the villages and made available to all the children at a small tuition fee. The rest of the school budget came from village funds— sometimes from ordinary income and sometimes from specially allocated funds such as rent of village land or profit from the granary. As the years went by, more and more villages established modern schools. In 1929 the Nationalist government made four years of lower primary education compulsory. Villages too small or too poor to support a separate school were to join with other villages until they had a sufficiently large group of families.

An increasing number of "returned students" who had studied abroad brought back many new social, political, and economic ideas and were anxious to have those ideas adopted locally; however, very few of this group lived in the villages.

Reforms under Sun Fa-hsü.—After the revolution of 1911 the situation was such that even a single dynamic individual could exert tremendous influence. Sun Fa-hsü was appointed magistrate in Ting Hsien in 1914 and immediately set about reforming the villages. At Chai Ch'eng he found a returned student who had studied in Japan and was intent on improving life in his village. This man was a member of the leading family of the village and so was making considerable headway with his plans. On the basis of the plans developed and the progress made, and on Sun's nomination, Chai Ch'eng was designated a "model village" in 1915. In 1916 Sun was granted permission to reorganize Ting Hsien as a "model hsien." In the fall of that year he was transferred to Shansi and there helped the governor, Yen Hsi-shan, put through plans for province-wide reorganization and for making Shansi a "model province."

During the time that he was in Ting Hsien, Sun put great pressure on the villages to establish schools and to give up their temples. The temple buildings were to be used to house the schools and the offices of the village administration. Forty-four per cent of the schools that we found in Ting Hsien in 1928 had been founded in 1914 and 1915 when Sun was the hsien magistrate.[4]

Effects of the student movement and civil war in the 1920's.— The development of a new national consciousness was stimulated by the student movement that began in 1918–1919. It forced some cabinet ministers out of office in Peking, carried its "Buy Native Goods" campaign to the villages throughout the country, and actively opposed giving Japan any rights in Shantung.

The civil war, banditry, and generally unsettled conditions around Peking during the 1920's encouraged considerable village self-defense activity. Some villages built new walls; others repaired their old ones. In some villages policemen were employed, put into uniform, and armed. Additional village guards were appointed and there was some experimenting with groups of guards employed and supported jointly by several villages. Some villages organized large numbers of volunteer guards, part of whom, in rotation, did the actual patrolling while the others were on call for emergencies.

At the end of our study there seemed to be a tendency to combine the police, guard, crop-watching, and night-watch functions and to employ one group of men on a year-round basis rather than have several seasonal groups.

VILLAGE FINANCES

Crop-money.—Most of the villages in North China obtained funds for their local activities by assessing the village green circle—land controlled by the village (crop-money), or, where the village controlled no land, by assessing the land owned by its resident families (land-money). The assessments usually were collected after the fall harvest, when the farming families had money available.

Handling of current expenses.—Because most villages received by far the largest part of their income after the fall harvest, providing money to pay for current operating expenses throughout the year presented a problem for many village administrations, especially in disturbed times such as prevailed during the 1920's. If the village had a surplus at the end of the year the money was very tempting to prowlers. When trouble was brewing in the area, village officers did not want to be responsible for the safekeeping of sums that might amount to several hundred dollars. Ordinarily no banks were available. If there were shops of moderate size, the money could be deposited with them and withdrawn as needed. When there were no shops, the money might be entrusted to a wealthy family in the village—with the possibility that it might not be available on call.

If no surplus was carried over into the new year, the money needed to pay some of the salaries and other items that could not be postponed until the end of the fiscal year would have to be obtained by borrowing, often at interest of 2.5 per cent per month, or more.

Some villages partly solved the problem by collecting "advance crop-money" at the time of the wheat harvest; some carried forward small balances and borrowed any additional sums needed; some borrowed all of the money required and paid the necessary interest, and in that case they usually borrowed several times, possibly from several sources, and arranged to repay at the end of the fiscal year.

Expenditures.—Our study did not include prices of food, fuel, cloth, etc., but, judging from various figures shown in the village accounts—such as the increase in the cost of crop-watching, the subsidy given a river ferry by one of the villages, and the salary paid its schoolteacher by another—the price level practically doubled in the ten years from 1920 to 1930. The total village expenditures went up almost four times during the same ten years, but a large part of that increase was owing to the heavy demands of the armies. Assessments levied by the military on the villages during the civil wars of the 1920's took a large part of the income and forced large increases in the crop-money rates.

Exchange rates.—Debasement of the copper coinage, which increased the silver-copper exchange rates by some 150 per cent between 1920 and 1926, brought continually rising copper prices. The final result, about 1926, was a general shift to silver as the money of account and the principal medium of exchange.[5]

REASONS FOR VILLAGE AUTONOMY

It has been interesting to speculate on how the villages were able to obtain the considerable amount of autonomy that our study showed them to possess. Was it a long-standing feature that had continued more or less consistently through several dynasties? Or was it connected with the decline of the strength and initiative of the Ch'ing dynasty, that had been tottering since the mid-nineteenth century and that went down in 1911, practically without a struggle?

The emperor nominally had complete autocratic power to legislate for the villages, and practically the same power was held by the Nationalist government that unified the country in 1928. The imperial bureaucrats, however, generally were not much interested in the villages beyond receiving their tax payments, especially since two of the three dynasties that ruled China through more than six centuries from 1280 to 1911 were not Chinese.

The emperor ordered the remission of taxes when flood, famine, or other disasters hit the countryside. When the peace of an area was threatened, decrees were issued for the renewal of the *pao-chia* system of self-defense and control in the villages, which was a strong feature during the early Ch'ing dynasty. This system, based on small groups of mutually responsible families, was reintroduced by the Nationalist government in 1928.

Several times the attempt was made, generally unsuccessfully, to require that a village have at least a hundred families before it should be given official recognition.

The village land-tax system was thoroughly revised early in the Ming dynasty. Five centuries later, under the republic, it was still practically unchanged. The official conversion rate from taels to dollars, or from amounts of grain to amounts of money, had been increased several times after 1911, but the basic system was undisturbed.

Officially, it was a long way from the capital to the village, even though the village might be just outside the walls of Peking. Any imperial decree had to pass through several official hands before it reached the area where it was to be enforced. The conservative villagers were known to be past masters at dragging their feet unless they were actively pushed. As was noted above, most hsien magistrates had no personal interest in the area they governed. This combination of factors made it possible for the villages to keep a varying amount of control over their local affairs and usually to recover gradually any that had been taken from them by reform programs developed in the capital. In some hsien the magistrate had to approve the appointment of the village officers. In others he selected a name from a list of nominations presented by the village. In still others the appointments were made without any reference to the hsien government. The weakness of the Ch'ing dynasty during its closing years discouraged the development of any active program from above and probably made it possible for the villages to recover and enlarge their autonomy—provided, of course, that they paid their taxes.

K. C. Hsiao, in his study *Rural China: Imperial Control in the Nineteenth Century*,[6] describes a situation very different from what we found in the late nineteenth and early twentieth century. He states that in the early part of the Ch'ing dynasty

Every local agency or organization whether sponsored by the government or of local origin was placed under the control or supervision of the magistrate [and] moreover, the selection of village headsmen and rural managers was usually subject to the review of the magistrate, if indeed the appointments were not actually made by the magistrate himself.

In later decades the morale of the administration declined to such an extent that "villagers and villages were left to shift for themselves" and a "partial administrative vacuum thus existed in the countryside," a vacuum in which the "local gentry or local bullies [were allowed] to dictate matters of the neighborhood, especially the matters that lay beyond the narrow scope of families or farms." Hsiao states, further:

Although organization appeared in many villages, it did not appear in all, and even in those where organizations existed, communal activities were limited in scope and were rarely if ever conducted by all the inhabitants on a basis of equality. It is difficult to find an instance in which associative efforts were conducted by a village-wide organization for the welfare of the inhabitants. Most of the organizations were set up only for special purposes and often to meet temporary emergencies. Then membership usually included only a segment of the inhabitants of a given village. Commoners were not precluded from participation or even leadership in village undertakings but the gentry usually dominated them. It was the gentry that determined to a large extent the pattern and direction of organized village life.

It will be interesting to see in the following pages how this description of village life, taken from historical documents, differed from what we found by a field study made in North China during the early years of the twentieth century.

China's isolation from the rest of the world long prevented new political and economic ideas from coming into the thinking of the national administration. When they were accepted, they became the basis of the vigorous program of the Nationalist government as it sought to apply them in the villages and, hopefully, to make possible a more democratic control of village politics and to improve the lot of the villagers. Energetic promotion of the program had, however, failed to gain compliance from all the villages, even in the Peiping area, by the time our study ended in 1933.

II: VILLAGES—GENERAL DESCRIPTION

THE TYPICAL North China village consisted of an aggregate of houses surrounded by a farming area that ordinarily was controlled by the village. There were no separate farmhouses. The farmland outside the village was often referred to as the *ch'ing-ch'uan*, the "green circle." Its size was more or less related to the number of families in the village.

TERMINOLOGY

The terms most generally used for "village" in North China were *ts'un* and *chuang*. It was said that both terms had been used for at least two thousand years. They could be applied to population groups of any size. *Ts'un* was possibly the more basic term, but in some areas *chuang* was more generally used. Thus in Tsou-p'ing Hsien, in Shantung, 270 places were known as *chuang* and only three as *ts'un*.

Chen ("town") was the term generally applied to areas that had a large number of families, a considerable number of shops, and a periodic market. The chen was often the seat of a district office of the hsien government. Village B, with 307 families and a considerable number of handicrafts, was called a ts'un; so was a village in Wu-t'ai Hsien, in Shansi, that had more than 1,000 families. Village H was once a hsien city, but had reverted to village status when the government offices were moved away and the market had to be given up because of competition from other markets nearby.

In T'ang dynasty times a minor officer who served as a gate-keeper and sheriff was called a *ts'un-chang* ("village head"). Villages with more than 100 families could have two such officers. Villages with fewer than 50 families were not entitled to have a ts'un-chang; they had to affiliate with larger villages. *Ts'un-chang* and *chuang-chang* were the terms used for the village heads appointed after 1900.

VILLAGE HISTORY

So few of the villages had any information about their founding or later history that the exceptions to the rule are worth noting. One of our sample cases, Village A, could place its founding exactly, as this coincided with the dedication of a new *Kuan Ling Miao*, and the date of the plaques in the temple was A.D. 1440. In several Hopei villages local tradition said that the first settlers were famine refugees from Shansi early in the fifteenth century. The immigrants could readily find unoccupied land south of Peking. Local fighting in 1401 had almost depopulated that area because it had held out, for a time, against the rebellious Yen Wang when he started for Nanking to dethrone his nephew. The people recalled that as the time when "the besom of Yen Wang swept the North," when the "red insects ate everything" (Yen Wang's soldiers wore red trousers), and when "the swallows nested in the trees" (because they could find no roofs).

Village J, in Shansi, reported that the family that gave its name to the village arrived sometime during the T'ang dynasty, or before 907. Village H became a hsien city under the Sung dynasty, during the decade 1021–1030.

SATELLITE VILLAGES

New villages were being formed in the 1930's. When the population increased after the area inside a village was fully occupied, new families started small residential areas outside. We have called these settlements satellites because they were still part of the political and economic organization of the original village. As the satellites increased in size and influence, they would reach a point where they wanted to have their own village organization and control their own affairs.

Because of intergroup rivalries some villages were in the process of splitting into two or even three parts and setting up separate administrations although officially, in the eyes of the hsien government, they were still single villages. Village B was a good example of this process.

In Ting Hsien, which had 453 villages, there were 19 satellites dependent on the original villages and 8 villages that had divided to the point where they had separate administrations, even though the hsien recorded them as single villages.[1]

Village D, with 99 families, had two satellite residential areas, with a total of 43 families, directly related to it and under its supervision and control. There were also two separate villages, with a total of 55 families, that had joined with it in order to reach the legal minimum for village organization.

In Yü-hsiang Hsien, in Shansi, there were 122 villages, but only 57 were recognized by the hsien government. Fourteen were large enough to be independent. Forty-three were compound villages of one major village and one or more smaller communities joined to it. There were 65 smaller villages.

EFFORTS TO ESTABLISH MINIMUM-SIZE VILLAGES

After 1917 the national government, on several occasions, tried to set 100 families as the minimum number for legally incorporated villages. Villages with less than that number were to unite to reach the required minimum. Attempts at enforcement usually broke down, owing to the number of exceptions that had to be made for small villages with a long history and a desire to maintain their

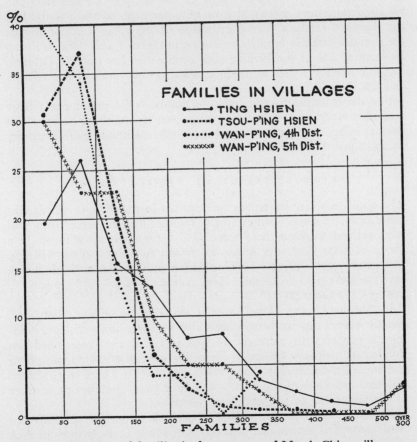

FIG. 1.—Number of families in four groups of North China villages.

identity and independence. The smallest village listed in our studies had only 3 families. The largest had 1,200.

Hsien Organization Act of 1929.—The Hsien Organization Act of 1929 provided that any population group with a minimum of 100 families could be incorporated as a hsiang, a political village. Groups with less than 100 families were required to join with other groups in order to attain the minimum. Together they would form a hsiang. A trading center with more than 100 families was to be called a chen, or town.

The strict enforcement of the 1929 act would have called for tremendous changes in the organization of the North China villages. For example, in four groups of villages, three in Hopei and one in Shantung, from 46 to 74 per cent of the villages had less than the required minimum. From 61.7 to 88.2 per cent of the groups had less than 150 families. The distribution of the villages, according to the number of their families, is shown in figure 1 and table 1. Forty per cent of one of the Peiping area groups had less than 50 families. In the other three groups, from 19.9 to 30.9 per cent of the villages had less than 50 families.

For the four groups the average number of families per village ranged from 80 to 150. In two groups, one in Shantung and the one near Peiping, the average was below the minimum established by the Nationalist government.

REPRESENTATION OF FAMILY NAMES

The number of family names represented in the villages varied tremendously. In some villages all the families had the same name and were related; in some there were 35 different names, or more. In a group of 100 villages in Shansi we found two single-name villages. In a group of 62 villages in Ting Hsien only one was single-name; the rest had up to 26 names.[2] The average was 8.5, the median 7.0 names. (See table 2.)

In Shu-lu Hsien, Hopei, was a single-name village that until shortly before our study had been also a single-family village, holding all property in common. It was said that the family had not divided its property for more than nine generations, or from about the time of the Emperor K'ang Hsi (1662–1721). There were several hundred members of the family, but how many families there were after the division of property was not stated.

In seven of our sample villages there was a total of 128 different name groups. This number was the sum of the name groups in each village; i.e., the Wangs who were found in all seven villages were counted as seven groups. We have no evidence of intervillage interest in same-name groups represented in more than one village.

The number of name groups in our seven sample villages ranged from 4 to 35. In four villages the number was more than 20, and in two it was 30 or more. The average was 18.3 name groups per village; the median, 21. The number of families in the different name groups ranged from one to 81. Sixty-two of the 128 groups, 48.4 per cent, had only one family; 57.1 per cent had one or two families, and 68.3 per cent had one, two, or three families. The average was 7.3 families per name group; the median, 2.

In the individual villages the proportion of single-family name groups ranged from 11.1 to 64 per cent, but for only one of the seven was the figure less than 43.5 per cent. The proportion with one or two families ranged from 22.2 to 72 per cent and was 50 per cent or more for five of the villages. The name groups with one, two, or three families ranged from 33 to 84 per cent. For four of the villages this figure was more than 61 per cent and for two it was 80 per cent or more.

The large proportion of name groups with only a few families suggests that there was a considerable amount of population movement going on in the North China villages and even in those that were not near Peiping. Some of the movement may have been of younger sons and their immediate families looking for land outside the home village.

Family activities.—The Chinese have long been noted for their close family ties. Family members have been ready to assist each other in times of economic need and when serious arguments arose with members of other family groups. The threat to "call out the clan" was one of the most serious that could be made when there was disagreement between different family factions in a village.

The most usual, certainly the most evident, large family activity was the maintenance of a joint family graveyard. Every year on the day before *Ch'ing Ming*, the spring tomb festival in April, each family sent a representative to help clean the graves and the graveyard. On Ch'ing Ming, the men and boys all came to offer food, incense, and paper money to the spirits of the ancestors.

Clan organization in North China.—In most villages even the largest family groups were hardly large enough or wealthy enough to have clan halls or clan land. So far as we could observe, such properties were not part of the general pattern in North China. An exception is Village H, in whose detailed story we have included clan material based on a family history, the earliest part dating from 1576.[3] We have also included the clan activity that we found in 1933. There were 69 families and 509 persons in this clan group.

It must be noted that the progenitor of the clan in Village H came from Kiangsu early in the Ming dynasty and would have brought with him the mores and traditions of central China. That fact, and considerable family wealth and position, may have been responsible for the long-continued clan activity. We have not attempted a special clan study, and there were no reports of special clan organizations or activities in our other sample villages. In some areas, however, the clan was the basis of representation in the village association.

VILLAGE PROTECTION SYSTEMS

Because of the need for protection from bandits and other marauders, many of the villages were surrounded by walls and had gates that could be closed at night. A few had moats, mostly dry. Around Peiping many villages had built no walls, relying for protection on proximity to the capital and the armed forces. After the revolution of 1911, however, many villages south of Peiping built walls to keep out the groups of bandits traveling through the area. To the east, the T'ung Hsien government went so far as to order its villages to build walls. During the fighting between the armies of Chiang Kai-shek and Feng Yü-hsiang in 1930 the walled villages in Honan were used as strong points by Feng's troops and had to be captured one by one. Village B rebuilt and repaired its wall in 1925, 1928, and 1932, raising $800 for the project by special subscription in 1925; during the three years $400 of ordinary village funds was used.

STREETS AND COURTYARDS

The number and length of the streets in the villages depended on the terrain and the number of families. Most streets were lined with walls whose only openings were gateways leading into courtyards. The wealthier families had their own separate courtyards. The poorer families lived two, three, four, or even five or more families in one courtyard. Village D had 99 families in 63 courtyards. There were 36 one-family, 21 two-family, 3 three-family, and 3 four-family courtyards. Village H had 375 families in 254 courtyards. Of these families, 191 had their own courtyard. Among the rest, up to 5 families lived in rows of rooms opening onto one courtyard.

The average frontage per house on the streets of Village C, the only one for which we have measurements, varied from 34 feet on the main street to 102 feet on one of the smaller roads. The average was about 55 feet per family.

WATER SUPPLY

Most villages in the Peiping and Ting Hsien areas obtained water for domestic use from wells inside the village. Some wealthy families had private wells inside their courtyards, but usually the wells were on the streets. Most streets had at least one well. In Village C, with 11 streets, 9 streets had one or more wells. The total was 16 wells for 248 families, an average of 15.5 families per well. For the different streets the averages ranged from 9.0 to 22.5 families per well.

In Village J, in Shansi, with 110 families, there were 8 wells; 6 of these were privately owned.

HOUSING

A study of the housing in Village C showed that, of its 276 families, 82.6 per cent owned their homes and 17.4 per cent were renters. This was a high proportion of renting families, especially since more than 90 per cent of the families had been living in the village for at

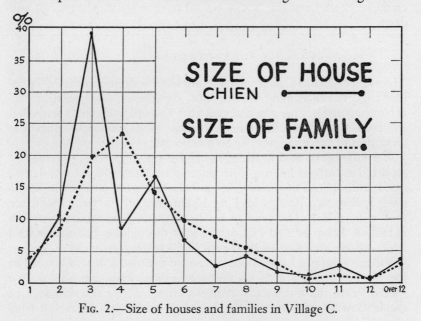

Fig. 2.—Size of houses and families in Village C.

least sixty years and all but 5.8 per cent for at least thirty years. In Ting Hsien the proportion renting their homes was 3.7 per cent in one group of families and only 1.2 per cent in another and larger group.[4] Nearness to Peiping undoubtedly was a large factor in Village C's ownership pattern. In a group of 283 families living in Peiping the proportion renting was 78.8 per cent. The figure was 92 per cent for families with incomes below $25 a month, 66 per cent for those with incomes between $50 and $100 a month, and 36 per cent for those with more than $200 a month.[5]

The size of the houses in Village C ranged from one *chien*—a space between two roof trusses and generally equal to one room—to 41 chien. The average was 4.95 chien per family, just under one chien per person, the average family having 4.97 members. There were 1,366 chien and 1,373 persons. The median family had three rooms. The rented houses averaged only 2.9 chien each. Thirty-nine per cent of the houses had three chien; 66.5 per cent had two, three, or five chien. There were tiled roofs on 10.5 per cent of the chien. The others had earthen roofs. Details of the housing study are given in figure 2 and table 27.

Practically all of the families used *k'angs*—built-in, raised brick beds that could accommodate five or six persons. The flue from the cooking stove went underneath the k'ang, so that in winter the bed could be heated and the family would have a warm place to sit and sleep.

GREEN CIRCLES

The typical North China village controlled a definite area of farmland that, in the Peiping area at least, constituted its "green circle" (*ch'ing ch'uan*). This was the area that the crop-watchers patrolled and from which the village derived most of its income through the collection of "crop-money" of so much a *mu*.

The amount of land in the green circle varied greatly. One village reported as little as 200 mu. The maximum that we found was 32,500 mu. Landholdings of the families in two groups of villages in Wanp'ing Hsien, two groups in Ting Hsien, and all of Ting Hsien are shown in table 3. The average amount per resident family is shown in table 4. From 24.2 to 45.1 per cent of the villages had fewer than 1,000 mu. From 8.4 to 24.2 per cent had 5,000 mu or more.

Village I did not have a definite area of farmland. It was located in the cotton-growing area of southern Hopei and, except for two special years, did not do any crop-watching. There the residence of the landowner rather than the location of the land was the basis of the village assessment. In other words, "land-money" rather than "crop-money" was collected. The area assessed by the village went up when its residents bought land and down when they sold to outsiders. Between 1907 and 1931 the area registered in the village land books ranged from a minimum of 3,586.5 mu to a maximum of 4,512.7 mu (see table 35).

LANDOWNERSHIP

Because of the variation in the number of families living in the different villages, the average amount of land per resident family is a much more significant figure than the amount of land in the village's green circle. Here, again, there was wide variation. In one Wan-p'ing Hsien district the range was from 6.4 to 35.1 mu per family; in another, from 17.4 to 87.5. In the Ting Hsien villages the range was from a minimum of 6 mu to a maximum of 76 mu per family. The over-all averages for the five groups of villages were 20.7 and 38.2 mu per family for the Wan-p'ing districts and 21.6, 22.8, and 20.4 mu for the Ting Hsien groups.[6] The distribution of the village

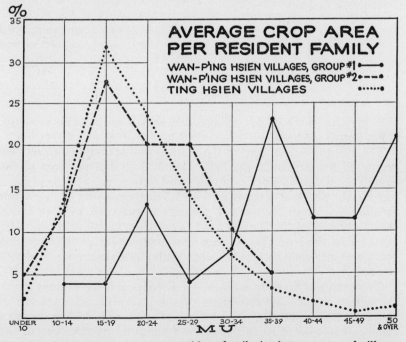

Fig. 3.—Average crop area per resident family in three groups of villages.

averages for three of the groups is shown in figure 3. Two of the curves are fairly similar. The third follows an entirely different pattern. The figures for the five groups of villages are given in table 4.[7]

The amount of land held by individual families varied widely, as might be expected, and the proportions of the families with different amounts of land fluctuated among the villages. The following figures which show that variation stress the large proportion of families with small holdings. The separate figures for the resident families are given, since most of the nonresident families held small areas and their inclusion would make the picture worse than it actually was.

All families (Six villages)	Maximum (Per cent)	Minimum (Per cent)
Under 10 mu	53.2	24.7
Under 20 mu	85.6	49.4
Under 30 mu (5 acres)	90.4	65.8
Under 50 mu	96.4	80.1
Resident families *(Three villages)*		
Under 10 mu	45.5	36.1
Under 20 mu	74.6	62.0
Under 30 mu (5 acres)	85.5	74.8
Under 50 mu	96.4	85.8

Holdings for three of our villages are shown graphically in figure 4. For details see table 5.

The 49.4 to 85.6 per cent of the families in our sample villages that registered fewer than 20 mu held from 22.2 to 43.2 per cent of the land. The 80.1 to 96.4 per cent that had fewer than 50 mu held from 45.6 to 80.1 per cent of the land. The 2.2 to 5.8 per cent with 100 mu or more held from 20.9 to 41.5 per cent of the land. In Ting Hsien the 72 per cent of the families with fewer than 25 mu held only 33.1 per cent of the land. The 91 per cent with fewer than 50 mu had 61.4 per cent while the 2.1 per cent with 100 or more mu had 17.1 per cent.[8]

Ownership of land by nonresident families usually did not affect the village control and assessment of the land involved. In seven of our sample villages the proportion of nonresident farm-owning families was from 6 to 46 per cent of the total number of families registering land with the village. (See table 6.) In another group of

eight villages the proportion of the landholding families who were
nonresident was from 36.0 to 90.7 per cent. The latter village registered 123 resident families and 1,193 nonresidents from six different
villages.

The proportion of the green circle owned by nonresident families
was usually much lower than the proportion of the families who
were nonresident; for most families, their extravillage holdings generally were relatively minor. In Village A the nonresident families
were 35 per cent of the families listed on the village land books, but
they held only 10.4 per cent of the village land. In Village F the nonresidents in 1928 were 41.5 per cent of the total list of families; their
holdings were some 28 per cent of the green circle. In Village G
they represented 43.6 per cent of the families and owned 34.4 per
cent of the land.

The considerable proportion of nonresident landowners and the
fact that the crop-money was used to pay for many village activities
besides crop-watching caused a number of people to feel that there
should be some difference between the rates charged the resident and

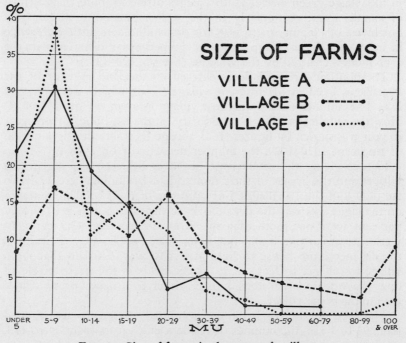

Fig. 4.—Size of farms in three sample villages.

nonresident owners. Why should nonresidents be assessed for school support, temple maintenance, the night watch, or payments to the military?

In line with this thinking, Village H assessed its nonresident owners only half the rate for resident families. In Village F assessments made for funds to meet the demands of the military were collected only from resident families; for all other village activities the resident and nonresident families paid the same rates.

Special studies of landholding.—Two studies of village land books gave a picture of the number and residence of the landholders registered with the village for their crop-money assessments. One study gave the figures for one year for 10 villages in the Peiping area; the other, the figures for one village, Village F, for ten years. The figures of resident and nonresident landholders in the 10 villages show a wide variation in the number of villages represented, in the number of landholders listed, and in the proportion of nonresident cultivators.

The villages generally were not concerned with the residence of the landowners as long as they paid the crop-money on their land in the village green circle. With villages often no more than a third of a mile apart, particularly in the well-populated suburban area northwest of Peiping, there was, for the landholders, little difference in intra- and extra-village land, except perhaps a difference in crop money charged by the villages. (See pp. 129–131.)

The nonresident landholders entered on the land registry of the 10 villages lived in 61 different villages, 7 of which were on two lists. The number on the different village lists ranged from 3 to 11. How the number of villages could vary on the land books from year to year was shown by figures from Village F, where during a period of ten years, 1920–1929, the number decreased from 9 to 4.

Figures giving the intervillage distances between the registering villages and the homes of their nonresident landholders are available for only 8 of the 10 villages. For only one of the 55 villages entered on the eight lists was the distance more than three li (1 mi.). Forty per cent were not more than one li away. Another 43.5 per cent were more than one li and not more than two li away. Naturally, the distance from house to field generally was less than that from village to village. In fact, many of the fields in the green circle of one village were often considerably closer to a neighboring village than to the home village.

The total number of landholders entered on the ten lists ranged from 94 to 1,316, the number of resident cultivators from 24 to 123, and the number of nonresident cultivators from 39 to 1,193; the proportion of residents was between 64 and 9.3 per cent. In 3 of the 10 villages the resident landholders were less than 10 per cent of the total list of names on the land books. In another 3 villages the proportion was between 17 and 19 per cent, and in still another 3 villages it was between 56 and 64 per cent. In the tenth village the figure was 34.8 per cent resident.

The village with 1,316 registrants was outstanding in having nearly four times as many as the next largest list and more than thirteen times the smallest. All but one of its six outside villages were represented by more than 100 families, two of them by more than 300 families. In the other nine lists there was only one village with more than 100 families.

The number of mu in the village green circle was available for only 2 of the ten villages. Village G had 2,154.5 mu. For Village F the total was between 1,550 and 1,600 mu. The detailed figures for its 55 resident landholding families were given by the list of a special intravillage assessment levied in 1928. The amount for the nonresident landholders can only be approximated from the number of families included in the groups with different-sized landholdings shown in table 5. The total for the resident landholders was 1,126.5 mu. For the nonresident families the possible minimum was some 355 mu and the possible maximum some 535 mu. The actual amount was probably about 450 mu.

The average holding of the resident landholding families was 20.4 mu in Village F and 18.2 mu in Village G, excluding any land owned in other villages. The nonresident average was 11.8 mu for Village G and between 9.1 mu and 13.7 mu, or about 11.5 mu, for Village F. For Village A the averages were: residents, 18.3 mu; nonresidents, 2.9 mu. One would expect smaller averages for the nonresident families, as most families owned more land in their own villages than they did outside.

If a family owned a considerable amount of land, its holdings usually were divided among several plots that might be located at some distance apart. In Village D the 104 resident families were cultivating 267 plots of land that totaled 2,010.5 mu. Thirty nonresident families had 50 plots totaling 482.5 mu. One family with 100 mu had 17 plots scattered all over the village area. One family with 90 mu had 12 plots, and another with the same amount had 8.

In Village D 22.7 per cent of the plots were below 5 mu in area and 69.7 per cent were below 10 mu. In four villages in Ting Hsien 70.3 per cent of the plots were below 5 mu and 90.3 per cent below 10 mu.[9] (See table 7.)

A study of the land books of Village F for the years 1920–1929 showed how the number of registering families and the size of their farms changed year by year. The number of families was different every year. The minimum was 84, the maximum 98 families. The proportion with fewer than 10 mu varied from 42.6 to 53.2 per cent, those with fewer than 20 mu from 65.1 to 80.6 per cent, and those with fewer than 50 mu from 91.0 to 97.6 per cent. (See table 33.)

Tenancy.—Tenancy ordinarily was not a serious problem in the Hopei area. In Ting Hsien more than 92 per cent of the families owned land and more than 96 per cent farmed some land. Rented land was farmed by 30 per cent of the farming families, but only 4.8 per cent were full tenants. Just under 6 per cent of the land-owning families rented land to others. Only 0.7 per cent were non-farming landlords. Twelve per cent of the crop area was rented.[10]

In Village A 6 of the 56 farming families cultivated rented land. The record did not definitely say whether they were part or full tenants, but seemed to imply that they were full tenants.

In Village B one of the wealthy families rented parts of its hold-ings to 10 tenants.

In Village D there were 26 full tenants. This was 22.6 per cent of the resident farming families and 20.3 per cent of both resident and nonresident farmers.

In Village F, where owned, mortgaged, and rented land was as-sessed for military expenses at different rates, the land books showed a tenancy rate for the resident families of 14.5 per cent full tenants and 41.9 per cent part tenants. Part tenants were renters who were also landowners or mortgagees. Mortgagees were classed with own-ers because, in lieu of interest on the loan, they took over and farmed the mortgaged land. Thirty-one per cent of the assessed land was listed as rented. Nearly 17 per cent was held under mortgage.

The only reported nonfarming landowners, complete landlords, were three in Village D and two in Village I. Four of the five were widows who had no sons to farm the family holdings.

Stability of ownership.—A very large majority of the village families were landowning farmers and were, therefore, usually a very stable group. In the one-name village in Shu-lu Hsien there had been no change for nine generations except possibly the emigration of some of the male members of the family. The females born to the family all married outside the village, but that would not be con-sidered a change in a patrilineal, exogamous family. In Village A all but 2 of the 64 families were descendants of the two cousins who founded the village in 1440. In Village C there were some fifteenth-generation families. In that village only 5.8 per cent of the families were first-generation immigrants who had moved in during the life-time of the then head of the family.

On the other hand, Village F showed a surprising amount of change in the number of families entered on the land books. During the ten years from 1920 to 1929 the total number of registrants and the number of resident families changed every year, the number of nonresidents every year but one. For the resident families the mini-mum number was 49, the maximum 57. The nonresidents ranged from 32 to 45 and the total number from 84 to 98. The percentage resident varied from 53.1 to 63.6.

The books also showed what seemed to be a very considerable number of transactions in farm real-estate. Probably most of this was connected with rented land. During the ten-year period the number of families registering fewer than 5 mu varied from 14 to 21, those with from 5 to 9 mu from 23 to 36 and those with 10 to 14 mu from 8 to 16. There were similar changes in the groups with

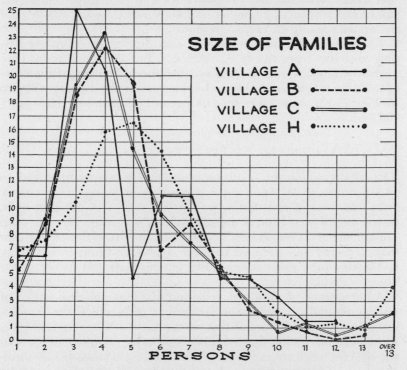

Fig. 5.—Size of families in four sample villages.

larger areas. The group with 300–399 mu was the only one with no change. That group had only one family. (See table 33.)

How the population could shift markedly in a single year was shown by the land books of Village D. From 1930 to 1931 the number of farming families went down by three, from 133 to 130. A further examination, however, showed that 17 families, 12.8 per cent, left the village during the winter and that 14 new families took their places before the next growing season. Such a large movement would certainly seem to indicate that the financial return from farming in that area was far from generous. Nearness to Peiping and possible employment there undoubtedly was also a factor.

SIZE OF FAMILIES

Population records regularly were kept in terms of families rather than individuals. Although the number of families in a village usually was readily available, special studies were needed to determine the size of the families, the number of family names in the village, and the age and sex of the family members.

The individual families in four of our sample villages in the Peiping area had from one to 32 members. In 5,255 families in Ting Hsien the range was from one to 65 members. The size of the average family ranged from 4.9 to 5.7 persons in the Peiping villages. In Ting Hsien the average was 5.8 persons per family.[11] (See fig. 5 and table 8.)

SEX AND AGE DISTRIBUTION IN VILLAGES

The sex division in three villages near Peiping ranged from 48.5 to 54.8 per cent male. Applying a correction in Village D for those away for work, the remaining group was only 40.6 per cent male. In the Ting Hsien families the sex division was male, 51.4 per cent; female, 48.6 per cent. Peking's population in 1918 was 63.5 per cent male and only 36.5 per cent female.[12] In North China a man going to the city for employment usually left his wife and family in the village with his parents.

A comparison of the age distribution of the population of two of our sample villages, of two other groups of North China families, and of the rural farm population of the United States in 1930 gives some very interesting figures. The outstanding differences are that the age of a much larger proportion of the Peiping-area family members was 50 years or more and of a much smaller proportion under 15 years. The proportion 50 years of age or older was 20.2 and 22.8

per cent for the two Peiping villages and from 16.2 to 16.8 per cent in the other three studies. For the group under 15 years the Peiping figures were 25.4 and 28.7 per cent, compared with 33.1 to 36.0 for the other studies. For the age group between 25 and 49 years the figures were quite similar. (See table 9.)

We are quite conscious of the possibility of underreporting for the younger groups in our villages, but we are inclined to believe that the unusually small groups reported by the Peiping families in the age groups from 5 to 9 years and from 10 to 14 years might very well have been the result not so much of underreporting as of the influence of famine and civil war on both the birth rate and the survival rate of young children. These two age groups were born between 1919 and 1928, a decade in which there was much military movement and considerable combat in the Peiping area and at least two serious crop shortages.

The age picture is shown graphically in figure 6 and numerically in table 10. The age and sex distribution is of the combined population of Villages A and C, put together in order to increase the size of the group and give a better sample. The sharp drop in the age group from 5 to 9 years and an even lower figure in the group from 10 to 14 years would hardly have been the result of mere under-

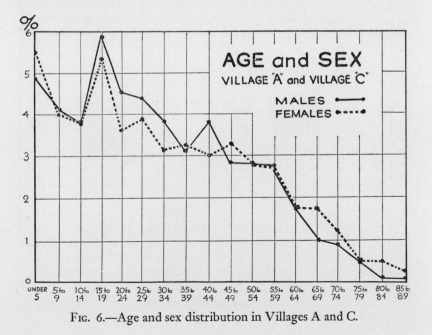

Fig. 6.—Age and sex distribution in Villages A and C.

reporting, especially when the male and female groups were so nearly equal. Our Peiping villages were outside the combat area, but were subject to occupation by several different armies, to looting, and to large exactions by the military. Then, too, there was a serious famine in 1919–1920 and a drought in 1924. The difficulties thus added to the usual hardships of village life around Peiping could be expected to affect the survival rate, especially of those in the younger age groups.

Besides the unusually small proportion in the younger age groups,

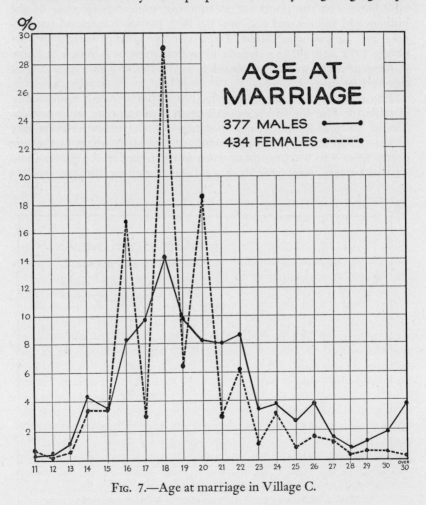

Fig. 7.—Age at marriage in Village C.

the age and sex figures had two outstanding features—the prepon- derance of males in the ages from 10 to 45 years and of females from 45 to 89 years. Those two differences were not unexpected, for we found the same situation in Ting Hsien[13] and it was also true of the Chihli (Hopei) families included in Buck's studies in North China.[14] In both the latter studies, however, the numerical superiority of females did not appear until the age group from 55 to 59 years.

A study of the age at marriage of 377 males and 434 females in Village C showed that 18 years was by far the most popular age for both sexes. Fourteen per cent of the males and 28.8 per cent of the females had married at that age, and 49.5 per cent of the males and 72.6 per cent of the females had married in the five-year period between the ages of 16 and 20 years. (See fig. 7 and table 11.)

The youngest age at marriage was 11 years, reported for one male and two females. Marriages at prepuberty ages, especially for girls, usually meant that the families could not afford the cost of a wed- ding and that the bride went to the husband's home without any special ceremony. Sometimes this arrangement was known as a "dry marriage." In most places it was detrimental to family social status. The prepuberty marriage of a boy might mean that his family was anxious to acquire a daughter-in-law who would serve his parents and take over a large part of the household work.

The oldest ages at marriage were 34 years, for one female, and 38 years, for two males. The average ages were 19 years, for females, and 22 years, for males.

In Ting Hsien for 766 couples the most popular age for marriage was 14 years for males and 18 years for females. The averages for that group were 17.2 years, for males, and 17.7 years, for females.[15]

POPULATION DENSITY

The population density of four of our sample villages, based on the amount of land entered on the books, varied from 430 to 1,450 per- sons per square mile of farmland. Village B, most of whose soil was poor and sandy, had the lowest figure. The next was 750 in Village C. The highest was for Village A, whose economy had been declin- ing and whose families had been gradually selling a considerable part of their land. The total village holding went down 12 per cent in six years. Usually land sold to outsiders remained under the control of the original village. Village A was an exception because it and two adjoining villages constituted a joint green circle. Any land sold to a resident of either of those two villages was transferred to its control and so reduced the land of Village A. Specifically, the population density was 1,270 in 1926 as against 1,450 in 1930. In Ting Hsien the figure was 850 persons per square mile.[16]

NONAGRICULTURAL OCCUPATIONS

Agriculture was the main occupation for most of the families in our sample villages, but in all of them there were some families who earned their living in other ways. In Village I about 4 per cent of the families owned no land. Of the Village B families, 6.5 per cent had no farm connection; of Village D, 10 per cent; and of Village A, 12.5 per cent. In Village H, 27 per cent of the families were not listed in the village land record.

Village K, in Shantung, did not report the number of its nonagricultural families. The village had an average of only 6.6 mu of land for each of its 380 families, so it is quite apparent that many of the residents had to seek work in the city, which was only three miles away.

Village D had 4 shops. Village H had 43 shops (table 34). In Village J, 100 of the 110 families made mats from the reeds grown in the village area. Village C, in which 18.8 per cent of the families were not on the land roll, reported 207 nonagricultural workers. Sixteen families were carrying on business activities in the village in shops, a teahouse, etc. Handicraft work occupied 43 persons; communications and professional and service jobs, 22; small trades, 22; there were 120 persons engaged in commercial work outside the village (table 28). Many of these workers were members of farming families, but others belonged to families that had no farm connections.

The combination of agricultural and nonagricultural occupations is well illustrated by two families in Village D. One family owned some 200 mu of land, cultivated 50 mu with hired labor and rented 150 mu to others, and had one member who was a government engineer and another who was an accountant for a coal mine. The other family owned some 50 mu of land, cultivating about 20 mu and renting out 30 mu; the family head had served as head of the village, as the head of the nearby town's chamber of commerce, and as manager of the town's Bureau of Official Measurement.

Families who owned no land ordinarily paid no crop-money and contributed nothing to the support of the village unless, as tenants, they were required to assume part of the assessment usually borne by the landowners. In many villages the number of landless families was so small that they were ignored by the village administration.

Elsewhere they were required to make a small contribution by means of a house tax collected from all resident families. In Village F the charge was 100 coppers (about 25 cents) per family in 1929 and 80 coppers in 1930. In some instances the retail shops, workshops, etc., registered with the village an amount of nonexistent land on which they paid the usual crop-money rate and so contributed to the support of local activities. In Village G, four shops registered 800 mu of nonexistent land and paid 27 per cent of the crop-money assessment.

III: THE VILLAGE ASSOCIATION

FOR THE CONCEPT of an association, in the sense of a group, the two most common Chinese equivalents were *she* and *hui*. The character for she is composed of two parts, one meaning "god of earth" and the other "land," an appropriate compound since the typical informal village association dealt with land and, often, with religion. The word *hui* means simply "meeting," or "association," and does not have the religious or economic implications of the term *she*.[1]

In Shansi she was the term most generally used. In Honan it had scattered use, but had been largely discontinued. In Shantung it was used only occasionally. In Hopei we found only one use, in an official document to be presented to the hsien court.

In connection with village activity, hui was the most popularly used term, especially in Shantung and Hopei. Another term was regularly added to describe the particular type of association. In the Peiping area there were the Green Crop Association (*Ch'ing-miao Hui*) and the Public Association, the United Association, the Public Welfare Association, and the Public Discussion Association. Many of the latter names replaced "Green Crop Association" as the organization originally formed to safeguard the crops developed into one which directed all the affairs of the village—social, economic, and political.

I-po Hui, the "Common Ground Association," or *Kung K'an I-po Hui*, the "Coöperative Crop-Watching Association," was the most prevalent type of village association in Shantung. In earlier days the crop-watching was done coöperatively, all the farmers contributing their services, but at the time of our study this custom had generally been given up and watchmen were hired to do the job.

In Honan the term *I-po Hui* was used occasionally. Other Honan crop-protective associations were sometimes called the Association for the Punishment of Crop Thieves, or the Cotton Association—a name used because cotton was one of the main crops of northern Honan.

Some Shansi villages called their group the Field Patrolling Association, or simply the Crop Association. Religious associations took their names from the particular god worshiped or the temple with which they were connected.

At the time that the system described below was in effect, matters that involved the village and the hsien government were handled by the *ti-pao*, the "local man," who was a village resident appointed by the hsien magistrate. All other village affairs were in the hands of informal local nonpolitical organizations.

In Shansi the old form of she, existing for the primary purpose of religious ceremonies and the secondary one of crop-watching, was still undisturbed. Rotation in office, whereby most of the family heads served in turn, was generally in effect throughout the province, and serving the village was the privilege or obligation of most family heads.

In Honan there were a variety of village organizations. Some were primarily religious in purpose and function; others were purely protective. The qualifying family heads usually served in rotation, but on a slightly different basis from that in Shansi. Specific associations for crop-watching functioned alongside those which were primarily concerned with religion.

In Hopei and Shantung crop-protection was the more important function of the village association and colored its organization and program. When compared with the associations in Honan and Shansi, those in Shantung and Hopei were quite alike in the emphasis they gave to crop-protection, though they differed in the way they carried it on. *I Po* ("common ground") were the generally adopted key words in Shantung, *Ch'ing Miao* ("green crop") in Hopei. The villagers contributed much more service to the coöperative crop-watching in Shantung than they did in Hopei, and that form of organization persisted much longer in Shantung. The Green Crop Associations of Hopei generally employed watchmen to protect the crops. That type of organization apparently reached its highest degree of development in the Peiping area. In Hopei any rotation in office was among the village leaders or among the members of their executive committee.

NATURE OF THE VILLAGE ASSOCIATION

While no two village associations were exactly alike, they all developed from the need of the villages for some organization or machinery to carry on the religious and economic activities that were not controlled by the official government organization. Because the village association was fundamentally social rather than political, a group based on local custom rather than law and with unwritten tradition rather than a written constitution, it evolved in different ways and at varying rates so that it was possible for us to find examples of all stages, from the purely social association to the purely political village administration. Through the years the general tendency was

for the association to take on more and more political features and
characteristics and to move from the informal to the formal and
from the customary to the legal basis.[2]

Since originally and basically the associations were informal, independent organizations that operated within a single village, they
developed their own programs and leaders and raised and spent their
own monies. Normally they carried on their work without the
supervision of any higher authority. Even in extreme cases they were
checked rather than managed until the promulgation of the Hsien
Organization Act of 1929.

Before 1929, however, it was quite evident that there was a growing trend for the village associations to become more and more political and for the higher governmental organizations to assume more
and more control of the activities of the villages, especially when
they wanted to introduce new ideas and programs. We even found
some hsien that had adopted regulations concerning crop-watching
and the collection of crop-money. In Yung-ch'ing Hsien, Hopei, the
government fixed the rate that the villagers paid as crop-money.
T'ung Hsien, near Peiping, published crop-protection regulations
that fixed the amounts of fines a village association could levy against
crop-thieves. The government also stepped into the religious field
and attempted to prohibit the worship of certain popular gods.

OPERATION OF THE VILLAGE ASSOCIATION

Without a written and legal constitution, the village associations
operated in a very loose fashion.[3] They had no fixed program except
as their activities were related to the crop seasons, to dates for ini-
tiating the night watch, and for religious and festival occasions.
Most associations had a head officer, and usually a treasurer, but
generally there was no secretary, no minutes of meetings (except as
they were being introduced after 1929), and nothing like parliamen-
tary practice. Whenever a problem arose, the leaders met, held a
frank discussion, and arrived at a collective opinion that became the
decision on the matter. Precedents were not evoked in determining
the treatment of cases brought before the leaders. One culprit might
be beaten, another fined, for the same offense. One might be heavily
fined, especially if he lived outside the village, while another, a resident, might have to pay only a light fine. An influential leader might
receive a large indemnity for a crop loss while an ordinary villager
might be paid only a small amount or given nothing.

The number of village leaders varied from time to time and from village to village. The usual number was from 5 to 8. We found extremes of 3 and 25.

Group control.—Group control of the business of the association and of village affairs was characteristic of the association's activities. Dictatorship in a village was practically unknown, though sometimes no action could be taken without the approval of the most influential resident. The process of rotation that was still prevalent in Shansi and Honan and in some places in Hopei, whereby the association executives were changed every year and sometimes oftener, made for widespread participation. Even when the village leaders were a self-perpetuating body, as in the Green Crop Associations in Hopei, it was the group rather than the individual that controlled. Generally, group decisions were made on the basis of unanimous rather than majority approval.

TYPES OF VILLAGE ASSOCIATIONS

The village associations, as we found them, could be divided into three main groups: the general, the specific, and the compound.

General associations.—The general association was one that took care of all of the interests of the village. The Green Crop Associations around Peiping, or their successors such as the Public Associations, are good examples of this form. Similar organizations were also common in Shansi.

In its simplest form the general association was a group of leaders who did not represent any specific sections, clans, or classes and who took care of social and economic matters directly and of political matters indirectly through the village head. In Hopei there generally was rotation among the leaders before 1900, but this was given up with the appointment of the village head (*ts'un-chang*) and the assistant (*ts'un-fu*). In Shansi the associations retained the regular rotation of their leaders, generally on an annual basis, much longer than those in Hopei.

There were some general associations where membership in the association was connected with other structural elements of the village, such as a clan, a street, or a section of the village. In one Shansi village there were seven different clan groups. Each group was represented in the general association by a delegate chosen by the clan. The offices of the association were filled by the delegates in rotation. In a village in Ta-t'ung Hsien the general association had five members—three from the Wang clan, one from the Shih clan, and one from the Li clan. Villages with only one clan often used the different lines of descent as the basis for choosing their association members. In a one-clan Shansi village with four family lines descended from the original ancestor, the village affairs were handled by two officers. One year they came from the first and second lines, the next year from the third and fourth.

When the clans were not strong, the unit was often a section of the village or possibly a street. One village was divided into the east and west sections, each of which had five representatives in the association. The ten men held office in rotation. In another village there were four officers who were changed every quarter: two from the front street, one from the rear street, and one from the east street. In still another village the north, south, and east sections each had two representatives in the association.

Specific associations.—Specific associations were independent groups with their own officers, finances, and programs and were organized for special services. Some were purely religious, related to the temple worship or temple maintenance; others handled economic matters, such as crop-watching, canal repair, or granaries. Honan had a particularly large number of specific associations. A village in Hsin Hsien, in Shansi, had four—two religious associations (one for the god of cows, another for the gods of heaven and earth) and two economic associations (one for protecting the spring harvest, the other for watching the fall crops). In another village in the same hsien the villagers watched their own crops, but had two independent religious associations. A third village had five religious associations and one association for economic affairs.

Compound associations.—The compound association consisted of an over-all association with semi-independent minor organizations operating under it. The minor units generally were organized on a territorial or clan basis. The over-all association handled only those matters that the minor units were unable to deal with. The villagers called the upper groups the "big associations," the lower groups the "small associations." We found compound associations only in Shansi.

Mixed type of association.—In addition to the general, specific, and compound associations there was a mixed type that was part village association and part village administration, part social and part political. On the whole it resembled the complex type of general association that had representatives from different parts of the village and one or two over-all administrative officers. These officers were known as village heads (*chuang-chang, ts'un-chang, pao-chang,* or *hsiang-chang*). They were elected by the villagers and in some areas were occasionally recognized by the hsien government. They administered both the political and the social affairs of the village. After 1900 this sort of mixed association gradually became the prevailing type of village organization in most parts of Hopei and Shantung. Its influence had not been felt, however, in any part of Honan or in most places in Shansi. In the Peking area the new officers, instead of being elected, were nominated from among their own group by the self-appointed leaders of the village, who had managed to absorb the new village administration rather than be absorbed by it, as was the case in most other areas.

ASSOCIATIONS CLASSIFIED BY SIZE

Large associations.—There were three types of "big associations." The first existed in fact, but not in name. In a Ting-hsiang Hsien village there were three small associations, each of which took care of an annual play and other matters within their part of the village; they united to deal with the affairs that involved the entire village.

In other places coöperative action took place through a supreme leader rather than through an over-all organization. In a Hsin Hsien village there were eight small associations and no big one, and here an over-all leader was appointed, in rotation, by the small associations.

The second type of large association had a definite organization, but no distinctive name. It was generally known as the *ta she* ("big association"). In a village of T'ai-ku Hsien, Shansi, there were five small she—East, North, Southwest, Front, and Rear. The large association above these had one elder and three assistants who were elected at large by the whole village. Another village in the same hsien had six small she and one large one.

The third type of large association had a religious connotation in its name. In a village of Ting-hsiang Hsien the three small associations were named for the streets, but the large association was the "Green Dragon" she. In another instance the large association was the *Lung Tung* ("Dragon Cave") she.

One village presented the peculiar case of a small association carrying on the work of a large one. There were three small organizations in the village—East, West, and Dragon. The East and West associations were composed of landowners. The members of the Dragon association were tenants. The East association acted as a large association and had the affairs of the village under its control.

Small associations.—There were three different kinds of small associations: clan, territorial, and religious. In one village there were the Shih and Lin clan associations and all other families belonged to the mixed association. In another village there were two small clan associations, but, as the clans were antagonistic to each other, there was no large association to coördinate their work.

The inhabitants of a street or section often formed a small association. One village had three street associations—Front, Middle, and Rear. Territorial designations such as North, South, Southwest, and Northwest were common.

In one village that was divided into six sections and had a small association for each section, a villager moving from one section to another was required to transfer his association membership to his new section. In another village, which had seven sections, a man kept his membership in his original association as long as he lived in the village, no matter how many times he moved.

The names of temples were often used to designate the third type of small association. In a Hsing Hsien village there were the *Nai-nai* ("Goddess"), *Shui Ts'ao* ("Water and Grass"), *Lung Wang* ("Dragon God"), and *Wan Shan* ("Ten Thousand Blessings") *Miao* ("Temples"). Correspondingly there was a Nai-nai she with twelve elders, a Shui Ts'ao she with six elders, and a combined Lung Wang–Wan Shan she with six elders. Of the six small associations in a T'ai-ku Hsien village, four were named the *San Kuan* ("Three Principles") she, one the *Shui Lu* ("Water and Land") she, and one the *Lung Teng* ("Dragon Lantern") she.

The names of months and of particular dates in the month were often given to small associations. Under the Lung Teng she mentioned above were six smaller associations called respectively the First Month, Second Month, Fifth Month, Seventh Month, First Eighth Month and Second Eighth Month associations.[4] These she were in charge of the plays given in those months. The Lung Teng she presented the dramatic offering for the sixth month. In a Nan Hsien village the names of the six small associations were the dates of the plays: the Second Day of the Second Month, the Fifth Day of the Fifth Month, the Sixth Day of the Sixth Month, the Fifteenth Day of the Seventh Month, the Fifteenth Day of the Ninth Month, and the Tenth Day of the Tenth Month.

CHANGES BEGINNING ABOUT 1900

The old associations began to change about 1900. Just when the change was first made could not be determined. It came gradually, and at different times in different villages. Both oral and written evidence indicated that it began not more than two or three years before 1900 at the earliest. It might possibly have been connected with the "Hundred Days of Reform" in 1898.

The first change, which seems to have originated in Hopei, was the creation of two new types of village officers, with the titles of village head and assistant village head—ts'un-chang and ts'un-fu—who were supposed to be elected by the village, but usually were appointed by the informal group of village leaders from among their own number. These new officers were to take over the work of the *ti-pao* or *ti-chia* ("local man") and were to represent the village when it had any dealings with the hsien government. That meant, of course, that the impetus for the change came from above, from the hsien government. It was the beginning of the shift from a non-political type of organization in the villages to one that was definitely connected with the government. The change from the old to the new type of organization went on at various rates in different areas and villages for the next thirty-five or more years. It was still going on when our study ended in 1933.

In Hopei and Shantung the new village officers and the village leaders who worked with them developed a mixed association that combined social and political activities. They ordinarily took over the village crop-watching and absorbed any crop-protective association that had previously organized that program.

In the years after 1900 there were practically no changes in the Honan villages. The ti-pao continued to take charge of all political matters and the village associations remained nonpolitical and independent. The she in Shansi continued to carry on their religious programs, to give numerous plays, and to protect the crops in the fields.

In the vicinity of Peking it was a different story. There the well-developed Green Crop Association continued to function and added the handling of political business and the control of political leadership to its other activities. The rotation in office of the association's executive officers was given up and the two village heads, who were selected by the self-perpetuating group of village leaders from among their own number, became the permanent leaders of the association as well as the political agents of the village. Village headquarters were called the association office, village affairs were association business, the income of the village came mainly from crop-money, and the village account books were labeled as the books of the association. There was no sectional representation. The village leaders, as a group, simply declared themselves the village council, elected or appointed the village heads, and directed all local affairs.

The village association gradually began to develop and control the educational program as the old private schools were abandoned and modern schools were established. The association also assumed control of the village temples and the temple land. Many of the associations combined educational and religious activities, using the temple buildings for schoolrooms and often turning over to the school the income received from the land owned by the temples and rented out to cultivators.

The revolution of 1911 transformed the national government from a monarchy to a republic, but it had little immediate effect on either the social or the political aspects of life in the villages. In Shansi and Honan the ti-pao still continued to work side-by-side with the village leaders who handled the nonpolitical activities. In Shantung and Hopei the mixed sociopolitical village associations were not affected.

CHANGES INITIATED IN SHANSI IN 1917

The next big change came in 1917 when the governor of Shansi, Yen Hsi-shan, launched his self-government program and established his "model province" and "model hsien" programs. In many villages the new political organization gradually took precedence over the old social or nonpolitical ones and absorbed many of the old she. In others, however, the she paralleled the political organization, so that in Village J we found the she collecting funds for its activities and the village administration levying assessments for its work. It was said that the people of Shansi, who were under more pressure from the local government than was felt elsewhere, clung the more steadfastly to their old customs and traditions, but did so by a process of nonresistance.

Effects of civil war.—Many of the village she activities fell victims to the civil war when Yen Hsi-shan and the Shansi forces were drawn into the conflict, especially in 1930 when Feng Yü-hsiang and Yen Hsi-shan fought against Chiang Kai-shek. Conscription of manpower and large and repeated assessments for funds to support the military program left the villages little or no money for the religious festivals and giving of plays that earlier had been such a big feature of their life.

In Hopei the influence of the civil war and the political unrest was perhaps even greater than in Shansi. Peking was the capital and therefore the center of the struggles that involved, at various times, Wu P'ei-fu, Chang Tso-lin, Feng Yü-hsiang, Yen Hsi-shan, and finally Chiang Kai-shek and the Nationalist forces. As the various armies entered the fighting, they made heavy demands on the countryside for men, wagons, and horses, food for men and animals, and money.

With the countryside disturbed and the economic life of the area badly upset, bandits became active and preyed on the villages for money and food, and often kidnaped members of the wealthier families and held them for ransom. Besides meeting the demands of the military and the depredations of the bandits, the villages had to undergo further financial strain in purchasing arms and employing guards, building walls and gates, and taking other measures for self-protection.

TERMS OF THE HSIEN ORGANIZATION ACT

The final blow for the village associations came when the national government promulgated on June 5, 1929, the Hsien Organization Act. It was largely based on the late Dr. Sun Yat-sen's principles of local self-government and was to apply to the entire country. Under the act each hsien was divided into several ch'ü, or districts, and each ch'ü into from 20 to 50 hsiang, or political villages, in the rural areas and chen, towns, in the urban districts. Villages of more than 100 families were to constitute a separate hsiang. Those with fewer than 100 families were to combine with one or more neighboring villages to form a hsiang.

The functions that were listed in the law to be carried on by the hsiang through its officers and committees included census taking, population registration, land surveying, public works, education, self-defense, physical training, public health, flood control and irrigation, forest preservation, industrial and commercial improvement, food storage and regulation, the development of coöperative organizations, and the improvement of customs and public beliefs, public enterprise, and financial control.

Under the new law the village head and his assistant (or assistants) were to be elected by the village assembly, which was to include all persons more than twenty years of age, both male and female, who had lived in the village for a year or who had maintained a residence there for two years. The assembly was also to elect an arbitration committee of four members to deal with village disputes, a finance committee of four members to look after the fiscal affairs, and an inspection committee of three members to supervise the school and village accounts. All officers and committees were to be elected annually by ballot, and the elections were to be supervised by a representative of the district government.

The hsiang were to be subdivided into *lü* of 25 families each and the lü into *lin* of five families each. The lü and the lin were to have elected heads, lü-chang and lin-chang, chosen by the members of the families in each group.

The law also provided for use of the initiative, referendum, and recall. These were new political features with which the villages had no experience, and we found no evidence of their use.

Acceptance of the Hsien Organization Act.—As might be expected, the new political organization decreed by the national government was not immediately accepted. Most of the villages included in our study, especially those in Shansi where the new system had been quite generally established during the years from 1917 to 1929, held an election every year or at least once every two or three years. There were, however, other villages that in 1933 still followed the old organization and probably would continue to do so at least until the village heads who had been chosen by the association members retired or died.

In other villages, although proper elections were held, all the old leaders managed to achieve some office. The offices they held might have different names, but the same group of leaders continued in control of village affairs.

In still other villages the elective system gave the poorer and more numerous families an opportunity to express themselves politically and to break the long-continued control of the wealthy families. Spirited elections were held, with first one group and then the other winning popular support. In one of our sample villages, Village B, the head was changed every year from 1929 through 1933.

Villages in Honan were slow in giving up their old type of organization because of their feeling that it was an advantage to the village to have a ti-pao who was wealthy and powerful. In form their organizations probably were midway between the older ones in Shansi and the more recently developed type found near Peiping.

Shantung continued to hold to its old, mixed sociopolitical type of organization, and though it tolerated some changes here and there, it was not making them on a large scale.

In several places the hsien officials were insisting that, as provided by law, a district officer should be present in the village when an election took place and that he should be the one to handle the ballots. They were finding that not a few villages were sending in what purported to be results of elections, but which were the decisions of the old association heads, reached without any vote by the village residents.

Some hsien were attempting to make the village administrations more democratic by preventing a village officer from serving for more than three consecutive years.

The regulations, given herewith, that T'ung Hsien adopted in implementing the laws of the national government, show how much some of the governmental agencies were taking over detailed control of the villages.

REGULATIONS FOR THE VILLAGE OFFICERS OF T'UNG HSIEN, HOPEI

ARTICLE 1. These regulations are derived from the forty-sixth article of the village self-government law.

ART. 2. Unless there are other laws, all village officers will administer their affairs according to these regulations.

ART. 3. The head of the town or village is to call a village or town meeting once a month. The rules will be decided by the meeting.

ART. 4. The duties of a village or town head and of a village or town assistant head are as follows:

1. The items from one to twenty-one in the self-government law as decided by the village or town meeting.

2. Making, sending, receiving, and keeping official documents, keeping seals, buying supplies.

3. To take charge of the village guards and appoint them their duties.

ART. 5. The more important documents will be drawn up by the village or town heads themselves. Ordinary documents will be drawn by the assistants, but must be presented to the heads for their approval.

ART. 6. The following books must be provided by the village officers:

1. Articles.
2. Contracts.
3. Income and expenditure.
4. Incoming documents.
5. Outgoing documents.
6. Messenger's record.
7. Seal record.
8. Document keeping.
9. Minutes and attendance.
10. Immigration and emigration register.
11. Register of village heads, street heads, neighborhood heads, villagers.
12. Checkbook.

Audited accounts must be presented before a treasurer transfers the funds to his successor.

ART. 7. Selections from all documents shall be recorded in the receiving and dispatching books. All documents must be numbered for filing.

ART. 8. Town and village officers must keep secret the contents of all documents until they are delivered.

ART. 9. Official business must be attended to immediately by town and village officers. No delay is permitted.

ART. 10. Village and town heads must not refuse to receive people who come on official business from other villages.

ART. 11. The village and town officers shall be responsible to help the villagers organize self-government associations and to direct them if necessary.

ART. 12. Whenever village or town heads are unable to be on active duty, the vice-heads will be appointed as acting heads by the head of the district. If the period of absence is for more than one month, the head of the district must report the matter to the magistrate and obtain his permission.

ART. 13. The vice-heads of the villages and towns must have permission from the heads to act in their stead. If the period is for more than one month, permission must be given by the head of the district who must report the matter to the magistrate.

ART. 14. Village and town officers will make their own detailed regulations, but these must be approved by the magistrate.

ART. 15. These regulations may be revised by the magistrate, but he shall report his action to the Civil Administration Department for its approval.

ART. 16. These regulations are to be effective after they have been approved and published by the Civil Administration Department.

(Published by the Hsien Government, June 2, 1931.)

Whatever the rate of change, it was evident that the hsien governments were putting increasing pressure on the villages to adopt the new form of democratic self-government outlined in the Hsien Organization Act. In spite of continued passive resistance in many villages, it would be only a matter of a few years at most before the pre-1929 forms of village management would entirely disappear.

IV: VILLAGE LEADERS

A CHINESE SAYING states, "In the court we respect rank, in the country we respect age, and for real work we respect ability." Because the recognized leaders of the Chinese villages were usually of middle age or older, they were often called, in English, "village elders," although men in their twenties or younger might be included in the group. Another name often used was "association head," which was closer to the Chinese *hui-t'ou*. In this discussion of the number, characteristics, methods of appointment, and functions of the men who were members of the group in charge of village activities or were village officers we have used the terms "village leaders," "village elders," and "association heads," interchangeably. In general these apply to men whose position was nonpolitical. The groups were primarily concerned with purely village matters and were not directly connected with the government. Political connections and implications increased, however, as the village organizations went through a period of transition from the form generally prevalent before 1900 toward that prescribed in detail by the Nationalist government in its Hsien Organization Act of 1929.

We have not used the term "gentry" to indicate the village leadership groups or the groups from which the village leaders came. It applies much more to town than to village groups. Very few gentry lived in the villages.

According to C. L. Chang, the gentry were those who had passed at least one of the classical examinations.[1] H. B. Morse says that "gentry seems to be the best word to describe men of family of means, and of education, living generally on inherited estates, controlling the thoughts and feelings of their poorer neighbors and able to influence the action of the officials." [2] K. S. Latourette defines "local gentry" as "scholars, retired officials, men of wealth, the elders of the leading clans," and differentiates them from the village administration, the chief organ of which he describes as "a council of elders or managers and a head man . . . often made up of the leaders of the more important families and of the men who were generally recognized as having the most influence in the village, scholars and those who had won esteem by their force of character, experience and administrative ability." [3]

Just as a variety of names were given to the village organization in different areas, so, too, the titles for the officers of those organizations varied. Some were different but synonymous; others were quite unlike; some had definite geographical relationships. In the following passage the Chinese terms we found used in our villages are listed, and the English equivalents are given to show our non-Chinese readers the variety and shades of meaning of these terms:

Where she is part of the name it usually, though not always, indicates a locality in Shansi. Only a very few Honan and Shantung villages used the term. Hui generally indicates a non-Shansi area.

The head of the village she usually was the *she-shou;* the head of the village hui was the hui-t'ou or *hui-shou.* Occasionally, but not often, the head of a she was called hui-t'ou or hui-shou, and the heads of a few hui were known as she-shou. The subordinates were known as *p'ang-she-shou.* The only use of she-shou that we found in Hopei was on a list of village elders prepared in 1923 in connection with a lawsuit in which the village was involved. In some villages the head she-shou was known as the *tsung-she-shou.*

Chiu-shou was also a common designation of the she heads. If there was a chief, he was the *tsung-chiu-shou.* In a village in Ning-wu Hsien the head of the she was called chiu-shou and his assistant hui-t'ou. (The next year the assistant became the head and a new assistant was appointed.) In a village in Wu-chai Hsien the chief was a she-shou, but his two assistants were chiu-shou. In a village in Wen-shui Hsien there was one chiu-shou who was in charge of the business of the entire village; his five assistants, the heads of five different she, were called she-shou.

Hui-shou was sometimes used interchangeably with she-shou. A village in Lu-ch'eng Hsien had three she whose thirteen heads were called either she-shou or hui-shou. The *nan* ("south") she had six heads, the *pei* ("north") she had four, and the *chuang-shou* ("main village") she had three. Another village in the same hsien used only the term hui-shou, and here each of the seven surnames in the village contributed one hui-shou; one of the seven ordinarily was appointed accountant, but if none could do the work the position was given to another villager; the accountant was in no way superior to the other hui-shou. By way of contrast, in a village in Tun-liu Hsien with one she and eight she-shou, the one who was appointed accountant had greater authority than the other seven.

Chu-chia ("chief," or "boss") was sometimes used to designate the head official of a she. An example was a Hsing Hsien village that had only one she. Its business was managed by a chu-chia, assisted by either three or five hui-shou. A village in Lan Hsien had six she, each with a chu-chia and a chiu-shou in charge of its affairs. In that village, administration was in the hands of a political leader, the *ts'un-t'ou* or village head.

The term *ts'ung-kuan* ("general manager") was used in some villages. In a village in Hsi-yang Hsien, Shansi, the ts'ung-kuan looked after the production of the village plays, the worship of the gods, and other village activities, and came in rotation from among four families. In Village B, in Hopei, the village association in earlier years was controlled by a number of hui-t'ou who in annual rotation became *hsiang-t'ou*, ("incense head") and ts'ung-kuan, the one a religious and the other a secular officer. In some villages hsiang-t'ou was the term used for manager; sometimes *hsiang-shou* ("incense head") was used instead. In Shansi the hsiang-shou, despite the religious signification of the title, was sometimes the chief village officer and had duties not only in religious matters, but also in the direction of the crop-watching and the supervision of the schools. In a village in Fen-hsi Hsien the hsiang-t'ou appointed the she-shou who served under him.

Ching-li ("manager") was the name given to the chief officer of some villages. He was chosen by all the villagers. The term evidently came into use after the revolution of 1911, and the office had enough of a political tinge to keep it from being merely that of an association head. A village in Hsin Hsien had two ching-li and three hui-shou. All the family heads were eligible to be hui-shou, and they served in rotation. A village in Ling-shih Hsien had six ching-li who were appointed by their predecessors. Besides the ching-li there were eight chiu-shou who came in rotation from the different families; their sole function was the preparation and presentation of the village plays.

Kung-cheng ("just and fair") was a title given a political leader who, upon nomination by his predecessor, was appointed by the *hsien-chang*, or magistrate. The kung-cheng sometimes had rotating hsiang-shou serving under him. In a village in Ch'in Hsien the kung-cheng had serving with him three hsiang-shou who came in rotation from twelve *shen-t'ou*. The exact translation of *shen-t'ou* is "god head," but in this instance it designated a land unit that was used as the basis for rotation of the hsiang-shou. The village was divided into twelve units, shen-t'ou, each of which consisted of at least 30 mu of land. A full unit was obliged to provide a hsiang-shou once every six years. A half unit, from 20 to 30 mu, had to provide one every twelve years. Families with less than 20 mu had no opportunity to serve, or rather escaped service, which in this village evidently was looked upon more as an obligation than a privilege.

In a village in T'ai-ku Hsien the five heads of the she were one *pao-chang* and four she-shou. The pao-chang was appointed by the hsien magistrate, and then he in turn appointed the four she-shou, who seem to have served indefinite terms—at least, they were not changed annually. When the pao-chang retired, he selected his successor and sent his name to the hsien magistrate for appointment. Although the pao-chang's appointment was political, he coöperated with the she-shou in the non-political activities of theatrical productions and crop-watching.

The political leader of a village in Ling-shih Hsien was known as *chia-chang* ("neighborhood head"). He was in charge of the political affairs of twelve small villages and appointed the chiu-shou who were responsible for other village matters.

In a village in Chao-ch'eng Hsien the term for the association head, *kung-cheng she-shou*, indicated a complete social and political mixture.

The heads of hui were generally known as hui-shou or hui-t'ou. In Honan the *Tuan Ch'ing Hui* ("Green Crop Cutting Society"), the *T'ien Ti Hui* ("Heaven and Earth Society") the *Niu Wang Hui* ("God-of-the-Cattle Association"), and other religious organizations had big and little hui-shou. The big hui-shou was the chief officer for a year. At the end of his term he was replaced by one of the small hui-shou; he then reverted to the position of a small hui-shou. The Niu Wang Hui of a village in Ting-hsiang Hsien had six hui-shou. When, after six years, each of them had served as big hui-shou, a new set of officers was appointed. The T'ien Ti Hui of the same village operated on a four-year cycle with one big and three small *hui-shou*. The T'ien Ti Hui and the *Kuan Ti Sheng Hui* ("Holy Society of the God Kuan Ti") in another village in the same hsien each had one big and three small hui-shou.

In the Peiping area the heads of the *Ching Miao Hui* ("Green Crop Associations"), the *Ho Hui* ("United Associations"), the *Ta Hui* ("General Associations"), and the *Kung Yi Hui* ("Common Discussion Associations" or "Common Welfare Associations," depending on which *yi* character was used) were occasionally called hui-shou, but more generally hui-t'ou. They were not divided into big and little hui-t'ou as in Honan, but, as in Village A, two of their number regularly served as *chih-nien-hui-t'ou* ("annual executive officers") of the hui. Sometimes their titles were hsiang-t'ou and tsung-kuan.

When village or temple fair associations had several leaders, instead of being called hui t'ou, they were sometimes called *pan-shih jen* ("men who conduct affairs") or *shou-shih jen* ("men who lead affairs").

New names were adopted with the appointment, beginning about 1900 in the Peking area, of village heads and assistant heads to take over the work of the ti-pao and represent the village in dealing with the upper governments. These appointments had a definitely political hue. In Hopei the village heads were known as ts'un-chang and their assistants as ts'un-fu. In Shantung the heads were called chuang-chang and their assistants were sometimes known as *kung-shih* ("public affairs officer") or *pai-t'ou* ("section head").

QUALIFICATIONS OF VILLAGE LEADERS AND OFFICERS

All villages, as far as we could find, had one or more qualifications that must be met by village leaders and officers. The most usual and basic requirements were that a man should be a native of the village and that he should be the head of his family. Others were age, ability, wealth.

In those villages where all the families were related and belonged to the same clan group, all family heads could serve. In a Ling-chiu Hsien village with several family groups, all the family heads met both the basic qualifications and were eligible. In the Hsin Hsien village that had no other reported qualifications, the heads of only 80 of the 91 resident families were reported to be eligible. Although no explanation was given as to why 11 family heads were disqualified, it seems probable that they were not natives of the village. Immigrants were ineligible to be association heads or to hold village office, but they could, if they had the necessary ability, serve as village accountant and, at least occasionally, use that position to influence policy and action.

Younger brothers of family heads were seldom allowed to serve. In a village in the Peking area we found that two brothers had served as village elders at the same time and that the younger was the village head. This, however, was an emergency situation.[4]

A son ordinarily could not become a village elder until after his father's death or retirement. Nevertheless, the newly appointed head of Village D included two of his sons in a group of five members that he added to the leadership group in 1926. He was able to do this because both sons technically were eligible to serve—one had been adopted by an uncle and so belonged to a different family, and the other represented an absentee landlord. The father and his sons attempted to monopolize the direction of the village affairs; they were forced to resign in 1929.

In Village B a son who was a middle-school graduate was a village elder rather than his father who was the head of the wealthiest family in the village.

Property ownership.—Property ownership was a qualification in a great many villages. Sometimes the amount was indefinite, and the heads of the richest families were the ones chosen. Sometimes the family had to own a fixed amount of land or number of oxen before the head could serve as elder. In one village in Ting-hsiang Hsien and another in Hsin Hsien the land needed was only 10 mu. In others it was 20 or 30 mu, 50 mu, 100 mu, and 160 mu. In a Hsin Hsien village where the land requirement was 30 mu, the heads of only 12 of the 75 families could qualify.

In a village in Kuo Hsien the minimum requirement was 100 mu or a team of oxen. In the eyes of the villagers the two were practically equivalent, as a team was needed to till 100 mu and a family would not have a team unless it had that much land. In that village more than 20 of the 48 families qualified. In another village in the same hsien the ownership of a pair of oxen was the only property qualification. Oxen were much easier to count than mu of land. In that village 62 families had 44 oxen, 22 teams.

In some villages in Shansi there was a relative qualification under which the heads of the poorer families could serve, but less often or for shorter terms than the heads of the wealthier families. In a village in Wu-t'ai Hsien there were two limits, 25 and 50 mu. The heads of families with fewer than 25 mu never served. Those with 25 to 50 mu were eligible for a term only half as often as those with 50 mu or more.

In Ch'in Hsien a village had twelve divisions called shen-t'ou. Families with 30 mu or more were a full shen-t'ou, those with from 20 to 30 mu were only half a shen-t'ou. The head of a half-division became eligible for office only half as often as the head of a division family. Family heads with fewer than 20 mu were ineligible.

In another village in Ch'in Hsien 30 mu of *shen-li* qualified a family head to be a she-shou. The size of a shen-li mu depended on the quality of the land. One mu of good land was one mu of shen-li. One mu of poor land was only one half-mu of shen-li.

In a Hsin Hsien village the nominal minimum for association heads was 160 mu, but families with less than that amount could combine to bring their united holdings up to the required minimum and so be eligible to have a representative hold office. There were 24 shares of 160 mu each in the village. Because there were several families in a combined unit, the head of each one, under the rotation system used in the village, had less chance to serve than the heads of the wealthier families that were able to qualify as a single property unit.

A village in Wu-hsiang Hsien, recognizing the part wealth played in determining family position and influence, required that the hsiang-t'ou rotate among all the village families and that the group of elders should always include an equal number of representatives of rich and poor families.

In some villages a poor man never was appointed, partly because of his small landholdings, but also because village service took a considerable amount of time and a man needed at least some leisure if he were to serve. A Hsin Hsien village disqualified those who owned no land; it also banned unmarried men and indecent ones.

Prestige qualifications.—Outside of Shansi, the property qualifications in general were not so specific and definite. The chief consideration was usually the wealth and prestige of a family, and the village leaders would often be the heads of the most well-to-do families. Village N, in its Green Crop Association regulations, required that an association head should own immovable property worth at least $1,000.[5]

In some villages, because of the influence of his family, a man's position in the leadership group would be passed on to his eldest son or in some cases to his eldest grandson. Hence, a fifteen-year-old boy might be asked to become a village elder immediately upon his father's death or retirement.

In Village H three of the six association heads were either the second or third generation of their family to have a place in the leadership group. In Village B, of six leaders who retired in 1922 and 1927, four were succeeded by their sons and two by their grandsons. In a Wan-p'ing Hsien village, sixteen of the thirty-seven hui-t'ou who served during almost a hundred years, from "before 1837" through 1932, had followed their fathers or grandfathers in the position. Ten of the sixteen were the second-generation and six the third-generation representatives of their families.

Personal qualifications.—While family wealth and prestige remained important, personal qualifications were, through the 1920's, gradually gaining recognition, especially as more people were getting a modern type of education. Thus, in one instance, a man who had only 14 mu of land in the village and not more than 40 mu outside served many years as an elder and twice was the village head. Although his wealth did not compare with that of two other families, who owned several hundred mu of land, he was chosen because he was "brave and wise, righteous and unselfish, experienced in affairs outside the village, and much praised by his fellow villagers."

In Village A the association heads owned from 7 to 46 mu of land. The average holding was only 27.5 mu. This low figure undoubtedly was directly connected with the declining economic condition of the village.

In Village C the landholdings of the twenty association heads varied from none to 560 mu. The average was 146.5 mu; the median,

80 mu. Nine of the twenty had 100 mu or more. The man with no land was the village schoolteacher. (See table 12.)

In Village D a man who owned only 5 mu of land was a village elder. It was said that he had been invited to participate in the affairs of the Green Crop Association because "in ordinary social intercourse he put on the air of a gentleman." Only five of the thirteen village elders owned more than 30 mu, and only seven cultivated more than 30 mu. (See table 29.)

A list of the landholdings of the village elders and association officers of Village B for the years 1926–1928 shows that the newly added members belonged to families with relatively smaller land holdings. Four of the eight new heads had fewer than 50 mu, seven had fewer than 100 mu, and the family of the eighth man had more than 100 mu but fewer than 200. In 1926 seven of the fifteen heads had 200 mu or more, and only one had fewer than 50 mu. In 1928 the proportions were seven and five, of twenty-three members.

There were sixteen families in Village B who owned more than 100 mu of land. In 1929 the heads of twelve of the sixteen families were serving as elders.

The schoolteacher, who ordinarily would own no land, was asked to serve as an elder in several villages in the later years of the period covered by our study.

Standards set by the Nationalist government.—In its laws concerning village officers the Nationalist government disregarded and wiped out the old qualifications of nativity, seniority, and, usually, property ownership and set forth its own list. To be eligible for election by the village voters a man had to be at least twenty-five years of age and have performed at least one of the following re-quirements:

Passed civil examinations
Served the Kuomintang
Served the Nationalist government as an officer of the fourth rank
Taught in a primary school or graduated from middle school
Taken training in self-government
Had a record of service in the local hsien government

In 1933, after four years, the government's list was far from being universally accepted. In Villages A and D there were only two or three men who could meet even one of the requirements. In Villages B and H there were some twenty to thirty men who could qualify. In Village D the village head in 1932 could not meet any of the requirements; in fact, he could neither read a newspaper nor write a letter.

NUMBER OF ACTIVE LEADERS

The number of leaders active at any one time usually was only a small fraction of the number of family heads who were qualified to serve. Some villages had only two active leaders. Other villages had twenty, twenty-four, and even thirty men functioning in various capacities in any given year. Part of the difference was related to the number of families in the village, part to the amount of village activity.

A Shen-ch'ih Hsien village with 62 families and a Ling-ch'iu Hsien village with 85 families had only two active leaders apiece. Another Ling-ch'iu Hsien village, with 600 families, had sixteen she-shou. Still other villages, with 270 and 730 families, had twenty. The village that had twenty-four active she-shou had only 200 families, but there were three she looking after the village temples—with twelve, six, and six workers. The village with thirty leaders presented five dramatic performances during the year, and there were six men in charge of the arrangements for each set of plays.

Sometimes the number of active leaders was determined by the number of clan families in the village. In a one-name village, ordinarily all the family heads would be eligible, especially if the number was small. One such village, with four lines of descent, had one leader from each group. Another village had three clan families and five leaders, one each from two smaller families and three from a family that was some three times as large as the others. The relative size of a clan family group was determined by the number of families in the group rather than the number of persons in the families.

Sometimes the arrangement of streets or sections in the village determined the number of leaders. One village had four she-shou because it was divided into four blocks. Another had seven leaders because it had seven sections. A village with twelve leaders, two each from six streets, had none from the seventh because that happened to be a street with only one family name. Another village had a large she with three divisions; each division had two leaders. Still another had ten she-shou, five from each of two sections.

In Village H, with 375 families, the village association was controlled by the representatives of six families. Three of the six belonged to the largest and richest clan-group (it included 69 families), two came from other wealthy families, and the sixth leader was the schoolteacher. Three of the six elders were second-generation leaders. Two had succeeded their fathers, and one had succeeded his older brother, who had succeeded their grandfather. Two of the three were heads of families that belonged to the largest clan group.

In a group of 25 villages northwest of Peiping we found the number of elders to vary from twenty in a village with 270 families to only three in a village with 68 families. In 16 of the 25 villages the number of village elders represented from 4 to 10 per cent of the number of families and for all except one village the figure was between 3 and 16 per cent.

The number of leaders in a given village was sometimes subject to relatively wide and rapid variation. In one village, over a period of almost a hundred years, the number of elders changed thirty-one times and varied from three to eleven. Village D had five elders in the first half of 1932, but added eight more in the last half of the year. Village B had eleven elders at the beginning of 1922 and twenty-three at the end of 1928, four being added in 1922, two in 1927, and six in 1928. The replacement of six elders who retired by four sons and two grandsons has already been mentioned.

In 1922 a group of families in Village H revolted against the continued close control of village affairs by the heads of six families and threatened a lawsuit, which they were persuaded to give that up only when they were promised that additional leaders would be appointed. The promise was not fulfilled until 1928, when the Nationalist government was beginning to introduce measures to give the people more power. Then six new association heads were added, doubling the number of the elders.

In Honan the village associations generally had more qualified leaders than those in the Peiping area, but fewer than those in Shansi. A village in Chi Hsien had ten hui-shou from 62 families. Only four of the group served at a time, one "big hui-shou" who held office for one year and three "small hui-shou" who served for three years before they in turn became the big hui-shou. In some villages the active leaders were one big and two small hui-shou; in others there might be as many as six small hui-shou.

The control of village activity by many leaders rather than by a single head was a significant fact in the nonpolitical village associations in North China and seems to have been a distinguishing characteristic of their organization.

ROTATION IN OFFICE

In Shansi and in part of Honan the village associations generally followed the principle of rotation in office, giving a large majority of the family heads an opportunity to participate in the management of village affairs. In Hopei and Shantung we found only a few traces of the system, and then the rotation was likely to be only among the village leaders, or even among a small executive committee of the group of leaders.

The term of service for a given set of officers ordinarily was one year. In some villages, however, the term was only for a season, which when calculated by the festivals was four months. In others, because of a landownership qualification, officers with small amounts of land served six months, while those with large amounts served for a year.

The time required for all of the eligible heads in a given village to fill a term in office depended, of course, on the number of positions and the number of those eligible. In one village in Hsin Hsien it took only two years to go round. There were 12 families who were qualified by the ownership of more than 30 mu of land and there were six offices to be filled. In a village in Ling-ch'iu Hsien all of the 85 families were eligible for two offices, and it would presumably take some forty-two years to go round once. This case, however, involved a one-name village in which the families were divided into four patriarchal groups. The first year the two village officers came one each from groups one and two, the next year from groups three and four. As the number of families in each group was different, it would take each group a different length of time to go completely round. Almost the same situation prevailed in another village, where there were seven family-name groups, each of which sent a representative to the village association; the representatives held office for one year only. In a Wu-t'ai Hsien village there were three family-name groups, in approximately a 1:2:2 ratio by the number of families in the groups; the association heads from the three groups numbered five, seven, and eight. In a Ta-t'ung Hsien village there were three name groups with 20, 20, and 70 families; the five village elders were from the three families in a 1:1:3 ratio.

In other villages the rotation method was based on regional divisions, rather than family or patriarchal divisions within the village. Some had the same number of elders from each section. Others attempted to adjust, at least slightly, to the differing numbers of families in the different sections. In a Hsin Hsien village with four sections the ratio was 7:4:3:2 for a total of sixteen elders; they held office for one year, then another sixteen took their places.

In the Ch'in Hsien village in which 30 mu or more was a full shen-t'ou and from 20 to 30 mu a half shen-t'ou, there were twelve shen-t'ou and three village officers. A full shen-t'ou served every four years, a half shen-t'ou every eight years.

In the Hsin Hsien village in which a full share was 160 mu, there were 24 shares and three hui-shou; thus the cycle was eight years. For the families who, because they had fewer than 160 mu, had to combine to make a full share, the chance that a particular family head would serve depended, of course, on the number of families in the share.

Some villages had a double system of rotation, first in the officers of the district she and then in the over-all grand she, the head of which came, in turn, from the district she. A Ch'i Hsien village had eight small district she and eight she-shou who came in rotation from the families living in the district. Over them was a grand she whose she-shou came from a given district once in eight years. In a Wen-shui Hsien village with five she the cycle for the chiu-shou, who was in charge of village affairs, was five years.

In some villages the term of service might be two years, the first as assistant and the second as chief official. In others it might be three, four, five, or even six years. In a Hui Hsien village in Honan there was a big hui-shou and three small hui-shou for the village. Each year the men advanced one step and so were in office for a total of four years; only one new man was appointed every year. In other villages the big hui-shou became a small hui-shou when his year's term was over; the group continued to serve until all in turn had been big hui-shou, then a new set of officers was appointed. The system of big and little hui-shou was widely used in northern Honan.

In some of the villages using this system of rotation the big hui-shou not only gave his time to the administration of the village affairs, but also had to spend some of his own money during his year in office. It was believed by the village elders that they would be specially blessed if they contributed to the village treasury, and they were equally afraid that the opposite would result if they underhandedly profited at the expense of the village. Our reporter noted that this attitude was an excellent safeguard against the misuse or embezzlement of village funds.

A village in Kuo Hsien had an unusual form of organization in its association for the worship of the god of fire. There were six big hui-shou and six small hui-shou. Each big hui-shou served in turn for one year. He was assisted by one of the small hui-shou, who owned less land and could never advance to be a big hui-shou.

A Hsin Hsien village had sixteen hui-shou, eight from the front street, four from the rear street, and four from the east street. These leaders served in teams of four for terms of three months each. The order of service was determined during the first month, probably about New Year's time. Men serving as chiu-shou of the associations that organized the village plays served even shorter terms.

There was some rotation in the Peiping area, but generally it was before 1900. So far as we could find, the rotation did not include all the families in the village, but only the group of influential, self-appointed village elders. Sometimes the rotation was only in what might be called the executive committee, a small inner group, two of whom were responsible for one year for the ordinary executive work of the village. They called on the entire group of elders only when there were unusual matters to handle. This was true in Village A and is more fully described in the account of that village. There, it will be noted, the power of the executive officers of the association was superior to that of the village head, who in most villages was in charge of all political matters.

In Village C the offices of village head and assistant head were rotated annually among an executive committee of six of the twenty members of the village association.

In earlier days in a Shantung village, there were twelve elders in the association and six local offices, permitting a two-year cycle of service. Later the number of elders was reduced to eight and the number of annual workers to four. Later still, the number of elders was reduced to five and the rotation plan was discontinued, as had been done earlier in most Shantung villages.

OTHER METHODS OF SELECTING VILLAGE LEADERS

Besides the rotation plan, we found other methods of selecting leaders. Under one, regular appointments were made, usually every year and for the duration of that year. Under another, appointments were indefinite and new ones were made only when vacancies occurred. The Shansi villages using selection rather than rotation usually followed the first type. Hopei villages generally conformed to the second type. The first was likely to be used where the leaders were few in number and where their offices were more or less political in nature. Ordinarily the same officers were chosen again and again, and there was little change even though the appointment was for only one year.

A Hsing Hsien village had no village association and no association heads. The only leader was called ts'ung-t'ou ("village head") and was chosen by the villagers to manage all their community affairs. His term was nominally for one year, but he usually held office for several years.

In several villages in Yü-tz'u Hsien the leaders were called kung-cheng. They usually were men who had gained some reputation, especially in the old-style civil service examinations. There was only one kung-cheng for each village, and he was chosen by the villagers for a one-year term.

Even where the village had the she type of association, the association heads might be selected rather than serve in rotation. A village in T'ai-ku Hsien was one of the few where this system was followed. It had five she with two she-shou in each. There was also a *kung-cheng*, chosen by all the villagers, for the entire community. The leaders of each she were selected by the she members and their appointments were for indefinite terms.

Still another method of electing village leaders was one in which the chief officer, the pao-chang, was appointed by the hsien magistrate upon nomination by the outgoing pao-chang. In his turn, the chief officer then selected the she-shou who were to assist him. This system was used by a village in T'ai-ku Hsien, Shansi. The appointed pao-chang and his assistants served indefinite terms and, with good behavior, could continue in office as long as they desired.

In another village in the same hsien the head of the big she of the village was a pao-chang who was appointed by the hsien magistrate upon nomination by the village. Public opinion determined the choice of the person to be nominated. The chiu-shou of the big she were appointed by the pao-chang. The she-shou of the six small she of the village came, in rotation, from the families in each of the she.

A village in Ling-shih Hsien had four chiu-shou who took care of all of the local affairs. They were selected by the li-chang, a political leader for an area that included several villages. He was appointed by the magistrate upon nomination by the outgoing li-chang.

Another village in Ling-shih Hsien had six ching-li, each of whom had been appointed by his predecessor. It also had eight chiu-shou whose function it was to superintend the dramatic performances of the village. They all served in rotation.

A village in Shen-chih Hsien, Hopei, was divided into several *p'ai* ("sections") of 10 families each. A leader, the *p'ai-t'ou*, was selected by the families in each p'ai. The several p'ai-t'ou then elected the village head, the ts'un-chang.

In a village in T'ai-an Hsien, Shantung, there were six p'ai with 30 to 50 families in each. The families in each chose a section head, *p'ai-chang*, and an assistant p'ai-chang. The six p'ai-chang and the six assistants chose the chuang-chang or village head.

In the Peiping area new village elders usually were co-opted by the elders already in office. Once appointed, they ordinarily served an indefinite period, often until they retired or died. A few served for a time, gave up office for one reason or another, and later were invited to rejoin the leadership group. Some positions more or less belonged to a family rather than to an individual, and so were handed down from father to son. Often the son became an elder immediately after the father's death or retirement; sometimes an interval of time elapsed.

In some villages membership in the group of leaders was not regularly passed on to the next generation, and when a leader died or retired, his family lost its position in the inner group. A member of the family might later be asked to serve, but because of his own personality and ability rather than solely on the basis of his family's wealth and influence.

Replacements were not necessarily made as soon as vacancies occurred. In Village D and the surrounding area it was a general practice to wait and make new appointments when a new village head took office. That gave him an opportunity to nominate his friends and have them help him with his program. In Village D five new members were appointed in 1926 when a new village head was installed. In 1929, when another head came in, three new appointments were made. Evidently some of the new appointees dropped out after very short terms, for the number of elders was down to five in the spring of 1932. Later in the year another new head was appointed and eight new members were added, bringing the total to thirteen. Two of the new appointees had previously been elders, and the ancestors of another two had been members of the leadership group.

Occasionally a village head attempted to force the retirement of some of the village elders so that he could appoint his friends, but such attempts generally were unsuccessful.

As the villages grew, the leadership group was often enlarged. Sometimes new members were co-opted because of their special ability to deal with a particular problem. In 1902 a subordinate officer of the hsien district was added to the leadership group of Village H, which was having trouble with a notorious member of the largest and most powerful family. In 1920 another man was asked to help the village in its struggle with the nearby town over the location of the district higher primary school. The village was successful: it offered to give the school a grant of $100, the income from the temple land, and the use of the Confucian temple, which was repaired by volunteer labor. Sometimes, as was the case in Village H, new members were added because of pressure from a group of dissatisfied villagers.

REWARDS FOR SERVICE

According to our records, all village elders and officers gave their services without pay. In one instance an assistant village head offered to keep the village accounts if he were given the $2 a month given to the previous accountant, but his offer was promptly refused on the grounds that no village officers were to be paid. Most of the elders belonged to the wealthier village families and had leisure time that they could devote to community service. The budget for ordinary village activities usually did not require any very sizable amounts, and except for some possible padding of expense accounts there ordinarily was little opportunity for personal gain. Whether those who delivered money collected for the military received or took a commission for their services is not known. It naturally would not be shown in the village account. The repairing of the village wall, the rebuilding of a temple, the purchase of guns for the local guard, involved fairly large amounts from which those directly involved might have had an opportunity to reward themselves. It has been reported that when town gentry organized, supervised, and raised the funds for large community works such as the repair of the river dikes or the organization and equipping of a hsien guard, their "opportunity for personal gain was considerable." [6] Our reports did not indicate similar practice in the villages. It was noted that official position often made it possible to appoint poor relatives to village jobs. The safekeeping of any surplus village funds was determined by the village leaders. The money and therefore its use, generally interest free, was often given to one or more of the wealthier families, a perquisite that seldom went outside the leadership group; the money, however, was repayable on demand.

AGE OF LEADERS

It was generally true that association members and village elders were of a relatively advanced age, especially when they were appointed or elected and did not succeed their fathers. If a man did not inherit property, he would need to be fairly well along in years before he could have had time to amass sufficient wealth or to acquire the experience and develop the personality that would make him a reasonable candidate for appointment.

In Village A the average age of the eight elders was 44 years; the range was 26 to 62 years. Their school education was from 4 to 11 years.

In Village C the average age of the twenty leaders was almost the same, 43.6 years. They had from 4 to 8 years of education. (See table 12.)

In Village D one man became an elder at 53 years and another at 74 years. The other elders said that the older man was appointed because of his age.

PROFILE OF VILLAGE LEADERS IN PEIPING AREA

Reports from twelve villages in the Peiping area gave us, for 1932, a sample profile of the village leaders—their number, the amount of land they owned, their age, age when appointed, length of service, and occupation. The number ranged from six to nineteen. The total was 142, the average twelve.[7]

The amount of land owned by the families of the leaders was none to 1,460 mu. Four families had no land. Seventeen had fewer than 20 mu. The average was 81 mu per family, 70 mu per family if the exceptional family with 1,460 mu were omitted. The next largest holding was 480 mu. The median was 50 mu. In the individual villages the averages were 34 to 201 mu per family, or from 34 to 125 mu if the 1,460-mu family were omitted.

The age of the leaders ranged from 16 to 84 years. The average for the twelve villages was 47 years. In individual villages the averages were 41 to 56 years.

The age when appointed ranged from 15 to 61 years. The average was 32 years. The individual-village averages were 26 to 44 years. For five of the villages the average was less than 30 years. Leaders appointed before they were 25 years of age were almost one out of four, 23.6 per cent; 9.4 per cent were appointed before the age of 20 years.

Length of service ranged from 2 to 58 years. Eight men had been association heads for 40 years or more. Twelve per cent had held office for more than 30 years, 45 per cent for not more than 10 years. The average was 15 years. In the different villages the average length of service ranged from 4 to 28 years; for two villages it was 8 years or less, and for three, 23 years or more.

We had data on the history of family leadership for only five of the villages. They had a total of forty-eight elders. One of the families had given eight generations of service to its village. Thirteen families had had a member among the association heads for five or more generations. (See table 13.)

In six villages, sixty-four of the seventy-six association heads were farmers, three were shopowners, six had formerly been shop workers, one was a grain merchant, one was a carpenter, and one had been a servant of the Imperial Family.

The records of one of the villages showed the changes in the number of leaders from "before 1837" through 1932. We were able to obtain personal notes on the leaders in office in 1932 and on their ancestors who had served in earlier years.

Thirty-seven men, from 21 families, had been association heads during the period. No single family had been represented during the entire time. The longest period of unbroken family service was fifty-four years, from 1861 to 1914. That family held office from before 1837 to 1914 with the exception of four years, 1857–1860, the time between a father's retirement and his son's appointment.

Another family was represented from before 1837 to 1932 except for a period of sixteen years, 1867–1882; another family from 1857 to 1932 with two breaks, one for a year, 1863, between the death of a father and the appointment of his son, the other for twenty-six years, 1888–1913.

Five families had provided association heads for three generations. Two of these had skipped the third generation and in 1932 were represented by a member of the fourth generation. Five families had served for two generations. Eleven of the leaders were the first of their family to hold the office, at least since "before 1837."

The number of association heads, at any one time, ranged from three to eleven. The average was 6.7. There were ten or eleven heads

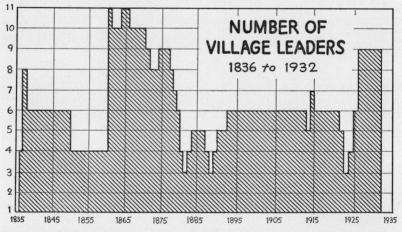

Fig. 8.—Changes in the number of village leaders (association heads) in one sample village, 1836 to 1932.

during the period 1861 through 1871. The number was down to three in 1882, 1889, and 1923, but each time an additional member was appointed the next year. From 1880 through 1925 the number was less than six except for one year. From 1926 through 1932 the number was nine. A chart of the changes is given in figure 8.

One wonders why, in 1837, the number of association heads was doubled, from four to eight. The seven new appointments made in 1861, which raised the number from four to eleven, probably were connected with war and the demands made on the village by invading foreign troops. The appointment of four new heads in 1926 came with the selection of a new village head to replace one whose program had been very unpopular; at the same time there was much local unrest brought about by the civil war in North China and the movement of large numbers of troops.

Marked fluctuation in the number of leaders alternated with long stretches of great stability. During the period, in five stretches of five years or more, 1838–1850, 1851–1856, 1893–1912, 1916–1920, and 1926–1932, there were no changes in the village leadership for a total of 51 out of 97 years.

Of the 21 families whose heads had been village elders, 15 had been represented for more than 10 years, 14 for more than 20 years, 13 for more than 25 years, 8 for more than 30 years, 5 for more than 40 years, and 2 for more than 70 years. Both of the last two had been represented by members of three generations, one for a total of 75 years, the other for 80 years.

Of the twenty-eight who retired before 1932 there were twenty-one who served for more than 10 years, thirteen for more than 20 years, and five for more than 30 years. The longest term was 38 years; there was one of 35 years. One head served for only a year, two for only 2 years.

The terms of the four men who were in office before 1837 probably would have had been longer if we could have carried the record farther back. In figuring time in office for those four, "before 1837" has been taken as 1836. On that basis two of the four had 21 years of service. The terms of the others were 2 years and 15 years.

Of the twelve men who followed their fathers as association heads, only three succeeded to the position immediately on the father's death or retirement. For the others there was a gap of at least 2 years. In one instance the gap was 27 years. In another it was 46 years. The three men who followed their grandfathers took office from 45 to 48 years after the grandfather's retirement. In their village the office evidently was not inherited automatically because of the family's wealth or position.

In 1932, at the end of our study, all nine leaders then in office had served for at least 7 years. Their average age was 44 years. The average age when they took office was 36 years. Only one man was less than 30 years of age when he was asked to serve. None of the leaders had served for more than 12 or less than 7 years. The average term, 8 years, was next to the lowest in the twelve villages included in our special leadership study. The difficulties of the countryside during the fighting in North China and the resignations of four leaders between 1922 and 1924 would account, in part at least, for the low average. Four of the leaders were the third generation of their family to serve the village as an association head. Two were of the second generation. The other three represented new families in the governing group.

Sketches of village elders.—The following are thumbnail sketches of the nine elders in office in 1932 in the village just discussed:

1. Y.S.T., age 43, was both the village head and the head of the village association. In 1932 he was the senior association head, with 12 years of service. He had been village head for 7 years. He was appointed in 1926 after his younger brother, Y.S.C., had been forced out as village head because of the actions he had taken to meet the demands of the military forces.

Y.S.T. had only one year of classical education. It was said that he was rather an ordinary person in his youth, had helped his father with the farming and indulged in bad habits with his friends, and was "just the ordinary type of country youth." He underwent a radical change at the age of 22 years, when he was admitted to the police training school. He completed the one-year course and then served as a training officer in one of the police districts of Wan-p'ing Hsien until he was transferred to a substation, to head the police force there. At the age of 26 years he was called home by his father, who wanted his help on the family farm and wanted to discipline him for his "romantic behavior of all sorts." Two years later, when the district head started a system of village police, Y.S.T. became the policeman for his village. The next year the village police were abolished and he became a village association head. Later he was made head of the local guards and vice-head of the district guards; in 1931 he tried, but failed, to get an appointment as head of the district office.

In 1926 he was made village head, succeeding his younger brother, who resigned. The same year, four new association heads were appointed, increasing the total to nine.

It was reported that Y.S.T.'s personal ability and his police experience made it possible for him to deal with the armed forces and to meet the emergencies created by their demands. His family owned 30 mu of land.

In 1924, when there was a great deal of fighting and disturbance around Peking, the then village head, who was one of the older leaders and had been serving for three years following the retirement of Y.S.T.'s father, found himself unable to deal with the village problems and resigned. Because of the difficulties involved, the other leaders refused to accept appointment as village head and so turned to Y.S.T.'s younger brother, Y.S.C., and asked his help in meeting the military demands. Even though he had had no previous connection with the village administration, they made him an association head and the village head at the same time. This was one of the few instances where two brothers were association heads at the same time and the younger, as village head, would take precedence over the older. The appointment evidently was an emergency measure resorted to because of disturbed conditions and the refusal of other leaders to take major responsibility.

Y.S.C. was described as a very able young man who had been nicknamed "Old Hen," a name that had belonged to a celebrated commander in the Han dynasty; he was also said to be slippery and undependable. The latter description came, in part at least, from the way in which he met the crises connected with the fighting around Peking. Demands were made on the village by the soldiers regularly quartered in the area and by the forces that were passing through. To meet these demands and other village needs, Y.S.C. sold some of the village land, an act which lost him the confidence and support of the older association heads. So many of them threatened to resign that he was forced out of office at the end of 1925. He was then succeeded by his older brother.

Y.S.T.'s father was only 16 years old when his father died. Because of his youth and inability to protect himself, he became a prey of the village bullies.[8] At the age of 19 years, he began to take singing lessons. At the age of 21 he was asked to serve as one of the heads of the village organization which was the predecessor of the Green Crop Association. He could not be active in the organization, since his singing took him away from the village a great deal of the time. When he was 26 years old he was asked by a well-to-do Peking family to supervise the construction of their cemetery near his village. While engaged in that work he was approached for a loan by one of the village bullies, who, when the loan was not forthcoming, threatened him with a knife. In self-defense he attacked the bully and, with the help of the men working on the cemetery, killed him. The laborers wanted to bury the body and keep the matter secret. Y.S.T.'s father, however, went to the police and reported the bully's death. In spite of the fact that he had acted in self-defense, he was jailed. It was only after two years' effort, with the expenditure of a large sum of money and the help of an influential friend, that he was able to regain his freedom. He obtained the money that was needed by selling most of the family land.

When he came home from jail, he was given an impressive welcome by the villagers. They killed a pig and offered sacrifices to give thanks to the god of heaven and to honor their returning hero. He joined a professional group of singers and actors who gave plays for the public. He was again asked to be one of the village association heads, a post he accepted but to which he could give little time or attention, for again his singing kept him away from the village most of the time.

When he was 46 years old he gave up his singing career and stayed at home. The next year he was made village head, a position that he held until he was 59 years of age, when he resigned on his own initiative. His eldest son took his place as a village elder. One of the older association heads succeeded him as village head. While in office Y.S.T.'s father bought some land for the village and some guns for its self-defense, and helped the village turn the private school into a public one.

Y.S.T.'s grandfather was one of the leaders in the establishment of the Little Temple about 1837. From that time on, a small but independent organization was maintained in the village. Neither records nor tradition gave its name or its activities, but evidently the later village association grew out of the organization first connected with the Little Temple. The grandfather resigned from the organization about 1867 and died in 1878.

Y.S.T.'s great-grandfather came to the village about 1800. There were then only about a dozen families in the village and they seem not to have made any attempt to develop a village organization. Gradually the great-grandfather bought "more than 200 mu of land." The exact amount probably was not known by his descendants; they reported it in general terms.

2. L.L.H., age 52, was an association head in name only. He had next to the longest term of service of the heads acting in 1932, eleven years, but he ordinarily sent his steward to association meetings and rarely appeared in person. Our reporters noted that he had neither the ability nor the intention of serving the village. He seemed to have been appointed to and continued in office because of the family's wealth. The family owned 1,460 mu, but was gradually

selling the land because L.L.H. was an opium addict and the income from the land was not enough to meet his needs.

The father of L.L.H. was trained in Chinese boxing and held the second military degree, *wu-chu*. He served as an association head for many years and did good work for the village. He and his family had to flee the Peking area in 1900 because of the fighting, and practically everything in his house was lost, including many contracts and deeds. He died soon afterward.

The grandfather of L.L.H. came from Shansi about 1850 and bought about 30 mu of land, which he farmed for some 10 years. In 1860 he became a eunuch and entered the Forbidden City as a servant of the emperor. He won the favor of the emperor and became very rich. Tradition, perhaps exaggerated, had it that at one time he owned 100,000 mu of land, 100 horses, 100 camels, 30 carts, 400 guns, 300 servants, and 50 shops. He was greatly interested in promoting the welfare of his village and paid most of the cost of building the Large Temple. To carry on his name and to have someone to inherit his property he adopted a son, who later became the father of L.L.H.

3. S.C.T., age 52, worked for many years in a grain shop. When the shop closed, he opened a small inn near the railroad station, but was unsuccessful in that venture. He then became a farmer, on 52 mu of land. His father was an accountant in a tea shop in the neighboring town. S.C.T. was asked to serve the village association in 1925. He was the first of his family to hold such a position.

4. H.Y.K., age 34, served an apprenticeship of three years in a grocery shop. He then went home because of illness and had not thereafter taken any outside work. He was asked to be an association head in 1926. In 1932 he was assistant village head. His great-grandfather and his grandfather's second brother were association heads. The family had a farm of 120 mu.

5. F.L.T., age 42, had two years of classical education. He farmed the 17 mu owned by his family and some 60 mu of rented land. Occasionally he worked as a donkey driver. He was one of the new association heads appointed in 1926.

6. S.H.C., age 44, came to the village in 1915 to help his father. He had spent his youth in the family's old home in Shansi. His grandfather was one of the founders of the Large Temple and had been a village head for some 22 years. S.H.C. became an association head in 1924. In 1932 he was one of the two association treasurers. His family had 37 mu of farm land.

7. L.K.T., age 46, had four years of classical education. His father

was an association head for some 19 years, but the family was not wealthy and so had little time to give to public affairs. L.K.T. became an association head in 1924. The family owned 32 mu of land.

8. C.H.C., age 42, came from a poor family. None of his ancestors had any connection with the village association. He served for two years as an apprentice in a Peking drug shop, then came home and made farming his career. He occasionally drove donkeys or carts in order to earn extra income. He became an association head in 1926. The family had 34 mu of land, but it possibly was of poorer quality than comparable amounts owned by other association heads.

9. W.S.C., age 41, became an association head in 1926. In 1932 he was serving as one of the two association treasurers. He owned 26 mu of land.

V: CROP-WATCHING

Ripening crops in open fields could not be left unguarded. They were too much of a temptation. In some villages every farm family watched its own fields, and a large part of the local population went out about dusk to spend the night on guard. Some villages made crop-watching a coöperative enterprise, a few men standing guard every night and the program so arranged that every farming family took part in the work. The number of nights a family furnished a watchman was determined by the number of mu in its farmland. Some villages hired watchmen and had them on duty during the entire growing season, in the spring for wheat and in the fall for millet, kaoliang, corn, beans, and other crops.

Kung K'an I Po ("Watch the Crops Together") was a slogan painted on the walls in many places in Shantung. Presumably in earlier days coöperative crop-watching was the practice in that area, but at the time of our study most of the villages employed watchmen.

In a Tsou-p'ing Hsien village the 1932 wheat crop was guarded by sixteen men, the villagers taking turns at the assignment, eight men in the north section, four in the west, and two each in the east and south. For the fall season the village engaged paid watchmen. Another village had given up coöperative crop-watching shortly before our study. A third village as late as 1921 had seven or eight groups of eight persons each watching the crops in rotation; each group was under the leadership of a village elder. In another village there were two crop-watching groups, one for the six sections at the west end of the village and one for the two sections at the eastern end. In still another village two of the eight sections of the village had coöperative crop-watching while the other six employed watchmen.

In Honan we found a village in Chi Hsien where, under the leadership of the "great family," the villagers drew lots to determine when they should serve. In Chieh-hsiu Hsien, Shansi, a special organization called *I-T'ien She* ("Public Field Association") carried on coöperative crop-watching. Hsi-yang Hsien in Shansi had a hsien-wide organization for crop-watching, with local associations in the villages. *Lien-chuan Hui* and *Ho-chuang Hui* ("United Association") were the names used for the hsien-wide organization.

In Hopei we found no examples of earlier coöperative crop-watching, but in 1933 a Shu-lu Hsien village was trying out, for the first time, a plan whereby groups of four villagers took turns in watching all the crops in the village area.

In Village J, in Shansi, the farmers in groups of five assisted one employed watchman whenever the crops were especially good and the single watchman could not protect them properly. The groups of volunteers were arranged by the head of the she; the amount of help required from each family was determined by the size of its farm.

CHARACTERISTICS OF HIRED WATCHMEN

In most villages the crop-watching was done by one or more hired watchmen. In our sample villages the number was from one to nine. The watchmen usually were poor men, most of whom owned no land and were without other regular employment. The ones chosen to serve were generally physically strong, so that they could cope with any crop thieves they might discover. Sometimes villages found it advisable to chose "big hands"—known crop thieves—in order to keep them occupied and stop their predatory activities. Some watchmen were poor relatives of the village leaders. One village report told of the appointment of a morphine addict as a watchman. One of the older men summarized the situation in his village when he said, "If they (the crop-watchers) are not rogues, they are favorites."

Most villages required that the watchmen should promise to compensate the owners of stolen or damaged crops if the culprits were not discovered and that the promise be assured by one or more guarantors. A sample contract to be signed by the village head, the watchman, and his guarantor is given in the account of Village K.

We found one watchman who had served for twenty years and another who had served for seventeen years.

CROP-WATCHING INCIDENT

An American friend reported a crop-watching experience in Shansi. Some peaches that he had growing near his house were, for a time, unmolested, and he was able to enjoy the fruit picked ripe from the tree. Then there were depredations by night raiders. On advice of the family cook a crop-watcher was hired to protect the peaches. The new employee slept soundly all night in the servants' quarters, but no fruit was stolen. When a protest was made to the cook, he calmly replied, "Your peaches are safe. The watcher comes from the village across the valley where the thieves come from. Now they know that you are paying the watcher to protect the peaches, so they won't come any more, as that would cause the watcher to lose his job."

AREA WATCHED

The area that the watchmen were to guard varied greatly from village to village. For the seven villages for which we have figures, the range was from 310 to 2,000 mu (some 50 to 335 acres) per man. For four of the villages the average area was 500 mu or less. It was possible for one man to cover the unusually large of 2,000 mu in Village B because most of the land was planted to trees and peanuts.

OTHER RULES ENFORCED BY WATCHMEN

Besides protecting the crops, the watchmen were called on to enforce certain village rules. For example, stripping of the lower kaoliang leaves was permitted by the village leaders in most years for about three days during midseason. At that time the fields were open to anyone who wanted to take the leaves for his own use, but the program for any particular year depended largely on the season and the condition of the crops.

At harvesttime if the crops were good the poor people of the village usually were allowed to glean in the harvested fields. Some years they might be allowed to go to the fields only on certain days. Other years no gleaning was allowed. As many of the poor people relied heavily on gleaning for at least part of their food supply, some villages used to give them grain if no gleaning was allowed. In later years there was no gift of grain. The regulations for the control of gleaning and theft at harvesttime were very strict, sometimes so strict that a farmer was not allowed to take his own grain stalks from the field during the days when gleaning was tabooed. In Hsin-hsiang Hsien, in Honan, the cultivators could pick only the cotton fiber from the plants. They had to leave the unripe bolls for the gleaners.

SEASONS FOR CROP-WATCHING

Around Peiping and in other areas where wheat was grown there regularly were two seasons when crop-watchmen were on duty. The first was for about six weeks in the spring, the second for about three months in the fall. The starting times differed among the villages, but usually were set for a definite date and generally were the same from year to year. The closing dates ordinarily depended on the season. Village A started its spring watching on the fourteenth day of the third month and ended it at the end of the fourth month. Village H began on the third day of the fifth month and ended on the second day of the sixth month. From the difference in dates it seems probable that Village A reported its dates according to the lunar calendar and Village H according to the solar one.

A number of villages began their fall season on the sixth day of the sixth month, Kuan Ti's birthday, and ended about the end of the ninth month. For other villages the fall starting-date was the twenty-fourth day of the sixth month, also said to be Kuan Ti's birthday. Village H gave its starting date as the fourteenth day of the seventh month and its closing date as the eighth day of the ninth month.

LAND-REGISTRATION CEREMONIES

The villages set different times for the registration of the land to be assessed for the next fiscal year. For some the first registration was made when the crop-money was paid at the end of the previous year. The leaders of some villages met during the New Year's holiday and prepared the land books for the year. Other villages made up the register when they started the spring watching. Still others, and perhaps the majority, did it at the opening of the fall season. Whether it was done in spring or fall, many of the villages made this a special day, with a feast for and worship of the gods. A special meal was prepared for those who came to register the family land. In a few instances the landowners made a small advance payment on the crop-money assessment so that the village authorities could have money available for expenses that had to be met before the end of the year.

Some villages charged 20 coppers (5 cents) to help defray the cost of the meal. They called it *mien-ch'ien* ("noodle money"), as the main dish was noodles made from wheat flour. The village elders paid 30 coppers, as they were on duty all day and had two meals. If they were busy a second day, they paid another 30 coppers. One village charged 15 cents for the spring meal of noodles and 20 cents for the more elaborate meal of eight dishes, with noodles, served for the fall thanksgiving. Another village provided that if the family representative did not partake of the special meal he would be given one catty of flour that he might take home to his family.

As space and equipment were limited, the registrants usually were served in relays and often the cooks were kept busy for the entire day and sometimes for a second day.

THANKSGIVING CELEBRATION

The actual crop-watching ended when the harvesting was finished, but the season and the fiscal year of the village association closed officially with a thanksgiving celebration held sometime toward the end of the ninth month or near the beginning of the tenth month. The exact date depended on the season and sometimes on the convenience of the village leaders. In some villages the thanksgiving activities went on for two days. In the Peiping area they included worship of the gods, the payment by the farmers of their crop-money assessments, the offering of food to the gods, and a special meal for the family representatives who came to the meeting. There were special tables for any women who came, either as landowners or as proxies for the heads of their families.

When worship of the gods was part of the program, candles, incense, and dishes of food were set out on the table in front of the altar. The village head would be the first to kneel and kowtow, usually bowing his head to the ground three times before the image. He also lit a bundle of incense and burned a long yellow paper on which were written prayers, the name of the village, and the date. The other village leaders would follow and make their obeisances. If there were several temples in the village, the elders often went in a body from temple to temple to burn incense and bow before the deities. Many of the villagers burned incense and kowtowed three times after they had paid their crop money.

In one village two offerings of food were set out in the temples, one in front of the image of the deity, the other outside the temple building. Later the inner offering went to the temple caretaker, the outer to the boys who stood round as spectators.

The close of the thanksgiving meeting was the end of the fiscal year of the association. Crop-money was collected. Bills were paid. Loans made during the year to provide operating funds were repaid. Accounts were completed and presented to the village leaders. If there was any rotation in office, the new incumbents generally took over at that time.

In some villages a summary of the accounts was posted on the wall near the temple, but in many others the elders were unwilling to let the villagers see the accounts lest it be inferred that there was lack of confidence in the handling of the money. If outsiders saw the accounts, the village might be subjected to loss of face in the event that the amounts recorded were small, or to other difficulties if the amounts were large.

The cost of the registration and thanksgiving meetings in Village A ranged from $30 in 1927 to $60 in 1929. In 1928 the meeting was omitted because conditions around Peiping were greatly disturbed and because the military had assessed the village $563. This was more than four times the amount demanded in 1927. In Village B the cost of the meeting ranged from $40 in 1923 to $86 in 1932.

TWO CASE STUDIES OF THANKSGIVING DAY

1. In 1932 the tenth day of the ninth month was the thanksgiving day for many of the villages north of Peiping. In one village, ten association heads met at seven o'clock in the morning at the Kuan Ti Miao, more generally known as Lao Yeh Miao, the "Old Master Temple." Paper horses, which later would be burned, and a square table on which were lighted candles, burning incense, and dishes of fruit and vegetables, were placed in front of the big images on the altar in the main room. The tables for the association account books and records were set up at one end.[1]

The charges to be collected from the farmers were 10 cents for food-money and 10 cents a mu for crop-money. At about eight o'clock the first landowner came, walked over to the association treasurer and gave him $2.10. The treasurer said, "Your bill is two dollars and fifty cents—ten cents for food-money and two dollars and forty cents for crop-money, or did you lease four mu?"

The landowner said that he had leased the four mu to Mr. Wang.

The money was counted again and recorded in the village account books.

The next man paid $3.10. The treasurer said that the bill was $3.30, so there was a shortage of 20 cents. "Three dollars for crop-money is enough—there is no shortage," the man replied.

"How about the two mu near Mr. Chen's land?" the treasurer asked.

"I leased them out so you had better shut your eyes," the man whispered. The money was accepted and recorded.

"Here's two dollars and sixty cents—ten cents food-money and the rest crop-money," said the next man. "I leased three mu to Mr. Lung."

The fourth man put 200 coppers (50 cents) on the table and said, "Ten cents for food-money and one dollar and fifty cents for crop-money. I still owe you one dollar and ten cents."

It was the custom for everyone to worship Kuan Ti after paying food-money and crop-money. One man said, "Let me pay my respects to Lao Yeh (another name for Kuan Ti)." He opened a bundle of incense, lighted it, and stuck it in the big incense burner. Then he knelt down and bowed his head to the ground three times. An association head rang the temple bell for him.

The next man who knelt down had no incense with him. The association head said, "Wait, let us light a bundle of incense for you. We have plenty of it."

The man replied, "It doesn't matter. My heart is quite grateful to Kuan Ti just the same."

To our field worker the association head remarked, "Every one of us believes in this custom. We are quite superstitious. This is the way we thank Kuan Ti, our god."

2. At the next village our field worker found a violent quarrel going on between the chief association head, the chief crop-watchman, who was a cripple, and one of the villagers, Mr. Ma, a native of Shantung. Several association heads tried to calm them down, but to no avail.

The association head said, "If no one is going to pay his crop-money, then we had better not have any association."

The farmer said, "How about my sweet potatoes? You know they were stolen from me. You are the chief association head, and you are unjust. Do you have any rules in your association? What's it for, anyway?"

In a loud voice the association head replied, "Where is your evidence that I am unjust? I have been one of the association leaders for twenty years, and no one has ever said that I am unjust. You are just making an excuse for not paying your crop-money."

The crop-watchman who was responsible for Mr. Ma's land was very angry and said, "You are getting very impertinent, Mr. Ma. Let me tell you, you must pay your crop-money, all of it and not one cent less. And let me ask you, just when did you lose your sweet potatoes? And when did you report to us? You are only trying to stir up trouble. That will never do. Come outside and let us see who will live or who will die."

Several of the association heads said to Mr. Ma, "Neither the association head nor anyone else is going to use your crop-money. It will all be used for the general expenses of the association. Our crop-watchmen began their work on the twenty-third day of the sixth month. Your sweet potatoes were stolen before that date, so our crop-watchmen are not to blame and the association is not responsible for your loss. Besides, the one who stole your crop was caught, but Village P took him away from us.[2] How can your refuse to pay your crop-money?"

Mr. Ma angrily asked, "Why did you give him to Village P? Who is going to pay my loss now?"

The crop-watchman could wait no longer and acted as if he were ready to fight. He said to Mr. Ma, "Still trying to find excuses for not paying your crop-money? Let us go outside."

The association head shouted in a loud and angry voice, "You pay no crop-money! That will never do!"

Mr. Ma realized there was no way out for him, so he said, "Oh, well, I shall pay my crop-money. What more do you want?"

The association head replied, "We have no more to say. All we want is your crop-money."

Several other association heads said, "It doesn't matter. You can pay it any time you please. You have lived in the village for more than twenty years, and we are all friends. You had better go home now, and we will see you in a few days."

The crop-watchman remarked, "Good. He is going to pay his crop-money. I have nothing more to say."

Mr. Ma was still quite angry when he left the temple. The watchman commented, "Don't pay any attention to him. If he doesn't pay his crop-money, I shall take him to court, or he can move out of the village."

Sometime later a policeman came in and said, "There is an annual telephone fee amounting to three dollars. I wonder if this village will contribute to it."

The association head replied, "Good! We have a man who is unwilling to pay his crop-money, which amounts to three dollars and seventy cents. You may collect it for us."

The policeman nodded and said, "I'll surely collect the money from him."

COST OF CROP-WATCHING

The annual expenditure for crop-watching was reported in the accounts of three of our sample villages in the Peiping area. The periods covered ranged from seven to eleven years. The figures ranged all the way from $31 to $222 per year. Because the accounts covered different periods of time and the amounts of land that were protected were very different, it has been difficult to develop any comparative figures; however, during the five years that were included in all three accounts, 1926–1930, the amount spent for crop-watching went up from 41 to 70 per cent. The cost per mu in 1926 was 3.8

cents for Village A, 4.8 cents for Village E, and only 1.4 cents for Village B. (As was noted above, a large part of Village B land was planted to trees and peanuts, and it was therefore possible for each watchman to guard an average of 2,000 mu.) In 1930 the cost was 7.3 cents per mu for Village A, 6.4 cents for Village E, and 1.7 cents for Village B.

The turbulent conditions around Peking in 1928 were reflected in the amounts spent for crop-watching. In two of the three villages the expenditures went up that year and down the next. For the third village, Village A, the increase did not come until 1929. Then the amount was twice that spent in 1928 and 55 per cent more than the amount spent in 1932.

CROP-WATCHMEN OF A VILLAGE IN THE PEIPING AREA, 1907–1924

The records of a village in the Peiping area gave, for the eighteen years from 1907 through 1924, lists of the full-time watchmen who were engaged for both the spring and the fall harvests and of the men who were hired for the fall season only, from the twenty-fourth day of the sixth month, Kuan Ti's birthday, until the harvest was completed in the ninth month. For most of the years the records also showed the wages paid and the amount of tips or special rewards given the watchmen.

Through 1912 there were only two full-time men. After 1912 there were three, except for 1924 when one man gave up his job and no successor was appointed. Ordinarily this village had three additional, fall-season watchmen. There were four in 1907, two in 1912 and 1919, and only one in 1920. The drought and famine in 1919–1920 probably were responsible for the dropping of some of the fall-season watchmen in those years.

The full-time watchmen were a permanent group. Only five names were on that list. One man served for seventeen of the eighteen years. Another served for twelve years. The other three had six years of service each.

The seasonal men, probably because they had only part-time work, were a much less regular group. There were 14 names on the list. Four men served only one year, another three for two years. One man served ten consecutive years. The next longest service was eight out of nine years. One man served five out of ten years. Only one seasonal watchman was promoted to annual service.

Wages of watchmen.—The full-time watchmen were paid 60 *tiao* per year from 1914 through 1923. In 1924 the rate was increased one third, to 80 tiao. For the seasonal men the regular wage was 15 tiao from 1909 through 1923. In 1924 their rate too was increased one third, to 20 tiao. The seasonal rate was regularly one quarter of the full-time rate. The full-time watchmen evidently were able to guard adequately the area planted to wheat and other spring crops, which usually was smaller than the fall-crop area, and also it was much easier to protect the wheat than some of the fall crops. The tall, closely planted rows of kaoliang made it very simple for thieves to hide and to get away.

The wages of both groups ordinarily were increased by bonuses or tips. For the annual watchmen the amount ranged from 10 to 30 tiao. For the seasonal men the bonus, when paid, ranged from 2.6 to 15 tiao. There were two years, 1909 and 1911, when no bonus was recorded. There were only three years when the extra amount was

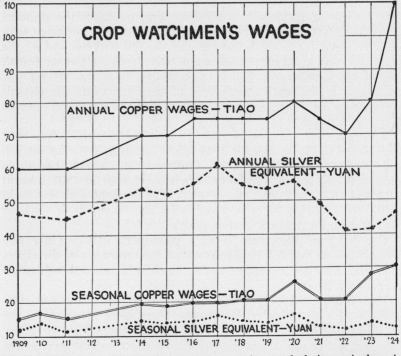

FIG. 9.—Fluctuations in the copper wages, tiao, and their equivalent in silver, yuan, paid to seasonal and annual watchmen in a village in the Peking area, 1909–1924.

more than 5 tiao. In 1920 there was only one seasonal watchman and a double bonus, 10 tiao, was given, evidently to compensate him for covering extra territory. The annual watchmen were also given an extra 5 tiao that year.

Wages plus bonus in 1914 were 70 tiao for the annual watchmen and 19.5 tiao for the seasonal men. In 1922 the totals were 70 and 20 tiao. In 1924 they were 110 and 30 tiao. The ten-year increase was practically the same for the two totals, 57 per cent for the annual and 54 per cent for the seasonal watchmen. The year-by-year changes are given in figure 9 and table 14.

From 1909 to 1924 the seasonal total increased 100 per cent. The records do not give any figures before 1914 for the annual watchmen, but, judging from those available and from the figures for the seasonal men, it seems probable that the increase for the 1909–1924 period was about 83 per cent.

It seems quite evident that the increases after 1922 were the result of depreciation in the copper coinage that began about 1920 and continued until 1927. In the fall of 1924 the Peking silver-copper exchange rate was 95 per cent higher than the fall rate of 1916, 81 per cent higher than the fall rate of 1920, and 51 per cent higher than that of 1922.

Exchange figures were not available for this particular village, but nearby the increase for the four-year period, 1920–1924, was only 2 per cent more than the rise in the Peking rate, 83 versus 81 per cent. We have therefore felt that the city exchange rates were reasonably applicable to this village. Changes in the silver-copper exchange rate are shown in figure 12.

How the silver equivalent of the copper wages varied from year to year is shown in figure 9. For the seasonal men the amount in 1924 was 10 per cent more than in 1909, $12.90 as compared with $11.70. From 1914 to 1924 the silver figure went down 12.8 per cent, from $14.20 to $12.90. The year when only one seasonal watchman was employed, 1920, was the only year when the silver figure was more than $16.00. That year, because of the extra bonus, it was $17.70.

For the full-time watchmen the silver equivalent of their copper wages plus their bonuses ranged between a maximum of $56.70 in 1920 and a minimum of $41.00 in 1922, with a possible $60.70 in 1917 if that year's bonus was the same as that for 1916. From 1914 to 1924 the silver equivalent of the copper wages declined 11 per cent. For the longer period from 1909 to 1924, the probable change was an increase of one per cent.

In 1930 the wage for the fall season was $12.00, or 90 cents less than the silver equivalent of the copper wages plus bonus paid in 1924.[3]

Real wages.—On the basis of Meng and Gamble's cost-of-living index numbers for Peking,[4] which showed an increase of 35.5 per cent from 1914 to 1924 and 41.5 per cent from 1909 to 1924, the real wages of the seasonal watchmen went down 22 per cent from 1909 to 1924 and 38 per cent from 1914 to 1924. For the full-time watchmen the decline was 34 per cent from 1914 to 1924, and from 1909 to 1924 it probably went down 29 per cent.

In Peking the decline in the real wages of unskilled workmen associated with the masons' and carpenters' guilds was only 3 per cent from 1909 to 1924 and 8.5 per cent from 1914 to 1924.

After 1932 all the watchmen of the village were hired on an annual basis, as the night watch and the protection of the village inhabitants during the winter and early spring were added to crop-watching.

OTHER EXAMPLES OF PAYMENTS TO CROP-WATCHERS

In 1932 one village paid $14 for the fall season. The same year another village paid $15 as wages and gave a food subsidy of $1 and a bonus of $5. A third paid its crop-watchers in kind, five or six *tou* of grain each for the fall season. The rate for the spring harvest was reported to be about $5 per watchman, but was not paid by the village, being collected directly from the farmers by the watchmen. Still another village paid $7 for the spring season.

Village A had only one watchman who protected the crops. He also looked after the fruit grown on hilly land that originally had belonged to the temple but was then under the control of the village association. For that work he received no pay from the village, but he was entitled to collect, from the purchaser of the fruit, a commission of 10 per cent of the price. On that basis he received $37.50 one year, but only $4.00 the next. The average for seven years was $18.50.

CONTRACTED CROP-WATCHING—A CASE STUDY

In 1931 the most influential man in one village became greatly concerned over the fact that the land registration was showing a declining total. He believed that almost a third of the land was unregistered and so failed to contribute to the cost of crop-watching and other village activities. He wanted to find some way, persuasion or force, to get the land back onto the records. He was convinced that the village leaders could not bring this about—they were too eager to compromise and unwilling to antagonize their fellow villagers. He finally persuaded the association heads to turn the problem over to a group of bullies who agreed to do the usual crop-watching and to attempt to force the registration of the omitted land. For their services the bullies were to receive, instead of the usual $12 per watchman, one half of the village land-assessment of 10 cents per mu. They were expected to increase the land registration by 2,000 mu, from 4,000 to 6,000 mu. If this increase was obtained, the village would still have the income it had regularly had after paying the crop-watchers and in later years would have additional income, as continuation of the contracted crop-watching system was not planned.

To facilitate the search for unregistered land the village adopted a rule that required every cultivator to register his land, pay his crop-money, and get a harvest permit before he went to the fields to gather his crop. The bullies were supposed to prevent the harvesting of any land not covered by a certificate. Instead of the expected 50 per cent increase, the amount of land registered actually decreased a few mu.

The village authorities asserted that the bullies had done such a poor job of crop-watching that there had been more than the usual amount of stealing, and that they had failed to carry out their agreement to increase the land registration. The head man refused to pay the half of land-assessment income, and the matter was finally compromised by paying $20 per man instead of the usual $12.

The next year when the two village heads, eight other leaders, and the two schoolteachers met to plan for the protection of the crops, there was no enthusiasm for contracting the crop-watching, and the old system of direct hiring of the watchers was reinstated. One leader suggested that the land registration should be according to the actual acreage of the deeds. Almost all the other leaders were opposed to such a suggestion. They said, "Do not speak of anything that is not workable. Only if Marshal Chang[5] comes can we practice your system. Now we can only work with our old country folks by persuasion and good will."

The village head proposed that the land registration be made part of the official government records, so that those who underregistered with the village would later be penalized by the government. Another leader suggested that they follow the old register, with the usual changes for sales, mortgaging, and rental, and this plan was adopted.

The village head pointed out that it would not be necessary to issue harvest certificates as was done the previous year. After discussion and argument, the suggestion was considered adopted without any official vote.

There was considerable discussion on the question of the extent of a field taboo. Should gleaners be allowed to go into the fields during the harvest? How long should the taboo be maintained? It was decided that the fields should be closed to both gleaners and stock during harvest days. Even landowners were not allowed to remove their cornstalks during the taboo period.

There was more discussion as to the length of the taboo. One man wanted it quite long, stating that the year before he had not had enough time to harvest all of his corn. Another man reminded the group that if the taboo were too long and the cornstalks were not removed from the fields, the planting of the winter wheat would be delayed. The village head effected a compromise by saying that if the taboo were kept for just a few days it would not be too late for the planting.

When the time came to nominate watchmen, one of the village leaders remarked that they did not want any drug addicts as watchmen. Later his son, a known addict and bully, was nominated, and he was asked, "Is your son still taking drugs?" To save face he had to answer in the negative.

Six of the seven nominations were accepted. The men were assigned by lot to the three crop-watching areas of the village, two to each area. The watchmen were required to offer a guarantor who would be responsible for their good conduct and for the payment for any crops lost through theft if the watchman could not find the thief and should be unable to pay for the loss. Three guarantors were village leaders who had nominated successful candidates. The leader who nominated the drug addict had left the meeting, so he would not be called on to act as guarantor for his candidate. Finally the addict's father had to act as his guarantor. The senior watchman, the most reliable man in the group, was guaranteed by all the village leaders.

The village head gave personal instructions to the watchmen, urging them to be diligent in their work and reminding them that they were responsible for lost crops, that they should not allow unauthorized persons to go to the fields during the harvest period, and that they should keep out all pigs and sheep. The addict was ordered to give up his injections. A carter was told to give up his work during the crop-watching period. The ti-pao was asked to accompany the watchmen to their respective areas and with them raise the symbolic pile of lime and earth to show the people that the village association's crop-watching was in force and that the theft of crops would be punished.

The crop-watchers' wages were finally set at $14 for the season. This was a compromise between the $20 paid the year before and the $12 previously paid. The increase was accepted on the grounds that the cost of living and other wages were going up. The village head decided that part of the wages should be paid at the mid-autumn festival and the rest at the end of the harvest season.

The senior watchman asked what the village leaders proposed to do about trespassing sheep and pigs. If they were impounded, would the owners be punished? The story of how he had rounded up a flock of sheep back in 1920 and had failed to receive the expected reward is told on pages 91–92.

DAMAGE BY THEFT AND TRESPASS

The amount of damage done to the crops by theft and trespass naturally varied greatly from village to village and from year to year. One village that had a group of nomadic Mohammedan neighbors came to expect a great deal of trouble. So also did another village that had several "big hands" among its residents.

Village H reported only two serious cases of theft, and these were some ten years apart. In 1932 there were several cases of trespass and 20 cases of minor theft reported. The theft losses totaled 859 stalks of kaoliang, 601 ears of corn, 150 stalks of beans, and one half-mu of peanuts. (See table 53.) In 1933 two minor cases of theft were reported; as the culprits were soldiers, the village declined to accept any responsibility.

Among the books of the village that gave us the list of the crop-watchmen and their wages from 1907 to 1924 we found one in which were recorded all the thefts reported for twenty-three years, from 1907 through 1929. The record gave the name of the family, the crop stolen, and the indemnity paid, or the amount deducted from the family's crop-money assessment. Separate lists were kept for the spring and the fall seasons.

For the spring season there were six years with no losses. For the other years the number of families reporting thefts ranged from one to 47. The total number of families claiming spring losses during the twenty-three years was 396, an average of 16 per year. For the fall season the number of reporting families ranged from 5 to 39. The twenty-three-year total was 441; the average, 19 per year. The annual totals, for both the spring and the fall seasons, were from 7 to

65 families, amounting to a total of 810 for the period and an average of 35 per year. The years with the maximum number of claims were 1918 for the spring season, 1909 for the fall, and 1920 for both periods. In 1920 the seasonal totals were spring, 29; fall, 36.

For nine of the twenty-three years the families with spring crop losses outnumbered those reporting theft of their fall crops. In 1918 the figures were spring, 47; fall, 11. In 1914 they were spring, 19; fall, 6. In 1929 the fall claims outnumbered those in the spring by 26 to one.

One year the families claiming indemnity amounted to 33.9 per cent of the total number registered in the village land books. Another year the percentage was only 3.6. For five of the last six years it was less than 10 per cent. The number of farming families registered varied from year to year between 187 and 207.

The total number of thefts was considerably more than the number of families reporting losses (810), since in any given season several families had more than one loss.

Losses reported and indemnities paid.—A detailed study was made of the losses reported and the indemnities paid in 1916. That year was chosen because it was the one with 72 claims, the largest number recorded. Losses were reported by 50 families, 16 in the spring and 34 in the fall. About a third of the reporting families made more than one claim. A Mr. Wu lost an elm tree, worth 200 cash, and 70 ears of corn.

Corn was the crop stolen in 43 cases out of 72. Thefts of millet, wheat, beans, and kaoliang together totaled 17. Trees and tree branches were also misappropriated. The amount of the individual losses ranged from between 100 and 200 cash ($0.07–0.15) to between 4,000 and 4,500 cash ($3.00–3.35). There were 10 claims between 200 and 299 cash and another 10 between 400 and 499 cash. Half the claims were for less than 50 cents each; only 12 were for more than $1. The total losses amounted to about $40.

In most villages the crop-watchmen were held responsible for any losses and the amount was deducted from their wages, unless they caught the thief. If the culprit was found, he was brought before the village authorities, who decided upon his punishment. The crop-watchmen, evidently, were quite ready to beat the suspect until he confessed. Some of the more serious cases were sent to the hsien government for punishment. Others were fined money or incense. The money was generally used to indemnify the crop-owner for his loss and to give a reward to the crop-watchman who captured the thief. Sometimes the other watchmen were given a small share of the reward. In several cases part of the money was kept by the village for its general expenses. Once the village and the watchmen divided the fine and the crop-owner got nothing for his loss. If the fine included incense, the benefit received when it was burned before the gods would be shared by the entire village.

There evidently was some general limit to the amount of the fine that a village could assess against a crop-thief, for it was reported that the hsien government had twice fined a village for attempting to collect unreasonable amounts. The reports of our villages told of fines of six tou of corn, of 300 packages of tea leaves worth about a half cent each, of $16 plus an indemnity for the actual crop loss, and of $30.

The account books that detailed the crop losses also showed that in 1916 the five village crop-watchmen were to have a total of 44,830 cash withheld from their wages because they had been unable to catch the culprits who had been stealing from the fields. The watchmen's wages were 15,000 cash ($11.15) each, plus a tip of 4,500 cash at festival time; thus they lost almost half the total amount due them. The man with the worst record was to be charged 15,790 cash, which would leave him only 3,710 cash for the season's work. Since he already had an advance of 5,000 cash, which the village could not recover, he was overpaid 1,290 cash. The other four watchmen were debited 11,890 cash, 9,420 cash, 3,890 cash, and 3,840 cash. One wonders why the men continued to keep their crop-watching jobs when their net return was so small.

Village D in 1931 paid a landowner 75 cents for damages to his kaoliang fields caused by a group of horses. It also paid $69 as indemnity for theft by soldiers. It collected a fine of $6 for trespass. Village B collected fines and indemnities amounting to a total of $299 during the ten years for which we have figures, but the accounts showed that only $21.25 was paid to landowners for damages.

SAMPLE CASES OF CROP-STEALING

Thirteen cases of crop-stealing were reported by five villages in the area west of Peiping. The majority came from one village. These seem to have been regarded as special occurrences, for they did not include instances of the usual petty thievery that occurred more or less regularly every season. The stories are interesting in that they show how the village authorities handled matters of varying gravity; how far the village authorities could go in punishing crop-thieves; the presence in the villages of recognized professional crop-thieves, sometimes called "big hands"; the disregard of theft along with gleaning on the part of dependent widows; a considerable and seemingly growing amount of drug addiction, to both opium and morphine, with the resultant degradation of the individual and his family, loss of family property, and often the death of not a few of the addicts. Additional cases of theft are noted in the descriptions of some of the individual villages.

1. *Treatment of crop-thieves.*—On the eleventh day of the eighth month, 1931, Mother Wang found that she had been robbed of 180 ears of corn and Mr. Li discovered that he had lost 1,730 ears. The next day they reported the matter to the authorities in the neighboring village, the center for the collective crop-watching of the area. The village head called a meeting of the leaders, and it was decided that the watchmen should go out and look for the thief.

On the evening of the fourteenth day, four watchmen found near Tsing Hua Yuan, west of Peiping, a man named Liu who was known as a professional thief. His actions, when he saw the watchmen, made them feel that he was not entirely innocent. They arrested him and brought him back to the village. The village leaders met again in the temple and finally decided to whip Liu in order to discover whether he had committed the theft. Almost immediately the prisoner acknowledged the charges against him.

On the fifteenth day a watchman from a nearby village came to report the loss of 400 sweet-potato vines. The authorities of his village had heard about the capture of a thief and thought that perhaps he was also responsible for their loss. Interrogated again, Liu admitted that he and two other men had worked together and named one of them, Chou, as the principal promoter of their activities. Liu insisted that he and the third man only helped in the actual theft. The confession was taken in writing by the village schoolteacher, and the thief signed it with his fingerprint.

Watchmen from the two villages were sent to the nearest city gate, Hsi Chih Men, on the theory that the thieves would be selling their loot in the market there. On the sixteenth day, the watchmen found Chou selling the stolen corn. He was arrested and taken first to the village that had reported the loss of the sweet potatoes. The village leaders held a short hearing, but did not attempt to handle the case. The next day, at the request of the authorities of the other village, the thief was turned over to them for judgment. It seems that the third man escaped; at least, no report was made of any attempt to locate him.

A short trial was held to confirm with Chou all that had been reported by Liu. It was decided that if someone would offer to guarantee the payment of indemnity for the goods stolen and of any fine levied by the village authorities, the culprits could be released. Otherwise they would be whipped once or twice a day for at least two weeks before they would be freed.

Faced with that prospect, Chou and Liu begged to be taken to their home villages so that they might find persons who would act as guarantors for them, saying that they were ready to pay for everything they had stolen and also to pay a fine. On the nineteenth day, four watchmen were delegated to take the culprits home. They went immediately to see a Mr. Chang and two others who regularly disposed of their loot, and asked them to act as guarantors. Fearing that the case might open up their own activities, the three men immediately promised to help out.

The next day the village authorities decided to parade the thieves through the neighboring villages, to make them lose face and to advertise them as confessed thieves. The men were bound with their hands behind their backs. Around their necks were hung signs describing their crimes. They had to announce their names, their home villages, and their crimes. If they were slow, they were encouraged with a whip.

The parade started at eight o'clock in the morning and lasted until about one in the afternoon. The thieves were accompanied by four watchmen who beat a big copper gong to attract the attention of the villagers. The parade ended at a nearby town where the watchmen had their noon meal and gave the prisoners something to eat.

About two o'clock Mr. Chang and his two companions came to the village office and, in the presence of the thieves, offered to act as guarantors for the payment of whatever amount the village authorities demanded for the thieves' freedom. A bond was written by the village teacher and signed by the fingerprints of the two thieves and the three guarantors. The bond read:

This is to certify that Liu and Chou have stolen two thousand ears of corn from Mr. Li and Mother Wang of X village and four hundred sweet-potato plants and eight hundred ears of corn from Mr. Liu, Mr. Wu, and Mr. Sun of Y village. According to the regulations of the association, all losses and expenses shall be paid by the thieves, together with the reward for the watchmen. We guarantee that the thieves will pay all the losses, expenses, and rewards that they should pay. If there is any delay or default, it will be our responsibility.

Indemnity:	....Dollars	Thieves:	Liu	[*fingerprint*]
Fine:	....Bundles of		Chou	"
	incense	Guarantors:	Chang	"
			Meng	"
			Ku	"

The 20th day of the 8th month of the 20th year of the Republic of China [August 20, 1931].

The oral agreement called for a total payment of $30 to indemnify the farmers whose crops had been stolen and reward the watchmen who had caught the thieves, and a fine of 200 bundles of incense, worth about $6. It will be noted that no amounts were entered on the bond, either as indemnity or fine. It was said that they were omitted because the authorities knew that the amounts would not be paid in full. Presumably, the fine was set in terms of bundles of incense because the head man did not levy money fines for the benefit of the village. The benefit came from burning the incense before the gods.

After the fall harvest the thieves sent one picul (100 catties) of corn to the village office and asked one of their friends to take $20 to the authorities. He declared that the thieves had only given him $18 and that he had lost $6 on the way. The picul of corn and the $12 in cash was all that the village could collect.

2. *Treatment of a habitual crop-stealer.*—A well-to-do farmer ruined himself by smoking opium and taking injections of morphine. He was forced to sell his 60 mu of land, and he came to rely on crop stealing for a bare existence. He stole crops in the spring and fall and wood from the trees in the winter. Gradually village sentiment turned very strongly against him.

In the fall of 1929 he stole a basket of more than 100 ears of corn. He was discovered by the village watchman, arrested, and locked in a small room in the temple. He got out by digging through the mud wall, but made no attempt to leave the village. He was then rearrested by the watchman. The village could get nothing out of him because he was so poor, and, being incorrigible, he could not be reformed. Finally he was sent to the hsien court and committed to prison on the recommendation of the village officers. After three months of confinement he became seriously ill and died. The village authorities had to bring his body back to the village and give it burial in the village cemetery.

3. *A marginal case of crop-stealing.*—In the seventh month of 1932 a crop-watchman went to a well about two li outside his village. His two small children, six and four years old, went with him. On the return trip the father walked so fast that the children could not keep up with him. They loitered along the way and, without the knowledge of their father, picked three ears of corn. They were carrying the corn in their hands when they came to the village gate. A Mr. Liu, who had cornland near the well, was standing at the gate, and, seeing the corn in the children's hands, he thought that the ears might have come from his land. Inspection showed that three ears were missing from his field. He reported the matter to the

village office and charged the watchman with the theft. The watchman said that he had no knowledge of the matter, that it was done by two ignorant children. The village heads said that he was at fault in taking the children with him and not supervising them while they were in the fields. He finally was fined six tou of corn and threatened with dismissal. He paid the fine and was allowed to keep his job, but only after friends interceded for him.

4. *Fighting between watchmen and thieves.*—A large number of willow trees around one of the villages became a popular prey of thieves. In 1931 the village authorities engaged two brothers to watch the crops and the trees. Both men were given guns, and their father, who was not a watchman, was also armed so that he could help in emergencies. The watchmen found five men cutting branches from the trees and fired on them. The thieves returned the fire and the shooting continued for some time, long enough for the father to get to the scene and join in the fray. The thieves were driven off without anyone being killed or hurt.

5. *False report of crop losses.*—In 1932 Wang Liang, of a village some seven li from one of the west gates of Peiping, rented five mu of land to Mrs. Chang, a widow. The rental was to run for three years for a total fee of $50. It was also agreed that Wang should continue to farm the land and receive half of the crop for his work. Toward the end of August he secretly sold 400 catties of sweet potatoes and the next day reported them to the village authorities as stolen. One of the purchasers, who heard of the reported loss, told the village officers that he bought the potatoes and believed that Mrs. Chang had agreed to the sale. When she was asked to come to a meeting of the village officers and was questioned about the matter, she insisted that she knew nothing about it and had not given Wang permission to sell the potatoes.

In discussing their possible lines of action, the village head told our field investigator that the village had the right to fine Wang if he were found guilty and that if he did not pay the fine they could take him to the hsien court or chase him out of the village. In connection with the latter possibility, the village head cited a previous case in which he had made a suggestion and then expelled a villager who opposed it. In that instance, the head had proposed that the private schoolhouse be turned into a modern public school, with the k'ang removed and twenty small tables installed. The expulsion brought quick acceptance of the "suggestion" by the other villagers.

At the next day's meeting of the village leaders, Mrs. Chang repeated her statement that she had leased the land from Mr. Wang, that he was farming it by agreement with her, and that she knew nothing about the sale of the sweet potatoes. One of the purchasers appeared and reported that Wang, when he offered the potatoes for sale, had stated that he was their sole owner.

Wang, when he was called, still maintained that he had lost the potatoes, but he had to change his story when he was confronted by Mrs. Chang and the purchaser. The village head said to him, "Wang, you have tried to fatten yourself on other people's property, but fortunately we have discovered the facts. Otherwise we would not have been able to collect any crop-money from you and would have had to reimburse you for your reported loss. Now we are going to treat you as you were attempting to treat us. If you do not obey us, you can go to court."

Wang replied, "I am willing to pay the fine."

The fine was set at 300 packages of tea leaves that cost two coppers (a half cent) per package. Mrs. Chang was to be paid for her half of the potatoes.

The village head refused to accept Wang's promise that he would pay and required him to provide three guarantors. He was accompanied by the village police-guard while he sought friends who would help him. In an hour's time he returned with three men who were willing to guarantee his payment of the tea leaf fine and Mrs. Chang's share of the potatoes. Both sums were paid within the next two days.

6. *Escape of a crop-thief.* Six days after Wang sold his potatoes, a village watchman on his way to the city gate saw a man with two bundles of sweet potatoes in a nearby field. The man started to leave, but the watchman ordered him to stop. An examination of the bundles disclosed that all the potatoes were big ones, still covered with dirt—a reasonable indication that they had been stolen. The watchman asked a passer-by to call the landowner, who quickly arrived with a club in his hand. The three men seized the suspected thief, tied him up, beat him, and forced him to admit that he had stolen 300 catties of potatoes, half of which he had already taken away. He was taken to the village temple and turned over to the association heads, who discussed the case but reached no decision.

That evening the head of a nearby village came and reported that the thief was a professional who had stolen many sweet potatoes. The thief was finally released to the visiting village head, who promised that there would be suitable punishment. The next day he set the thief free without notifying the village that had captured him.

When this news was received, some of the association heads blamed the village head for having turned the thief over to the other village and accused him of having accepted money from the head of the other village or from the thief. Two of the association heads handed in their resignations.

The village head felt that he was unjustly accused and complained that as chief secretary of the local Kuomintang organization and business manager of the Farmer's Association he was required to go to the city several times every month for meetings, but had not been reimbursed for any of his traveling expenses. He said that he was so disgusted that he was handing in his letter of resignation for at least the second time. His resignation was not accepted.

At the end of the month the case was still pending. One of the association heads was very dubious about getting anything done. He said that the village head who released the thief had made many promises and then done nothing more, and that they could not rearrest the thief. The village head, it was also reported, had accepted $30 from the thief, but that, of course, was denied and could not be proven.

7. *Sheep trespass.*—The inhabitants of a small village, part of the "green crop" area of a neighboring larger village, were very poor, having only a small amount of infertile land. The richest family had not more than 30 mu of sandy land. Some of the villagers were raising sheep and pigs to add to their income, but since they had no pasturage in their own area, they had to drive the sheep to other villages. In the process, the crops of the neighboring villages suffered damage from the trespassing sheep.

After the wheat harvest, in 1920, a low-lying piece of land that was regularly flooded by the summer rains or by the river was left uncultivated. The sheep owners were anxious to use its weeds for sheep pasturage, but there was no road leading to it. Finally, in the early part of the seventh month, the boys who were herding the sheep drove about 200 of them along the river dike and then across a kaoliang field to the weedy land. The sheep ate the kaoliang leaves and broke the brittle stalks so that the field was almost completely ruined.

The landowner discovered what had happened, informed the watchman, and asked him to inspect the damage and report it to the village authorities. He said that they must do something about it if they expected him to pay his crop-money at the end of the season. The watchman found five of the village leaders in the drugstore, the recognized center of local politics. Even though the group included the village head and all of them wanted to impound the sheep, no action could be taken until Mr. Chen, the most influential man in the village, approved. Thereupon two of the crop-watchmen were sent to drive the sheep to the village and lock them in an empty shop. By way of encouragement, the watchmen were told that their efforts would not be wasted, because they would share in the fine. The village leaders discussed the problem over their evening meal, but were unable to decide upon any definite course of action.

The next morning a group of more than ten persons came from the small village. They called on all the village leaders and were most apologetic about the damage caused by the sheep. They laid the responsibility on the ignorant shepherd children who had been warned time and time again to see that the sheep did not damage growing crops. They made great promises that it would not happen again and said that the sheep, if they ever returned, could be eaten. By soft words and many promises the village leaders were persuaded to release the sheep before any definite terms of indemnity had been agreed to or guaranteed. The sheep owners then refused to make any payment. The watchmen received no reward for their efforts, the farmer lost his crop, and the leaders were criticized for cowardice, lack of foresight, and ineptness.

The only thing salvaged was an indemnity for the loss of 80 ears of corn that ordinarily would have been paid to one of the farmers living in the sheep owners' village. The village authorities kept that amount to offset the damage done by the sheep.

The shepherds must have taken the matter seriously, for there was no further trespassing reported during the next thirteen years. Eleven years later the chief watchman was still reminding the village elders of the matter.[6]

8. *Crop-stealing by husband and wife.*—The wife of a Mr. Wang stole a basket of corn from the field of another Mr. Wang in the fall of 1920. She was caught by the village watchman, a third Mr. Wang, who reported the matter to the village head, a fourth Mr. Wang. He decided to fine her, but she refused to pay anything. At night she went to the home of the village head and threatened to kill herself by eating *hung-fan,* a common poison.[7] She disturbed the household for half the night and left only on the persuasion of several friends of the village head. As a result of the commotion, the village head resigned and from then on refused to serve in any public office.

Mrs. Wang's husband was also a crop stealer. When he was caught, the village authorities immediately put him in a wagon and sent him to the hsien authorities, fearing that he would follow his wife's example and make a great to-do in the village. He was put in prison, but was released when he paid the fine levied against him by the hsien authorities.

9. *Conspiracy to steal crops.*—In 1921 Mr. Liu, who was both the village head and an association head, offended Mr. Wang, the son of

an old bully living in a village about three li (one mile) away. During the fall season the revengeful Mr. Wang sent a bully, nicknamed "The Cat," from his village to create trouble by stealing crops in Mr. Liu's village.

The bully started work near the north gate of the village. He was caught by the watchman before he had picked more than half a bag of corn. The village authorities discussed the case briefly, but because the thief was a known bully and came from nearby, they turned him over to the district office. The matter became an intervillage issue. The authorities of The Cat's village felt that they could not appear in the matter and asked some of the men of another neighboring village to represent them, apologize for The Cat's behavior, and negotiate a settlement for them. It was finally agreed by both parties, and guaranteed by a third group, that all the losses suffered during the fall season by the damaged village were to be made good by The Cat's village whether the theft was committed by him or by someone else.

Mr. Liu recognized the name on the bag used by The Cat as that of the man he had offended. He attempted to investigate how it was that the bag was in the hands of the thief, thinking that the bag's owner might have had something to do with the incident. Mr. Wang, however, was clever enough to have reported to the district office the loss of a bag of grain and identified The Cat's bag as the one he had lost. Mr. Liu was finally persuaded by his friends to drop the matter of the bag.

10. *Newcomer to the village turns thief.*—Mr. Sun, a potmaker by profession, was a newcomer to the village. He roomed with one of the local families. The head of the family observed his actions for a time and became convinced that he was stealing crops. He told his suspicions to the crop-watchman, who paid special attention to Sun and also was convinced that he was a thief. When the matter was reported to the village authorities, they ordered that Sun should be watched and be arrested when an opportunity arose.

Toward the end of the seventh month of 1928 the landlord and the watchman felt sure that Sun was going out to the fields. They reported their convictions to the village head, who sent the watchman to the fields and said that he would wait in the village drugstore. Sun was caught with a half-filled bag of corn. When his room was searched, fifty more ears of corn were found. Sun was fined $16. Of this, $10 went to the farmers for their corn; the six watchmen each received $1 as a reward.

11. *Female crop-stealers.*—The village had two well-known female crop-stealers. One was old Mother Wang, not of the Wang

family in the earlier story. The other was an old aunt of the Sun family. Mother Wang was about seventy years old, very fat and strong. She had been a widow for many years. Her brother-in-law, the eldest of the family, died a drug addict. Her eldest son, who succeeded his uncle as head of the family, had died of the same habit. Her second son was dying from drugs, and her grandson was also an addict. With no property to rely on for her livelihood, no one to support her, and no public provision for the care of indigent widows, her only alternative was to help herself by stealing. The farmers did not object if she took small amounts, and the village authorities could not punish her if she took a lot.

Mother Wang had bound feet, but they did not impede her in crop-stealing. She had a very bad temper and was always quarreling or fighting with her neighbors. The villagers called her "an eagle with five claws." She usually stole only small amounts, did not "dig a big hole," and generally did not go to the fields until harvesttime, when she could insist that she was only gleaning. She picked up ears that had fallen on the ground, but when no one was about she would pick ears from the standing crops. She was nearsighted and partly deaf. When people yelled at her, she would not heed their protest. If they came near and still yelled, she would stop picking and move on, then resume picking until her basket was full. Neither the cultivators, the watchmen, nor the village authorities could do anything with her. She had been arrested several times, but they could not beat her because of her age, and they could not collect any fine. All they could do was release her.

In the spring of 1932, instead of moving about, she took a whole basketful from one field. The watchman saw what she was doing and arrested her, but again all that the village heads could do was scold her and release her.

Aunt Sun, as she was called by the villagers, was as old as Mother Wang, but not so strong or obstreperous, and so was less hated by the authorities and the people. She was a native of the village and had returned many years before, when the death of her husband left her without property. Her son had not been heard from for several years. Her father had had a brother and sister-in-law, but they had been dead for many years. Her only surviving relative was a nephew who was a guard in another village, but he was a drug addict and could give her no help. Her stealing technique was very much like that of Mother Wang.

12. *Misuse of permission to glean doddered bean-vines.*—In the early part of the sixth month of 1931 a landowner found a young man in his field with a basketful of beans, some good and some from

vines infected with dodder.[8] The boy's family was "quite well-to-do," owning 30 to 40 mu of land, but he and his older brother made a practice of going to the fields with the announced purpose of picking doddered bean-vines. They never cleared out all of the doddered vines, always leaving some of the young vines to grow back and provide an excuse for future expeditions. They also took some of the good beans and, in picking the scattered doddered vines, went over the entire field and did considerable damage. The brothers were hated by most of the cultivators, but the Green Crop Association of the village had never adopted regulations or had any understanding on the question of whether doddered beans were open to free picking by anyone. Evidently the cultivators had not made an issue of it with the association.

When the landowner saw that most of the beans in the young man's basket were uninfected, he became very angry and took the basket to the village office. He told his story to three of the village leaders—the most influential man, the village head, and one other. They heard his statement of the case and then sent for the young man. They scolded him, reminded him that it was not easy for the cultivators to tend their crops, and said that if he were not one of their fellow villagers they would certainly fine him for his misconduct. They finally told him to go home and to have the older brother send the beans back to the owner and apologize for the younger brother's conduct. They also warned him that he would not be excused for another offense.

The landlord and the other cultivators had a very poor opinion of the brothers and had hoped that they would be fined. The return of the beans and an oral apology were not what they wanted, but nothing more could be done. The villagers murmured that the authorities were afraid of making enemies, were weak, and were not doing their duty.

13. *An attempt to prevent crop-stealing.*—Before the fall harvest of 1931 the village head, Mr. Liu, decided that something must be done to stop the rapidly increasing crop-stealing. Mr. Liu had been appointed to his position in 1920, when the previous head had resigned because of the woman crop-stealer's threat to commit suicide at his gate. The village authorities had noted that most of the crop-stealers were drug addicts and also that the number of addicts was increasing. To keep the addicts from the fields, Mr. Liu organized a new institution called the Village Sanitarium, in which he proposed to confine all the drug addicts during the harvest season. He rented some rooms on the east street of the village to house the sanitarium.

When the drug addicts heard about the plan, some ran away and some came to the village office. Most of them, however, had to be brought in by the village guards. Eleven addicts were finally assembled. The village head told them that the village was putting them into the sanitarium for their own good and at considerable expense, as it was providing them two meals of corn flour a day. Other food they could buy for themselves. The patients all answered: "We know it is for our good. We will not inject any morphine from now on." A search of the group by the village guard found one packet of morphine.

The first day, two patients slipped out. One, Mr. Wang, was found the same day and brought back. The other, Mr. Ch'en, came back on his own initiative after three days. Another Mr. Wang ran away on the second day and did not come back. After five days Mr. Ch'en was allowed to go home to get some money to send to his father, who was working in Manchuria. Two Wus, father and son, stayed in the sanitarium for nine days and then were allowed to go home before their family's food ran out. Another Mr. Ch'en, who had only recently developed the habit, gave it up; he was released. Six patients stayed in the sanitarium during the entire crop-watching period.

The experiment was successful in cutting down the damage to the fields, but was a failure in treating the addicts. One man gave up the morphine injections, but only because his father had come home after the Manchurian incident and was able to supervise him. Another gave up morphine, but continued with opium.

REGULATIONS OF GREEN CROP ASSOCIATIONS

The printed and published regulations of some of the Hopei Green Crop Associations indicate that over the years the morale of the associations was often subject to gradual and many times serious deterioration. The association heads evidently tried to improve conditions by adopting and displaying a new set of regulations so that the villagers would be reminded of their part in the program. Differences between even neighboring villages are illustrated by the variety of points covered.

One set of regulations provided that the association heads must all be natives of the village. Another specified that the number of association heads should be twelve and that three should come from each of four presumably united villages. Four of the twelve heads were to hold office in rotation for a year at a time, two charged with the care of the money and two with the care of the accounts. Ordinary administrative affairs were to be handled by the four officers. More serious matters were to be decided by a majority vote of all twelve heads.

Under one set of regulations the village collected two kinds of crop-money—for crop-watching and for other village affairs. Cultivators, whether owners or tenants, paid the crop-watching charge for the land they farmed. The charge for other village affairs was divided between owner and tenant on rented land. Village shops paid the other-activity charge, nothing for the crop-watching. The cost of the religious part of the meetings at the opening of the crop-watching seasons was paid from crop-money, that of the thanksgiving meetings at the end of the seasons from other village funds.

One village provided that the cultivators were to pay one *kuan* of grain per mu as crop-money and give the watchmen, if satisfied with their work, some bundles of grain stalks.

Two village announcements provided that treasurer's accounts were to be posted on the wall of the village temple.

Several villages provided penalties for cultivators who did not register all their land.

One set of regulations established fines of $1 to $5 if animals trespassed on the fields; $2 to $8 if the animals were found feeding in the wheatfields, except in winter; $4 for crop-stealing by an adult; and $2 for crop-stealing by a child—but another paragraph provided for a warning to a child for a first offense and the same fine as an adult for a second offense. Another village fixed fines for crop-stealing at $20 for adults and $10 for children. A grasscutter found concealing crops in his grass was to be fined ten times the value of his loot. Special punishment was provided for thieving crop-watchers.

One village provided that a watchman who captured a crop-thief should receive three tenths of the fine for an arrest made in the day, half if he caught the culprit at night.

Another village provided that the watchman was to receive two tenths of the fine as his reward and that one tenth was to go to the cultivator; seven tenths was to be kept by the village. A different set of rules stated that one kuan of grain would be paid to the crop-grower for the loss of eight heads of kaoliang, eight ears of corn, or fifty heads of millet. Still another announcement fixed the owner's remuneration at the rate of eight *sheng* (pints) of grain for the loss of one mu of crops.

The full texts of the regulations of four villages were as follows:[9]

REGULATIONS OF THE GREEN CROP ASSOCIATION
OF VILLAGE M, HOPEI

The principle that trees will not grow without roots and water will not run without a spring cannot be changed. It is good that this village has established the Green Crop Association, but in order to make this association strong and permanent, twenty-three articles or regulations have been adopted after careful consideration by a group of the village residents. All the village people should obey the following regulations.

ARTICLE 1. The villagers should elect some just, honest, and capable men to organize and operate the association. If one of these men is guilty of misconduct, he should be dismissed by the villagers.

ART. 2. The purpose of the association is to organize the people to carry on local welfare work and to get rid of the bad men.

ART. 3. The green crops must be well protected. Animals are forbidden to tread on the growing crops under penalty of a fine of from one to five dollars.

ART. 4. Except in winter no animals are allowed to feed in the wheatfields. If this rule is violated and the animals are brought to the association by the landowner, a fine of from two to eight dollars will be levied on the owner of the animals.

ART. 5. No kaoliang leaves are to be taken except as ordered by the association. The taking of kaoliang leaves is to be treated as stealing. If such stealing is discovered, the leaves taken are to be confiscated.

ART. 6. Crop-stealers, when caught, must be brought to the association headquarters. Adults will be fined four dollars, children two dollars. The fine will be doubled if the thief is caught at night.

ART. 7. A watchman who catches a thief during the day will receive three tenths of the fine. If he catches the thief at night, he will receive one half of the fine as a special reward.

ART. 8. The head watchman must inspect the work of the watchmen. If they are found stealing any of the green crops, they will be punished by the association. All of their fine will go to the head watchman as a reward. If the head watchman conspires with other watchmen and is caught stealing, he is to be handed over to the hsien government for punishment.

ART. 9. If a landowner catches a watchman stealing crops or stalks, the association will consult the landowner before it determines the fine to be levied.

ART. 10. If children steal crops or destroy the trees, the association will warn their parents the first time, but will levy an adult's fine for the second offense.

ART. 11. Kung K'an I P'o (coöperative crop-watching) means that if

A sees *B* stealing somebody's crops, but, to save *B*'s face, does not arrest him, and *C* proves this to be the case, then both *A* and *B* are to be fined five dollars each. Two tenths of the fine will go to *C* as a reward.

ART. 12. The true number of mu must be registered with the association. If the association finds that a landowner has reported less than his actual holdings, he shall be fined twice the amount of the crop-money on the unreported land.

ART. 13. The watchmen must be specially diligent in watching any "closed fields" and prevent the gleaners from entering the fields before dawn. If the gleaners do not obey the rules, the association can punish them.

ART. 14. The gleaners must not enter the fields while the owners are loading the crops. If the gleaners insist on doing so, the watchmen have the authority to prevent them. If they do not obey, the association will punish them.

ART. 15. The landowners may give some grain stalks to the watchmen as a present, but if the watchmen become quarrelsome and attempt to compel an owner to give them stalks, they are to be punished.

ART. 16. The winter night watchman will protect the trees. If anyone steals trees or branches, he will be fined by the association.

ART. 17. Food money of fifty or sixty cents a day will be provided by the association for its officers when they are on official business. Ricksha fare will be paid according to the distance.

ART. 18. There are two kinds of crop-money assessments: (1) for crop-watching and (2) for village expenses. Land cultivators, both owners and tenants, pay the green-crop assessment. The owners pay half of the assessment for village expenses. The other half of the expense assessment is paid by the tenants. The cultivators of cemetery land pay both crop-money and village-expense assessments. Shops will pay only the village-expense assessment.

ART. 19. The green-crop money and the village-expense money are public funds. All assessments must be paid promptly. The head of the association should set an example and be the first one to pay his taxes. If the villagers find that he violates this rule, they can dismiss him from the chairmanship.

ART. 20. The green-crop-money is paid by the land cultivators. It is to be used only to pay the watchmen's wages and the expenses of the religious services at the opening of the crop season.

ART. 21. The village-expense money is used for policemen's wages, thanksgiving expenses, repairing temples, school subsidy, the Public Safety Bureau fund, winter night watchman's wages, planting trees, repairing bridges, traveling expenses, military and miscellaneous expenditures.

Art. 22. In order to avoid improper expenditure the public funds should be paid through several processes and supervised by more than one officer.

Art. 23. At the end of the year the treasurer must give the villagers a clear report of all income and expenses. His report should be posted on the wall.

REGULATIONS OF THE GREEN CROP ASSOCIATION OF VILLAGE N (NORTH SUBURB OF PEIPING)

Article 1. The purpose of the association is to supplement the police force in maintaining public safety and in the protection of the green crops.

Art. 2. The number of the association heads is limited to twelve. Three heads are to be elected from each village. (Village N was a compound village.)

Art. 3. In order to avoid having irresponsible leaders, those selected to be association heads must be just, honest, and popular; in addition they should own immovable property worth at least one thousand dollars.

Art. 4. The association heads are to take charge of the village affairs in turn. Four are in charge of the money and accounts for one year. In order to avoid corruption, the accounts shall be turned over to the succeeding heads on the first day of the second month.

Art. 5. Two of the four head men are to be in charge of the accounts and two of the money. After the fall harvest the income and expenditure accounts shall be posted on the temple wall.

Art. 6. Although the four head men are to be in charge of the routine association affairs, more important business shall be decided by a majority of the twelve heads. A meeting of all the heads shall be called by the four officers.

Art. 7. When an association head is obliged to leave the village, he shall resign from the association and his village shall elect his successor.

Art. 8. If an association head speculates with association funds and is reported by another head or by anyone else, he must pay double compensation to the association and he will be turned over to the hsien government for further treatment.

Art. 9. Ten crop-watchmen are to be employed by the association. The head watchman will appoint the others. In case any watchman steals any of the crops, the head watchman will be held responsible for the loss.

Art. 10. If a watchman is injured in the performance of his duties, the association must pay compensation for his injuries unless they are received in connection with personal vengeance. If the case is serious, the association will discharge the watchman and turn him over to the hsien government.

ART. 11. Association heads must be natives of the village. Immigrants from other provinces and other places are not allowed to serve in village affairs.

ART. 12. The villagers must report the true number of mu of land that they hold in the village area. If a landowner is found to have reported less than the true number of mu, he shall pay the crop-money for the unreported area plus an equal amount as a fine.

ART. 13. If crops are stolen from the protected area, the association will compensate the owner at the rate of eight sheng of grain, local market measure, for the loss of one mu of crops. If the loss is under one mu, it shall be estimated and paid for at the rate of eight sheng per mu.

ART. 14. When thieves are caught by the watchmen, they shall be brought to the association headquarters. The association heads will decide, according to the nature of the case, whether to fine them an incense fee or to send them to the hsien government.

ART. 15. For the convenience of the association, the heads from the different villages will collect the crop-money right after the fall harvest.

ART. 16. These regulations will become effective as soon as they are adopted and published. They may be revised whenever they do not meet the situation.

REGULATIONS OF THE GREEN CROP ASSOCIATION OF VILLAGE O

This announcement of the Green Crop Association [of Village O] is made on the fifteenth day of the seventh month of 1932.

ARTICLE 1. Eight watchmen will protect the green crops this year. If thieves are caught they will be fined twenty dollars if adults, ten dollars if children.

ART. 2. If a grasscutter conceals green crops inside his grass, he will be fined as much as ten times the value of the crops taken.

ART. 3. If a thief is released by a landowner, the association will fine the owner twice the usual amount.

ART. 4. If a watchman is caught stealing by a landowner, he will be fined twice the usual amount.

ART. 5. If a thief is proved guilty and refuses to pay the amount of his fine, the village officers will send him to the hsien government for punishment.

REGULATIONS OF THE GREEN CROP ASSOCIATION OF VILLAGE P, SHEN-TSE HSIEN, HOPEI

ARTICLE 1. Those who intend to be watchmen must register. No one is allowed to withdraw after registration.

ART. 2. The number of watchmen is not limited. The watchmen must elect a head and an assistant head who will be responsible.

ART. 3. One *kuan* of grain will be paid for the loss of eight heads of kaoliang, eight ears of corn, fifty heads of millet. The rate for panicled and glutinous millet is the same as for the regular millet.

ART. 4. All cultivators shall pay one kuan of grain per mu as crop-money and give some grain stalks to the watchmen if they are satisfied with their service.

ART. 5. The landowner and the watchmen will investigate any crop losses. The village head and the assistant head will record the amount of the loss so that compensation can be paid after the harvest.

ART. 6. If the watchman is caught stealing cotton, he will be fined as much as ten times the value of the theft. Grain or cotton thieves, if caught by the watchman, will be fined. Half of the fine will go to the watchman as a reward.

ART. 7. The watchmen are not allowed to engage in other duties.

> *Signed* . . . Head watchman
> . . . Assistant head watchman

In 1931 the government of T'ung Hsien drew up and passed a series of regulations for the village crop-watching and asked the provincial government to approve. These rules made crop-watching an integral part of the work of the village administration, legalizing and putting under government supervision activities that had been carried on informally by the leaders of most villages for many years.

The tentative regulations for the Green Crop Associations of the villages of T'ung Hsien provided:

ARTICLE 1. After the seed is sown the village heads will appoint watchmen to protect the green crops of the village area.

ART. 2. When crop-stealers are caught by the watchmen, the village head can fine them from one to ten times the amount of their loot. If they refuse to pay the fine they will be sent to the branch office of the District Bureau of Public Safety where the fine will be collected.

ART. 3. One tenth of the fine will go to the landowner, two tenths to the watchman as a reward, and the rest will be used for the educational expenses of the village.

ART. 4. If the thieves are caught by the landowner or the village head, they will be fined according to Article 2, but no rewards will be given.

ART. 5. If the thieves are a group of more than three persons, they are to be sent to the hsien government for severe punishment.

ART. 6. If the watchmen conspire with the thieves, or make false reports, the village head and the assistant head can send them to the hsien government for severe punishment.

ART. 7. No kaoliang leaves are to be taken before the *fu t'ien* ("mid-summer") days, otherwise the takers will be treated as thieves. The association will decide how many leaves can be taken from each kaoliang stalk.

ART. 8. During the harvesttime the villages will restrict the gleaners according to the local regulations.

ART. 9. These regulations will be effective after they are approved by the provincial Civil Administration Department.

ART. 10. If any of these regulations are unsatisfactory they may be changed by the magistrate.

VI: OTHER VILLAGE FUNCTIONS

BESIDES CROP-WATCHING, other functions or activities that were administered by the village associations or officers included, to name the chief ones, the education of the children, mutual protection and self-defense as provided by the night watch and the local guard, the arbitration of disputes, and religious observances.

EDUCATION

Education underwent the greatest change in content and control of any of the village activities. Before 1900 the Chinese classics were taught in private schools by teachers who usually earned only a meager livelihood from the fees paid by their students. At that time there were limitations on education. The sons of servants of government officials, of actors, of prostitutes, and of those in other inferior occupations could not enter any official school. While they might attend private schools, they were not allowed to take the classical examinations and so qualify for official position.

Establishment of modern schools.—Signs of change appeared in some villages as early as 1894. Progressive families were providing support for schools teaching the new "modern" or "western" type of education. Soon after 1900 some of the hsien governments began to urge their villages to establish modern schools and to finance them from village funds. In 1923 the Chihli provincial Department of Education ordered that the hsien "Bureaus for Urging the People to Learn" be reorganized as hsien bureaus of education. By a decree dated September 6, 1928, the Nationalist government made four years of lower primary education compulsory for all children. Every village was to have a school of its own or was to join with neighboring villages to establish a united school. The village boards or committees responsible for the schools were to keep detailed accounts and make regular reports to the hsien bureau of education. Higher governmental agencies took over almost complete control of village education. In one of our sample villages the hsien bureau of education even appointed one of the two teachers.

All our sample villages had "modern" schools. The dates of establishment were from "after 1900" to 1929. The last opened was that of Village A, which felt that it was too small and too poor to have its own school. When orders came from the hsien government requiring a school, Village A joined with two small neighbors in organizing a school that each village supported according to the number of its students. Village A paid $28 the first year and $68 the third year. Ordinarily Village A would have joined with a larger neighbor, but local tensions and jealousies made that impossible.

Besides their modern schools, two sample villages still had old-style schools teaching the Chinese classics. They were privately supported.

Management.—In some villages the village head ran the school along with his other duties. In others a special committee of several village leaders was appointed to manage the school, handle its finances, and make the required financial reports to the hsien bureau of education. In one instance a three-member management committee consisted of a village leader who was changed every year, an old man, and a very enthusiastic young man.

School buildings.—Most village schools were housed in the temple. They usually had one room, one teacher, and four grades. There was normally a wide range in the ages of the students. In Village C the span was from seven to nineteen years. The number of students in the four grades in that village showed a year-to-year drop of about 45 per cent. Forty-eight per cent of the students were in the first

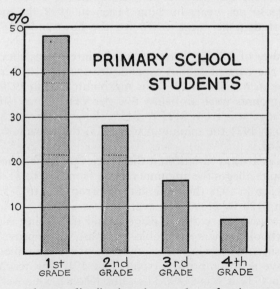

Fig. 10.—Proportionate distribution, by grades, of primary school students in Village C.

grade. Only about 7 per cent were in the fourth grade. (See fig. 10.)

Only one of our sample villages had used local funds to build a separate schoolhouse. Village I had paid $12 a year for rent for its schoolhouse from 1910 through 1915 and $15 a year from 1916 through 1922. In 1922 it spent 1,000,000 cash ($294) for a site and in 1923 and 1924 spent 2,495,156 cash ($542) for the erection of a school building. Equipment costing 320,950 cash ($52) was purchased in 1925.

Vacations.—The school vacation schedule was adjusted to the agricultural activities of the village. Village C had 100 days of vacation during the year—one month, from the twentieth day of the twelfth month to the twentieth day of the first month, for New Year's; 19 days, from the twentieth day of the fourth month to the ninth day of the fifth month, for the spring harvest; 40 days, from the fifteenth day of the seventh month to the twenty-fifth day of the eighth month, for the fall harvest. The other 11 days were scattered throughout the year and were for the days when fairs were held in the area.

School budgets.—School budgets varied widely from village to village. Some were only $100 per year, others about $200, still others more than $300. The amount per student in the 1930's varied from $3.80 to $8.30 per year. In Ting Hsien in 1928 the average was $8.20 per student per year, $7.70 for the boys and $10.50 for the girls.[1]

The figures of Village I are of special interest, as they show the change in the current school expenditure from 1910 through 1931. The minimum was $79 in 1915, the maximum $349 in 1929. Through 1915 the amounts were all below $90 per year. From 1916 through 1921 the range was from $125 to $155; the average was $142. From 1922 through 1931 the minimum was $215; the maximum, $349; the average, $265.

There was a wide variation in the salaries paid the schoolteachers. In our sample villages the amounts ranged from $70 to $180 per year. In Ting Hsien in 1928 the minimum was from $50 to $59, the maximum from $120 to $139. The average was $90.[2]

The increased salary that Village I paid its teacher suggests that primary-school teachers were able materially to improve their economic position following the government's requirement that all villages have a lower primary school. In 1910 the teacher's salary was $32. In 1930 it was $180. The same teacher who was employed by the village from 1916 to 1919 and paid 180,320 cash per year

($61 in 1916) was rehired in 1931 at a salary of $165. This was an increase of 170 per cent in fifteen years.

Besides the teacher's salary, school expenditures were relatively small. In 1932 one village paid $18.00 for coal, $3.60 for a special meal, $2.40 for books, and $20.00 for miscellaneous items. Another village paid the school attendant $24 and spent $10 for books, $4 for equipment, and $24 for all other items. In Village I the nonsalary items ranged from $29 in 1910 to $189 in 1928.

Sources of school income.—Small tuition fees were regularly charged by the village schools. In most places the fees were graded according to the amount of land owned by the pupil's family. In 1910 Village I charged 3,000 cash if the family had fewer than 15 mu, 4,000 cash if they had from 15 to 50 mu, and 5,000 cash if they had more than 50 mu. The cash amounts were equivalent to $1.20, $1.60, and $2.00. In 1925 the charges were $3.00, $3.50, and $4.00 In another village, in 1931–1932, the fee was from 50 cents to $5.50 and averaged $2.40. In a third village the fee was $1.

Additional support for the schools came from a variety of sources. If the village had taken over the temple lands, the income from their rental usually was allocated to the school. In one village the basic school-support came from the income from trees growing in the dry moat outside the village wall; in another from the commission charged on the sale of charcoal, lumber, and peanuts; in another from the sale of reeds grown in a pond controlled by the village; in another from a 2 per cent commission collected from buyers of land in the village "green circle"; in another from the profits of the village granaries. Judging by our sample villages, only a small amount came from crop-money.

Availability of education.—Universal education, although decreed, was far from being a fact. In our sample villages 25 per cent was the largest proportion of families that had children in school. In one village the figure was only 10.5 per cent. Our sample villages had no schools for girls, although one reported that eleven of its girls were studying in a "vocational school." At the urging of Magistrate T'ang of Wan-ping Hsien, Village B had opened a girls' school in 1922, but closed it two years later; there were no regular funds for the support of the school and there was almost no enthusiasm on the part of the parents for education for their daughters. In Ting Hsien in 1928 there were schools for girls in 23 per cent of the villages.[3]

In Village C, 460 persons, 33.5 per cent of the 1,373 inhabitants, had at least one year of schooling. Some had as much as twelve years.

The educational record of the group is shown graphically in figure 11. The totals with some school experience were 442 of the 675 males in the village, but only 18 of the 698 females. None of the females had more than four years of education, i.e., they had not gone beyond the lower school.

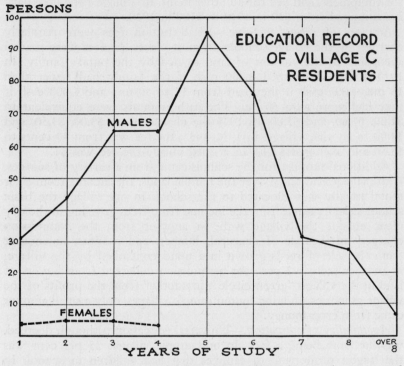

FIG. 11.—Education record of Village C residents, by number, sex, and years of study.

Sixty-three per cent of all the males living in the village had some education, but only 2.6 per cent of all the females. For those of more than five years of age the figures were males, 73.4 per cent; females, 3.0 per cent. The figures for the males were unusually high, especially when compared with nearby villages. Undoubtedly one of the reasons was the fact that Village C had opened its modern school soon after 1900, when the teacher of one of the old-style schools merged the two existing schools into one modern school.

SELF PROTECTION — THE NIGHT WATCH

The protection of life and property was a constant problem in the villages of North China. It varied in intensity with the time of year and the general economic and political conditions. Scattered across the countryside, the villages had to provide most of their protection themselves. Any forces that the hsien government might have were usually small and, being based in the hsien city or a district town, could give little help to the villages in case of trouble. The first protective measure of the farming families was the aggregation of their houses into compact villages, some of them surrounded by walls.

When the crops were growing in the fields there was little threat to property inside the village. That was the busy time of the year. The nights were short. People were constantly coming and going. Almost everyone had work and there was relatively little pressure from want. Theft of crops during the growing season was prevented by the organized system described in chapter v. Losses generally were kept close to the minimum, and often it was possible to apprehend the culprits when there was theft or trespass.

By the end of the ninth month, when the harvest was over, there was nothing left in the fields to steal. It was beginning to be cold. The nights were long. Few people were about. Many men were idle, as little work was available. Then property inside the village was threatened, and losses might range from petty thievery to looting by organized bands of marauders.

In peaceful times most villages attempted to meet the post-harvest threat to property inside the village by having the streets patrolled at night by unarmed watchmen (*keng-fu*) equipped with a metal gong (*lo*) and a wooden rattle (*pang*). The rattle was a hollow wooden tube that was hit with a wooden stick. Beginning about the first night of the tenth month, the two-hour watches were rung on the gong and the rattle. The noise and the presence of the watchmen were to scare away any prowlers who might be about. The first watch began at seven in the evening, the sixth at five o'clock the next morning. The watchmen were also expected to look out for fires and warn the householders that they, too, should be alert to protect their property.

Organization of the night watch.—It was said that the night watch was one of the oldest of the village functions and that it had been used for "one or two thousand years." It was also said that originally the night watch was a wholly coöperative activity to which all the village families contributed personnel. Later the wealthier families were allowed to make their contributions in money, and finally all the watchmen were employed by the village and paid from general funds. We found examples of the first and last of these types of night watch in our sample villages, and one that used both employed and volunteer watchmen.

In Village B all of the able-bodied men were expected to serve. About two hundred participated. Half of the group came out for a parade every evening, but only twelve men kept watch, two for each of the six sections of the village. Each section was expected to raise the money needed to supply meals for those on duty.

In Village H there were 120 men in the volunteer night watch. Each man served once in six days. The twenty men on duty were divided into four groups, five men for each of the village gates. As each man completed the tour of his section of the village, he sent his *keng p'ai* (wooden identification board) to the village office to show that he had fulfilled his duty.

In Village J there was one head watchman who was employed for four months, from the first of the tenth month to the end of the second month. He kept only the second, third, and fourth watches. During the third watch he knocked on every door in the village to be sure that every family was "alert." During the eleventh and twelfth months he was joined by seven or eight volunteers every night. The order of their service was arranged by the village head. A slip of paper passed from one family to the next showed whose turn it was to furnish a volunteer for the night watch. The number of times a family had to provide a watchman was determined by the amount of land it had registered in the village books.

Village I usually hired three men for its night watch, one man for each section of the village. In 1911, the year of the revolution, seven men were employed, two watchmen for each section and one as superintendent of the operation.

Village D hired four watchmen and a superintendent.

A few villages whose walls were in good shape and whose gates could be firmly closed and locked at night felt sufficiently secure against marauders and prowlers to dispense with the night watch. They paid a small wage to a group of men who were engaged to close and bar the gates every night.

Duration of the night watch.—The work of the watch usually began on *han-chieh* ("cold festival"), the first night of the tenth month, and continued at least to the end of the twelfth month. Some villages stopped then, for they said, "Everybody behaves better at New Year's." Others carried on the work until the second night of the second month, when the great dragon god, the god of water, "lifted up his head." Farm work usually started at that time, so there was more employment available.

If conditions were badly disturbed, some villages continued the night watch until the beginning of the third month. This was true of Village I in 1926, 1927, and 1928, when there was trouble in southern Hopei.

Wages paid to watchmen.—The villages paid various amounts to their watchmen. Village J paid its one employed man $2 per month and gave him and each of the seven or eight volunteers who served with him a half catty of wheat flour per day.

Village D paid $5 each to four of its five watchmen and $4 to the fifth man for three months' service in 1932. The total cost that year was $45.00—$24.00 for wages, $9.38 for coal, $6.70 for ammunition, and $4.67 for repairs to the watch room and the installation of a stove.

In 1911 Village I paid 4,800 cash ($1.85) each to four of its seven watchmen and 3,200 cash ($1.28) each to the other three, for the winter watch period. The total cost was $11.09. The next year there were three regular watchmen, paid 10,800 cash ($4) each. In 1913 the rate was increased to 15,000 cash per man. Then there was no change for ten years. In 1913 the 15,000 cash were equivalent to $5.77, but in 1922 they were worth only $4.41, because of the decrease in the silver value of the cash. In 1923 and 1924 the rate was only $4 per man. In 1925 the rate was officially set at $15 for each of the three sections of the village, but in only one section was the watchman paid the official rate; the two other men were paid $14 each.

In 1926 the winter rates remained the same, $15.00 and $14.00, but the night watch was continued for an extra two months, for which one section paid $11.60 and the other two paid $10.85 each. The same disparity continued in 1927, when the spring rates were $10.00 for one section and $9.32 each for the other two.

In 1928 four men were paid $12 each for the winter season and three men were paid $11 each for the spring season. In 1929 the night watch was made one of the duties of the village guard.

From 1910 to 1928 the cost of the winter night watch went up 290 per cent, but all of the increase came after 1924, as the total for that year was 40 cents less than the silver equivalent of the amount paid in 1910. If we add the extra cost of the two months' extension in 1928, the 1910–1928 increase in the cost of the night watch was 550 per cent.

In 1910 Village I spent only nine cents per family for the night watch. In 1925 the wages were increased 275 per cent; evidently, large and dramatic changes were taking place in the wage scale in the area. By 1928 the amount per family was 27 cents for the usual three months of the winter and 46 cents per family for the extended period of five months.

In 1933 Village D spent 32 cents per family for its night watch.

VILLAGE GUARD

During the 1920's the unarmed night watch maintained during the winter months was unable to give many of the villages the protection that they needed. At this time our sample villages reported that, in addition to their night watch, they had groups of armed guards. The village guards showed the same variety of organization that we found in the programs for crop protection and the night watch. Some were purely volunteer, some were partly hired and partly volunteer, some were fully hired. Some were set up by a single village, some were united guards organized jointly by several villages. Some shifted from the single-village to the united program and then back. In our sample villages organization of the guards took place at various times from 1920 through 1926.

In 1920 Village H organized a collective training program to which every family that had either modern or old-fashioned weapons sent representatives. Some sixty men took part. Neighboring villages followed suit and instituted similar programs. Village H was chosen as the leader in developing a federated protection system. Every night a number of volunteers went out to patrol the villages. The next year the volunteer feature was discontinued and a united guard of five armed men was employed to patrol an area that included several villages.

In 1922 the hsien government organized guard groups for each of its districts and required the villages to contribute to their support. At that time the united volunteer village-guard set up by Village H and its neighbors was abandoned, but the work was continued by the individual villages.

Revival of old system ordered by the central government.—In 1926, by order of the central government, the old system of village guards, long used during times of disturbance and emergency, was revived for the Peking area. The order was sent to the hsien governments and by them passed on to the villages. Village D hired two men, put them into uniform, and had them ready to answer any call from the hsien government. Village I organized its guard under the direction of the village head, but did so under supervision by the hsien government. The field report stated that in Village I the guard was expected to serve only for the winter months "when there was need for armed protection."

Village A, a small village, joined with six others to maintain a united guard of one head man and two assistants.

Village B set up its guard organization in 1928. It had seven men on duty inside the village walls and contributed three more to a united guard of seventeen men organized by eight villages. The two large villages in the union, of which Village B was one, were to contribute three men each, the five medium-sized villages two men each, while the one small village sent one man.

In 1929 the united guard was continued, but the village guard was given up. The next year the united system was discontinued and the village guard was reëstablished. In 1931 the system was reversed again and the united guard reorganized, but then without the one small village.

In 1932, when quiet had been restored in the area, the united guard was again discontinued and the village guard reactivated, but at that time no special men were hired. The work of the guard was added to that of the five village crop-watchmen.

Village C had a combined hired and volunteer guard. Two former soldiers were employed to take care of the details of the self-defense corps. They were put into uniform and each paid a salary of $6 a month. The corps consisted of some 150 members who belonged to the 44 families owning 30 or more mu of land. Every member was expected to give one night a week to the work. They carried guns when on duty. Each of the seven groups of guards was headed by a member of the village association. Any corps member who had to be absent when his turn came was expected to find a substitute to serve for him.

In Village J, in Shansi, males between eighteen and thirty-five years of age were to join the "Self-Protection Organization" and one of every three brothers was called on to serve in the village militia or guard. Both organizations were set up on paper only.

In Village K, in Shantung, the members of the Red Spears, a secret society, acted as village guards. That village reported a pitched battle with and the defeat of a band of some two hundred bandits on the twentieth day of the third month, 1926. The bandits lost twenty-nine men killed; the Red Spear Society, five.

Reorganization under the Nationalist government.—After its final struggle with Feng Yü-hsiang in 1930 the Nationalist government forced the Red Spear Society to disband and worked to organize the district guard as an official self-defense corps. All adult males between twenty and forty years of age were expected to take part in the village program. In Village K, there were 490 men eligible. Ordinarily thirty-two men kept watch every night. In time of emergency the guard was doubled and sixty-four men were on duty. The hsien government gave the village four rifles, one for each section. Other arms were broad knives and red spears.

In 1931 a strong group of bandits in Shantung was inducted into the regular army. On the way to the army depot the bandits robbed and disturbed many villages. At Village K about ten thousand guards were assembled from the area to greet the bandits and escort them. They went peacefully on their way.

After 1926 many villages found themselves with two groups of protectors on duty at the same time, the guard and the night watch. It was not long before the two were consolidated and both programs were carried on by one group of men. In several villages the same men also watched the crops.

Expenses of the guard.—The expenses of the guard naturally varied among the villages. Village A paid an average of only $31 a year for its part in a united guard program. Village B averaged $314 per year for four years of village guards and $294 per year for four years of a united guard program. In addition it raised, by special subscription, $1,000 for the purchase of guns and ammunition. Village I spent an average of $186 a year for the period 1926–1931. In 1932 Village D's outlay was only $13 for wages and $2 for expenses.

Only Village D included a policeman in its self-protection program. Although he was given the title, he was not in uniform and his work was more that of a village servant than a police officer. Part of his time was spent running errands for the village head, calling the village elders to meetings, and entertaining any hsien or district government representatives who came to the village. Occasionally he represented the village in minor matters at the hsien and district offices. The predecessor of the man who held the position in 1932 had represented the village so often that he was generally known as "Mr. Representative." He was literate and so was able to keep the village books, a service for which he was paid $2 per month.

In 1932 the policeman was also the head of the crop watch, the night watch, and the village guard. His salary as policeman was $5 a month. His total income from his four activities was about $87 for the year.

District police force.—Besides their guard, the hsien districts had organized a district police force, supported by collections from the villages. Five of our sample villages reported that they contributed to the district police budget. Village A's average, for seven years, was $12 per year. Village B's average, for ten years, had been $55 per year, but the 1926–1932 average was $60 per year. There was an increase of almost 50 per cent in 1926 when the amount jumped from $42 to $62. Village D paid $38 in 1932, Village C $80 in 1933. We have not been able to find any relationship between the amounts paid by the different villages, the number of mu recorded in the local land books, or the number of resident families. It is possible that the amounts might have been based on the number of mu that the district office had on its land books, but those figures were not available.

GRANARIES

Public granaries, in which were stored the surplus of the grain paid as taxes and from which grain might be distributed in time of need, were an ancient part of the Chinese economy. T'ang T'ai Tsung (A.D. 627–650) reëstablished the system. Kublai Khan used it as part of his economic organization.

In the latter part of the twelfth century Chu Hsi (1130–1200) started a system of *she-ts'ang*, village granaries. When there was a great famine in eastern Chekiang Province, where he was commissioner of education, he obtained 600 *tan* of grain from the provincial government and supplied village people during the winter, with the grain to be repaid in kind with interest after the next harvest. The rate of interest varied with the state of the harvest, being reduced for years of bad harvest and waived entirely when there was famine. It may have averaged between 10 and 15 per cent, for after fifteen years the granary had collected enough as interest and as gifts from wealthy families to return the original 600 tan and still have 2,100 tan on hand. Thereafter the interest was only three sheng per tan, 3 per cent, presumably enough to cover waste and loss and to maintain the stock of the granary at 2,100 tan.

Although procedure varied from village to village, generally families that wanted to borrow grain filed applications during the first month of the year, listing the number and ages of the persons in the family. Those who were sick or whose conduct was questionable were not permitted to apply.

The families requesting loans banded into *chia*, groups of ten families, and elected a *chia-shou*, or head. Five chia were united to form a she that had a capable, educated man as she-shou. The she-shou, after examining and verifying the applications, took them to the she-ts'ang for further checking and final approval.

Loans were made twice a year, the first at plowing time, the second at cultivating time. Each adult member of a borrowing family was entitled to a loan of one tan of grain; for children more than five years of age the amount was a half tan. Because of his service to the group, the chia-shou could borrow double the amount allowed an ordinary adult. Loans were to be repaid with interest after the fall harvest. One district set the date as not later than the end of the eighth month.

Because of its effectiveness in helping poor farmers in normal times and preventing starvation during famines, the she-ts'ang system initiated by Chu Hsi was continued and extended by the Yuan, Ming, and Ch'ing emperors, with varying degrees of success.

In the Yuan dynasty the central government ordered the establishment of a she-ts'ang in every village. In years when there was a good harvest every family was to contribute grain to the granary. In famine years grain was to be lent and distributed to needy families. Detailed decrees were issued regarding fairness in the collection and distribution of the grain and prescribing methods of storage and care to prevent spoilage and waste. Government officials were prohibited from using grain from the she-ts'ang.

In the Ming dynasty the government attempted to strengthen the she-ts'ang organization by adding two associates to assist the she-shou and by specifying the amount of grain to be contributed by the village families, who for this purpose were divided into three classes.

The Ch'ing emperors also attempted to expand the system throughout the country, emphasizing in their decrees the need to elect fair and just men to take charge of "getting rid of the old grain (through loans in the spring) and taking in the new" in the fall after the harvest.

The granaries maintained earlier by many villages in North China had, for the most part, been given up before 1933. Their grain had been requisitioned by the military or been sold to obtain money to meet army demands. We found three still operating in Village J, in Shansi. Two were run by the village authorities and were managed by the eight village elders. The third was under the control of the most influential family in the village. The combined storage capacity of the three granaries was some 2,000 tou, about 26 tons.

The grain was regularly distributed in the late spring to make room for the new harvest. How the grain was handled depended largely upon the year. In normal years it was lent to poor farmers in neighboring villages as well as to those in Village J. In poor years and in very good years it was available only to Village J residents.

The recipients of the grain ordinarily were expected to return it after the harvest. Whether or not they paid interest depended on the season and the decision of the village elders. In very good years and in very bad years there generally was no interest charge. The family-run granary regularly charged 30 per cent interest for its grain. For every 10 tou of grain lent in the spring, 13 tou were to be returned after the harvest. This was not considered an excessive charge, both because of the yield from the borrowed grain and because, in terms of money, the repaid grain and that paid as interest together often had less value after the harvest than the borrowed grain had early in the season.

The profits of the village granaries were used for the village school. Those from the family granary went to repair temples and bridges.

ARBITRATION OF DISPUTES

The settlement of disputes by arbitration was a very important activity of the village association. It was reported that there were a great many arguments in the villages and that people were often ready to spend money and time in court on disputes of little material value, but which they felt to be of importance for personal and family prestige.

To reduce the adverse effect of lawsuits on neighborhood harmony and agricultural production, and to avoid an unnecessary burden on both the government agencies and the villagers involved, the village elders had the traditional and legal responsibility to arbitrate and settle disputes relating to marriages, debts, land, fighting, and other matters which were not in violation of law and order. The village head was given the power to punish those who continued to misbehave or to remain idle after repeated advice and warning. Only serious cases were to be reported to the government officials. If there had been no attempt at arbitration, the court officials in many instances referred the case to the village leaders, hoping for its settlement by them.

In the Ming dynasty a just and able village leader (*li lao*) was especially assigned to act as arbitrator. In some villages special pavilions were built where the leader would hear and settle disputes and punish villagers who misbehaved.

Arbitration was still an important village function at the time of our study. The Hsien Organization Act of 1929 called for the yearly election by every village of an arbitration committee of four members. We are unable to report on the extent and success of the procedure, as our material dealing with village litigation and arbitration was destroyed by the invading Japanese forces before it could be compiled and analyzed.

HSIANG-YÜEH

Hsiang-yüeh, a village contract system advocated by a famous scholar in the Sung dynasty, had great influence in developing and preserving social and moral virtues in Chinese villages. The four major elements in the hsiang-yüeh consisted of mutual encouragement in virtues, mutual correction of mistakes, mutual exchange of courtesies, and mutual help in time of difficulty.

Under the hsiang-yüeh the village people voluntarily entered into a contract agreement to observe these four practices in their daily life. Each village of a hundred families was to elect two fair and honest persons to serve as *yüeh-cheng* ("contract chief") and *yüeh-fu* ("associate contract chief"), and two persons who could write and were eloquent as *yüeh-chiang* ("contract lecturer") and *yüeh-shih* ("contract recorder"). These four officers were responsible for the promotion and preservation of the social conduct and moral virtues of the people in the village. They were assisted by the *chia-chang*, heads of ten families. Any person in the village who violated the contract was first advised and corrected by his nearest neighbors. If he failed to change and improve, he would be reported to the chia-chang, who would in turn report the case to the yüeh-cheng. If the advice of the yüeh-cheng was still not accepted, the case would be brought to the attention of the officials for appropriate punishment.

In the village temple there were two bulletin boards—one to announce the good deeds of individuals and the other, the bad deeds. There were also two books—one for recording the names of persons who performed good deeds and the other for those whose deeds were bad.

On the first and fifteenth day of each month everyone gathered in a public place, usually at the temple, to listen to lectures encouraging them to be good and to avoid misconduct. Public announcements were made then about important examples of both the good and the bad deeds of the village people during the month. The troubles of individual villagers, if any, were also brought up for solution.

The hsiang-yüeh system was used for centuries with varying degrees of effort and success. An imperial decree of the first Ch'ing emperor ordered the strengthening and expansion of the system, but by 1911, the end of the dynasty, the hsiang-yüeh had practically disappeared. The hsiang-yüeh, village officer, appointed by village heads in Shansi for a one-year term of unpaid service, may be a remnant of the earlier system.

RELIGION

Most of the villages in North China had one or more temples, and the activities connected with religious observances often surpassed all other programs, even crop-watching. In some villages the crop-watching was only a minor function of one of the religious associations.

Number and purpose of temples.—Six of our sample villages had a total of 38 temples—from 2 to 15 each. No reports were available for the others.

The temples were dedicated to a wide variety of deities—Buddhist, Taoist, official, and individual gods. Kuan Yin, the goddess of Mercy, was the principal Buddhist deity. Kuan Yü or Kuan Ti, the Chinese god of war who was also looked on as a god of literature and by some of the village people as a god of wealth, and the dragon god, who controlled the rain, were the most popular of the official deities. Many of the villages started their main crop-watching activities on Kuan Ti's birthday.[4] At least four of the six reporting villages had Kuan Ti temples.

The chief Taoist gods were the Wu Tao, the gods of the five elements, of heaven, hell, men, animals, and hungry devils, to whom all deaths were reported, and the Niang Niang, a group of female deities who granted children, protected the eyes, etc. Others were the god of cattle, gods of medicine, and the god of literature.

Besides the gods to whom the temples were dedicated, there were figures of many other deities on the secondary altars in the temples, such as the god of earth, the god of the hills, the god of horses, and the god of insects. These were the individual gods, not strictly associated with the Buddhist, Taoist, or official pantheons.

Health and safety of men and animals, good crops, and wealth were some of the things for which the villagers prayed to the various gods who through the years had given help and protection. Collectively they offered food, incense, prayers, and the entertainment of theatrical plays.

The Big Temple in Village A was built in 1440. The Kuan Ti Miao, at the north end of the main street of Village C, was rebuilt in 1838; it had four buildings, with twelve chien. The T'ien Ch'i Miao ("Heavenly Air Temple"), at the south end of the street, was given major repairs in 1845; it had six buildings, with twenty-four chien. The one-room shrine at the east end of the main street of Village D was rebuilt in 1928; it was dedicated to Kuan Yin. The temple of the god of medicine, at the west end of the street, was refurbished in 1932 at a cost of $582.

The financing of the work on the temple of the god of medicine suggests how other temple building and repairing may have been handled. Contributions amounting to $560 were collected, but of this only $85 was given by residents of Village D. The $22 needed to finish the job, hang the bell and the tablets, and pay for the dedication exercises came from village funds—crop-money—collected from the farming families.

Temple management.—In only two of our sample villages were priests living in the temples. Village D had two monks in its Kuan Ti Miao, and Village A had a monk and a servant in its big Kuang Ning Miao. Two other villages had caretakers look after the buildings. In Ting Hsien there was one priest per 10,000 population.[5] When Village C held its annual service to propitiate and control the wandering spirits of those who had died by drowning in the nearby pond, the priests came from neighboring villages.

In 1932 Village A gave its temple servant $25 and his food. Village C paid its temple caretaker $100 a year, but he had to provide his own food. Village J supplied a room in the temple and the free use of 10 mu of temple land. Village D allocated 10 mu of temple land to the support of its two priests.

In another village it was believed that the elders who organized and cared for the details of worship received a special blessing from the gods. Some of the wealthy families or families in urgent need of help from the god of the cows or the goddess of earth would often obtain the appointment by twice inviting the village elders to a feast.

The management and control of the temples, their property, and their activities were, in earlier days, usually in the hands of separate organizations. In later years, as the village administrations in the Hopei area developed in strength and influence, most of them took over the temples' affairs. In Shansi the separate organizations were much more numerous and active, and they seemed to have been able to continue their programs. At the close of our study, however, when the demands of the military were increasing, many of them had had to discontinue most of their activities for lack of funds. Also, the village administrations were increasing their power, aided by the hsien government and the decrees of the higher governmental echelons. It seemed probable that the separate temple organizations would slowly disappear as the villages gradually took over the temples.

We found an example of this process in Village B. There the "Association for the Fourth-Month Fair" was controlled by a group composed mostly of the heads of landless families. The leader was the village bully. To secure funds for the fair and the plays that were offered to the two gods of medicine on their birthday, this association levied arbitrary assessments on the wealthier families of the village. The poorer ones were not asked to contribute. Those who were assessed grumbled over the amount they were called on to pay, but it was "pay or stay away," and they did not want to deprive their families of the pleasure and excitement of the fair and its plays. Finally the village authorities, backed by the larger landowners, brought suit against the heads of the fair association and forced them to discontinue the fair and the plays.

Through the years many of the larger and more popular temples received gifts of land, the income from which was to be used for the support of the temple and its activities. The temples in Village B had 300 mu. Those in Village C had 90 mu. The renting of the land and the collection of the rents were handled usually by separate groups of leaders, but because of favoritism and poor administration many of the tenants had come to regard the land as almost their own and often paid little or no rent. An evident decline in the general interest in religion in many of the villages helped to make this possible. Later, when new schools were opened and money was needed for their support, the leaders of many villages took over the temple land and allocated the income to the support of the school. In some villages a special subcommittee of the administration was set up to handle school finances and to collect the rents on former temple land that had become village land. In the village where the committee consisted of an association leader, an old man, and a very enthusiastic young man, the association member was changed every year.

The yearly expenditure for the maintenance of the temples in Village A doubled between 1926 and 1932, increasing from $95 to $191. In 1932 the expenses were $61 for repairing the temple wall, $25 for the wages of the temple servant, $22 for various items used for worship, and $83 for 102 different items, most of which were for the food and maintenance of the monk and the temple servant.

In 1915 the priest then in Village A was defeated in an attempt to take over the temple and its lands for his personal use and advantage. The elders called the heads of all the families together to discuss the matter. After sharing a simple meal and hearing the details of the problem, they all agreed to join in the lawsuit and signed the complaint against the priest. It outlined the importance of Buddhism and the rights to village property. The document bore the signature of the village head and the assistant head, the two annual officers of the village association, the seven other village elders and the heads of 48 households, a total of 59 names.[6]

In a similar case, the priest's assistant, who had been dismissed for violation of Buddhist discipline, returned after the death of his superior and attempted to claim the temple and its lands for himself. This effort was also defeated by legal action.

After the lawsuits the village associations assumed the control of the temples and their lands. Such action by village authorities seems to have been widespread in the Peiping area. The available data does not indicate whether there was a similar move in Shansi, where there were many more temple associations and much more religious activity.

Religious services.—Offerings of fruit, cakes and other food, excluding meat, were usually set out on tables in front of the altars of the gods honored by special services. In Ta-t'ung Hsien we found some villages, in the sheep-raising area, that added animal sacrifice to the ceremonies and included meat in the feast set before the gods. In one village five sheep were slaughtered on the eighth day of the fifth month as an offering to the dragon god. On the twenty-fourth day of the sixth month one sheep was sacrificed to the god of insects and on the fifteenth day of the seventh month the dragon god was again propitiated with a sheep. After the services the mutton was divided among the livestock-owning families who had contributed to the cost of the sacrifice.

In another village in the same hsien three offerings of sheep were made to the dragon god as a prayer for rain and to give thanks afterwards. The cost of the sacrifices was borne by the twenty elders who held office in annual rotation. They were the only ones to share in the distribution of the meat after the service.

In Village J the she leaders arranged each year for eleven special celebrations at the village temples. The fourth and eleventh months were the only ones with no services. Offerings of cakes and fruit were set before the gods and were, after the service, usually divided among the she leaders; but the special offerings to Kuan Ti on the eleventh day of the first month, to the dragon god on the sixth day of the sixth month, and for the thanksgiving day were shared by all the villagers. In another village two sets of food were placed before the gods, one outside the temple, the other inside directly in front of the altar. After the service the inner offering went to the temple caretaker, and the outer one was divided among the boys who came as spectators.

Theatrical activities.—Giving plays to pay homage to the gods

and to entertain the villagers was one of the religious activities connected with many temples. In Hopei only Village B and a few others
had plays every year. The more usual practice was to perform them
on special occasions, such as the dedication of a rebuilt temple. Village I had four performances of plays in twenty-five years. In Shansi,
on the other hand, practically every village gave plays once a year
at least, and some gave them each month. It was estimated by some
village leaders that before 1911 a fairly large village would have
from eight to ten plays per year. The number reported to our field
men ranged from one to thirteen. The number of performances at
64 villages were as follows:

Sets of plays performed per year	Villages	Sets of plays performed per year	Villages
1	17	6	5
2	15	7	1
3	12	13	1
4	5	Total	64
5	8	Average: 3 plays per village per year	

A Lin Hsien village in Honan had six series of dramatic performances per year. On the nineteenth, twentieth, and twenty-first
days of the first month, plays were offered to the god of the cows,
to pray for the health of the cattle. The assessment was 20 cents for
a cow, 17 cents for a horse, 15 cents for a mule, 10 cents for a
donkey, and 7 cents for a sheep. In the second month, plays were
given for the goddess of earth. On the fourth, fifth, and sixth days
of the fifth month, a series of plays was given for the Buddhist god
of earth, who was no relation to the goddess of earth. After the
harvest, plays were performed to thank the dragon god for sending
the rains. In the tenth month a second series of plays was given for
the goddess of earth.[7] For the last four series the assessments were
based on the number of mu in a family's farm. If there were any
surplus funds, these were used in the twelfth month for additional
plays for the enjoyment of all the gods honored earlier.

In a Ta-t'ung Hsien village, play assessments were made according
to the number of men, animals, and mu of land. The plays given to
the gods in the second month were to ask for health for both men
and animals. In figuring the amounts to be charged to the village
families, a man, a horse, or a mule was counted as one unit, a donkey
or a cow as two thirds of a unit, and a child as a half unit. A later
series of plays was an offering to the dragon god. Crops were the

chief concern at that time, so the assessment was by mu of land. If the year turned out to be a prosperous one, a further series of plays might be given after the harvest, to thank the gods for their bounty. This series usually was paid for from surplus funds left from the other two.

Village I paid $72 for its plays in 1910, $208 in 1922, and $185 in 1923. The assessment was 60 cash (2.4 cents) per mu in 1910, 140 cash (4.1 cents) in 1922, and 200 cash (5.0 cents) in 1923. The totals collected were $88.28, $176.12, and $224.73.

The actors were paid 347,200 cash ($102) in 1922 and 300,000 cash ($75) in 1923. Other expenses were 358,588 cash ($105) in 1922 and 405,285 cash ($101) in 1923. Most of the other expenses were for food for the players and for the village leaders who were in charge of the activities.

Special accounts were kept for the plays, but any surplus or deficit was made part of the regular village income and expenses. In 1910 the surplus was $15.97. In 1922 there was a deficit of $31, but in 1923 there was a surplus of $48. Plays were given in 1914, but no figures were available, as the account books had been lost.

Village D gave a series of plays in 1928 as part of the celebration held when the rebuilt Kuan Yin temple was opened. In 1932 booking agents for a group of actors tried to persuade the village elders to put on a special celebration, but without success; the price of grain was low and the village was hard up.

In a Ta-t'ung Hsien village we found a local group of amateur or semi-amateur players who were trained to give *yang-ke*. Originally these were planting songs that tradition in Ting-Hsien said were written by the poet Su Tung-p'o (1036–1101) when he was magistrate there. As we found them, they were plays given in costume by village residents for the entertainment of their neighbors. The plays often had a religious connection, for they were given at the time of special temple celebration, at the time of the spring or fall festivals, or after the harvest. We did not attempt any study of the Shansi yang-ke, as basically they were the same as those that we had recorded earlier in Ting Hsien.[8]

Theft of the dragon god.—On the thirteenth day of the seventh month [1932 ?] a newly painted mud image, about one foot high, was seen in the Kuan Ti Miao in a village near Peiping. The temple keeper, generally known as Lao Tao ("Old Taoist"), said that it was the dragon god that had been stolen from a temple in another village and left in his temple. He also said that the dry weather was caused by the dragon god's getting lazy, going to sleep, and not attending to his duty. To wake him up, his image had been taken off the altar and out of the temple so that he could see how dry the fields were. Sometimes it was thrown into a deep well or under a high bridge, but this time it had been left at another temple. After the god had done his duty and brought rain, his image could be returned to its proper place.

When the temple keeper was asked whether stealing the dragon god's image would bring rain, he replied, "Everyone says so and everyone believes it."

The village elders wished very much that they could find out who stole the image, so that they could make him pay for the ceremonies connected with the god's return and possibly fine him. To send the image back properly would require that it be given a new coat of paint, and that it ride in a sedan chair and be accompanied by music all the way. The total cost would be about $10.

Not knowing the necessary details, the village elders were trying to please the god by giving the image a new coat of paint. They hired a man from the nearby town to do the work for sixty cents. Obviously the god could not be returned until the village learned from whence he had come. Then they had to be willing to escort him back in proper style.

Pressure for secularization of temples.—Many of the North China temples were being secularized, and the images of the gods were removed and services and worship discontinued, but our sample villages reported only one temple that had been closed—it had fallen down many years before our study. Without discontinuing the religious features, parts of the larger temples had been taken over for village schools, village administration offices, and quarters for village guards. In Ting Hsien, activities in 245 temples in 62 villages were given up in 1914 and 1915 when Sun Fa-hsü was magistrate there.[9]

In Honan, Feng Yü-hsiang, who was a Christian, tried to suppress the old religious activities. The images were taken out of many of the temples, and the land and buildings were turned over to the schools and the village administrations.

After the Nationalist government unified the country in 1928, it adopted a law which called for the closing of temples in which purely legendary persons and spirits were worshiped. This act met with considerable passive resistance on the part of the villagers, and seemingly no great effort was made to enforce it. In a village in Chen Hsien, Honan, however, it was considered to be enough of a threat that the temple of the god of fire was converted into what looked like an ancestral hall for one of the village clans. The villagers continued to meet there every year on the seventh day of the first month for worship and a feast.

VII: MONEY, EXCHANGE, AND VILLAGE FINANCE

THE COINS earlier used as money in the North China villages were single *cash* pieces—small, round, cast bronze coins with a square hole in the middle. These were later replaced by minted copper 10- and 20-cash pieces. The cash still in circulation at the time of World War I disappeared rapidly when their bullion value rose above their monetary worth. A few very light ones were still used in Peking in the early 1920's, but only in places such as the post office, where it was necessary to make exact change.

The silver unit was the *yuan* or dollar, containing 0.72 ounces of silver. The fractional silver currency consisted of 10-, 20-, and 50-cent pieces. These were seldom exchanged at par. Sometimes the rate was as high as twelve dimes to the dollar. For a time a new issue of Yüan Shih-kai pieces exchanged at ten dimes for a dollar, but it was not long before they, too, were quoted at a discount.

The copper money of account was the *tiao*, which ordinarily was 1,000 cash. In some of our sample villages, however, the tiao was only 500 cash.

The silver money of account for larger business and wholesale transactions was the *tael*, one ounce of silver bullion. For general use the tael was gradually displaced by the coined yuan. In Shanghai the use of the tael was discontinued in April, 1933.

The par of exchange between the different currencies was one tiao per tael, $1.3888 per tael, 72 tael cents per yuan (dollar), unless there was a difference in the fineness of the silver.

The actual exchange rates varied widely above and below par, depending upon supply and demand and other factors of the money market. For the years 1927 through 1932 the variation of the annual average dollar-tael rate was from 1.374272 to 1.417151 dollars per tael, a range of 3.12 per cent from minimum to maximum. In 1932 the monthly averages ranged from a high of 1.45296 in August to a low of 1.319887 in October. The value of the dollar varied from 68.82 to 75.76 tael cents, a difference of just a little more than 10 per cent.[1]

Although the official tiao-tael exchange rate was one tiao per tael, the rate had long been more than 1,000 cash per tael. In 1900 the average rate for the year was 1,060 cash per tael. Soon after, the yuan had so thoroughly become the silver unit for ordinary transactions that the silver-copper exchange rate was quoted in terms of cash per dollar. The last year that the Peking annual average rate was less than 1,000 cash per dollar was 1906. From 1909 through 1918 the annual averages were between 1,235 and 1,354. The lowest rate was for 1917. After that the annual average went up every year as the copper coinage was more and more depreciated. By 1925 the rate had reached 2,855 cash per dollar, almost two-and-one-third times the rate for 1917. In 1929 the annual average was 4,060. The maximum monthly average that year was 4,140 cash per dollar.

The above rates are all for Peking, but we found that the village

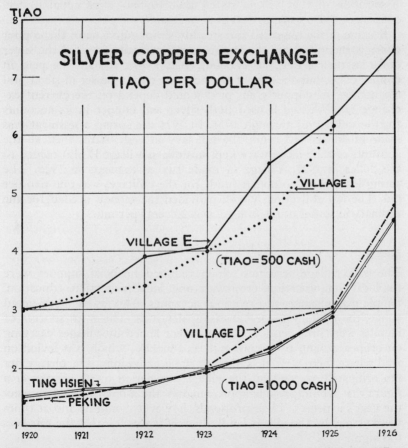

FIG. 12.—Changes in the silver-copper exchange rates, in tiao per dollar, for Peking, Ting Hsien, and Villages D, E, and I, 1920–1926.

rates followed the city figures closely, except that the village rates generally were slightly higher. Figure 12 shows the changes in village, town, and city rates for the years 1920 through 1926. The rates for Village I from 1907 are given in table 35.

It will be noted that the rates for Village E, which was in the Peiping area but at a considerable distance from the city, and for Village I, which was in southern Hopei, were generally about twice the city and town rates. This would seem to indicate the use of a 500-cash tiao by those two villages and possibly by many of the rural villages in Hopei province. So far as Village E was concerned, this was clearly the case, since the regulations of the Green Crop Association of that village stated that 10 tiao were equal to 500 coppers or 5,000 cash, or 500 cash per tiao.[2]

Because of the unsettled and steadily shrinking value of the copper coinage, the villages in the Peiping area gradually adopted the silver dollar as their money of account. Bills might actually be paid in copper coins, but the size of the account would be set in silver and the number of copper coins paid would depend on the current exchange rate. Village E used both silver and copper in its accounts for the years 1923 through 1926. In 1926 the spring assessment was made in dollars and cents, the fall levy in cash. After that, all the accounts of the village were kept in dollars. Village D also turned to the dollar in 1927. Village G made two assessments in 1928. The spring levy, made to obtain funds for the military, was one tiao per mu. The fall collection, which provided the money needed for the ordinary expenses of the village, was 20 cents per mu.

VILLAGE FINANCE

The main village activities which required financial support were the local administration, crop-watching, local protection, education, temple maintenance, and religious activities. Also, as has been noted above, the military made increasing demands. The main sources of income were crop-money, an assessment levied by villages carrying on crop-watching programs, and land-money, which was levied on land where there were no crop-watching provisions. The charge per mu ordinarily was set by the village association or its officers at a figure that would provide approximately the money needed to meet the year's expenses. Their proposals, however, could be and at times were vetoed by the village landholders if it was felt that the rate was too high.

When the tiao was the money of account, the rates per mu generally were set in multiples of 10 cash, one one-hundredth of a tiao. When the dollar was the monetary unit, the assessments usually were multiples of 5 cents per mu. The copper rates were from 10 to 200 cash per mu. The silver rates ranged from 8 to 70 cents. It is possible that the rate in Village E reached 90 cents per mu.

CROP-MONEY ASSESSMENTS

Some villages collected a small part of their crop-money in the spring when the farmers registered their land for the coming season or at the thanksgiving meeting held at the end of the spring wheat harvest. This gave the village some funds with which to pay for the spring crop-watching and other current expenses, but usually most if not all of the assessment was paid in the fall after the main harvest had been gathered and the farming families had the necessary funds available.

The basis of the crop-money assessments varied from village to village. Village A, with only a small crop area, collected from both owners and tenants. Some other villages collected from the owners

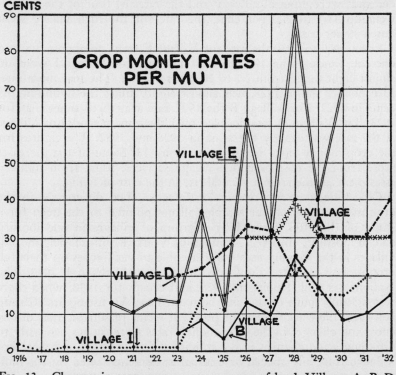

FIG. 13.—Changes in crop-money rates per mu of land, Villages A, B, D, E, and I, through 1932.

only. Still others charged those who cultivated the land, whether owner or tenant. Village H charged nonresident families who owned land in the village area only half the rate for residents because the nonresidents benefited only from the crop-watching, not from any of the other village programs. The crop-money of some villages included the money required for the armed forces in the area. Others made special assessments for that purpose and charged only the resident families, since nonresident families would be assessed in their own villages. One village charged different rates for owned, mortgaged, and rented land when it was raising money for the military, but charged a single rate for its crop-money assessment.

The crop-money rates for three of our sample villages, A, B, and D, the land-money rates for Village I, and the estimated crop-money rates for Village E for a number of years during the period 1916–1932 are shown in figure 13. The 1907–1931 figures for Village I are given in table 35. The available data show no uniformity whatsoever in the year-to-year changes. Even in 1928, when the military demands were especially heavy and the rates of four of the villages went up 33.3 to 200 per cent, the rate for the fifth village went down 38 per cent.

From 1920 to 1930 the rate for Village E went up almost five and one-half times. From 1907 to 1931 the rate for Village I went up almost eight times, from 2.7 to 20 cents per mu. The maximum rate, 23 cents per mu in 1928, was almost eighty times the minimum 0.3 cents in 1922. For Village B the 1932 rate was three times that for 1923. The Village D rate doubled over the same period. For Village A the rate was exactly the same in 1926 and 1932. The figures for the crop-money rates are given in figure 13. Some of the increases arose from the cost of added village services, some from military assessments, some from a general rise in the cost of living.

Crop-money assessments in 21 villages.—The differences in the crop-money rates of our sample villages pointed to the need for a study of the rates charged by a group of villages in one locality and, if possible, during a number of years. From 21 neighboring villages in the Peiping area we were able to get figures on their fall crop-money rates for the five years from 1929 through 1933. The Nationalists took Peiping in 1928, and except for 1930, when there was fighting south of the city between Feng Yü-hsiang and Chiang Kai-shek, these were years of peace. It seems reasonable that differences and changes in the crop-money rates were owing primarily to differences and changes in the activities of the villages and were not influenced by any special or unusual assessments levied by the military forces in the area.

No two villages had the same rate-history. In any one year not more than 7 of the 21 villages charged the same rate. The number of different rates charged per year varied from seven to ten.

In 1929 the rates were from 15 to 70 cents per mu. In 1931 the range was 10 to 65 cents per mu; in 1933 it was 20 to 50 cents per mu.

Every village changed its rate at least once. There were 4 villages with only one change—three up, one down. The four changes were made in three different years. Three villages changed their rate every year. There were 55 changes out of a possible 84 (four for each of the 21 villages). Twenty-nine of the 55 changes were increases. Twenty-six were decreases. The year 1930 had the largest proportion of decreases—twelve reductions and only three increases. In 1933 there were nine increases and only two decreases.

The maximum increase from one year to the next was 40 cents, from 20 to 60 cents per mu. There was another rise of 30 cents, from 35 to 65 cents. The largest decrease, 35 cents, was a 50 per cent reduction, from 70 to 35 cents per mu. At the other end of the scale there were four increases and two decreases of less than 5 cents a mu. Forty-two of the 55 changes were for either five or 10 cents per mu.

In only 4 of the 21 villages was the 1933 rate the same as that for 1929. It was higher in 8 villages and lower in 9. In 3 villages the 1933 rate was twice that for 1929, while in one it was half the 1929 figure.

There were sixteen different five-year averages for the 21 villages. In no case did more than two villages have the same average. The range was from 19.6 to 54 cents per mu; the median was 32 cents per mu.

The average fall crop-money charge for all 21 villages was 36.4 cents per mu in 1929, 30.6 cents per mu in 1930, and 36.2 cents per mu in 1933. The over-all five-year average was 33.3 cents per mu. (See table 15.)

The differences in the crop-money rates charged by these groups of villages strongly reëmphasizes our thesis that no two villages were alike and that each one, though geographically close to its neighbors, had been free to develop an individuality of its own.

CHANGES IN NUMBER OF FAMILIES
PAYING CROP-MONEY

The number of families, resident and nonresident, paying crop-money to any given village was subject to almost constant change. The total number registered in Village A changed every year from

1926 through 1932. The resident families changed every year, varying in number between 51 and 56. The only change in the number
of nonresident families was from 27 to 30 in 1931.

Over a period of ten years the number of farming families registered with Village F also changed every year. The minimum was 84,
the maximum 98. In the twenty-two years from 1910 through 1931
the number of resident landowning families registered with Village
I changed every year but two and ranged from a minimum of 134
to a maximum of 177 (see table 35). The figures went up in a way
that indicated a distinct increase in the number of families in the
village. During the nine years after 1919 the number increased every
year but one. From 1921 through 1925 it was in the 150's, during
1926 and 1927 in the 160's, and from 1928 through 1931 in the 170's.
Some of the old, large families probably divided, forming several
new families. There was possibly some immigration, and some landless families may have become landowners.

The year-by-year changes in the number of families paying fall
crop-money to one village are shown in figure 14. It will be noted

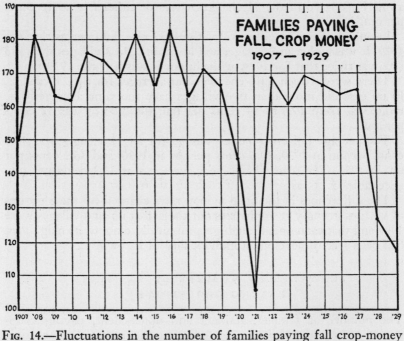

FIG. 14.—Fluctuations in the number of families paying fall crop-money
in one village, 1907–1929.

that the number changed every year. Unfortunately the records gave no explanation for the very large decreases in 1920, 1921, and 1928 and the large increase in 1922. Assuming that the large decreases resulted from some temporary conditions, the figures for the other years seem to indicate a small but continuing decline in the number of families in that village.

PAYMENT OF CROP-MONEY IN KIND

The records of one village gave us a complete picture of how the families paid their crop-money from 1907 through 1929. Figure 15 shows the proportions paying in kind, in copper coins, and in silver. For most years the total was more than 100 per cent, as many

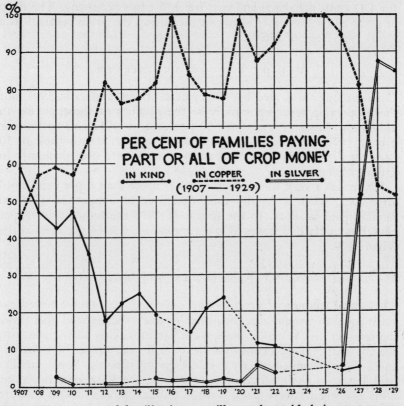

FIG. 15.—Per cent of families in one village who paid their crop-money in kind, in copper, and in silver, 1907–1929.

families paid part in kind and part in money, or part in copper and part in silver. Payment in kind was made by 60 per cent of the families in 1907; in 1923 no families paid that way.

The field reports stated that in 1911 some 98.7 per cent of the families of Village D paid their crop-money in kind, but that by the 1920's the number doing so was small and declining.

Several days before the fall thanksgiving meeting of 1932 the head of Village D announced that the fall crop-money rate had been set at 40 cents or 8 sheng of corn per mu. Between the announcement and the meeting the price of corn dropped almost 10 per cent, so the owners of about half the village land decided to save on their crop-money and pay the assessment in grain. The village leaders had to hire a wagon to go from house to house to collect the grain, which amounted to 10,000 sheng (100 tan) of corn. It was sold, part for 4.47 cents per sheng and part for 4.35 cents per sheng. The drop in price and a loss of 36 sheng in measuring the grain resulted in a loss to the village of $56.92.

USE OF COPPER AND SILVER

Copper money was used by 45 per cent of the families in 1907, but the proportion went up rapidly as the number of those paying in kind went down. It was up to 80 per cent by 1912 and to 100 per cent in 1923, after which it went down rapidly. It was back to 50 per cent in 1929. By that time, copper coins were used primarily in making change.

Silver was a very minor factor, never more than 6 per cent, until after 1925, when it rapidly took the place of copper. In 1925 no families paid in silver. In the spring of 1928 the figure was 18 per cent, but by the fall it was 87 per cent, and it was 86 per cent in the fall of 1929.

DELINQUENT PAYMENTS OF CROP-MONEY

The actual amount of crop-money collected was almost never exactly equal to the amount theoretically due—the assessed area times the rate per mu. When families were late in making their payments, the amounts went over into the next fiscal year since, for most villages, the year ended after the thanksgiving meeting. Some families paid less than their official assessment. In the long run, however, most assessments were paid. Village public opinion would tolerate some delinquencies if they were not too blatant. A village elder said, "We can only work with our old country folks by persuasion and good will." A crop-watcher gave the other side of the picture, saying, "If so-and-so doesn't pay his crop-money, I will take him to court or he can move out of the village." Public opinion, persuasion, and official pressure from the village administration, tempered with understanding of the financial problems of some of the families, kept the system of village assessments working, with nearly every family bearing its share of the load.

In Village A the actual collections for seven years were only $9 less than the assessments. Three years with surpluses almost balanced out four years with deficits. One deficit was $31 another only $1. The largest surplus was $17.

In 1928 Village F collected $494.50 on an assessment that totaled $494.38. Four families paid more than the amount due, one family by $1.10, which probably was a carry-over from the year before. One family underpaid $1.90.

Other account books for Village F showed that every year during the decade 1920–1929 some families were delinquent. The number ranged from 7 to 34 and averaged 14.4 per year. The proportion of families delinquent ranged from 7.5 to 39.5 per cent and averaged 16.0 per cent, a rather surprising amount of delinquency, even when we remember that the figures are for families and not for money. No information is available to show what proportion of the money due was unpaid or how many of the families who were delinquent at the end of one year paid up during the next year.

There was a deficit in the crop-money collected by Village B every year for the six years 1926–1931. The amounts ranged from $38 to $280. The total for the six years was $1,051. The average was $175 per year. The total delinquency was 13.2 per cent of the amount due. For the different years the shortage varied, from a minimum of 4.5 per cent in 1927 to a maximum of 17.5 per cent in 1926.

In the sixth month of 1928 Village G levied a special assessment of one tiao per mu to raise money for the military. Only 73.8 per cent of the money due was collected at that time. Many families said that they did not have the money. In the ninth month the village collected its fall crop-money of 20 cents per mu plus delinquencies on the earlier assessment.

When the fall collection ended, eleven families, 7.9 per cent, were delinquent in whole or in part on their spring assessment. Four had paid part of the amount due, seven had paid nothing, and one family had overpaid 6.16 tiao. The total shortage was 93.4 tiao, 4.3 per cent.

Six families were delinquent on their crop-money payments. The shortage came to $10.45 and was 1.8 per cent of the amount due.

Thirteen families, 9.2 per cent, were delinquent on one or both of their crop-money and assessment payments. Four families were short on both, seven on their assessment but not on their crop-money, two on their crop-money but not on their assessment.

Village I had much the best record on its collection of land-money. From 1907 through 1931 there were only four years when the difference between the amount due and the amount received was more than 40 cents. In three of the four years there were surpluses. The maximum overage was $6.70. The largest deficit was $3.96 in 1910. For the twenty-five years the difference was a surplus of $9.64.

OTHER SOURCES OF VILLAGE INCOME

Besides their crop-money our sample villages reported a wide variety of other sources of income. Two sold timber, one fruit, another reeds grown on village land. Others collected fees—for recording mortgages, for making the official measurement of land when it was sold, etc.—and the equivalent of a sales tax on land, charcoal, lumber, peanuts, etc. One village invested some of its surplus funds in land mortgages and collected interest on the loans. Another reported interest on bonds that the government had required it to buy. Another received additional payments from its mortgagees because the value of the mortgaged land had gone up and the village would have received the additional amount if the old mortgage had been paid off and a new one negotiated. One village collected a fee of $3 each for watching the water wheels in its area, in a program similar to crop-watching. Several villages reported rent from village-owned land, from fines collected from crop-thieves or for trespass, and from "noodle-money."

In some villages, shops registered an amount of nonexistent land and paid crop-money on it in order to contribute to the village expenses. In one village the shops thus provided 27 per cent of the village income. Some villages, especially those with a large proportion of nonagricultural families, collected a small amount from every resident family. One village collected $1 from the farmers who slaughtered five pigs. This, however, was a losing transaction, as the collection of the hsien-levied pig-slaughtering tax of 20 cents per animal had been farmed to the village for $2.30. Occasionally the military made small payments for some of the supplies they received, but almost always this was much less than the amount demanded of the villages.

Some villages raised very considerable amounts for special projects by subscription, even as much as $800 or $1,000. Such projects in-

cluded repairing the village wall, restoring a temple, purchasing
guns for the protection of the village, and giving theatrical performances. These collections were outside the regular accounts, though
sometimes the village would have to contribute from its ordinary
funds to finish the project. In the case of the repair of a temple a
large part of the money was often raised outside the village.

When money was collected to pay for the plays given to honor
the gods and entertain the villagers, several different bases were used
in determining the amount of each family's subscription. When plays
were given for the gods who looked after the health and welfare of
men and animals, the amount was calculated in some villages according to the number of persons in the family and the number of their
animals. Usually there was an allowance for children and for animals
of different sizes.

For plays given for the dragon god, who controlled the rain, or

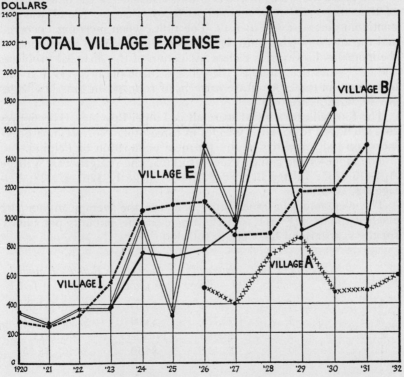

FIG. 16.—Total annual expenditures of Villages A, B, E, and I for various
periods between 1920 and 1932.

for the gods who protected crops, the assessments usually were pro-rated according to the size of the family farm.

In some villages the charges for the plays or the assessments for the military were made on the basis of the hsien tax levied annually on the family land, in tan of grain or taels of silver.

Occasionally the association giving the plays raised the necessary funds by making arbitrary assessments on the wealthier families of the village. The poorer families paid nothing.

In Shansi some villages raised money for their schools by collect-ing 700 cash per tou of land tax. For taxes paid to the hsien gov-ernment the rate was 600 cash per tou for the first half of the year and from 600 to 900 cash per tou for the second half. The date when these rates were in effect is not known, but the figures indicate how the old tax rates in kind were continued year after year and were adjusted to varying monetary conditions.

The expenditure side of the accounts also showed the individuality of the villages. The only common factor that we found was the continuing increase in expenses. The times when increases occurred and the amounts were entirely different. The general magnitude of the increases, however, is a clear indication of the financial problems and difficulties that troubled the villages throughout the 1920's. The differences in the expenditure patterns of four of our sample villages are shown in figure 16.

The four villages studied were all in Hopei Province. The figures that we hoped to have for villages in three other North China prov-inces were all casualties of the Japanese occupation of Peiping.

The range of the annual expenditure for the villages was: Village A, $400–$835; Village B, $388–$2,200; Village E, $267–$2,428; Vil-lage I, $241–$1,469.

The average village expenditure per year, the average amount per resident family per year, and the range of the amounts per family for the years after 1925 were as follows:

Village	Number of years	Average expenditure	Average per family	Range of annual average per family
A	7	$576	$9.00	$6.20–$13.00
B	7	$1,223	$4.00	$2.50– $7.13
E	5	$1,580	No data	No data
I	6	$1,112	$6.50	$4.10– $8.00

The average per family for Village A was by far the highest, but only $4.80 of this was paid by the farming families. The remaining

$4.20 came from the sale of fruit and lumber grown on village land. These items were not found in the accounts of the other villages.

MILITARY ASSESSMENTS

Because of the demands made on the villages by the armies when there was fighting in or near the area, one would expect that 1928, when the Manchurian forces left and the Nationalist forces arrived, would be the year of maximum total expenditure for villages in the Peking area. It was the peak for two of our villages. The year 1929 was the peak for the third village, and in the fourth village, Village I in southern Hopei, the 1928 expenditure was only $10 more than that for 1927, which was the lowest of any year after 1923. (See fig. 16.)

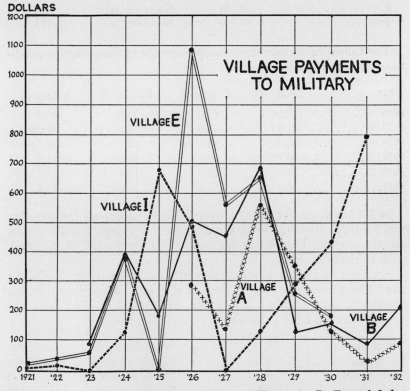

Fig. 17.—Payments to military forces by Villages A, B, E, and I for various periods between 1921 and 1932.

Since the military assessments usually were levied first on the hsien and then passed down through the districts to the villages, one might expect that the amounts paid by the different villages would be based on a percentage system and that, even if the actual amounts varied from year to year, the relative amounts would be similar. There was, however, no such common pattern. Villages A and B made their peak contribution in 1928. Village E paid the largest amount in 1926 and Village I in 1931. (See fig. 17.)

The amounts paid to the military forces after 1925 were:

Village	Number of years	Total amount paid	Minimum and maximum annual amounts	Per cent to military
A........... 7		$1,545	$29–$563	38.4
B.......... 7		$2,189	$77–$688	25.5
E.......... 5		$2,738	None—$1,058	34.1
I.......... 6		$2,119	None—$798	31.8

The following figures show the percentage of the village expenditure taken by the military after 1925:

Year	Village A	Village B	Village E	Village I
1926............	57.0	65.0	73.4	44.2
1927............	31.5	49.0	52.3	None
1928............	76.0	36.8	26.8	14.5
1929............	40.3	13.1	19.9	25.0
1930............	25.6	14.5	10.5	24.2
1931............	6.1	9.8	None	54.4

In 1926 Village E collected from its landholders an amount that was 5.4 times the 1925 total. Expenditure for village activities went up 34 per cent. The rest of the money, 73.4 per cent of the total, went to the military.

A village in Honan reported that in 1930, when Feng Yü-hsiang and Chiang Kai-shek were fighting in that area, it had to make nine assessments in order to satisfy the military. The time and the amounts per mu were as follows:

Third month	$0.455	Seventh month	$0.293
Fourth month	0.385	Eighth month	0.391
Fifth month	0.228	Tenth month	0.340
Sixth month	0.187	Twelfth month	0.137
Leap month[3]	0.292	Total	$2.708

One wonders how the village families were able to get the money to pay the assessments.

The village expenditures for their major functions of crop-watching, education, self-protection, and religion have been discussed in chapters v and vi. Their miscellaneous expenditures covered such a wide range that we have not attempted an analysis of them as a group. We have outlined the details in the descriptions of the individual villages.

The accounts of three of our four sample villages showed a surplus over the period covered. Village A collected $493 more than it spent in seven years; it also carried over a balance of $70 from previous years. For Village E the amount was $95 in eleven years. Village I accumulated $567 during twenty-five years. Only Village B showed a deficit. Its ordinary expenditure showed a surplus of $444 for ten years, but during that time the village paid back on loans, presumably as interest, $1,003 more than it had received. If this is included, the village had a deficit of $559. There seems to be good evidence that there was an error in copying the amount repaid one year, making it $780 rather than $280. This adjustment would make the deficit only $59 for a period of ten years. One would naturally expect the total income and expenses to be approximately equal over a period of years. The deficit of $559 discussed here was the ten-year difference between cash income and expense. The $1,051 deficit reported earlier in this chapter was the six-year total of the difference between the crop-money assessments and the amounts collected.

The two villages with the larger surpluses invested part of the money in land, in interest-bearing mortgages on land, and in loans to individuals.

Most of the villages in North China were faced with a difficult problem in handling the money they needed to pay for village operations. Most of their income came at the very end of the fiscal year. A considerable part of the bills could be postponed until that time, but from $200 to $300 ordinarily was needed for bills that had to be paid before the next thanksgiving meeting, even if the military did not call for special contributions. The village officials did not like to hold that much money during the winter months, when there might be considerable thievery. Most of the villages lacked access to banks. Sometimes a local shop or one in a nearby town might accept deposits and be ready to return the money on demand. Some villages deposited surplus cash with one or more of their wealthier families, but then there was always the chance that a family might not have the money available when it was needed and might have difficulty in raising it.

Many of the villages found it better to resort to deficit financing and borrow money as needed, paying interest if necessary. In 1932 village D borrowed eight times, for a total of $615. The year before, the total was $422, of which $162 was borrowed without interest.

The 1932 loans were from $50 to $150 each. Three loans, totaling $125, were for funds for the armed forces. A loan of $50 was for money to pay for a roadbuilding program ordered by the army; one of $150 was for funds to be advanced to the hsien government. Only three loans, totaling $200, were for village expenses.

All the 1932 loans bore interest, seven of them at 2.5 per cent per month and one at 2.7 per cent. The loans were repaid on seven different dates between October 20 and November 11. The total interest charge for the $615 borrowed was $69.58.

The money was borrowed from four shops in the village, from the richest families, and from nonresident money lenders. The notes were endorsed with from two to ten signatures. Even the village policeman put his name on one of them.

In the fourth district of Wan-p'ing Hsien an effort was made in 1923 to set up a committee of local officials and gentry to which the villages of the district were to present their budgets for the succeeding fiscal year for review and their accounts for audit after the close of the year. The proposed regulations were as follows:

REGULATIONS OF THE ASSOCIATION FOR THE AUDITING OF VILLAGE FINANCES, FOURTH DISTRICT, WAN-P'ING HSIEN

ARTICLE 1. The name of the association shall be the Association for the Auditing of Village Finances, Fourth District, Wan-p'ing Hsien.

ART. 2. The purpose of the association is to approve the budgets and audit the income and expense accounts of the crop-money of the villages in the Fourth District.

ART. 3. The membership of the association shall be composed of local officials and gentry.

ART. 4. At the beginning of each crop-season all Green Crop Associations must send in their budgets for approval.

ART. 5. When the crop-money has been collected, all Green Crop Associations must send in their ledgers for auditing. When the items have been found to be correct, they will be stamped with the seal of the association. Otherwise the village heads must personally explain the items in detail.

ART. 6. Ledgers will be distributed annually by the association to all Green Crop Associations. Each ledger must bear an imprint of the hsien government seal before it is used.

ART. 7. When their accounts have been audited, the Green Crop Associations shall report their income and expenses to the village people.

ART. 8. All expenditures above budget figures must be properly explained. Otherwise the village heads and assistant heads must refund the money.

ART. 9. Changes in these regulations can be made only by majority vote.

ART. 10. The association comes into existence when approved by the hsien government.

So far as we could find, the effort was futile and the committee existed only on paper. None of the village account books that we saw bore the imprint of the hsien seal as required by the proposed regulations, and we know from personal experience how loath the leaders of many villages would be to have outsiders examine and audit their accounts and thereby be in a position to question their handling of the village finances.

Although the auditing committee seemed to have failed to come into being, the attempt to create such an agency was indicative of the various forces that were attempting to introduce new ideas to the countryside. Such encroachments on the villages from above would have limited their very considerable autonomy and reduced their individuality, two of their outstanding characteristics in the years before 1933.

VIII: VILLAGE A

WE HAVE DESIGNATED Village A as our first sample because it, more than any other village we studied, had kept the pre-1900 type of organization and control. Officially the village-head and assistant-head form of administration had been adopted, as required by the higher government authorities, but this was a false front behind which the leaders of the unofficial, self-perpetuating group of village leaders, variously known as the United Association, the Public Association, or simply "the Association," continued to exercise their power and control. The fact that all but two of the 64 families in the village were descended from the same ancestor undoubtedly had much to do with the continuance of the old form of administration. At the same time the village was an interesting example of the maintenance of an earlier form of political control in spite of pressure from above and in contrast to the changes that had taken place in the vicinity.

The village was located northeast of Peiping at the edge of the plain, and the land was divided roughly in half between hills and plain. The usual farm crops of the Peiping area—wheat, millet, corn, and kaoliang—were grown on the level area. Most of the hilly area was given over to fruit and timber trees. Such crops as were grown there were primarily intended to provide green fertilizer for the trees.

VILLAGE HISTORY

The tablets in the big Kuang Ling Miao recorded that the temple was completed and the village founded in the year 1440. The famous eunuch Wang Yen, after a long and glorious military career under the third, fourth, and fifth Ming emperors (1403–1436), retired and turned his activities toward religion. He built six temples and made major repairs on at least another five. The temple in Village A was the sixth to be built and was erected when Wang Yen was about seventy years old. He bought a large tract of land around the temple and sent two of his nephews, one fraternal and one sororal, and their families to look after the land and the temple. They were the first families in Village A. Since both families had the same grandfather, the temple and the land belonged to both and were the common property of the entire village. Even so, the two families

A North China village

Village shrine

Memorial arch

Courtyard

Cross-country travel

Passenger cart

Crop-watcher's field house

Work cart

Winnowing grain

Threshing floor

Spectator

Spinning thread

Temple pilgrim

Wheelwright

Image of temple gate guardian worshiped as a weather god

Temple gate

and their descendants evidently recognized that they belonged to different patrilineal lines, for as the clans grew each expanded in a separate part of the village and continued to maintain that division through the years. At the time of our study they were completely distinct, the Sungs in the eastern part of the village and the Changs in the western part (the names have been changed). Politically the Sung patrilineal line, descended from Wang Yen's fraternal nephew, was dominant with a seven-to-three, and later a three-to-one, representation in the village association or leadership group.

In the period of almost five hundred years since the building of the temple and the founding of the village the two original families had increased to 62 in number: 53 families were descendants of Wang Yen's brother and 9 were descendants of his sister. Two unrelated families were living in the village. There was no report on when they arrived, or how or why they were admitted. Other unrelated families who came to the area originally purchased by Wang Yen had built their homes in a nearby village that was a satellite of Village A until 1911. The two villages were still economically integrated in that they had a joint "green circle" and jointly levied and collected their crop-money. In 1900 Village A was the larger and more prosperous, but by 1933 it had dropped to second place, both in the number of residents and in the amount of land and other wealth owned. The neighboring village had even grown to the point where a third, still smaller, village had been started.

Before 1900 Village A and its neighbor were managed as a unit by the unofficial group of village leaders. When the post-1900 form of administration was set up, with a village head and an assistant, the head came from Village A and the assistant from the other village. After the revolution of 1911 each village had its own head and assistant, but as late as 1933 the farmland of Village A and of its two neighbors was still administered as a unit for the collection of crop-money from the farming families. Each village, however, received only the money collected on the land owned by its residents or taken over by rental or purchase by nonresident families. Each village appointed and paid its own crop-watchers who worked cooperatively in covering the different sections of the farm area.

COMPOSITION OF FAMILIES

The 64 families in Village A had from one to 12 members. Forty-five per cent of the families had 3 or 4 members. One family in eight had fewer than 3 members; only one in sixteen had 10 or more. The distribution of the families by number of members is shown in figure 5 and table 8.

The total number of persons in the 64 families was 312. The average family had 4.9 members and the median family, 4—figures which would indicate that the economic status of the village was probably on the low side. This was borne out by the small size of the average farm of the 56 farming families, 11.9 mu per family, and by the fact that 51.7 per cent of the families had fewer than 10 mu. Only 3 families in the village owned a cart, and only 7 families could afford to hire a full-time worker to help with the farming. The 7 families with the largest farm area included all those with 25 mu or more.

The sex division of the 312 family members was 171 males and 141 females, or 54.8 per cent male, a masculinity rate of 121.2 males per 100 females. The masculinity rate for those under fifteen years of age was 140. For those fifty years of age and older it was 82, the females outnumbering the males 39 to 32. The proportion fifty years of age and older was 22.8 per cent, in contrast to 16.8 per cent in 5,255 Ting Hsien families[1] and 16.3 per cent in another group of Hopei (Chihli) families.[2] A comparison of the age distribution of Village A families and four other rural groups, Chinese and American, is given in table 9.

We were permitted to take detailed figures from the village land-registration books and the cash books for the years 1926 through 1932. The books were kept on a crop-year basis covering the period from the end of one fall harvest to the end of the next. The date for the closing of the books varied from year to year, from the latter part of the ninth month to the early part of the tenth month, depending on when the harvest was completed. The slight difference in the period covered would not make any appreciable difference in the year's income or expenditure.

LAND DISTRIBUTION

In 1932 the village registered a total of 829 mu (138 acres) of land in its books. Some thirty or forty years before, it had more than 1,000 mu, but during the intervening years more and more of its farm area had been sold by the resident families to people living in the growing village nearby. By 1926 the total was down to 942 mu. From then until 1932 the registered total went down in every year except 1931, when it went up 6 mu; in 1932 it went down 27 mu. The decline in the village farm area was entirely in the amount held by village residents, from 856 mu in 1926 to 743 mu in 1932.

The area registered by nonresidents was the same in 1926 and 1932, 86 mu, but was up to 92 mu in 1928 and the two years following.

Some of the variation in the number of mu registered in the village was undoubtedly owing to changes in the amount of land leased to tenants. Because of the small and decreasing amount of land contributing to the village finances, the elders collected double crop-money on rented land—from both the owner and the tenant.

While the number of registered mu was going down, the number of farming families went up from 80 in 1926 to 86 in 1932. The increase was evenly divided between residents and nonresidents. There were 27 nonresident families in the 1926–1930 period and 30 in 1931 and 1932. The resident farming families increased from 53 in 1926 to 56 in 1932. The number was different every year, with the minimum of 51 in 1929. Some of the difference came as the result of the division, in 1932, of one of the large families living in the village. Eleven years after the death of their father the three sons divided the family property and set up separate households and farms. We were told that before the family was divided it owned almost one third of the village farmland.

In 1932 six of the 56 resident farming families rented land. Eight families had no direct connection with agriculture. Some had handicraft work; some went to Peiping for employment. The year-by-year changes in the number of farming families and the number of mu registered are shown in table 16.

The distribution of the landholdings is shown in table 5. Seventy-one per cent of the families had fewer than 15 mu (2.5 acres). Only one family had as much as 10 acres. For the nonresident families the average landholding was only 2.9 mu. Only 5 or 6 resident families held land in other village farm areas. The total farm area of the 56 families was reported to be 664 mu, an average of 11.9 mu per family.

EDUCATION

Village A was unable to support a school by itself. Ordinarily the village would have joined with its larger neighbor in establishing a school, but intervillage jealousy and disagreement regarding the sharing of expenses prevented joint action, and the other village established a school of its own. Finally, in response to orders from the hsien government, Village A joined with two small nearby villages in opening a joint school in 1929. The three villages were to share the school expenses, over and above receipts from tuition, according to

the number of their children registered. The amount contributed
by Village A was $28.00 in 1930, $52.70 in 1931, and $69.00 in 1932.
The village was dissatisfied with the school arrangement and was
threatening to discontinue its support in 1933.

RELIGION

The religious aspect of the village life was well organized; in fact,
it was perhaps the best-organized aspect. Both the Sung and Chang
clans carried on annual ancestor worship. Neither group of families
had an ancestral hall, but both groups had family burying-grounds,
where they met during Ch'ing Ming, the spring festival in April, to
tend the graves and worship their ancestors. The Sung clan, with the
larger number of families, carried on the more elaborate ceremonies.
They roasted a whole pig and added many other kinds of food for
the feast. Each participating family was asked to contribute one
sheng (pint) of black beans, 20 coppers toward the cost of the pig,
and 10 coppers for general expenses. A representative from every
family was expected to help in clearing the weeds and bushes from
the graves and to join the others in paying homage to the family
ancestors. He shared in the feast served to all present and was given
a portion of the food offered to the ancestors. The organization and
direction of the Ch'ing Ming worship and activities was in the
hands of a director appointed by lot for a term of one year. The
appointment was regularly made at the end of each year's service
and carried through to the next year's meeting.

Temples.—There were two temples in the village, the big one to
which the village owed its existence, and another which was much
smaller. The small temple was dedicated to the Wu Tao—heaven,
hell, men, animals, and hungry devils—but in it there were also
figures of six other gods—the dragon god, the god of horses, the
god of crops, the god of insects, the god of earth, and the god of
the hills, a group of deities closely related to the everyday life of
the village. The dragon god, who was the god of water and so the
god of rain, occupied a central position in the temple, but the Wu
Tao and the god of the hills seemed to be the deities most often
turned to by the people. When anyone died, the women in the
deceased's family went to the temple to report the death to the Wu
Tao. Three days later they came again to the temple to escort the
spirit of the deceased back home for a final visit before the coffin
was taken to the cemetery. In other villages it was the men in the
family who reported the deaths to the Wu Tao. The god of the
hills, who had at his feet a tiger with a chain round its neck, con-

trolled the wild animals and protected the villagers when they went up into the hills that adjoined the village.

The Big Temple was dedicated to the Buddhist deities. They occupied the altar in the main building, but there were other gods in the other buildings of the same courtyard. A figure of Kuan Ti, the Chinese god of war and a hero of the Three Kingdoms period, was in one of the side buildings. He died A.D. 220, was deified by the Ming emperor Wan Li, and was given high honors by the Ch'ing emperors. He did not have the popularity in Village A that he enjoyed in many other villages. The god of medicine was in still another hall. He was the more popular of the two, for he was both doctor and apothecary for the village people.

The offices of the village association were also located in the Big Temple.

The village association and the temple management.—The land and buildings of the temple were controlled by the village association at the time of our study. Much of the original large tract of land bought by Wang Yen when he founded the temple had been sold to private owners, but there was still some temple grainland that the village rented to tenants and substantial fruit orchards and timber tracts on the hillsides. Income from the sale of the fruit and timber crops belonged to the village and was used to meet the general village budget, which included repairs to the temple, the cost of an occasional major rebuilding, the support of the priest, and the wages of a servant attached to the temple.

Before 1915 the income from the temple lands, the cost of the maintenance of the building, and the support of the priest seem not to have been part of the regular village budget, being handled as a separate account either by the village association or by a special committee of the association, or possibly by an entirely separate group of village leaders. When, in 1915, the priest attached to the temple tried to appropriate the temple lands and buildings for his own benefit, the leaders of the village association, representing all the families in the village, opposed his claim and eventually settled the matter by taking it to the hsien court, where they won their case. The association then took control of the temple property, and by the time of our study both the income from the temple land and the expenses of temple maintenance were included in the village budget. The temple expense was $95 in 1926, $216 in 1929, and $191 in 1932. Expenses for the intervening years are shown in table 17.

The struggle with the priest was a case of such importance that the association leaders did not attempt to handle it themselves, but called for an assembly of the heads of all the families in the village.

After a simple meal and a brief discussion it was agreed that the entire village would join in refusing to let the priest take over the temple and the temple land. They all signed a legal document that was to be used in a lawsuit against the priest. The preface to the document was a discussion of the importance of Buddhism and of the rights to temple land. It was signed by the village head and the assistant head, the two elders who for that year were the executive officers of the association, the seven other village elders, and forty-eight other heads of families. The total of 59 signatures would seem to indicate that the number of families in the village increased by five between 1915 and 1932, when there were 64 families. Division of some of the old families and possibly the immigration of the two unrelated families could account for the increase.

VILLAGE ADMINISTRATION

On the surface the administrative organization of Village A was like that of many of its neighbors. Although it had less than the minimum 100 families required for village status by the higher government regulations, it was recognized by the district and hsien governments as one of the village communities of the third district of the hsien. It had a village head and an assistant head who were appointed by the self-perpetuating group of local leaders. Any business coming to the village from the district or hsien government, such as demands for fodder and wagons for the army or requests for advance payment of taxes, was received by the village head. Although he held the office of village head, he could do nothing about these matters himself. He had to refer them to the members of the village association for decision and action. In fact, the village head, who if he had been serving in another village would ordinarily have been in charge of the village finances, had to go to the association officers for money to pay for his transportation when he was required to go to district or hsien headquarters. When two district policemen arrested a wanted criminal in the village, they could not remove him without having the village seal on their papers and the village head could not affix the seal without having the permission of the officers of the association.

In 1933 there were eight men, the association heads, who controlled association affairs. Two of the eight were appointed as the executive officers of the group for one year, at the end of which time another two were appointed. The time when the men should serve was fixed by lot. After all had served one term, lots were drawn again to determine the order of service for the next four-year period. Of the eight, six were Sungs and two were Changs. From the end of 1924 through 1929 there were ten heads, seven Sungs and three Changs. At the end of 1929, after two of the heads had resigned and another had died, only one of the three was replaced. A son of the deceased head was appointed to fill his place. It seemed to be customary that an association head who retired or died should be succeeded by his son. Six of the eight heads in 1933 had succeeded their fathers in office, one of them at the age of seventeen years and another at the age of twenty-two years.

The two new heads who had not inherited their offices seemed to have been appointed because of their ability. Their fathers had not been association heads and neither was a member of a wealthy family. One had 7 mu of land; the other, 19 mu. Table 12 shows the ages of the association heads in 1933, the extent of their education, and the amount of their land holdings. It is interesting to note that neither of the two families with the largest amounts of land was represented among the association heads. This probably was owing to the fact that the family that at one time held a large part of the total land area of the village had in 1932 divided its holdings between three brothers, only one of whom, continuing in the position he had filled as the representative of the large family, was an association head.

Leadership crises.—In 1932 the association faced a leadership crisis. One of its executive officers for the year was a merchant in Peiping and so could give little time to village affairs; the other, having hurt several members of his family during a severe fit, had been sent away to be cared for by his mother's family. It was the younger brother of the ill man who finished out the year's service rather than one of the regular association heads. After the year was completed, the brother had no further connection with the association. Among the six active association heads left after the 1932 harvest there were three who were clearly the most influential leaders of the village, two Sungs and one Chang. If one was absent from a meeting of the association heads, he would be consulted later about the matter, while if any one of the three objected to a proposal, the scheme would be dropped or modified.

Another crisis arose in October, 1932, when the village head, who was fifty-five years old and had been in office for more than ten years, wanted to retire from public service. He had sent his resignation to the district government twice and they were about ready to accept it. They sent a representative to the village to discuss the appointment of a successor. The hsien agent pointed out that the new head would have to be elected by the vote of all the adult villagers, as required by the Hsien Organization Act of 1929. In fact, he would have held the election then and there if he had had ballots and a ballot box with him. The association heads had no desire for an election and a drastic change in the setup of the village administration, so they persuaded the village head to withdraw his resignation. They promised that he would have three informal assistants from among the village leaders, who would attend all meetings at which the village head or his representative should be present, and would handle all matters requiring the attention of the village head. When the resignation was withdrawn, the proposed election was called off. One wonders whether, having weathered this crisis, the association leaders were able to retain their control until the Japanese invasion in 1937 completely changed all political organization and control.

Temporary members were added to the group of regular association leaders when they were needed. Some twenty persons worked on the case against the temple priest in 1915. In 1933 four were added to help with the reconstruction and repair of the temple; all four belonged to the Sung family. The entire group, permanent and temporary members, was divided into five committees—purchasing, accounting, supervision, labor distribution, and miscellaneous—with two or three members each.

Work of the association.—The ordinary work of the village association was quite regular and generally followed the seasonal order of the year. At Chinese New Year the association heads met together to pay homage to the various gods and to have a feast together. Each man paid 20 coppers toward the feast, for which the association spent several dollars. The ordinary villagers had no part in the meeting, though in some years they were expected to come to the village office at that time and register the land they would be farming during the coming season.

During the spring season the crop watchman, who was also the village policeman and the local guard, started his work of protection for the wheat crop. No special registration was made of the wheat area, however, and no special charge was made for the wheat protection. It was all included in the payment made at the end of the fall harvest. Wheat was a minor crop in Village A and not so much subject to theft and trespass as corn and kaoliang.

The fall season began on the sixth day of the sixth month of the lunar calendar, the birthday of Kuan Ti, the god of war. In North China the villagers have a proverb, *Liu yueh liu k'an shu*, meaning that on the sixth day of the sixth month you can look at the millet heads and know what the harvest will be. On that day the association heads met together to pay homage to Kuan Ti and other gods. Again they shared in the food offered to the gods. This was also a date on which the cultivators could register their land with the association. The crop watchman again took up his field duty, which had been temporarily suspended after the wheat harvest.

Crop regulations.—There were numerous regulations for the fall season that were determined by the association heads. First were the rules governing the stripping of the kaoliang leaves. In some years no one was allowed to take them. In other years the fields were completely open and the people could go to any field to strip off the unnecessary leaves for their own use. The height to which the leaves could be taken and the days on which they could be gathered were set by the association.

Then there were the gleaning regulations. In some seasons the fields were declared open to anyone after the ninth day of the ninth month. In others, the fields were open to gleaners only once in five days. Occasionally, no gleaning was allowed. In earlier years if the fields were closed the association heads arranged to give food to the poor families who regularly counted on gleaning to help meet their needs. In 1932 there were no restrictions on taking the kaoliang leaves, but the fields were closed to gleaners at harvesttime and no grain was given to the poor families.

THANKSGIVING CEREMONY

The thanksgiving held at the end of the harvest was the most important public gathering and ceremony of the year. It was held toward the end of the ninth month or beginning of the tenth month, depending on the date of the local harvest, and was a two-day affair. In 1932 it was held on the fourth and fifth days of the tenth month. The detailed preparation for the celebration was the responsibility of the two association heads who were serving as executive officers.

The religious ceremony usually was observed on the first morning. Dishes of food were placed on the altar as a feast for the gods. Then the two executive officers knelt before the altar and paid homage to the gods by kowtowing and burning incense and a printed prayer. The other village heads followed and some of the villagers joined in the ceremony. The food set before the gods was later divided among the association heads.

After the ceremony the farmers who had registered land with the association paid 20 coppers *mien-ch'ien*, noodle-money, each toward the feast of eight dishes with noodles in which they all shared, one member from each family. The family representative might be the head of the family, his son, or his wife. Any women who came were served at separate tables apart from the men. If they sent no representative, the family did not have to pay the special feast fee. The association heads were charged 30 coppers each, since they were served two meals during the day while they were busy with association business. If they were on duty the second day of the celebration, they had another two meals for which they paid another 30 coppers. They had special food only if the supply for the general feast was exhausted.

The expenditure for the thanksgiving feast, offerings to the gods, etc., ranged from $30 in 1927 to $60 in 1929 and averaged $43. There was no thanksgiving in 1928—the political changes that took place in May and June when the Manchurian forces left and the Nationalists took over, the heavy demands of the military, and the generally unsettled condition of the countryside made the people feel there was little cause for thanksgiving, and the leaders omitted the usual feast and worship.

CROP-MONEY

At the same time that they paid for the feast, the family representatives usually paid the crop-money due on the land they had registered earlier in the year. Occasionally a family would want to postpone the payment for a few days or longer. This would have the effect of putting it over into the next year's business, as the close of the second day of the thanksgiving celebration was the end of the fiscal year and the association heads in charge of the money then made up their accounts for presentation to the leaders on the following day.

In 1926 the net difference between the amount brought over from the previous year and the amount postponed to the next year was a deficit of $30.11 or 10.5 per cent of the crop-money receivable at the then current rate on the amount of land registered. The next year there was a surplus of $10.40. Deficit and surplus alternated for the next five years for which we have the accounts. In 1931 there was a surplus of $16.31, 6.2 per cent, and in 1932 a deficit of $16.58, 6.5 per cent. For the seven years 1926–1932 the net deficit was $9.08, less than 0.5 per cent.

The crop-money charge was regularly 30 cents a mu except in 1928, when it was raised to 40 cents a mu because of heavy assessments by the armed forces. (See fig. 13.) As the amount of land registered with the association decreased every year but one, the amount of crop-money receivable went down from $283 in 1926 to

$249 in 1932. When the rate was 40 cents a mu in 1928, the amount was $355. For the seven years the total amount due was $1,932. The actual receipts were $1,923.

SOURCES OF VILLAGE INCOME

Besides its income from crop-money, the village regularly received considerable amounts from the apricots and persimmons grown on the temple land controlled by the village. The persimmon crop brought in from $40 to $375, averaged $184 per year, and totaled $1,290 for 1926–1932. The return from the apricot crop ranged from nothing in 1926 to $50 in 1932, averaged $23 per year, and totaled $161. The income from the fruit trees was 32 per cent of the total village income for the seven years. The accounts had no record of any cultivation expense for the fruit trees.

Timber grown on the village's temple land was another occasional source of income. It produced $10 in 1926 and $475 in 1929. The larger amount probably came from a fairly general cutting of the timber crop. Part of that income was needed to cover the 1928 deficit, but much of it went for special items. Almost $150 was spent for unusual temple expenses; $150 was used for the purchase of additional village land; another $50 to $75 was used for extraordinary items included under miscellaneous charges.

Income from land rent varied from $12.00 to $38.00, was entirely omitted in two years, and averaged $14.30 for the period.

An unusual item of income was money received from land mortgaged by the village, $10 in 1926 and $180 in 1932. This came not from newly mortgaged land, but from 7 mu of garden land mortgaged years before. The new payments by the mortgagees were made to cover at least a considerable proportion of the increase in the value of the land. They made the extra investment in their mortgages in order to insure their continuing control of the land. Otherwise the village leaders could redeem the land by paying off the old loan and then remortgage it for a larger amount.

The several types of income from the village land, from the fruit orchards, land rent, and mortgage increases, represented 49.5 per cent of the total village income. This was a most unusual figure and was made possible only because all of the original village land was purchased as temple land when the village was founded.

Some years the military made small payments for the forage and other supplies provided by the village. The total for four years was $134.35.

The accounts also included a variety of small income items that have been classed as miscellaneous. The annual totals varied from $5.14 to $64.37. As a sample the figures for 1932 are shown in table 18.

The tax item was the repayment by the village families of amounts earlier advanced by the village to the hsien authorities. The amount, $28.37, was $4.63 short of the $33.00 advanced by the villages.

The $4 for land cultivation was to pay for work that should have been done by a lessee. The village had cultivated the land before renting it the previous year. Rather than do the work himself, the tenant paid the $4 when he gave up the land.

The hsien assessed a tax of 80 coppers, about 20 cents, on each pig slaughtered and then farmed the collection of the tax to the villages. Village A paid $2.30 in advance; but only five pigs were slaughtered that year, so the village collected $1.00 and lost the difference.

The 40 cents from the New Year's feast was the 20 coppers or 5 cents paid by the village leaders for the meal served them when they were busy with the land registration at that time.

For the seven years 1926–1932 the village income totaled $4,526. Of this amount, 42.5 per cent was crop money, 32.0 per cent came from the sale of apricots and persimmons, 10.7 per cent from the sale of trees, 2.2 per cent from land rent, and 12.7 per cent from miscellaneous sources. If the $195 received from the mortgaging of village land is subtracted as capital rather than current income, the percentage were 44.4 per cent from crop-money, 33.5 per cent from the sale of apricots and persimmons, 11.2 per cent from the sale of trees, 2.3 per cent from land rent, and 8.6 per cent from miscellaneous sources. The details are shown in table 17.

OPERATING EXPENSES

The total operating expenditures of Village A for the years 1926–1932 were $4,033. The yearly totals were from $400 to $835. The year with the highest expenditure was not 1928, when the Nationalist forces took over the area and the military was particularly active, but the next year when there were unusually large expenditures for the maintenance and repair of the temple and for miscellaneous needs. How the expenditures for watchman, guard, police, military, temple, thanksgiving, school, and miscellaneous items varied from year to year are also shown in table 17.

Crop-watching was the basic item in the village finances, but was only the fourth in amount. The yearly totals varied from $31 to $62. It was reported that the watchman was supposed to receive $50 a year—$30 as land watchman and local policeman and $20 as local guard. Early in the century, before he had a police title, his wage was about $10 a year. Besides his wages from the village, the watchman collected a 10 per cent commission on apricot and persimmon sales. Besides protecting the farm crops, he was responsible for the persimmons and apricots. His pay for that work came from the purchaser of the fruit rather than from the village. From his income he had to spend $10 to obtain the services of an assistant crop-watchman for two months during the fall crop season.

Expenditures for the guard were not for the local guard, who was also the crop-watchman of the village, but were for Village A's share of the cost of a united guard of one head man and two assistants supported by seven villages. The men were expected to be a mobile force and to give assistance where needed. Their budget included uniforms, ammunition, and other items, as well as wages.

Expenditure for police was a small amount, averaging $12 a year, paid by the village toward the budget of the district police.

Military expenses, the assessments paid to the army occupying the area, were the largest item of village expenditure, amounting to $1,545 for the seven years and more than 38 per cent of the total village expenditure. It reached a peak of $563 in 1928, the year the Nationalist forces took Peking, but it was down only to $336 in 1929. In 1930, when there was fighting between Chiang Kai-shek and Feng Yü-hsiang, it was $122. The low point was $29 in 1931.

Temple expenditures were the second largest item, averaging $149 a year and accounting for almost 26 per cent of the total expenditure. When the village took over the temple land in 1915, it became responsible for the upkeep of the building and the support of the monk. The totals also included the wages of a servant. The $191 spent in 1932 included $61 for wall repair, $25 for the servant, $22 for the items used for worship, and $83 for 102 different items, most of which were for the food and maintenance of the monk—items such as $1 for cabbage and 210 coppers for salt.

The thanksgiving ceremonies cost an average of $43 for the years they were held. The 1932 accounts had 19 different items of expense for the celebration. All but one were dated the twenty-eighth day of the ninth month. Almost all were for food and the work of preparing it. The one item entered on the day before was for paste for putting up the public announcement of the celebration.

Miscellaneous expenditure, which included a wide variety of generally minor or irregular expenses, amounted to $450. This was 11.2 per cent of the total expense for the seven years studied. In order to show some of the special village activities, we have detailed in table 18 the larger items for 1931–1932, a year when miscellaneous expenditure accounted for 20.4 per cent of the total.

When the army wanted to improve a road and provide better transport facilities to the area, they called on Village A to send a specified number of men to help with the work. The villagers, who were satisfied with the road, or at least had no enthusiasm about coöperating with the army, refused to volunteer for the job. The village then had to hire the necessary men and pay them a total of $55.08. On the other hand, the villagers regularly contributed their services when the nine bridges nearby were in need of repair. The $4.20 spent for that item all went for the purchase of material.

The district government called on all its villages to support a district school. This was possibly a higher primary school. Village A paid $7. The charge was first made in 1932 and there was some question as to whether it would be continued the next year.

The district also called on the villages to subscribe toward the capital needed to open an agricultural and industrial bank for the hsien. Village A's share was only $3.43.

Travel costs for village representatives going to district and hsien meetings or on other village business amounted to only $2.41.

Expenditures for tea leaves, account books, and other items too small and varied to group or analyze were included in the $14.05 miscellaneous outlay.

In 1931 the village had only 399.5 mu of taxable land registered with the hsien government, less than half the actual amount. The hsien tax on that amount of land was 8.964 taels. At the official exchange rate of $2.30 per tael,[3] the tax amounted to $20.60, considerably less than the $33.00 reported in village accounts as paid for 1932.

Loans of $1 and $5 were made to the village servant during the year. It would seem that no repayment was made before the year ended.

When the village received a payment of $180 from the mortgagee of some village land, the village elders promptly lent the entire amount to one borrower, who presumably would be paying interest the next year.

Three small loans totaling $39.35 were made in earlier years. Of this amount, $26 had been repaid. At the end of 1932 the village had just under $200 due from individual borrowers.

The records show that the village borrowed $138.84 in 1926 and $120.00 in 1929. Low cash balances from the previous year and the need for operating funds were evidently the reasons for borrowing.

Both loans were repaid before the end of the year. Interest of $3.80 was paid in 1926, but none was shown in the 1929 accounts.

Village A was able to maintain a cash surplus through all the seven years covered in our study. Even a deficit of $134 in 1928 did not exhaust the reserve. In only one other year, 1930, did expenses exceed income. Then the difference was $66. For the seven years, the total income exceeded the total operating expense by $493. A balance of $70 on hand at the end of 1925 made the total balance $563 at the end of 1932. Only some $214 of this was in cash, however, for in 1929 the village had used $150 to purchase land and had made several loans with a net outstanding amount of $199. From the figures it appears that a cash balance at the end of the year of between $200 and $300 would make it possible for the village to pay the expenses that had to be met before the thanksgiving celebration and the annual collection of crop money at the end of the year.

CHINESE APPRAISAL OF VILLAGE A

The author of the Chinese report of our village study closed his description of Village A with this statement:

Such is the simple picture of a small village of only 64 families. It is a small bird indeed, but still it has a head, a tail, wings, claws, and other organs, as do the larger birds. The only difference that we can detect is the lack of differentiation and progress in the collective action of the whole village. The informal village organization is still holding on very nicely. The legal officers, village head and village assistant, have never once been voted on by the people and have no control at all over the finances of the village. It is the association, the association of natural leaders, who are the village organization, who are the collective body of the whole village. The process of change from customary to legal control, from informal to formal organization, is so slow in this village that we wonder how many more years it will take before this village catches up with the other bigger villages.

IX: VILLAGE B

VILLAGE B was large, with 307 families and a farming area of some 12,700 mu of land. Its political organization had gone through the complete transition from informal, self-perpetuating leadership groups to an annually elected village government, as provided by national law. It was one that showed severe internal tensions among intravillage groups and a strong and growing tendency toward fission. We were permitted to see and study its land books for the six years from 1926 through 1931 and its financial records for the ten years from 1923 through 1932.

AGRICULTURAL SITUATION

Village B was located in the fourth district of Wan-p'ing Hsien, some twenty-five miles from Peiping. The southwestern corner of its farm area was a little less than three miles from the troublesome Yung-ting Ho ("Permanently Settled River"). In 1892 the river had broken out of its banks, flooded the area, destroyed all the buildings in the village, and covered much of the good loam land with white sand. As a result, the best land was in the northeastern corner of the village area, the worst in the corner nearest the river.

The sand left by the flood spoiled a large part of the land for wheat, kaoliang, or corn, so the villagers took to raising peanuts and trees and to part-time industry to supplement their reduced income from agriculture. It was said that this village had more trees than any of the neighboring villages, more even than those for whom lumber was a major agricultural product. While one would ordinarily see an almost endless sea of grain when approaching other North China villages, the area around Village B showed nothing but trees. Willow trees, which do well in sandy soil, were the most numerous, followed by poplar, elm, and pine. There were also some fruit trees, pears and peaches. Peanuts, which do well in sandy soil, were one of the main annual crops.

Of the approximately 12,700 mu of village land, about 2,000 mu were reported to be good, about 3,000 mu were average, and the rest, about 7,700 mu, were poor.

ORGANIZATION INSIDE THE VILLAGE WALL

The residence area of the village was surrounded by a wall that was built about 1885 and given major repairs in 1925 when there was much turmoil, banditry, and civil war in the area. Inside the wall, the village was divided by two main east-and-west streets with connecting lanes. The north or back street was the home of the 170 wealthier families, belonging to four name-groups. The other 137 families, who were poorer, lived on the front street. Of the 137 families, 61 belonged to the largest name-group in the village; they were numerous, but not wealthy.

The differences in financial status between the families living on the two streets were the basis of political and social tensions that had, at the time of our study, practically split the village in two. That development will be described later.

FAMILY COMPOSITION

The 307 families in the village had a total membership of 1,402 persons, an average of 4.6 persons per family. The families ranged in size from one to thirteen persons, with four the median and the mode. Just under one third of the families had less than four persons, while just above 10 per cent had more than seven members. The complete family distribution is shown in figure 5 and table 8. No figures were available for the sex division or the age distribution.

There were 23 family names represented. The largest group had 61 families; the two next largest had 58 and 50. Together, the three groups had a total of 169 families, 55.6 per cent of all the families in the village. There were 10 names with only one family each. No group had enough families or enough family tradition to have a clan organization with an ancestral hall and a clan history.

PATTERN OF LANDOWNERSHIP

The village land books listed 287 resident landowning families. There were also 30 nonresident families who owned land in the village area. The average holding was 40 mu (6.66 acres) per landowning family. This was a high average, almost twice that found in another study,[1] but it would be expected because of the poor quality of the soil.

The names of the lessees of the public land, previously owned by the temples, but later taken over by the village government, were entered in the land account as they paid the crop-money on any land they farmed. The lessees tended to look upon the land as almost their own; the rent was below that current for similar land, and the leases seemed to be for an indeterminate period. The rent was allocated to the support of the village school and was collected by the school authorities.

The amounts of land held by the registered owners are shown in table 8. Thirty-nine per cent of the families had fewer than 15 mu; almost 75 per cent had fewer than 40 mu. Nine per cent had 100 mu or more. Seven families, 2.5 per cent of the total number, each had 200 mu or more and together held more than 25 per cent of the village land area. The largest family in the village, with thirteen members, had the largest holding, more than 900 mu, and was reported to own a substantial amount of land in other villages as well.

The concentration of ownership probably had been much more serious in earlier years, for it was reported that a century ago the families in one name-group had held some 6,000 mu, practically half the village farming area. No family of that name was on the 1933 list of families holding 250 mu or more. Sixty years before our study another name-group held some 8,000 mu, or approximately two thirds of the area. Three families of this name-group were among the seven largest landholders in 1933. The other four families with 250 mu or more all belonged to another family group.

Sharecropping.—It was reported that in the village there was very little renting of agricultural land. Several large landowners cultivated all or part of their holdings with hired labor. The report tells of some twenty full-time laborers and several dozen at the busy seasons. Most of the laborers came from outside the village. There was a considerable amount of sharecropping in which the owner supplied the land, some equipment, all seeds, and a wagon and horses when needed. The produce, after the seed for the next planting had been taken out, was divided either 60-40 in favor of the landlord or on a 50-50 basis. There were no records to give any indication of the amount of sharecropping, and no estimates were reported. The village land books recorded only the name of the owner.

NONAGRICULTURAL OCCUPATIONS

Seventy-five of the 307 families reported 18 different kinds of nonagricultural occupations. Camel drivers, charcoal burners, and bean-curd makers were the most numerous. The full list is given in table 19. This is a much longer list and larger proportion of families than ordinarily was reported by the agricultural villages, and no doubt the poor quality of the land in the village "green circle" was responsible.

Before 1900 the village organizations included the Green Crop Association, four or five temple associations, an "Association for the Fair of the Fourth Month," and two private schools. Communications between the village and the hsien government were handled by two ti-pao, local men, rather than the customary one.

The Green Crop Association, handling the agricultural affairs of the village, was the strongest of the organizations. Its group of leaders numbered between ten and twenty men. The association organized the village crop-protection program and collected the necessary "crop-money" from the farm owners. Two of the association heads served in rotation for a year as executive officers. The head of the association was known as the hsiang-t'ou (incense head), even though the association seemingly had no religious connections or activities. The second officer was known as the ts'ung-kuan ("general manager") and was responsible for the collection and spending of the crop-money. All routine business of the association was handled by the two officers. Only when some special problem had to be dealt with were the other association leaders called together to discuss the matter.

The actual crop protection was done by the two ti-pao and some four temporary assistants. The official duties of the "local men" were not onerous, and they were glad to have extra work and extra income. The prestige of their official position was helpful to them when they were acting as crop watchmen. The crop-watchers were paid in kind, five or six tan of grain each.

Temple associations.—The four or five temple associations were informal groups of village leaders who were in charge of the fifteen temples in the village. Seven of these were small Wu Tao shrines. Of the eight large temples (there had been a ninth, but it had fallen into ruin long ago), only two were specially related to the life of the village. They were the Chen Wu Miao and the temple of the gods of medicine. The latter attracted the largest number of pilgrims of any of the temples. It was on the eighth day of the fourth month, the birthday of the two gods of medicine, and the three succeeding days that the village fair was held.

Most of the large temples had received gifts of land at some time. Altogether the temples owned more than 300 mu. The land was all rented out, but as there was no pressing need for the income, the groups in charge of the temples had become very lax in their administration of the property. Some tenants did not pay their rent, and some paid only a small part of the amount due. It was said that any village resident who was rough enough could get the use of some of the temple land. The situation had reached the point where the tenants were looking on the land as a permanent holding. They paid only a minimum rental. Most of the land was held by residents of the front street.

The first change in organization came about the year 1900, when the hsien government sent orders to the village that it was to appoint a village head and an assistant head who would handle local affairs and take over the functions of the ti-pao in dealings between the village and the hsien government. The Green Crop Association, which was the strongest group in the village, was the one to respond to these orders, and its leaders appointed two of their number to the new positions. The old system of annual rotation of the headship positions among the association leaders was given up and the village head and his assistant served more or less indefinitely. The old terms of hsiang-t'ou and ts'ung-kuan disappeared, and the name of the association was changed from Green Crop Association to Village Public Assembly. The two ti-pao lost their positions and perquisites, but continued as seasonal crop watchmen and later became a sort of police force entirely under the direction of the village heads.

CHANGES IN VILLAGE ORGANIZATION AND ADMINISTRATION

In 1933, instead of these various organizations, the village administration followed the plan of the Nationalists' Hsien Organization Act of 1929. There was a village assembly made up, officially, of all the adult residents, but actually no women participated. The assembly annually elected a village head and, in 1933, two assistant heads, a four-member committee for the arbitration of village disputes, a four-member finance committee, and a three-member inspection committee. The village's 307 families were divided into 61 lin of five families each and 12 lü of approximately 25 families each. The heads of the lin and lü were chosen by the members of the groups.

Educational system.—In 1913 the private school on the back street was replaced by a new village school. This school gave modern courses that were very different from the former classical education. The teacher of the old school was employed by the village to teach the new courses and, for a time, the school was conducted in his home. In 1919 the second and better of the two private schools was discontinued and its pupils were shifted to the new village school; in 1920 the school was transferred to the Chen Wu Miao.

When the village school was established, the local leaders appointed a principal to take charge of it and selected four of their group to act as trustees to oversee his work and assist in administration. The school was to be financed by the tuition paid by the pupils, by the rental of the temple lands, and by commissions on the sale of charcoal, lumber, and peanuts, the three most salable village products. The village leaders decided that, as there was no special religious use for the rental received from the temple land, this income should be taken over by the village and applied to the support of the school. This meant the disappearance of the groups who had been looking after the temples and their property. If the tenants had been paying the going rental for the temple land, the income would undoubtedly have been more than sufficient to cover the school budget. Long-continued undercollection, however, had established a pattern that was difficult to change, and so the village leaders also allocated to the school the charcoal, lumber, and peanut commissions.

The collection of the rents on the temple lands was assigned to the school trustees. A separate fiscal organization and program were set up which, while technically under the direction of the village officers, actually was operated independently. The school's income from tuitions, land rents, and commissions, as shown in the account books for the years 1923–1931, ranged from $296 to $440 and averaged $387. Its expenses ranged from $182 to $570 and averaged $363. For the nine years there was surplus of some $210. The annual figures are given in table 22.

A girls' school was opened in 1922 at the instigation of Magistrate T'ang of Wan-p'ing Hsien. Some of the income of the village school (for boys) was allocated for its support, as well as a small amount from the general village funds—$63 in 1923 and $21 in 1924. At the end of 1924, the girls' school was discontinued, partly because there were no assured funds for its support and partly because the villagers had but little enthusiasm for the education of their daughters.

Association for the Fair of the Fourth Month.—The Association for the Fair of the Fourth Month had long been run by an entirely independent group of leaders. Most of them belonged to landless families. They collected contributions to pay for the fair and for the three or four days of plays, performed by a professional troupe of actors, that were put on to pay homage to the gods of medicine and to provide amusement for the villagers.

This fair was one of the big events of the year, as it meant several days of activity, excitement, and entertainment. It opened on the eighth day of the month, the birthday of Sun and Liu, the two gods of medicine. The basis of the fair was religious, the worship of the gods of medicine so that they would grant the village freedom from sickness.

While the Green Crop Association and its successor, the Village Public Assembly, were controlled by the wealthy men of the village, the Fair Association was run by leaders from the landless group. At the time of our study, one of the most boisterous of the local bullies headed the Fair Association. He was helped by his wife, who was known as a notorious character both at home and in the nearby district.

The Fair Association leaders obtained the money needed for its activities by arbitrary assessments on the wealthy families, deciding how much each family should pay and then proceeding to collect that amount. The poor families presumably were not asked to contribute. A leader of the Green Crop Association, feeling that he was being overcharged, once refused to pay the amount assessed him by the Fair Association. He was told to pay the full amount or nothing, but at the same time he was warned that if he paid nothing, any member of his family or any of his relatives who came to the plays would be beaten. The full amount was finally paid, as the head of the family did not feel that he should deprive his family and other relatives of the pleasure they would get from the plays.

The arbitrary assessments of the Fair Association and the large sums that had to be spent entertaining friends and relatives who came for the celebration were a constant annoyance to the leaders of the Village Public Assembly, and there had long been irritation and ill feeling between the leaders of the two groups. In 1929 the village authorities, backed by the landowners, brought suit against the head of the Fair Association before the district government and asked that the bully and his wife be punished for their misdeeds. The case was finally dropped when a group of people came forward to plead for the accused and to guarantee their good behavior.

The open conflict brought about the discontinuance of the fair and the plays, but could not force the dissolution of the Fair Association. Every year its leaders tried to resurrect the fair and plays but for three years, at least, the village authorities were able to forestall their efforts. In 1933, as we were ending our study, there were persistent rumors that the fair and plays were to be revived, especially since the front street residents had been able to force other concessions from the village administration and the residents of the back street.

Village officials.—At the beginning of 1922 there were eleven village elders. During the year four retired. Three were succeeded by their sons and one by his grandson. Four other new members were added to the group. In 1927 there were two more retirements. One was succeeded by his son, the other by his grandson. Two other new members were appointed. In 1928 six new elders were added, bringing the total number to twenty-three.

Four of the eight new members added in 1927 and 1928 owned fewer than 50 mu of land, three had between 50 and 100 mu, and one had between 100 and 200 mu. All the families with 200 mu or more already belonged to the group in 1926. The appointment of the four leaders with fewer than 50 mu of land would seem to indicate that personal ability was gradually being accepted as a basis for choosing at least some of the village leaders.

Village elections.—The Nationalists' Hsien Organization Act of 1929 called for the annual election of village officers by universal adult suffrage. That gave the residents of the front street a long-awaited opportunity to challenge the political control held by the wealthy families of the back street. The first election took place in 1929, soon after the promulgation of the new law. There was a large turnout of male voters, but no females came to vote. When voting was done on a family basis or by family heads, the women often represented their husbands or their sons, but they did not accept the privilege of voting as individuals.

At the first election the men chosen as village head and assistant head were both residents of the front street. As it happened, the village head was liked by both streets and was elected practically without opposition.

The second election was held the next spring, not long after the Chinese New Year. The incumbent officers were not reëlected. In fact, in the five elections held before the end of our study no incumbent was reëlected for a second successive year. Some were returned to office, but only after an interval of at least a year.

The village head chosen at the second election was a back street resident who was only twenty-four years of age. He had some high school education and was an able person, and his family was the richest in the village. Our investigator commented on the fact that the new head could manage and control village affairs, but was still subject to his father and uncle when at home.

At the third election the front street man who had been the assistant the year before was chosen to be village head. The new assistant was a back street man.

For the fourth election the front street put on a political campaign and won both top offices. The village head was the popular man chosen by both streets in the first election.

Both sides worked hard to get out the voters for the fifth election. At that time the village decided to take advantage of the section of the law that permitted a village with more than 100 families to have additional assistant heads. Three candidates were proposed, one by the back street and two by the front street. Evidently the office of village head went to the man who received the largest number of votes. The back street concentrated its votes on one candidate. He was easily elected head, as the front street divided its votes between its two candidates, who consequently became assistant heads.

The first four elections had been carried on informally by the village authorities. The fifth election was conducted by representatives of the district government. They brought with them ballots that had been printed beforehand. They distributed, collected, and counted the votes and were present throughout the election to insure proper procedure.

Committees.—Three committees were chosen at the same time that the village head and assistant heads were elected: the committee for the settlement of village disputes, with four members; the finance committee, with four members; and the committee on financial inspection, with three members. As there had always been someone in the village who heard complaints and helped settle quarrels, the first committee continued this informal service on a formal basis. The second committee took over the work that had been done by the accountants and treasurers previously appointed by the village association. The third committee was something entirely new and consequently had but little to do.[2]

In the 1929 elections all the old leaders—the members of the Village Public Assembly—managed to get some position in the new administration. They were members of one of the three committees and heads of the lü groups of 25 families into which the village was divided. They were called together as a village council when serious matters came up that could not be handled by the village head and his assistants.

Internal dissension.—In 1933 representatives of the front street, encouraged by their political success in the elections, came to the village leaders with the demand that a separate school be set up for children from the front street and that half the land held by the village be turned over to them for the support of the new school. The temple lands which had been taken over by the village and allocated to the support of the existing school provided most of the school financing and were farmed, for the most part, by front street residents. The demand was one that the village administration could not well refuse, and a teacher was engaged for the new school. Both schools, however, were under the supervision of one principal and one set of trustees.

The demand for a second school was followed by one for control of the village income collected from residents of the front street. Again the demand had to be granted, and the village funds were divided into two sections, with two treasurers and two sets of accounts. Those who lived on the front street paid their crop-money to the front street authorities. The back street residents paid their assessments directly to the village office.

From the reports it appeared that the front street also took over the supervision of and payment for part of the crop-watching. The intravillage administration was evidently well on its way to splitting into two separate units, even though, in the eyes of the hsien government, there was only one official organization.

Village finance.—The land books for the six years from 1926 through 1931 and the account books for the ten years from 1923 through 1932 gave us a picture of the financial side of the story up to the time that the village activities and funds were divided between the front and back streets.

The land books for 1926–1929 showed an area of between 8,579 and 8,761 mu. Then in 1930 the total dropped to 6,350 mu.[3] A drop of almost 28 per cent in one year could only mean some unusual change in the registration system. Investigation showed that instead of an apparent loss of some 28 per cent there actually had been a gain of 46 per cent. What had happened was that the village officers had decided that something needed to be done about the large amount of unregistered land that, up to that point, had by more or less common consent been omitted from the land books. To bring about registration of the omitted land, it seems that an understanding was reached with the owners whereby they would register all of their land, but only 50 per cent of the actual amount would be entered in the books. It evidently was hoped that by registering only half the amount of their actual holdings the owners might escape the heavy taxation that was expected if the Nationalist government decided to change the basic method of land assessment in use since early in the Ming dynasty. The change in the village system of registration was a closely kept secret and was not known even in the immediate neighborhood. We were able to get the information only because the village was the home of one of our assistants.

In collecting its crop-money Village B assessed only the landowners, with the exception that tenants who were farming village land were expected to register their land and pay their crop-money.

The crop-money rates shown in the land books ranged from 10 cents a mu in 1927 to 25 cents a mu in 1928. In 1930, while the official rate was 16 cents, the actual rate was only 8 cents, owing to the 50 per cent underreporting. In 1931 the official rate was 20 cents per mu plus a surcharge of seven tenths of a cent that was levied to provide money for the purchase of a rifle. Actually the extra $44.45 was used to help meet the heavy expenses of the local guard for that year, amounting to $976.00.

For the four years for which we saw the account books but not the land books it has been possible to estimate fairly closely from the amount of crop-money received the probable crop-money rates. From 1923 through 1925 the estimated rate ranged from 3.5 to 8.5 cents. In 1932 it was 15 cents actual, 30 cents official. The changes in the rate are shown in figure 13.

If the earlier rates are adjusted to the larger area of 1930 and 1931, the range was from 2.4 cents per mu in 1925 to 17 cents in 1928.

The amounts recorded in the account books ranged from $278 in 1925 to $1,865 in 1928 and $1,783 in 1932. The total for the ten years from 1923 through 1932 was $10,010. The amount collected in 1932 was almost five times the total for 1923.

The amount of crop-money due, according to the number of mu entered in the land book and the crop-money rate for the particular year, was always higher than the amount collected as shown in the cash book. The smallest undercollection was 4.5 per cent; the largest, 27.5 per cent. For the six years from 1926 through 1931 the amount due was $7,955; the amount collected, $6,899 or 86.6 per cent of the amount due. (See table 20.)

The total village income for 1923–1932 was $10,862. All but $852 or 7.8 per cent came from crop-money. Fines and indemnities, bonds, and miscellaneous sources supplied the rest. The minimum total was $363 in 1925; the maximum, $2,003 in 1932. In 1928, the year of maximum assessment for most villages in the area, the total was $1,942. In 1930 it was down nearly 50 per cent from 1928, but from 1930 to 1932 the amount increased almost 100 per cent.

The largest item in the expenditure list was the money given to the army. It amounted to $2,843 for 1923–1932 and accounted for more than 27 per cent of the total expenditure. In the last two years it took only 9 per cent, but in 1926 it was 65 per cent of the total. In 1928, the year with the largest amount, it was $688 or 37 per cent of the year's total expense, but was the second largest item in the account, being exceeded by the $744 spent for the local guards. (See table 21.)

Village guards.—The three different groups of guards, village, united village, and district, did not appear in the accounts until 1927. Then the amount was $77 paid for the district guard. In 1928 the contribution to the district guard was reduced slightly, to $71. At the same time, because of the disturbed conditions connected with the withdrawal of the Manchurian forces, the arrival of the Nationalist troops, and the banditry and kidnaping that were rife in the area, the village felt the need for extra protection and helped organize two groups of guards, one inside and the other outside the walls.

Six guards and a head man were employed to keep watch inside the village.

A united guard was set up in coöperation with seven neighboring villages and had seventeen men. The two large villages in the union, of which Village B was one, were to contribute three men each, the five medium-sized villages, two men each, and the one small village was to supply one man. The headquarters of the united guard was not in Village B, but in the other large village. The guard was divided into two units who in turn patrolled the several villages. Three shots signaled an emergency, and the whole force was expected to come to the rescue.

In 1928 Village B paid $327 for its share of the cost. The group was organized with a commander who was given $6.00 a month for food money and $3.00 a month for office expenses, a head guard and assistant head who were paid $7.50 a month, and fourteen guards who received $7.00 a month.

In 1929 the united guard was continued, but the village guard was demobilized. That year the cost to Village B was $270.

In 1930 the united guard was discontinued, but the village guard was reëstablished. It cost $219.

In 1931 the system was reversed again, the village guard being given up and the united guard reëstablished; also the small village dropped out. The cost to Village B was $281.

In May, 1932, the united guard was again discontinued, as quiet had been restored to the area. The village guard was reëstablished once more, but no guards were hired. The guard function was added to the work of the five crop watchmen. This increased the cost of crop-watching by $130, or 60 per cent more than the amount for 1931. The guards were armed with newly purchased rifles that cost $1,292. One thousand dollars of that amount was collected from the landowners, outside the regular village budget. The expenditures for the different guard groups are shown in table 23.

The village contribution to the hsien police averaged $55 per year. Before 1926 the amount was $42 a year. That year the amount went up almost 50 per cent, to $62. The average stayed at about $60 for the next six years. In 1931 the amount was only $13. But the 1932 contribution of $124 offset the small payment of the previous year.

The cost of the crop-watching more than doubled, rising from $99 in 1923 to $222 in 1931. In 1932, after the crop-watchers had guard responsibilities, the amount was $352. The cost of collecting the crop-money went up from $40 in 1923 to $86 in 1932, an increase of 115 per cent.

Other expenditures.—For a number of items, such as wall repairing, village litigation, and repayment of mortgages, the total expenditures and the number of times they appeared in the ten-year accounts are shown in table 24. It is to be noted that the village paid only $21 in indemnities for crop-thefts, while it collected $158 under that heading. It also collected $141 in fines. The $86 spent for buying a small piece of land and for redeeming a plot that had been mortgaged were evidently paid from current expense. The $166 lent to the hsien government and to individuals probably had been repaid, but the payments, if any, would be classified as miscellaneous receipts and were not shown separately. The details of the village litigation were not reported, but for four years, beginning in 1929, there were expenditures ranging from $18 to $100 and totaling $200.

Repairing the wall and making five new gates cost some $926. Of this amount, $800 was paid by raising a special fund outside the regular village financing. Minor repairs in 1928 cost $53. A larger job in 1932 cost $221. It was surprising to find such a large expenditure made in 1932, four years after the Nationalist forces had taken over the area and two years after the final fighting between Chiang K'ai-shek and Feng Yü-hsiang.

For the major repairs the village was divided into six sections, each of which was assigned a part of the work. The villagers supplied the labor; the village provided the materials and the workers' food.

The total annual expenditure ranged from $388 in 1923 to $1,877 in 1928 and reached $2,200 in 1932. The 1928 total was a sharp peak, $937 or 99.7 per cent more than the 1927 total and $1,000 or 112.4 per cent more than the 1929 figure. The 1932 figure was more than twice that for 1931. Both of these big increases resulted from extraordinary expenditures connected with the army and the self-protection activities. Except for the two peaks, the expenditure went up in steps from approximately $400 in 1923 to about $750 for the next three years and then to about $950.

In seven of the ten years the accounts showed a surplus, ranging from $7 to $442. The three deficits ranged from $45 to $355. The net surplus for the ten years was $444.

In spite of the fact that the cumulative balance in the current accounts showed a surplus of more than $400 every year after 1928 and in only one year before had there been a deficit of more than $55, the village borrowed money every year in amounts ranging from $60 to $1,175 and made payments on loans from $15 to $1,287. The total received was $3,926; the total paid, $4,930. (See table 21.) Some of this difference of about $1,000 undoubtedly represented interest paid on the amounts borrowed, but even when the going interest rates were from 2 to 3 per cent a month, it is unlikely that the village would pay 2 per cent or more a month for the full year. The money would be required only as payments had to be made, not all at the beginning of the year. Furthermore, the yearly differences between receipts and payments were not consistent. In one year only 8.5 per cent was returned. In other years the payments were from 103 to 168 per cent of the receipts. The most extreme case was the payment of almost three times the amount received, $780 as against $263. The figures do not show any direct relationship between the surplus or deficit in the village accounts and the difference between the loans received and repaid. Some factor other than the payment of interest must have been involved.

We are inclined to think that this factor might have been an error in copying the 1929 payment and that the $780 shown might have been $280. If that were the case, the entire loan picture would be much more reasonable. Then the average interest would be $50 a year on the amount due if the average loan of $373 was made at 2.5 per cent a month and carried for an average period of a little more than five months.

The accounts gave no indication as to how the village authorities met the cash deficit they faced every year from 1923 through 1932. Loans received, plus other income, was larger than loans paid, plus other expenses, for only three of the ten years. At the end of 1923 the total expenditures were $143 more than the total income. From then on, the cumulative expenditure total was larger than the cumulative income total every year. The minimum cash deficit was $58 in 1924; the maximum, $561 in 1932. The amount was not more than $165 until 1929. From then on, it was $335 or more. This cash problem may have been at least partly responsible for the high interest total.

If the 1929 loan repayment was only $280 instead of the $780 reported, there would have been a cash surplus of $150 or more for three years and the final deficit would have been only $61.

Official approval of account books.—We were interested to find that two of the account books of the village had been stamped with the official seal of the hsien. The village officials explained that the magistrate T'ang Hsiao-chin had tried to do something to improve the lot of the people and had visited many of the villages. When he was in Village B he inspected and put his seal on the accounts for two years. He also wrote comments on the account book.

In 1923 a committee on financial inspection was organized for the fourth district of Wan-p'ing Hsien and was approved by the hsien government. According to the regulations of this committee, all village accounts were to be inspected and approved by the committee and then stamped with a seal. None of the account books that we saw bore the seal of the committee. Presumably, the committee on financial inspection was not much more than a good idea and its constitution and rules a bit of waste paper.

X: VILLAGE C

VILLAGE C was chosen as one of our samples because we were able to obtain very complete information on its history, the origin of its families, its housing, population, schooling and literacy, and religious activity. Another reason for choosing it was that a large majority of the families originally came from Shansi Province and the Shansi pattern of rotation in office was maintained in the village administration. We were, however, not able to get detailed information on the finances, as the elders would not let our representative or any other outsider see the account books.

The village was a suburban one, in the fifth district of Wan-p'ing Hsien, some ten miles northwest of Peiping. Nearness to the city was undoubtedly the chief reason for the large proportion of nonagricultural families, 18.9 per cent, and possibly for the high proportion of families who lived in rented houses.

The village was a compound one, with four residence areas. Three small satellite villages, with 4, 6, and 18 families, and all less than three li from Village C, were included in its political organization and green-crop area. There was a large independent village only a half li from Village C, but communication between the two had been almost entirely cut off because of an intervillage feud over the ownership of a pond.

VILLAGE HISTORY

According to tradition, the village was founded during the later years of the Ming emperor Ch'eng Hua (1465–1488). About 1483 two families, driven out by famine in the northwest, came from Hung-t'ung Hsien in Shansi to the Peking area. They set up temporary quarters on vacant land that was sometimes used as grazing ground for the horses belonging to the Imperial Family. Here they managed to provide food and shelter for some of their fellow refugees.

During the next 450 years the village grew from 2 to 276 families. There were 248 families in the main village and 28 in the three satellites. Seventy-two per cent of the families said that their ancestors came from Shansi Province. Twenty-seven per cent were Hopei families. The others came from Shantung. (See table 25.)

Nine families, 3.3 per cent, said that their ancestors came to the village before 1513, more than 420 years ago. This would be a span of fifteen or more generations. Thirty-six per cent of the families had lived in the village for more than 300 years. Twelve per cent had been there for not more than 90 years, and 16 families, 5.8 per cent, were first-generation families that had immigrated during the 30 years before. (See table 26.)

Somehow and at some time, but local tradition did not say how or when, the village had acquired control of an area of 7,342 mu of land, divided as follows:

	Mu	Per cent
Farmland	7,033	95.8
Village	258	3.5
Graves	51	0.7
Total	7,342	100.0

The 258 mu of the village residence area was divided as follows:

	Mu	Per cent
Houses	22	8.5
Yards	117	45.4
Streets	11	4.3
Empty	108	41.8
Total	258	100.0

The field report made special note of the fact that the graves of the dead occupied almost 2.5 times as much space as the houses of the living.

The main village was divided by a ten-foot-wide ditch that ran down the main street and provided drainage for the pond to the north. There were three stone bridges across the ditch.

VILLAGE STREETS

The houses of the 248 families in the main village faced on eleven streets. The two longest streets were little more than a fifth of a mile in length. Together they totaled one third of the length of all the streets. The shortest street was only 150 feet long. The average frontage per house ranged from a minimum of 34 feet to a maximum of 102 feet. As might be expected, the lowest average was on the main and longest street.

WATER SUPPLY

There were water wells on all but the two shortest streets. On one street a single well served 9 families. On the main street there were three wells for 65 families. The average number of families per well was 15.5 in the main village and 4.6 in the satellite villages.

HOUSING

The housing of the 276 families in the main and satellite villages totaled 1,366 chien, an average of 5 chien per family and one chien per person. The individual houses varied in size from one to 41 chien. Thirty-nine per cent of the houses had 3 chien; 16.6 per cent had 5 chien. Two thirds of the houses had 2, 3, or 5 chien. Only 6.8 per cent had more than 10 chien.

Forty-eight houses, 17.4 per cent, were rented by the occupants. This was quite a high proportion, especially in view of the fact that more than 90 per cent of the families had been living in the village for more than sixty years and all but 5.8 per cent had been there for more than thirty years.

There were earthen roofs on 89.5 per cent of the houses. The others were tiled. No tile-roofed house had more than 11 chien.

The earthen-roofed houses had an average of 5.0 chien. The tile-roofed houses averaged 4.2 chien. The medians for both were 3 chien. The rented houses had an average of only 2.9 chien, and none had more than 6 chien. Besides the family homes there were 36 chien in the two village temples, 24 in the T'ien Ch'i Miao ("Heavenly Air Temple") and 12 in the temple dedicated to Kuan Ti. The housing details are shown in figure 2 and table 27.

DEMOGRAPHIC DATA

The population of the village was 1,373 persons. The 276 families had from one to 23 members. The average family had 4.97 members. The median family had 4 members. The largest group of families, 23.2 per cent, had 4 members. The three-, four-, and five-member families were 56.9 per cent of the total number. The families with more than 10 members were only 4.9 per cent of the group. The complete numerical distribution of the families is shown in figure 5 and table 8.

The population density of the village area was 720 persons per square mile for the entire village area of 7,342 mu and 750 persons per square mile for the farming area of 7,033 mu.

The sex distribution of the village population was 675 males and 698 females, or 49.0 per cent male. The masculinity rate was 96.7 males per 100 females. Approximately a quarter of each group was under 15 years of age. The proportion 60 or more years of age was females, 11.5 per cent; males, 8.5 per cent. Of those 45 years of age or more, males were 25.0 per cent; females, 29.1 per cent.

Our population study did not give any figures for marital status, but did give the age at marriage for 377 males and 434 females. The ages ranged from 11 through 38 years for males and from 11 through 34 years for females. The most popular age for both males and females was 18 years. Fifty-one per cent of the males and 62.8 per cent of the females were less than 20 years of age when they married. Sixty-one per cent of the males and 81.6 per cent of the females were in the age group of 16 through 22 years. Age at marriage was 23 years or more for 24.3 per cent of the males and 25 years or more for 17.1 per cent. The corresponding figures for females were 10.0 and 5.6 per cent. The average ages at marriage were: males, 22 years; females, 19 years. The median ages were 19 and 18 years. (See fig. 7 and table 11.) It is our understanding that the figures are for first marriages only.

Proximity to Peiping probably was responsible for the fact that these figures were considerably higher than those in the more rural areas. In Ting Hsien, 175 miles south of Peiping, the average ages at marriage in a group of 515 families were males, 17.2 years; females, 17.7 years. In another group of 1,843 men and 2,059 women, the average ages were males, 18.6 years; females, 17.7 years.[1]

Farming was the chief occupation of the village. Of the 276 families, 224 (81.2 per cent) cultivated some land. Within the limits of Village C they farmed an area of 5,952 mu, an average of 26.6 mu per family. How much farmland they had in neighboring villages was not learned, but families from other villages farmed 1,081 mu (15.4 per cent) of the farm area of Village C.

The average land per farming family was 26.6 mu, the amounts per family ranging from 3 to 560 mu. There were 157 families, 70.1 per cent of the farming families, who had fewer than 20 mu; 80.4 per cent had fewer than 30 mu (5 acres). This group held 25.6 per cent of the farm area, while the 4 families with 200 mu or more held 20.1 per cent. There were 3 families with only 3 mu, half an acre, each. (See table 5.)

Sixteen families were carrying on business activity in the village—grocery shops, meat shops, a teahouse, a small inn, an undertaker's shop, and peddling. The total number of workers was 22, of whom

7 were peddlers. The total capital employed was reported as $4,916; the amount per family ranged from $30 to $1,000.

There were 120 persons engaged in commercial work outside the village. Forty-three persons were occupied with handicrafts—vermicelli and bean-curd makers, tile workers, carpenters; 14 of the 43 were employed in a government woolen factory in the nearby town. Another 22 persons were engaged in communications, professional, or service jobs. The total nonagricultural workers was 207. (See table 28.)

EDUCATION

Of the 1,373 persons living in the village, 460 had at least one year of schooling. This was one third of the population. There were 306 persons, 22.2 per cent, who had more than three years of school work. Almost two thirds, 65.5 per cent, of all the males in the village and almost 75 per cent of those more than 5 years of age had had at least one year of schooling. This was an unusually high proportion. Some of the males had as much as twelve years of study.

Only 18 of the 698 females, 2.6 per cent, had any formal education. Four of them had four years of study, but none had as much as five years, i.e., had attended a higher primary school. (See fig. 11.)

EDUCATIONAL FACILITIES

In 1900 the village had two private, old-fashioned schools, supported by the fees paid by the pupils. Shortly thereafter the hsien government urged the villages to open modern primary schools. One of the teachers then took advantage of the situation to merge the two private schools into a new modern school, which was held first in the Kuan Ti Miao, but in 1917, because of the increased number of students, was moved to the larger T'ien Ch'i Miao. There it occupied four chien, three as a classroom and one for the teacher. The rooms were reconstructed in 1928 in spite of the fact that the civil disturbances and military levies that year left most villages without funds for any such construction work. Across the courtyard from the school were four chien that were being kept for future expansion.

In 1933 the school had four grades. The 54 students ranged in age from 7 to 19 years. The first grade had 26 students, almost half the total number. The second grade had 15 students; the third 9; the fourth, only 4. There were no girls in the school. (See fig. 10.)

The school was directed by a three-member committee. One of the committeemen was an association leader who served for one year and then was replaced by another member of the leader group. The others were an old man and a very enthusiastic young man. Any important school problems, of course, were dealt with by all the members of the village association.

There was only one teacher for the school. He was expected to teach four grades and nine courses, Chinese, arithmetic, general knowledge, the Three People's Principles, music, physical exercise, manual training, and composition. The students also spent considerable time in practicing penmanship and calculation on the abacus.

The Chinese report said that the boys went to school seven days a week, arriving about daybreak and staying until 9:00 P.M., with two breaks of an hour each at 11:00 A.M. and 4:00 P.M. for meals.

School was in session for 265 days of the year. The fall vacation of 40 days was from the fifteenth day of the seventh month to the twenty-fifth day of the eighth month and was planned to coincide with the fall harvest. The spring vacation for the wheat harvest was for 19 days, from the twentieth day of the fourth month to the ninth day of the fifth month. The New Year vacation was for 30 days, from the twentieth day of the twelfth month to the twentieth day of the first month. The other 11 days of vacation were arranged to enable the students to go to the different fairs in the area. When a neighboring village held a boxing procession on the fifteenth day of the fourth month, the teacher and students all went together. Sundays were used for reviewing lessons.

The finances of the school seemed to be in unusually good shape. The income included $180 from the rent of 90 mu of temple land, $300 from the sale of reeds grown in a pond near the Kuan Ti Miao, and $54 from tuition fees of $1 per student. The total was $534. The expenses totaled only $206: salaries, $144; servant's wages, $24; books, $10; other equipment, $4; miscellaneous, $24. This left a balance of $328 which was held as a contingent sum to meet the military levies. Even though there was a balance of $274 without tuition, this presumably was not considered large enough to meet the army's assessment. Thus the tuition was collected and added to the balance.

Any pupils attending school past the lower primary grades went to the higher primary school in the nearby town, which was run by the district government but supported by assessments paid by all the villages in the district.

TEMPLES

The village had two temples, the Kuan Ti Miao at the north end of the main street and the T'ien Ch'i Miao at the south end.

The Kuan Ti Miao, dedicated to the god of war, was last rebuilt in 1838. It had four buildings, each with three chien. The altar was in the main building. The east building housed the village self-government office. The west building was the headquarters of the self-protection organization. The fourth building was used for storage. On the main altar were the images of Kuan Ti and his two attendants, Kuan P'ing and Chou Ts'ang and on side altars were those of Yen Wang, T'u Ti, Erh Lang, and the gods of fire, of animals, and of wealth. Kuan Ti was worshiped because of his loyalty to his two sworn brothers, Liu Pei and Chang Fei.

T'ien Ch'i Miao is another name for Tung Yueh Miao ("Eastern Peak Temple"), which signified the worship of the sacred mountain, T'ai Shan. K'ai Huang deified T'ai Shan as T'ien Ch'i. A Tung Yueh Miao often had, around one of its courtyards, a three-dimensional depiction of the punishments of hell.

This temple was last rebuilt in 1845. It had six buildings, around two courtyards. With 24 chien, it was twice the size of the Kuan Ti Miao. In the front courtyard the main altar room had three chien. The two side-buildings had four chien each. One was used for the village school; the other was reserved for the future use of the school.

The back courtyard had 13 chien, used for a secondary altar room, for storage, and for the living quarters of the temple servant —described as "usually a worthy fellow without relatives to depend upon and therefore employed by the village association." The servant was paid about $100 a year in 1932.

Huang Fei-hu, the god in charge of life and death and the king of the nether regions, was the principal figure on the front altar of the T'ien Ch'i Miao. The secondary altar room was the more popular, for it had the images of the three Niang-niang, goddesses in charge of smallpox, eyesight, and childbearing. They had fourteen attendant figures.

In general, the T'ien Ch'i Miao was frequented by individual worshipers and the Kuan Ti Miao was the place for public worship.

Some of the wealthier families of the village had a Buddhist shrine hanging on the wall of their houses directly opposite the main doorway. The poorer families put up colored pictures of the deities they worshiped.

Feast of Departed Spirits.—On the fifteenth day of the seventh month, the time of the Feast of Departed Spirits, Village C held a Yu Lan P'en Hui to feed, quiet, and control the wandering souls of those who, in earlier years, had drowned in the nearby pond. It was said that these spirits were always trying to lure people into the pond and that by providing a substitute the wandering spirit could be released and become eligible for reincarnation. The ceremonies consisted of dancing, singing, the chanting of prayers, the offering of food to hungry spirits and devils, the distribution of food to the needy, and the burning of a *fa-ch'uan*—the paper boat that would ferry across the river of the nether world the spirits of those who were to be reincarnated.

It was said that the festival commemorated the filial piety of Mu Lien, a Buddhist monk who tried to get relief for his mother, Yu Lan, who, when she died, was sent to hell for punishment. The judge of hell before whom her spirit appeared decreed that everything she tried to eat would turn to fire. Mu Lien's piety was so great that finally the god of hell was moved to rescind part of Yu Lan's punishment and give her spirit something to eat that did not ignite.

The boat, which was made of kaoliang stalks and dark yellow paper, was fifteen feet long, six feet wide, and three feet high. On its prow were three figures. The chief one, in the center, was that of Yeh Ch'a, the ugliest of the devils, of which there were two kinds, heavenly devils who could fly and earthly devils who could not. Yeh Ch'a had long stringy hair, wore dark clothes, and held a big sword in his hand. On the left was the figure of a *t'iao-ssu kuei*, a man who had committed suicide by hanging himself, in white clothes and a tall hat; his tongue stuck out three inches and over his right shoulder he carried a bag hooked onto the handle of an umbrella. On the right was the figure of a *chu-ssu kuei*, a man who had died under unnatural conditions. All three figures looked as though they were travelers.

On the foredeck of the boat was a pavilion in which sat four figures. The first was Li Ching, a Buddhist worthy, who was the deification of a very good and successful T'ang dynasty general. As a spirit he had magical lifesaving powers. His image usually held a pagoda in its hand. Next to him was the figure of T'ang Chen, a T'ang dynasty monk, whose spirit also had great lifesaving power. The third figure was O Cha, a great general and a son of Li Ching. His spirit gave special protection to monks. One of the first manifestations of this occurred when a T'ang dynasty monk named Ch'ien, who had been on a long and arduous trip, had walked until he was completely exhausted—he was able to reach his destination only because he was upheld and supported by a figure who said that he was O Cha. The fourth figure was of Erh Lang Shen, another renowned general. Once when he was a magistrate, it was said, he built a huge dam and saved a large area from flood. He was later deified for this accomplishment. Another legend said that he was a spirit who had helped a Sung emperor win a war. Later the emperor made a god of Erh Lang's spirit because of the help that he had given.

In the center of the boat was a large pavilion in which the figures of eighteen Buddhist monks were seated.

On the afterdeck in a small pavilion was a figure of Yu Lan, the "sage mother," a Buddhist worthy for whom the festival was named. At the stern of the boat was a small house in which stood a female figure called by the villagers the "mistress of the ship."

It was about 7:00 P.M. when the four men carrying the boat reached the T'ien Ch'i Miao. Many of the people climbed over the wall to see the boat.

In the center of the village more than a dozen men, in costume and with painted faces, were singing and dancing to the accompaniment of the clicking of lotus-petal-shaped bamboo castinets. They were singing a song called *Kuang Hua Yuan* ("Strolling in the Garden") to the *Lien Hua Lao* type of tune.[2] They were joined in the singing and dancing by some people from the neighboring villages. The music kept up until about midnight. The crowd of visitors was policed by some of the members of the village association carrying rifles.

Outside the T'ien Ch'i Miao a low table and some long benches were set up for seven monks who were chanting prayers and playing musical instruments. The prayers were to be carried over to Ti Ts'ang Wang, the king of hell, so that he might be influenced to restrain and placate the wandering spirits of those who had drowned in the village pond. The priests came from a neighboring village, as Village C had only a caretaker in the T'ien Ch'i Miao. The monk who formerly lived in the temple had died and his disciple had been expelled from the village by the association heads because of his low morals and his infraction of Buddhist discipline. The only compensation given the priests for their part in the service was their food, which cost $4. The other expenses of the festival were $11 for the paper boat and $1 for miscellaneous items.

At 12:30 A.M., when the singing and dancing in the village was over and the monks had finished chanting their prayers, the boat was burned, so that it could be used by the spirits in their world.

INCOME PROPERTY

The pond associated with the Yu Lan P'en Hui covered an area of some 100 mu and was village property. Every year it produced a crop of reeds said to be worth about $300. This amount was reported as part of the village income. A smaller pond, covering 15 mu, lay between Village C and the nearby village on the south. Some years before, the two villages had gone to court over the ownership of this pond. Each spent about $400 on the case, only to have it decided that the pond belonged to both. The value of the pond was said to be about $400. Feelings ran very high over the case, and after it was decided, relations between the villages were broken to the point were employees were discharged if they lived in the other village.

Some 90 mu of "incense land" was owned by the two temples, 70 mu by the T'ien Ch'i Miao and 20 mu by the Kuan Ti Miao. The village association controlled the use of the land and regularly rented it for an annual cash payment that in 1933 averaged about $2 a mu. Before 1924 the land was managed by the temples and the rental income was used by the priest who lived in the T'ien Ch'i Miao for his support and that of his assistant. About 1919 the assistant was dismissed for violating the Buddhist discipline. When the priest died in 1924 the former assistant came back to the village and attempted to appropriate the temples and the temple lands. The village leaders defeated him and took over the property for the village association. The rent from the land, as part of the village income, was allocated to the support of the village school.

POLITICAL HISTORY

The political history of the village followed the usual pattern of the area. Before 1900 the village association was run by an informal group of village leaders and was concerned almost entirely with crop-protection. The most important officers of the association were the accountant and the cashier. Political relations between the village and the hsien government were in the hands of the ti-pao, who received all material sent by the hsien magistrate and reported any unusual occurrences in the village, such as murder or theft. Whenever messengers came to the village from the hsien headquarters, they were given money for "expenses." The ti-pao collected the necessary funds, and more, from the villagers. His relation to the hsien government naturally gave him considerable power in the village. The ti-pao in Village C was a man whose family had been resident there for ten generations.

The year 1900, with the antiforeign activity of the Boxers and the presence of foreign troops in the Peking area, brought about an upheaval that permanently altered the political pattern of the area. One unit of foreign troops had headquarters in the town near Village C. They demanded that the neighboring villages deliver 20,000 eggs a day and threatened that, if responsible persons did not arrange for the delivery of the eggs, they would themselves do the collecting. A former *pa-tsung* ("lieutenant") in the Chinese army, who had taken care of the Imperial granaries, then proposed and carried through the organization of an intervillage league of 72 villages located near the boundary between Wan-p'ing Hsien and Ch'ang-p'ing Hsien. The league not only dealt with the foreign troops, but also with bandits who attempted to take advantage of the anarchy around the capital.

Every member village chose its own leaders to represent it in the league and to handle the problems in the village. The village association was thus established in a strong position, which the leaders were not willing to give up when the emergency had passed. Other problems requiring action continued to arise, and the village leaders assumed more and more authority, even going directly to the hsien magistrate. Gradually they took over the powers of the ti-pao and eliminated his position and influence.

At the time of our study the over-all political and financial affairs of the village association were directed by a general committee of twenty leaders. Earlier the number had been eighteen and then twenty-two.

CHARACTERIZATIONS OF VILLAGE LEADERS

The village report gave an interesting series of characterizations of some of the leaders. Leaders *A-F* constituted the executive committee. Leader *A* had a good memory, was shy with strangers but fluent with his acquaintances, was alert and reliable, and was obeyed by everyone when there was any emergency. Leader *B* also had a good memory, and was alert and reliable; he was good in conversation and was relied on for his ability in external transactions. Leader *D* was noted for his exactitude and open-mindedness. He was bold in words and actions. When the allied troops of Chihli and Shantung provinces, feared by all because of their rudeness and because they treated the farmer folk with blows, were quartered in a neighboring village, he was the village representative who dealt with them. His uncle, Leader *P*, was also revered by his associates for his exactness and open-mindedness. His cousin had sometimes been one of the village leaders.

Leader *E* had a very good memory. Only twenty-one years old, he had not developed other outstanding characteristics. Leader *F*, a member of the executive committee, evidently had taken his young brother's place as an association leader. The younger brother was alert and reliable and had worked in Chinese medicine stores in Peking and Tientsin. Leader *H* had a good memory and was alert and reliable, but was quite shy. Leader *J* was exact and open-minded. He tried to resign as a village leader, but because of his business ability the group would not let him go. Leader *M* was particularly noted for his goodheartedness. His nickname was "Old Hen." Leader *Q* was very artistic. He was a brother of Leader *J*, but had been adopted by another family and so had another name. Leader *S* owned a coffin shop and a small inn. He was reported to be of mediocre ability in public affairs, but very able in private transactions—even though he had lost 70 mu of land in business ventures. He had two wives, but no son. Leader *T* owned the most land of any of the village leaders, 560 mu, but he lived in the nearby town, came to the village only occasionally to look after his farm, and did not want to accept the public responsibility connected with membership in the executive group.

The ages, landholdings, and extent of education of the twenty village leaders are shown in table 12. The ages ranged from 21 to 70 years, their schooling from 4 to 8 years, and their landholdings from none to 560 mu. The average age when we made our study was 43.5 years; the average education, 6.5 years; and the average landholding, 146.5 mu. They represented the wealthier part of the village, for although they came from only 7.2 per cent of all the families in the village and 8.9 per cent of the farming families, they held 41.7 per cent of the total village farm area of 7,033 mu and 49.2 per cent of the farm area held by the families resident in the village.

These figures, however, undoubtedly overstate the case, for a comparison of the landholding figures in tables 5 and 12 makes it evident that the first set of figures represents the families' holdings as entered in the village land-assessment books. The second set of figures includes also land owned in the village area but rented to others and therefore entered in their names, since they were to pay the crop-money assessment. Possibly some landholdings in other villages are reflected in this listing. Thus in table 8 there is only one family in the group with 75–99 mu, while four of the leaders' families were listed as having 80 mu each. Both tables had four families with more than 200 mu, but the total area held by the four families was 1,196 mu in one table and 1,610 mu in the other.

It seems probable that 18 of the 26 families having 50 mu or more of village land were represented in the leadership group. Our reporter stated that it seemed clear to him that wealth was the primary quality in the selection of a village leader. Ability was a secondary consideration. It will be noted, however, that although the man with the largest landholdings, 560 mu, was one of the twenty leaders, he was by his own choice not a member of the executive group.

VILLAGE ADMINISTRATION

The chief village officers were the village head (ts'un-chang) and his assistant (ts'un-fu), but the control was actually in an executive committee of six elders, who held the offices of village head and assistant head for one-year terms in rotation among themselves. Another leader was in charge of the landownership records and current accounts, and there were more than ten leaders who helped handle the public funds.

The continued use of the rotation system reflected the fact that 71 per cent of the families in Village C came from Shansi. In that province the offices of the village she, or association, had long been rotated among a larger or smaller proportion of the family heads of the village, the size of the qualifying group depending on the restrictions imposed by the particular village. Judging from the other villages studied, the heads of most villages in the Peiping area held office for indefinite periods.

The executive committee was a closely related group. Elder B was the uncle of C, a cousin of A, a brother-in-law of F, and the father-in-law of a child of D. Only one of the six members of the group had no family connection with the other five, even though he had the same family name as three of them. He was also only twenty-one years old, but his family owned 350 mu of land.

The routine village business was handled by the village head and his assistant or by the executive committee of six. Occasionally the village head called meetings of the entire group of twenty leaders. Notice of the meeting would be delivered either by a uniformed member of the local guard, by the Kuan Ti Miao servant, or by one of the crop-watchers. Meetings were held in the village offices in the temple and usually after sunset. The problem would be presented and generally discussed by the group, sometimes for several hours without their reaching a definite conclusion or solution. The village heads then would have to solve the problem as best they could, but they would feel that they had the backing of the entire group, who had been made aware of the difficulty. For instance, in April, 1932, a regiment of government troops stationed at the nearby town wanted to hold field exercises near Village C. All the village leaders were against the proposal, and finally they sent a petition to the officials, asking that it be given up. It was reported, however, that the meeting at which the leaders discussed the problem was quite chaotic, with everyone talking at once and one grumbling leader saying that the troops ought to go and fight the Japanese instead of bringing trouble to the villagers.

After the Nationalist government took over in Peking, several committees of leaders were formed as part of the village administration. The committee on arbitration attempted to solve all but major village conflicts. The committee on discipline dealt with those who did harm to crops or broke the rules of the association. The finance and inspection committees called for by the Nationalist government's plan of village organization were not mentioned in the village report.

CROP-WATCHING

The fundamental and continuing activity of the village association was, of course, protecting the crops. Crop-watchers were hired for the spring wheat season as well as for the period before the larger fall harvest. The amount of land farmed by the individual families was entered in the land book at the association office on the twenty-eighth day of the fourth month. The actual crop-watching period for wheat usually lasted for about six weeks, from the fourteenth day of the third month until harvesttime, which usually came near the end of the fourth month. The number of watchmen depended on the size of the area planted to wheat. In some years, if the area was very small, no watchers would be hired. The men engaged for the spring season of 1933 were paid $7 each.

The fall crop-watching season regularly began on Kuan Ti's birthday, which in Village C was celebrated on the twenty-fourth day of the sixth month. (Village A celebrated Kuan Ti's brithday and started crop-watching on the sixth day of the sixth month.) The gong was rung and the whole village was warned that "the watchmen are going to oversee the fields and protect the crops." The season lasted until harvesttime in the ninth month. Usually six watchmen were hired. In 1933 they each received $15 and a share of the fines levied on any crop-thieves they were able to catch, and also the gifts of small bundles of grain straw given as tips by the farmers. The number of bundles ordinarily depended on the size of the donor's farm. They were worth about a half cent apiece. It was impossible to get an estimate of the number of bundles each man collected or how far they would go in providing fuel for cooking and heating. In many villages the crop-watchers were village rascals, "big hands," who were hired to prevent them from raiding the fields. Village C, however, used small farmers who did not have enough land to keep them busy.

Punishment of crop-thieves.—Any crop-thieves that the watchmen apprehended were brought before the village elders for determination of their punishment. Fines were levied on persons whose animals trampled the crops or whose children stole grain from the fields. The amount of the fine depended upon the seriousness of the offense and the residence and economic status of person responsible. For a serious offense a wealthy man might be called on to pay for a feast for several tables of guests and to give candles and incense to the temple. A less wealthy man might be assessed a money fine. A fine of more than $2 was called an incense fee and used for public purposes. A smaller fine was known as wine-money, and the wine ordinarily went to the crop-watchers.

For trespass and theft, a local resident might have a sign detailing his crime hung round his neck and then be paraded through the neighboring villages as well as through Village C. Those who did not live in the area and would not be shamed by such treatment were ordinarily given a thorough beating, although officially this was not supposed to be permitted. The crop-watchers regularly expected some monetary reward for catching a thief, generally part of the fine levied by the village authorities.

The fees for the crop-watching in 1932 were 3 cents a mu for the spring season and 30 cents a mu for the fall season. In some villages only the wheat growers paid for the spring season, but in Village C all the farmers paid. The crop-money was paid by those who farmed the land, whether landlord or tenant.

OTHER INCOME

Although the largest part of village expenses was borne by the farming families, the nonfarming families were required to contribute toward the local administration sums that ranged from 50 cents to $2 per family. The amount for each family was determined according to the size of the family and its economic status. The 52 nonfarming families paid about $50 altogether, an average of about

$1 per family. For the farm families the average contribution was $10.60 per family.

THANKSGIVING CEREMONIES

The thanksgiving for the wheat harvest had no set date, but usually came near the end of the fourth month. Besides paying their crop-money, the representatives of the farming families paid 15 cents for a meal of noodles served in the Kuan Ti Miao. The village leaders were kept busy recording the payments as made and presenting sacrifices to Kuan Ti and the other deities.

The service took place about two o'clock in the afternoon. The temple servant placed incense, candles, and other offerings on the table in front of the altar. Then the village head, as the representative of the village, took a long, hollow rectangular paper prayer about five inches square and from three to five feet long which had the name of the village written on it and burned this in front of the altar while he kowtowed before the image of Kuan Ti. The other village leaders followed him and kowtowed one by one. The group then went to present sacrifices before the other altars. Two sets of offerings regularly were arranged, one inside, in front of the image of the deity, and the other in front of the temple. The inner offering later went to the temple caretaker, the other one to the village boys who came to watch the ceremony.

The fall thanksgiving, which usually came toward the end of the ninth month, followed very much the same pattern as that for the spring service, except that the crop-money was 30 cents a mu instead of 3 cents and the feast was more elaborate—eight dishes besides noodles. The fee for the feast was also larger, 20 cents instead of 15 cents.

When they paid their fall crop-money, most of the farmers reported to the village authorities the number of mu they expected to cultivate the next year.

SELF-DEFENSE CORPS

Besides the crop-watchers, the village employed two former soldiers to take care of the activities of the village volunteer self-defense corps. They were put into uniform and were paid a monthly salary of $6 each. Their headquarters was in the west building of the Kuan Ti Miao, across from the office of the village administration.

The corps consisted of some 150 volunteer members who belonged to the farming families with 30 or more mu of land. In Vil-

lage C this was a group of 44 families, so each family was expected
to furnish, on the average, three members to give one night a week
each to the work of the corps.

The night patrols consisted of twenty men. They carried guns
when on duty. Each of the seven teams was headed by a member of
the village association appointed by the village head or the assistant
head. Any corps member who had to be absent when his turn came
was expected to find a substitute to serve for him.

The village was required to pay $80 toward the expense of the
guard maintained by the district government.

It was impossible to get a detailed report on the village finances.
The leaders felt that anyone's asking for a statement of their handling of funds was the same as questioning their honesty. Furthermore, inasmuch as Village C was one of the wealthier villages in the
area and regularly carried over a sizable cash balance, there was fear
that the military and higher political authorities might find ways to
draw the money off for dubious "public" use. From the information
obtained, we have roughly estimated the village income for 1932 as
follows:

Rent of temple land	$ 180
Reeds from pond	300
School tuition	54
Crop-money—7,033 mu @ 33 cents per mu	2,320
Nonfarming families	50
Total	$2,904

The expenditure for the same year was verbally reported to be
somewhat smaller: about $2,360, or just under $200 a month. The
largest item was the sum paid to the army. That, together with the
amounts paid for special assessments levied by the higher government, accounted for some 70 per cent of the total. The school cost
about $206; the crop-watching, about $104 for wages; the local
guard, $144 for wages plus additional amounts for equipment and
ammunition. The district police required $80. Besides these items
there were expenses for the thanksgiving celebrations, for the offerings and sacrifices in the temples, for the village office, and for travel
expenses for village representatives going to conferences called by
district and hsien officials. Although the 1932 income and expense
figures for Village C seem to be about $500 apart, with income the
larger, it seems evident that over the years the totals undoubtedly
stayed close together and that the crop-money rate was adjusted as
needed.

XI: VILLAGE D

HOW OTHER LEADERS could curb village heads when they attempted to assume autocratic power and how the families could refuse to accept a program proposed by the leaders were both clearly shown in Village D.

Situated some seven miles northwest of Peiping, Village D was basically an agricultural community. There were indications, however, that more and more of its families were being influenced by proximity to the city and the market town, where opportunities for employment might be more remunerative than the return from farming. Two small neighboring residence areas or "satellites" were under Village D's control. They were one and three li from the main village.

After 1929 two other small villages had been required by law to join Village D, as they had a total of only 55 families, not enough to qualify as separate villages. Although they were politically attached to Village D, they had not in any way moved to amalgamate with their larger neighbor. They maintained their own associations, collected their own crop-money, and had a separately elected political head who, however, in the eyes of the district and hsien governments, was only one of the assistant heads of Village D.

DEMOGRAPHIC DATA

In 1933 there were 142 families living in Village D and its two integrated residence units: 99 in the main village, 43 in the two smaller units. In 1902 there had been only 108 families.

There were thirty-five different family names in the village, but eighteen of these names had only one family each. Nearly half of the families were included in the three largest name groups. Two had 24 families each. One had 22 families. Only one other name group had more than 10 families. The six largest name groups included 64.8 of the families in the village. So far as we could find, there was no clan organization in any of the name groups. One sixth or more of the families in the four largest name groups had moved into the village fairly recently and were only distantly related to the other families with the same name.

There were 46 families, 33.4 per cent of the entire group, who were first-generation residents, having come to the village during the lifetime of the then head of the family, and 16 families, 11.2 per cent, who had lived in the village for not more than ten years. Sixty-one per cent of the immigrant families came from a distance of less than five miles. Thirteen per cent came from other provinces in North China. Fifteen of the families came because the wife was a native of the village.

The 99 families in the main village lived in 63 different courtyards, each of which had a separate gate opening onto a village street. There were 36 families in single-family homes and 42 in two-family, 9 in three-family, and 12 in four-family courtyards. Most of the buildings were of brick. The total village area was some 80 mu.

The population of the village was 627 persons, an average of only 4.4 persons per family. There were 108 persons, 17 per cent of the total, who spent most of the year outside of the village, in the neighboring market town, in Peiping, or farther afield. Even so, they were counted as part of their village family, and they contributed to its support and had an undivided interest in the family property. Fifteen of the absentees were females. If the absentees are omitted, the average family had only 3.7 persons, an unusually low average.

Including the absentees, the families ranged in size from one to 25 members. Four families had 10 or more members; seven had only one. There were two old bachlors and five old widows. The median was 4 members, and 77.5 per cent of the families included fewer than 6 persons.

In sex division the village was 48.5 per cent male. If those absent most of the year are omitted, the ratio was only 40.6 per cent male. When men sought employment elsewhere they usually left their families in the village.

In 11 families the head was a female.

In age distribution those 15 years of age or younger were 29 per cent of the population and those 50 years of age or older, 20 per cent. In the first group the females outnumbered the males 97 to 86 and in the second 71 to 53.

It was reported that for those more than 13 years old the literacy rate for the village was 41 per cent: 79.8 per cent for the males and only 3.5 per cent for the females. The absentee males were 87.5 per cent literate; the resident males, 74.6 per cent.

LANDOWNERSHIP PATTERN

The farm area of the village, as registered in the village land books, was 2,492.5 mu (415.4 acres), divided into 317 plots. There were 267 plots, containing 2,010 mu, owned by resident families. Nonresidents held 50 plots, totaling 482.5 mu. The size distribution of the plots was as follows:

Size of plot	Number of plots	Per cent of farm area
Less than 5 mu.................	72	22.7
5– 9.9 mu.................	149	47.0
10–14.9 mu.................	62	19.6
15–19.9 mu.................	31	9.8
20 and more mu.................	3	0.9
Total.................	317	100.0

Size of average plot: 7.9 mu

The 1930 land books listed 98 resident and 35 nonresident land-owning families. For an earlier year the division was 104 resident and 30 nonresident families. Of the resident farm-owning families, who were 69 per cent of all the village families, 75 lived in the main village and 23 in the satellites, or 76 per cent of the families in the main village and 54 per cent of the families in the satellites. These figures would seem to indicate a considerably lower financial status for the satellite families.

The nonresident families lived in five neighboring villages, 21 in one village, 7 in another, 5 in a third, and one each in the other two.

Only 10 of the resident landowners, 10.4 per cent, had more than 30 mu (5 acres) and only 5 had more than 60 mu. The largest family holding was 196 mu (32.7 acres). That family had 25 members and was the largest in the village. The 196 mu were divided into 17 different plots. The two families with the next largest holdings, between 80 and 90 mu, had 8 and 12 different plots.

The 5 families with more than 60 mu all employed full-time farm laborers who were given their room and board and from $30 to $40 a year. Day wages, other than at harvesttime, ordinarily were 30 cents for men and 15 cents for women.

Ten mu of public land were owned by the largest temple in the village. The income was used for the support of the two monks who lived there.

There were four shops in the village: a brewery making kaoliang wine, an oil and grocery shop, a cloth shop, and a salt shop. According to the field notes the brewery had a capital of some $20,000 and did an annual business of some $40,000. It had been started in the late 1870's with a capital of 3,000 taels, $4,165. It was said to produce about 500 catties of wine per day from some 1,200 catties of kaoliang.

The oil shop daily pressed some 500 catties of oil from some 1,500 catties of sesamum seed. It was said to have a capital of $2,000 and yearly sales of some $8,000.

The clothing shop had been developed by a Shantung man who started out as a peddlar and, when he had a surplus of $100, joined two other men in opening a small clothing shop. The other men later sold out, so that in 1933 the Shantung man was the sole owner of the business, which had a capital of $600. He also owned the store building. As he was getting to the age when he wanted to retire, he was turning the business over to his two nephews, whom he had pursuaded to leave Shantung and come to Peiping.

The salt shop was part of the distribution system of the government monopoly. The dealer had to get his license from the hsien government. To protect his monopoly and prevent people from bringing into his area salt bought in Peiping or in the nearby town, he employed four inspectors who probably worked on a part-time basis, as they also had jobs with the village administration.

To help carry some of the cost of the village activities, the brewery, even though it had no land, registered 400 mu in the village land books and paid the regular crop-money on that amount of "land." The oil shop registered 300 mu. The other two shops did not actually register any "land," but they each paid crop-money equivalent to the amount due on 250 mu.

The village head hired several men to make noodles from the corn and green peas that he grew on his farm. His brother, who had been crippled in an accident, acted as his secretary and accountant. There was no noodle shop in the village, so the output all had to be sold in other villages or to some of the nearby academic institutions.

It was reported that 114 of the 142 families living in the village were farm operators—owners, part owners, or tenants. Actually the number should have been 115, as one family's land was registered with that of an older brother. It might even have been increased to 118, as 2 families were farming cemetery land and one had a vegetable garden, neither of which activities would be recorded in the village land books. Of the other 24 families, 3 were landlords who rented out all of their land, 7 were hired farm laborers, and 14 presumably got their incomes from nonagricultural sources.

Two of the landlords were widows who had no one in the family to farm the land. Three other women were listed as landowners, but they must have had sons who did the necessary work. Five females were listed as full-time workers.

The number of families registered in the village land books regularly showed a year-to-year change and a very considerable increase over a longer period. In 1902 the number was 100 families. In 1928 it was 141. It dropped to 133 in 1930, to 130 in 1931 and to 128 in 1932. While the change from 1930 to 1931 was only 3 families, the records showed that 17 families left the village and 14 new ones moved in. A drop-out of 12.8 per cent was, of course, a very high turnover; however, the books also showed that only 50 per cent of the families registered the same amount of land in 1930 and 1931. Besides the 17 who dropped out, 26 families reported an increase and 22 families a decrease in the amount of land they were farming. Three families made a change in their fields without affecting their total area. These figures would seem to show an unusually large amount of shifting, a large amount of tenancy, and a surprising lack of permanency in the tenants. One wonders to what extent job opportunities in the nearby town and city were contributing factors.

TEMPLES

There were five temples in the village. The largest was dedicated to Kuan Ti, the god of war, but also a patron saint of art and literature and, for the villagers, a god of wealth. Two monks, attached to the temple, lived in one of its courtyards. The headquarters of the village association and of the local administration were also housed in the temple buildings.

The next largest temple was dedicated to the god of longevity. It had been a large temple, but had gradually fallen into decay. A fire in 1921 burned many of the temple's old books and destroyed a considerable part of the main building. In 1932 the village leaders and the village monk decided to rebuild the temple, but on a much smaller scale. They collected $560 in contributions, but only $85 of this amount came from Village D residents. The building cost $582. The final $22 came from general village funds. The amount was needed to pay for such items as the temple tablets, the hanging of the tablets, and bell, and the dedication exercises. The other three were small, one-room shrines. The shrine erected at the east end of the main street to prevent the good luck of the village from leaving by that road was dedicated to Kuan Yin. It was rebuilt in 1928. Theatrical plays were given as part of the celebration and thanksgiving when the work was completed and the temple was reopened.

The temple at the west end of the street was dedicated to the god of medicine. He, however, shared the altar with Kuan Ti and the "Mysterious Goddess."

The third small temple was erected by the village opposite the brewery to prevent some topographical changes made by that organization from affecting the *feng-shui* of the village—natural influences for good and evil. The shrine was dedicated to the dragon god, who was in charge of the waters and so could oversee and control the spirits in the pond dug by the brewery. The dragon evidently was doing his work well—so well, in fact, that no pilgrims came to worship at this temple and the building was badly neglected.

VILLAGE SCHOOL

The village school had one teacher and 22 students. It was held in some rather dilapidated rooms in a side building of the temple of the god of longevity. Before 1929 the village allowed the school to meet in the temple, but up to that time it was a private activity and the teacher was expected to exist on the fees paid by his pupils.

In 1929 the village was required by law to open a school. The village head, hoping to improve the quality of the school, arranged with the teacher that the village should guarantee him an income of $120 a year. If the tuition fees, which ranged from 50 cents to $5.50 per pupil, depending on the economic status of the family, were more than the $120, the teacher would keep the whole amount. If total was less than $120, the village would make up the difference. Actually the fees totaled only $35.90. In 1931–1932 the tuition fees and subsidy amounted to $89.50, and the teacher was importuning the village head to pay the rest. Besides the teacher's salary, other school expenses, amounting to $43.00, were $18.00 for coal, $14.00 for a new ceiling, $1.80 for matting, $2.40 for books, $3.60 for a special meal, and $3.20 for miscellaneous items.

In 1932, repairs of the rooms used by the school were paid for, in part, from a fund of $50 raised by the former village head among his relatives. Because this was a special fund, it was not recorded in the general village accounts. To finish the repairs and buy new tables for the school, $23 more was needed. As there was no money in the village treasury at the time, the $23 was advanced by six village elders who were reimbursed from village funds later in the year. At the insistence of one of the elders, the money was lent without interest.

There were no girls in the village school, but eleven girls were studying in a special vocational class.

VILLAGE ASSOCIATION

The village association, earlier known as the Green Crop Association, was a self-perpetuating group of village leaders. It naturally included those who, because of wealth, education, or personal influence, held a prominent position in the community. Members of the association needed to have considerable leisure, for they all contributed their services. The number of members was not definitely fixed, but once a man was asked to join the group he ordinarily stayed on until he died or retired.

In Village D it had become more or less the established practice for a newly appointed village head to recruit a new group of members soon after he took office and then make no more appointments. This was especially true in the 1920's and early 1930's when the tenure of the village heads was shorter than it had been previously. Thus five new members were appointed in 1926, three in 1929, and eight in 1932.

At the beginning of 1932 there were only five members and, before that, the number had been down to four. With the eight new members appointed during the latter part of the year, the total at the end of the year was thirteen. The new members usually joined either on the opening day of the crop-watching in the sixth month or on the thanksgiving day in the fall.

Descriptions of members of the association.—The members of the association were an interesting group. Two brothers, one representing the family that had adopted him, were sons of a man who had been village head for many years and had participated in village affairs for an even longer time. The family was not exactly wealthy, but had a long background of village service. Another leader was one of the rich men of the village who only lately had become an association member. His father had been the accountant of the village association, but not one of the regular members.

The richest man in the village had been an association member for many years and assistant head for a long period, but had retired because of age. Because his sons were away from home, his family was not represented in the association. A nephew of this man was a member, but he had no economic connection with his uncle and could not be said to be well-to-do. The father of another association member was an actor who had recently become rich and made this position possible for his son. Two other recent appointments were from families who earlier had suffered economic depression, but had recovered.

Other new members hardly fulfilled traditional requirements for association members. One had started life as a hired laborer and then become a peddler. Another, who had been a tenant farmer, had recently purchased land and hired others to help in tilling it, and this, of course, had raised his social status. Another member owned only a small parcel of land, and another was a renter. One member owned no land, rented no land, did not work on a farm, and was, in fact, said to be a vagabond who lived by meddling in the affairs of others. One of the newly enlisted members of the association was not even a native of the village. His prestige came from the fact that his brother was a brigadier general.

In age, the association members ranged from under thirty to more than seventy years. Two were in their thirties, four in their forties, five in their fifties. One was only nineteen years old when he first became a member.

The land owned by the members varied from none to 132 mu. The median holding was 29 mu; the average, 43.5 mu. Seven members rented out from 10 to 78 mu. Four were lessees of from 19 to 65 mu. The plots the members cultivated ranged from 5 to 84 mu. (See table 29.)

Before 1900 the village association had been concerned almost exclusively with crop-watching. Political matters had been handled by the ti-pao living in the village. The members of the association served in rotation as executive officer and treasurer, ordinarily for a one-year term. After 1900 a village head and assistant head were appointed by the members from among their number, to hold office for an unspecified period. When an officer gave up his post, he had to file a resignation with the hsien magistrate and have it accepted by him. After 1929 and the adoption of the Hsien Organization Act, the village head was supposed to be elected annually.

In 1926 the village association reappointed as head a man who earlier had held the same position. One of his first moves was to add five new members to the association, two of whom were his sons. One son represented another family, as he had been adopted by an uncle. The other represented the farmstead of an absentee landlord. Together the three attempted to monopolize control of local affairs and to force their opponents out of the association.

A crisis arose in 1929 when the village head spent an unusually large amount of public funds early in the year and then proposed a special assessment of 10 cents a mu. The families refused the assessment, and the opposition members in the association filed suit with the magistrate against the village head, accusing him of extravagance in his handling of civic affairs. Rather than hold an official trial, the magistrate persuaded both parties to settle the matter between them.

The pressure was severe enough to force the village head to resign, and he and his two sons left the association. The affair very definitely weakened the power and position of the village head.

When the association decided on a successor, he invoked the new law and insisted that he be elected by the village assembly as well as be appointed by the association. He was reëlected in 1930, but was replaced in 1932.

In the 1932 election two ballots were taken, as the man first elected declined to serve. There were 45 votes cast at the meeting. There was supposed to be universal suffrage, but actually the voters represented a family, a business, the temple, or a relative. No family sent more than one representative to the meeting. There were 27 family heads present and 13 persons who were acting as substitutes for family heads (3 wives, 5 mothers, one younger brother, one older brother, and 3 sons). The four shop-managers, who originally came as observers, were allowed to vote as representatives of the shops. The monk, who was present because the meeting was held in the temple, was given a vote representing the temple.

The hsien government was becoming more and more insistent that it be notified of the dates of village elections and that it have a representative present with ballots and ballot box to see that the election was properly conducted. Even so, the village head elected in 1932 fell far below the minimum requirements set by law; he could not meet any of the six conditions of eligibility.[1] His main failing was the fact that he could not read or write.

The principal and almost the only direct political control in the hands of the villagers was their ability to accept or reject the crop-money rates or the special assessments proposed by the village leaders. In Village D they refused the special assessment proposed in 1929, and again in 1933 they would not accept an advance in the crop-money rate from 30 to 50 cents a mu and forced a compromise rate of 40 cents.[2]

After the 1932 election the two men who, with their father, had been forced out of office in 1929 were reappointed as members of the village association. When he was thus bypassed, the father decided that the time had come for him to relinquish his position as family head. He divided his property between his first and third sons and lived with the third. The second son was not included in the property division, as he had been adopted by his uncle and so belonged to that family. Occasionally the father went to village association meetings, not in his own right but as the representative of his son.

Acting as a proxy, it was he who strenuously objected to the proposal that a special grant of $23 be given to the village school for the purchase of tables and chairs. Only after it had been explained that the amount was to supplement some $50 of contributions raised by the recently retired village head would he give his consent to the expenditure. Even then he insisted that the amount be advanced by the village leaders rather than be borrowed at interest.

Village accounts were regularly kept by a man who received a small salary or present for his work. In Village D this was done by the man who also was the village policeman. He received an extra $2 a month for his accounting services. When this man left the village in 1928, the assistant village head offered to do the work if he were paid the same amount. His offer was rejected on the ground that no village head or assistant head should receive money for his services. Because his offer was refused, the assistant head resigned. His successor did the accounting work, but without pay. He had two men working with him, one of whom served without pay. That man, a Mr. Liu, had come some fifteen years before from Shantung, where he had gained experience as a government official of low rank. He owned some 50 mu of land and was said to have an intellect much superior to that of the local teacher. He was an influential man in the village and thoroughly qualified to be a member of the association, but the fact that he was born in Shantung evidently barred him from that position.

While he did not have official position, Mr. Liu unofficially contributed a great deal of leadership to the village. He initiated and promoted the campaign to raise funds for the rebuilding of the West Temple. He developed a set of written bylaws for the village association, most of which were adopted. But Mr. Liu failed to win acceptance of his suggestion that the village finance its projects from two types of levies, crop-money and a special assessment. Crop-money was to be paid by the cultivators of the land in the village area, and half the special assessment was to be paid by the landowners and half by the cultivators. The shops would contribute only to the special assessment. Those who cultivated cemetery land were to contribute to both funds. The crop-money was to be used only for the opening exercises of the crop-protection program and for the wages of the crop-watchers. The special-assessment funds were to be used for the thanksgiving meeting after the harvest, for paying indemnity for crop losses, for the support of the night watch, for the maintenance of the temples, for road and bridge repair, for tree planting, for the travel expenses of the village officers, and for the armed forces. The village leaders rejected his suggestion with the plea that it would be difficult to change the assessment rules. Also, the landlords were opposed.

In the 1932 election Mr. Liu was chosen acting village head, but he declined the honor. He was also considered to be the best possible candidate for permanent village head, but again he declined, on the ground that his deteriorating economic condition made it necessary for him to seek remunerative employment. Judging from the reports, this probably was not just an alibi.

CROP-WATCHING

Wheat, which was planted on some 300 to 400 mu, was not given official crop protection. The head crop-watcher usually had two or three of his fellow workers help him carry on an unofficial watching program for which they would solicit contributions from the wheat growers. The amount collected was usually about 5 cents per mu, which would give the men from $4 to $5 each for about six weeks' work. Sometimes the village officials would help with the collection of the money for the wheat watchers, but this was not an official matter and the money was not entered in the village account books.

The official crop-watching program of Village D began with an opening meeting held on the twenty-fourth day of the sixth month, Kuan Ti's birthday. The meeting, organized by the leaders, was attended by representatives of all the families with land in the village area. As they came to the association headquarters in the Kuan Ti Miao they registered with the association accountant the number of mu they would be farming during the coming season. They paid 10 coppers (2.5 cents) a mu as advance crop-money in order to provide some working funds for the association and 60 coppers (15 cents) as mien-ch'ien, noodle money, for the feast that was part of the program.

As space and equipment were limited, the family representatives were served in relays at two or three tables set up in the temple courtyard. Any women who came as family representatives were served at a separate table. Those who did not stay for the feast were entitled to receive one catty of flour.

At the end of the day the members of the association, who had been busy with the details of the land registration and entering all the cash payments, went in a body, escorted by the second priest, to all the other village temples to burn paper prayers and incense before the altars, to pray for a bountiful harvest, and to ask for

help in protecting the village crops. Worship at the Kuan Ti Miao
was led by the head priest. When their duties were completed, the
members were given a second and appreciably better meal than that
served the family representatives.

After the twenty-fourth day of the sixth month the fields in the
village area were tabooed to all persons who were not cultivators,
except that on certain days fixed by the village authorities the people
were allowed to go to the fields to strip off the lower leaves of the
kaoliang and take them away for their own use. In 1932 the dates
for the leaf gathering were set for the fourteenth, fifteenth, and
sixteenth days of the seventh month. Gleaning privileges at harvesttime were also fixed by the village authorities.

The crop-watching was done by five men, each of whom was
responsible for a section of the village land. A sixth man, who was
the village policeman and the head of the village winter night-watch,
was employed as superintendent of the watchers. Four of the five
crop-watchers had no land; one, with 7 mu, earlier had 60 mu. One
watchman was also a shoemaker; another was a donkey driver; two
had been hired farm-laborers. Political connections evidently helped
in getting and keeping the crop-watching jobs. One watchman was
the maternal uncle of the assistant head of the village; one was the
brother of the village accountant; another was a relative of a former
village head. Such nepotism was the basis of the earlier quoted statement of an older man who said, "If they are not rascals, they are
favorites." One of the men had been a crop-watcher for twenty
years, one for eight years, and two for three years. The fifth man
had just been appointed to the job.

In 1932 each watchman was paid $15 for three months' work and
received $1 as a food subsidy. One report said they expected a
bonus of $5, but the wage account did not show it. If they caught
any thieves or trespassers, the watchmen were rewarded by being
given part of the fine collected from the culprit.

In 1932 an old crop-watcher who had been away from the village
came home. Since he was evidently in need, a former village head
helped get him appointed as an assistant watchman. He was given
$5 for work during the fall season. The total amount paid to the
crop-watchers that year was $103.50.

The watchmen evidently did a very efficient job, for we were
able to learn of surprisingly few thefts or trespasses. During the
1932 season only three thefts were reported. One was committed by
a boy who took a few ears of corn, the others by soldiers who helped
themselves as they went through the fields. Nothing could be done
about these culprits.

In 1930 one of the women landowners reported that one mu of her beans had been taken at night. Detective work on the part of the crop-watchmen led to the finding of a cache of beans in the home of a man who had no beans growing on his land. He was arrested and taken before the village heads, and at first he denied the charge, but finally admitted it when he was given the choice of confessing or being taken to the hsien yamen for trial by the magistrate. The case was settled by his paying a fine of $7 to the village and giving $4 to the crop-watchman.

Sheep-trespassing case.—The fields west of Village D were near the Peiping-Kalgan road and so were liable to trespass by sheep, cattle, and horses being driven to the city. In the tenth month of 1931 the manager of a mutton shop in the nearby town and his two assistants were driving a herd of 107 sheep down the road. Four of the sheep ran off the road into one of the wheatfields. The brother of the owner of the land saw the trespass and, with the help of three or four farm employees, captured the three men driving the sheep. After being beaten, the men were taken before the village leaders for formal punishment. Their plea that very little damage had been done was countered by the argument that it was the trespass, not the damage, that counted. Ultimately the fine was fixed at $25, to be divided $15 for the crop-watchmen and $10 for the village. Three men were sent with the sheep owner while he tried to get the money for his fine. The sheep and the other two men were held by the village.

The owner found only about $7 in his shop. He begged the watchmen to take that sum back to the village and let him bring the rest of the money the next morning. Since he was still short $7 in the morning, he took with him 10 catties of mutton and a sheep's stomach and pleaded that the village authorities have mercy on him and accept the meat as final payment. The owner of the field was given 24,000 cash (about $6) to be divided among his workers, the village received $5 (but it was not entered in the accounts), the crop-watchmen divided $7, and the association heads enjoyed the mutton and tripe.

Horse trespass and other problems.—In the fall the same man who discovered the sheep trespass found a group of horses in his kaoliang field. He went to the temple to report the matter to the village heads. By the time they reached the fields the horses had gone. Nothing was done about the matter until the fall thanksgiving day. Then the owner claimed indemnity for the damage done to his crop. To forestall further trouble the village paid him 75 cents.

In September, 1932, two men and two horses were apprehended

for trespass by a group of men from one of the satellite villages. A special meeting of the local authorities was called to deal with the case immediately. Fortunately the horse owner knew a man in a nearby village who would come and plead for him. The fine was set at $20 and was paid the next day. So many people were involved that it was difficult to arrive at a satisfactory division of the money. The final decision was to give 50 cents apiece to the twenty-three men who had helped capture the horses and $3.50 to the crop-watch-men and let the village keep $5.00.

With neighbors the authorities were usually less severe. When cattle from a nearby village broke away from the small boy who was watching them and came into the fields of Village D, the crop-watchmen who saw the trespass took the boy to the temple and sent for his father. As no serious damage had been done, the father was fined only $1.

A poor man caught stealing corn in 1920 was given a beating, but was not fined.

In 1932 the brewers declared that their shop had suffered $1,000 in damages from soldiers in 1926 and threatened that if the village did not do something about it they would refuse to pay the crop-money on their 400 mu of "land." The matter was compromised by reducing their annual charge by 30 per cent for a number of years. Others who entered claims for the 1926 depredations by the soldiers were paid $68.52.

THANKSGIVING CEREMONY

The crop-watching season officially closed with a thanksgiving meeting held after the harvest was completed. The date of the meeting varied with the season. The available records showed it coming as early as the tenth day of the ninth month and as late as the first day of the tenth month. The thanksgiving meeting usually marked the end of the association's fiscal year.

The procedure of the meeting was very similar to the opening meeting. The cultivators paid their crop-money and noodle-money, and enjoyed a feast. At the end of the day the village leaders gave thanks to the gods and then had another meal together. In 1932 they skipped the run-down Dragon Temple when they were paying their homage to the gods.

The thanksgiving meeting was a time when various problems that had been left unsettled during the season came up for final settlement —such as claims for crop-damage and arguments between the land-holders and the village leaders. There were two cases in 1932. One man lost 18 ears of corn and one of the women owners lost 50 ears. Both cases had been reported to the crop-watchmen, but they had failed to pass the information on to the village leaders. They excused themselves with the plea that the loss had been caused by soldiers. The landholders threatened to refuse to pay their crop-money unless they were given some compensation for their loss.

In 1932 the village head resigned at the thanksgiving meeting and the village leaders had to meet and elect an acting head to serve until an official election could be arranged. At the 1932 thanksgiving meeting it was proposed that the village have a special celebration with plays given by professional actors. The village was hard up and the price of grain was down, so the play promoters failed to get their idea adopted even though they spent most of a day at the temple attempting to persuade the village heads and the landholders.

The expenses for the thanksgiving meeting amounted to $23.28, almost 50 per cent more than for the opening meeting.

RATE OF CROP-MONEY ASSESSMENT

The records showed that in 1902 the crop-money assessment was only 8.5 cents a mu. It was 10.2 cents in 1911, 20 cents in 1923, 32.4 cents in 1926, 20 cents in 1928, and then 30 cents until 1932, when it was raised to 40 cents. The rates were set in terms of copper cash through 1927 and then in silver. The exchange rate went from 936 cash per dollar in 1902 to 3,760 in 1927. The rate for 1932 was 4.7 times the silver equivalent of the rate charged in 1902. (See table 30.)

The village leaders had tried to increase the crop-money payable at the 1932 Thanksgiving meeting to 50 cents a mu, as the village needed the money, but the landholders grumbled and refused to accept that rate. The villagers were so incensed that, in their daily conversation, they hurled abuse at their leaders. Anticipating trouble if they insisted on the 50 cent rate, the leaders compromised and set the rate at 40 cents a mu, an increase of 10 cents over the previous year. It was definitely a case where the group was able to exert enough pressure to force the village leaders, who usually were quite independent in making their decisions, to listen and accede to the force of public opinion.

Some days before the thanksgiving meeting the crop-money rate was announced as 40 cents per mu, or 8 sheng, pints, of corn for those who wanted to pay in kind. On the day of the meeting the price of corn was below 5 cents per sheng, so more than half of the cultivators elected to pay their crop-money in kind. This was a much larger proportion than usual. In 1911, however, 78.7 per cent of the families paid their crop-money in grain.

The village leaders had to get a wagon and go from house to house to collect the grain. The accounts, dated eight days after the thanksgiving meeting, showed that 10,001 sheng of corn had been collected and sold, part for 4.47 cents per sheng and part for 4.35 cents per sheng. There was also a loss of 36 sheng in measuring the grain. The total loss was $56.92.

The total crop-money income was $1,057. The land area assessed would seem to have been some 2,785 mu. The year before, the crop-money receipts were $883.68. This with the crop-money rate set at 30 cents per mu would seem to make the assessed area some 2,945. Advance crop-money was paid on 2,396 mu. Some under-payment at one collection and some overpayment at another would make the difference in the number of mu assessed.

VILLAGE POLICE AND GUARD PROGRAM

The position of village policeman in 1932 was somewhat similar to that of the ti-pao before 1900, but without the prestige that the ti-pao had because of his connection with the hsien government. The policeman had no uniform and no arms. He ran errands for the village heads, and summoned the village association members when-ever the head wanted them to meet. He was expected to receive and entertain any subordinate person or messenger who came from the district or hsien government. He could handle minor matters for the village at the district or hsien offices.

In 1932 the policeman was also the head of the crop-watchers, the night watch, and the local guard.

The 1932 salary of the policeman was set at $4 a month, but he was given an extra bonus of $12 at the end of the year that brought the year's total to $60. For his work as head of the crop-watchers, the night watch, and the village guard he received an additional $27.

The night watch was kept for the last three months of the lunar year by four watchmen and a supervisor. The field report said that they did not go beyond the end of the old year, because "everybody behaved better at Chinese New Year." The principal duty of the unarmed night watch was to mark the time, look out for fires, and scare away any thieves who might be about. The watchmen regu-larly made their rounds every two hours from seven o'clock until three and then the final morning round at four. Sometimes they marked every hour.

For their three months' service the night watchmen were paid $5 each. In 1932 the total wage cost was $24, since one man received only $4. Other expenses were coal, $9.38; ammunition, $6.70; and $4.67 for repairs to the watch room and the installation of a stove.

In 1926 the hsien government, because of disturbances in the Peking area, asked each village to organize a local guard. Village D put two men in uniform, employed them by the day, and had them ready to answer any call from the hsien government. Then in 1928 the village head and his son worked out a guard system to which all the village families should contribute. The contribution was to be one day's service or 100 coppers for every 10 mu of land. "Rich families," those with more than 50 mu of land, were allowed to make their entire contribution in money. Families with fewer than 50 mu were required to contribute at least one day of service unless there was no one in the family who was able to serve. This allotment brought out ten persons per day. They were divided into two groups who took turns making the night rounds of the village. If anyone failed to appear, he was fined 100 coppers, and also he had to put in the time later.

This guard program was carried on from the twelfth day of the seventh month to the twentieth day of the ninth month. By then the area had quieted down and the guard was discontinued. Later on, in the winter months of that year, there was renewed fear of robbery and banditry, and the village guard was revived. At that time three men were employed to serve under the village policeman. The four men were put into uniform and were armed with two guns that the village association owned and two that were borrowed. After three months the guard was again discontinued.

The accounts for 1931–1932 show the employment of three men as guards during the winter months, the village policeman and two others. The policeman was paid $2; the others, $3 and $8. Other expenses amounted to $2.08, making the total for the guard $15.08. The policeman was paid only $2 for his supplemental guard service because he received a regular salary for his police duties. The crop-watching, night watch, police, and guard duties were distributed among ten men. Only one man served in all four capacities. Five of the ten men participated in only one of the four activities, and three in two activities. The wages of the ten men ranged from $3 to $27, but only three men were paid more than $20.

OTHER EXPENDITURES

Other expenditures for village activities in 1931–1932 included $22.00 for repair of the temples and $28.30 for planting 80 willows and 5 pine trees in the sandy area behind the Kuan Ti Miao. The trees cost $11.50; the labor, $17.80.

Most of the $44 for supplies was for items purchased from the village shops. Some $57 of the $122 paid for items charged in previous years went to the shops. Another $53 was used to finish paying the expenses of the lawsuit whereby the village head had been ousted in 1929.

The miscellaneous expenditure reported by Village D was $65.96. This included 53 items costing from 10 cents to $3. Six items totaling $8 were connected with the collection of the crop-money which was paid in kind.

The hsien government had but little direct financial connection with the village administration. The land taxes payable to the hsien were assessed against individuals rather than the village, but sometimes the village advanced the money due from its people and later recovered it by issuing to the landholder a certificate showing the amount of tax paid. This certificate could be presented to the hsien tax office to satisfy the landholder's assessment. The village administration also forwarded to the hsien government the money collected for the army. In 1932 the total amount advanced was $125.

Relation of district government to village.—The district government had a much closer connection with the village. In general it was the intermediary between the village and any matters sent down from the hsien government. The district program evidently was developing in 1931–1932, for village representatives were called to attend some twenty meetings. Usually the village head was expected to go to such meetings, but the head of Village D in 1932 was so busy with his business in the nearby town that he regularly sent someone to represent him. The assistant village head, the representatives of the two satellite villages, and the village policeman-accountant were some of those sent. The village paid 50 cents toward the travel cost of its representatives. This would account for $10.50 of the $20.90 spent for travel expense. The "cart-money" for a trip to the hsien office was $1.50.

The district received a small amount of support from the hsien, but had to obtain most of its money from the villages. In 1931–1932, Village D paid $31.14 for the support of the district office and $37.54 for the district police. An item of $20 listed as a loan to the district office was reported to be a contribution rather than a loan.

The district police patrolled the Village D area, at least occasionally, for it was reported that they had surprised a group of the village leaders playing cards (i.e., gambling) in the temple and they had arrested one of the village monks for opium smoking. The monk was held for a time and released only after he had given a considerable sum of money to the police.

Military expenses.—The last item of expense, and in 1931–1932 by far the largest, was the amount needed to satisfy the army's requirements for forage, for the transportation of the forage, for horses and wagons, and for cash. The straw forage that Village D had to provide cost $33.39; its transportation, $45.50. Wagons and money together totaled $271.57. Part of the cost of the straw, $16.22, was repaid by the army, together with $3.06 for losses on horses and carts.

The army purchasing agents endeavored to buy the needed amounts of straw and fodder for the animals, but if supplies were not forthcoming, or if there was an extraordinary demand for fodder and carts, allocations were sent to the hsien magistrates and passed on to the districts and from the districts to the villages. Because a cart was a large item worth some $200, several villages usually combined to furnish one or two. In May of 1932 Village D joined with five neighboring villages to pay for one. In July Village D and six neighbors worked together for the same purpose. The other villages looked to Village D as their leader and asked its head men to obtain the horses, carts, and drivers.

The villages seem to have paid the owner for the cart and the animals that went with it and to have paid the driver some $30. If the driver was fortunate enough to bring the cart and horses back within a month, he would be rewarded for making a saving for the village. If he had to be away for more than a month, he would keep the cart and the animals. If he did not come back, or if he came back disabled, his family could not look to the village for help.

Borrowing funds.—The total expense for Village D for 1931 was $1,301. The income from crop-money, advance crop-money, noodle-money, fine for trespass, tuition from pupils, and refund from the army was $1,022. The deficit was financed by borrowing. (See table 30.)

During the year before, the village had to borrow $422 to provide operating funds. Of that amount, $162 was lent without interest by twelve different persons. Since the interest charge on the other $260 was only $18, the money probably was borrowed near the end of the year. The repayment of the loan and interest took almost 80 per cent of the crop-money collected.

It was only about three months after the thanksgiving meeting and the close of the previous fiscal year that the village had to borrow to meet current expenses. Between January 29 and September 4 the village borrowed eight times, for a total of $615. That year all the loans were interest-bearing, seven at the rate of 2.5 per cent per month and one at 2.7 per cent per month.

Three of the loans, totaling $175, were used for military expenses. Another three, amounting to $200, were used for village expenses. When the hsien government asked the village to pay the land tax in advance, $150 was borrowed, but only $60 was sent on to the tax office. Another $11 was used to buy stock in the People's Bank, and the rest went for village expenses. When an army general proposed that the village and the army coöperate in a road-building project, the village borrowed $90, but used only $52 for its share of the road expenses.

The terms of the loans ranged from two to ten months. Five were to become due in November, two in October, and one in September. The earliest loan was due September 24; the latest, November 29. The actual payment dates were between October 20 and November 11. Three loans were paid before they were due, three were paid when due, and two were past due. The total interest charge was $69.58, or 11.3 per cent of the total borrowed.

The four village shops lent the village a total of $215, about one third of the total. The four richest families of the village lent $180. Ninety dollars was advanced by a prominent family. Two loans for $130 came from outside the village.

The notes for the loans carried a wide variety of endorsements. One was signed by the village head and the assistant head; three notes were signed by the village head and the head men of the two satellite villages. One note was signed by all the village leaders and another by all the leaders, the second richest man in the village, and the assistant accountant. There were ten names on the note for the first loan of the year: the village head, the assistant head, three association members, the village accountant, two of the four shops, a former association member, and the policeman.

When the new village head, who was elected at the thanksgiving meeting in October, 1932, found in December that there was only about $40 available for operating expenses, he adopted an austerity program. The rate for a horse and wagon was cut from $2 to $1 a day. Expense-money for a trip to the district office was cut from 50 cents to 30 cents and from $1.50 to $1.00 for a trip to the hsien city. Tea leaves, cigarettes, and meals for the village leaders were eliminated. He wanted to raise the crop-money from 30 cents to 50 cents a mu, but, as was noted earlier, the most that the landholders would permit was 40 cents a mu.

When money was needed for expenses, some of the association

members wanted to borrow at interest, but the village head persuaded the shops and the association members to advance various amounts from $2 to $10 and in that way obtained $72 in interest-free money. Another interest-free loan, for $23, was made by four village heads to pay part of the cost of the renovation of the schoolroom and the purchase of desks. Another $50 used for that purpose came from gifts collected by the former village head.

If, after paying off the loans from the previous year and other immediate expenses, the village had any surplus money at the beginning of the new crop year, it was deposited in the four village shops in amounts somewhat proportionate to the wealth of the shops. In 1931–1932 the $112 so deposited was divided $60 to the brewery, $30 to the grocery shop, $12 to the clothing shop, and $10 to the salt shop. This system put the money where it would be safe and at the same time available for use when needed, which might not be the case if the money were lent to one of the well-to-do families. The village did not have a close control of the withdrawal of the money; the village head, the assistant head, the accountant, and even the policeman could go to the shops and withdraw small amounts or take commodities that would be charged against the village account. The use of the money had to be reported later to the accountant for entry in the village books.

XII: VILLAGE E

ALL THAT WE KNOW of Village E, located in the fourth district of Wan-p'ing Hsien, is told by the village account books for the eleven years from 1920 through 1930 and by the printed regulations of the Green Crop Association. The earlier years give a picture of village activities, income, and expenses during relatively quiet times. The middle years, 1924–1928, reflect the disturbances connected with the struggles of Chang Tso-lin, Wu P'ei-fu, Feng Yü-hsiang, and later the Nationalist forces for the control of Peking. The last two years, 1929 and 1930, show how local conditions affected the village financing. The Nationalists had taken over the area, and peace had been restored locally, but Feng Yü-hsiang and Chiang Kai-shek were still fighting farther south.

CROP-MONEY COLLECTION

The village ordinarily collected crop-money in both spring and fall. The dates varied somewhat with the season, but generally the spring payments were made in the fifth or sixth month, after the spring harvest, and the fall payments in the ninth or tenth month. For three of the eleven years studied there was only one collection, in the fall of 1921 and 1922 and in the spring of 1928. It was in May, 1928, that Chang Tso-lin withdrew his Manchurian forces from Peking. The Nationalist army arrived in June. The departing army forced the village associations to furnish fodder, transportation, and money. The $2,518 that Village E collected that year was more than 50 per cent higher than the largest amount in any previous year, almost seven times the largest amount for any year up to 1924, and almost nine times the village income of $281 in 1921. Eighty-five per cent of the 1928 expense went for self-defense and to the army; for the eleven years the average was 63.7 per cent.

The one assessment for 1928 was made in the fifth month, but in the account books it was labeled "spring and fall." The total amount collected was enough to pay $653 for the military assessment and more than twice as much, $1,376, for local self-defense. It also covered the other village expenses for the year and left a balance of $89. The village elders evidently decided that the extra $200 to $300 needed for the ordinary fall expenses would not add too much to the spring total and that, in view of the chaotic conditions, they had better be prepared for later difficulties and hope that the land-owners would get enough income from the spring harvest to meet the heavy and unusual assessment.

EXTRA ASSESSMENTS

In other years extra assessments were made to meet special needs. There was one for $100.84 in the spring of 1920, of which $100.00 was used for construction and repairs, $1.27 for police and self-defense, and $1.34 for office and miscellaneous expenses, leaving a deficit of $1.77. There were two extra assessments in the fall of 1924 totaling $331.56. The military took $293.00; construction and repair, $12.80; office and miscellaneous expenses, $10.00. This was an under-expenditure of $16.56. In the first month of 1929 there was an extra expenditure of $160 for police and self-defense and $60 for military and political purposes. No extra receipts were reported at that time, and the year showed a deficit of $185. That amount was covered by the receipts in the spring of 1930.

MONETARY UNIT USED

Through 1923 the accounts were kept entirely in terms of tiao, a copper monetary unit ordinarily of 1,000 cash. For the next three years part of the accounts were in tiao and part in silver dollars. After 1926 all the amounts were given in silver. The reason for the shift from one monetary unit to another was the rapid depreciation of the copper coinage from 1920 through 1926 and the consequent rapid increase in the exchange rate between the dollar and the tiao. In the third month of 1920 the exchange rate was 28 tiao per dollar. In the ninth month of 1926 it was 74 tiao per dollar. Every rate shown on the village books between those dates was higher than the one before. The detailed rates are shown in figure 12.

While the books were kept in terms of 1,000 cash to the tiao, the exchange figures, when compared with those current in Peking, seem to indicate that the tiao used in Village E was actually only 500 cash. The village rates were just about twice the exchange rates in the city. From 1920 through 1925 the annual average for the city went up from 1,410 to 2,855 cash per dollar,[1] and the village averages went from 2,885 to 6,150 during the same time. The wider difference in the 1925 figures, when the village rate was 213 per cent of the city average as compared with 205 per cent in 1920, was largely owing to the accelerated rate of increase in the exchange figures and the fact that the city average was based on a large number of quotations covering the entire year, while for the village there were only two quotations, one in the sixth month and one in the tenth month.

The use of the 500-cash tiao was confirmed in the printed regulations of the village Green Crop Association. In that document it was stated that 10 tiao were equal to 500 coppers, 5,000 cash.

The crop-money collections varied so from season to season and from year to year and totaled such odd amounts that it was not possible for us to find a definite land area and a series of rates that would fit the reported receipts. It was only after allowing for a varying amount of underpayment and some possible overpayment to cover earlier delinquencies that we were able to arrive at a possible series of crop-money rates that would show a reasonably consistent amount of land area sharing in the village expenses and to determine approximately the amount of land in the village "green circle."

Crop-money figures for other villages indicated that the copper rates were regularly set in multiples of 10 cash, while the silver rates were almost always in multiples of 5 and 10 cents. Assuming that this was true for Village E and also that the fall rates for 1929 and 1930 would not be less than the minimum fall rates for the 21 villages listed in table 15, we get a series of crop-money rates and the number of mu which, paying at those rates, would contribute the income reported for the twenty-two collections during the eleven years covered by the village account books. These figures are given in figure 13 and table 31. The copper rates ranged from 100 to 900 cash per mu. The silver equivalent of these rates went from a minimum of 3.5 cents to a maximum of 16.38 cents per mu. The silver rates went from 2 cents a mu for an extra assessment to 90 cents a mu for a combined spring and fall collection. For five of the eleven years the total annual assessment was below 14 cents per mu. For three years the total was between 30 and 40 cents per mu. For the three highest years, 1926, 1928, and 1930, the rates were more than 60 cents per mu, with the maximum 90 cents in 1928.

The number of mu, as determined by dividing the total receipts by the rate per unit, varied from 2,550 to 2,842. The average of the figures shown for the twenty-two assessments was 2,712 mu. The median area was between 2,712 and 2,732 mu; the eleven yearly totals averaged 2,722 mu. If we make allowance for overpayment in the collections showing the largest area, we can reasonably estimate that the village held somewhere between 2,700 and 2,750 mu of land under its control.

It is recognized that it would be equally possible to make another table similar to table 31 with the rates half those shown and with the area figures twice as large. To do that, however, we would have to postulate that the fall rates for 1929 and 1930 were 33.3 per cent or more below the minimum fall rate of the twenty-one villages listed in table 31, and that does not seem to be a reasonable assumption.

ANNUAL INCOME

The annual income of Village E for the eleven-year period, 1920–1930, ranged from $281 to $2,518. For five of the first six years the amounts were less than $380. Only in 1924 did the amount go over $1,000. The big jump undoubtedly was a result of the fighting in the Peking area. The next year, when there was no fighting, the amount was down 71 per cent. With peace temporarily restored, the village budget returned to a more normal level. Furthermore, a surplus of $53 accumulated from 1920 through 1924 made it possible to give the landholders some extra relief. The 1925 collection was only $296 (table 32). (In the tables and in this discussion all amounts are rounded to the nearest dollar.)

The military movements around Peking during the next three years meant high expenses and high assessments. As noted above, the maximum came in 1928, when $2,518 was collected. Even after the Nationalists took Peking, the village felt it necessary to spend, in 1930, more than $1,000 for local police and self-defense, and the amount of crop-money collected was just under $2,000, the second highest assessment for the eleven-year period. The military item was only $181, even though Feng Yü-hsiang and Chiang Kai-shek were still fighting.

The total amount of crop-money collected during the eleven years was $10,650, an average of $968 per year. For the first six years the average was only $447 per year; for the last five years it was $1,593, or more than 3.5 times the earlier figure.

VILLAGE EXPENDITURES

The village expenditures totaled $10,555, or $95 less than the amount collected. For seven years the receipts were larger than the expenditures. For two years the excess was less than $2.00—$1.81 in 1920 and $1.61 in 1922. For the last nine of the eleven years surplus and deficit alternated. With the fall crop-money collection coming after the harvest and at the end of the fiscal year, the village elders could estimate the total expenditure with considerable accuracy. The crop-money rate could then be fixed at a point where it would produce approximately the amount of money needed to meet the expenses and take care of any carried-over deficits. With crop-money rates regularly set in amounts divisible by ten for the cash rates and by five for the dollar rates, and with some under- and overpayment, the amount could seldom be exact. It was only in the spring of 1927 that income and expenditure were exactly equal, $266. For only three of the eleven years did the cumulative income and expense totals show an over-all deficit. One of those was only $5. The difference was always less than $140 and for only four years was the difference more than $50. In three of these four years there was a surplus remaining. The total year-by-year expenditure is shown in figure 16.

In table 32 the village expenses are divided into seven categories—crop-watching, ferry subsidy, school fund, local police and self-defense, office and miscellaneous, military and political, and construction and repair. Local police and self-defense accounted for exactly one third of the total expense of the eleven years. Another 30.4 per cent went for military and political purposes. Only one eighth, 12.6 per cent, was spent for the basic crop-watching. The village school received 11.1 per cent of the total.

If we take the total for five of the first six years, omitting 1924 when the requirements of the armies fighting around Peking upset the village budget, and then do the same for the last five years and include 1924, we get the following series of percentage figures:

Expense	1920–1925 (omitting 1924) Per cent	1926–1930 (adding 1924) Per cent
Crop-watching	23.8	10.4
Ferry subsidy	3.6	1.4
School	33.1	6.9
Self-defense	16.9	36.4
Military and political	7.1	34.9
Construction	9.6	1.4
Office and miscellaneous	5.9	8.6
Total	100.0	100.0

Self-defense and military expenditures totaled $407 for the five-year period and $6,308 for the six years. They rose from 24.0 per cent of an over-all total of $1,700 to 71.3 per cent of $8,885.

In 1926 there was a big increase, practically a doubling, in the expenditure for crop-watching and in the ferry subsidy. The crop-watching expense averaged $83 a year for the first six years, 1920–1925. For the last five years, 1926–1930, the average was $145 a year. Up to 1926 the ferry subsidy seems to have been $1 a month. For the next five years it was just under $2 a month.[2] Village E paid a subsidy to the ferry even though it was some 15 li (5 miles) from the river. The villagers had to use the ferry when they went to the neighboring hsien city.

The school expenditure did not follow the same pattern. The amount for 1930, $95, was only $15, 17.7 per cent, more than the $80 shown in the 1920 account.

The $2,981 spent for local police and self-defense in 1928–1930 must have been used, at least in part, for the purchase of arms for the village police. For the eight years up to 1928 the total was only $529 and in only one of the eight years was the amount more than $75. With the Nationalist forces in control of Peiping after June, 1928, and peace restored to the countryside, one would not expect such large local-defense expenditure unless it included a considerable amount for the purchase of arms.

The "extra" income entered in the 1920 and 1924 accounts totaled $433. The extra expenditure in 1920, 1924, and 1929 amounted to $638. It seems that the difference came about because there was no income to offset the $220 spent in the first month of 1929. The deficit was not included in either the spring or fall collection of 1929, but was more than covered in the spring of 1930. Of the extra expenditure, $353 went to the army, $160 to local self-defense, $115 to construction and repair, and $10 to office and miscellaneous items.

The published regulations of the Green Crop Association of Village E give a picture of the official basis for the operation of the crop-protection program of the village. Besides giving the general rules and regulations, they indicate the influence of the hsien magistrate, T'ang Hsiao-chin, who, according to the Village B report, was very active in attempting to improve the lot of the villagers in Wan-p'ing Hsien. They also confirm what had been indicated by the exchange figures: that the village monetary unit was a tiao of 500 rather than 1,000 cash. We have not been able to determine who paid the court fees and expenses of entertainment that Article 10 said would not be paid by the village.

REGULATIONS OF THE GREEN CROP ASSOCIATION OF VILLAGE E

The Green Crop Association of Village E, of the Fourth District of Wan-p'ing Hsien, has been organized ever since the Ch'ing dynasty. The original members were very coöperative and everything was in good shape. Gradually the membership has changed from a homogeneous to a heterogeneous group. Some members are jealous of others. Some do not care very much for the activities of the association. Weak families must pay their crop-money in full. Strong families may not pay even a single cent. The ruining and loss of the crops are neglected. Countless occasions of misbehavior have reduced the morale of the association to a ridiculous state.

Recently Magistrate T'ang has ordered us to reform and to reorganize all Green Crop Associations, and we have decided to follow his order. The reformation of the Green Crop Association is to protect the life and property of the people. No one can afford to neglect his property, which is the foundation of his life. No one can afford to neglect his crops, which are the foundation of his property. After we have reformed the association, every member must be coöperative and impartial in order to follow the good will of the magistrate and to protect our life and property.

The following articles constitute the simple regulations of the association.

ARTICLE 1. Every cultivator must report to the association the actual area, location, and number of plots in his farm, so that they may have the careful protection of the watchman.

ART. 2. Any report of crop-damage or stealing must be thoroughly investigated immediately. The loss of the cultivator will be repaid and the crop-stealers fined according to the regulations of the association and the decision of the association heads.

ART. 3. Any increase or decrease in the annual crop-money is to be cided by the association. Every cultivator must pay in full according to the announced rate.

ART. 4. Crop-money for both spring and fall seasons shall be paid not later than the market days following the thanksgiving day.

ART. 5. Each watchman is to be assigned a particular locality. Losses in his territory shall be deducted from his wages. Losses in greater amount must be made good by the head watchman.

ART. 6. Men with other business or duties are not qualified for employment as watchmen.

ART. 7. Watchmen are responsible for anything left in the fields after the grain has been collected. Losses of this sort must also be paid for by the watchmen. Watchmen are not allowed to ask the landlord or cultivator for any of the leftovers, unless they are relatives or special friends of the landlord.

ART. 8. When a crop-stealer is caught and proved to be guilty, he will be fined. If the sum is below 10 tiao, 500 coppers (5,000 cash), the watchman will be rewarded with half the sum. If the amount of the fine is more than 10 tiao, the watchman's reward will be specially determined according to the merits of the case. If the charge of stealing is not true and the proof is not adequate, no fine will be collected.

ART. 9. The wages of all the watchmen are to be paid by the association. No watchman is allowed to ask a landlord or cultivator for his wages. If such private negotiations occur, the association is not responsible for them.

ART. 10. If a crop-stealer who has been found guilty refuses to pay his fine, the association will take the responsibility of bringing the case to the hsien court. All expenses except the court fee and the expenses of entertainment will be paid by the association upon the decision of the association heads.

Registered members (heads) of the Green Crop Association.

[Sixteen names]

[NOTE: Five of the names were followed by the notation "not registered"; one was noted as "concealed." There were seven different family names among the sixteen heads listed, one name appearing five times, one name four times, two names twice, and three names once.]

XIII: VILLAGE F

THE LAND BOOKS of Village F for the ten years from 1920 through 1929, together with the registers for seven assessments made to collect money for the army from the ninth month of 1928 through the fifth month of 1930, provided us with a surprising amount of information about the village. These sources gave the number of families and name groups, the number of landholding families both resident and nonresident, the size of the family farms and how the size changed from year to year, the amount of tenancy among resident families, the crop-money and assessment rates, and the amount of delinquency in both crop-money and assessment payments.

FAMILY DATA

The village was a relatively small one, with only 64 families listed in 1928 and 61 in 1930. Presumably, three families left the village during a period of twenty months.

There were 11 different family-name groups. Thirty-eight of the 64 families, 59 per cent, had the same name. In the next largest groups were eight and four families. Five names were borne by one family each.

LAND REGISTRATION

The total number of registered resident and nonresident landholders changed every year. The number of resident families also changed every year and the number of nonresidents every year but one. The totals ranged from 84 families in 1922 to 98 in 1927. Fifty-two resident landholding families registered in 1920, 49 in 1921, 57 in 1927, 55 in 1928, and 51 in 1929. The minimum for nonresident families was 32 in 1924; the maximum, 45 in 1929.

The nonresident families came from eight different villages in 1920, but for the last three years of the ten-year period only four outside villages were represented on the land books of Village F.

Because of the annual changes in the number of resident and nonresident landholding families, the proportion of resident families changed every year, from a maximum of 63.6 per cent in 1924 to a minimum of 53.1 per cent in 1929.

The number of families with different amounts of land changed almost every year. During the ten years, 1920–1929, those registering fewer than 5 mu changed every year, from a minimum of 14 to a maximum of 21. In 1921 there was a decrease of 5 such families, 23.8 per cent, from the 1920 total. The number in the group holding 5–9 mu also changed every year but one. It went up by 13 families, from 23 to 36, in two years, 1926–1928, and then down by 9 families in the next year. The group holding 10–14 mu varied from 8 to 16; the group holding 15–19 mu, from 8 to 14; the group holding 20–29 mu, from 7 to 15; and the group holding 30–39 mu, from 3 to 8. In the 6 groups with fewer than 40 mu the numbers were the same in two successive years only six times out of a possible 54, nine years for 6 groups. (See table 33.)

There was but little chance for year-to-year differences in the groups with 40 mu or more, as together they included a total of not more than four families. The records did show, however, enough change to indicate considerable shifting in the amount of land held by these families.

The proportion of families with fewer than 15 mu ranged from 52.5 to 65.3 per cent. The figure was different every year, but in general it decreased from 65.3 per cent in 1920 to 52.5 per cent in 1925 and then went up again to 63.8 per cent in 1928 and 63.5 per cent in 1929 (see table 33).

With the number of outside villages represented on the land books decreasing from 8 to 4, the number of resident families registered changing every year, and the number of nonresident families changing every year but one, and with the changes in the farm groups of different sizes detailed above, it seems clear that there was a great deal of activity in farm real estate in Village F. It seems also that the farming families registered under their name the land they rented as well as the land they owned, and that probably most of the shifting was in the rented land. The reports do not give any reason for the changes.

The records for the assessment made in the ninth month of 1928 were transcribed to make possible a detailed study of the relationship of the resident families, their landholdings, the assessment rates, and the actual amounts paid by each family.

TYPES OF LANDHOLDING

An interesting feature of the 1928 assessment book was the fact that it listed the land under three headings—owned, held under mortgage, and rented.

The resident landholding families registered a total of 1,126.5 mu (about 188 acres), divided as follows:

	Mu	Per cent
Owned	582.5	51.7
Mortgaged	190.0	16.9
Rented	354.0	31.4
Total	1,126.5	100.0

Forty-one families, 64 per cent, owned from one to 236 mu. Twenty-five families held from 1.5 to 32.5 mu under mortgage. Thirty families rented from one to 100 mu.

The total family holdings ranged from one to 336 mu. The second largest amount was 61 mu. Only 7 families had more than 30 mu (5 acres).

The families with the different combinations of landholdings were:

Owner	12	Mortgagee	3
Owner, mortgagee	9	Mortgagee, renter	3
Owner, mortgagee, renter	11	Renter	8
Owner, renter	9	Total	55

If the mortgaged land is classed with owned land, the division of the families was as follows:

	Number of families	Per cent
Owner	24	43.6
Part-owner	23	41.9
Tenant	8	14.5
Total	55	100.0

If the mortgaged land is counted as leased land, the division was as follows:

	Number of families	Per cent
Owner	12	21.8
Part-owner	29	52.8
Tenant	14	25.4
Total	55	100.0

For the 55 families the average landholding was 20.5 mu. The distribution of the farms according to size is shown in table 5. It will be noted that 47.3 per cent of the families, those with not more than 10 mu, held only 14 per cent of the land. The 3 families with the largest holdings, all of more than 40 mu, held 39.2 per cent of the land; the one family with 336 mu held 29.9 per cent.

The largest group of families (38 with the same name) owned, held under mortgage, or rented 74 per cent of the land held by residents of the village. Three families in that name group had no land. One family rented one mu.

CROP-MONEY RATES

The village crop-money was collected in the seventh month in seven of the ten years, 1920–1929, in the sixth month in 1925 and 1926 and in the ninth month in 1920. It was reported that the crop-money charge was 10 cents per mu and that the proceeds were used primarily for the expenses of the crop-watching, but also for other nonmilitary functions and expenses of the village. The crop-money was collected from both resident and nonresident families. Unfortunately, we were not able to persuade the village head to let us see the cash books.

DELINQUENCIES

The books we did see showed that a surprising number of families were delinquent in paying their crop-money. The records of other villages and one of the special-assessment records of Village F had shown close to 100 per cent payment. It seemed to be generally indicated that, with the payments being made at harvesttime when the landholders would have money available, the influence of the village association was such that landholders generally paid without question. "What would the village do if a landholder didn't pay his crop-money?" seemed to be just a foolish question. In Village F, however, for the years 1920 through 1929 the number of delinquent families ranged from 7 to 34. The largest number was for 1925 and was 39.5 per cent of the families registered that year. There was a spring drought and crops were short. In 1926 the delinquency was almost as bad, 33.3 per cent. In both years there was fighting around Peking. In other years the proportion of delinquent families ranged from 8.2 to 14.8 per cent. For the collection made in the seventh month of 1928, very shortly after the Nationalist forces had taken Peking, the delinquency rate was only 7.5 per cent, the lowest for any of the ten years under review. We have no information on the amount of the delinquencies, only the number of delinquent families.

The records do not show whether the delinquencies of one year were carried forward to the next year and collected then or later. We feel certain, however, that most of the amounts were paid, even though an occasional family might refuse to pay part or even all of its assessment. The reasons for such refusal might have been that the watchmen had not prevented theft from their fields or that they did not have the necessary cash. Some families arbitrarily stated how much they would pay, regardless of the charges.

ASSESSMENT RATES

To raise money for military needs Village F levied seven special assessments on its resident families in the ninth month of 1928, the first and ninth months of 1929, and the first, second, fourth, and fifth months of 1930. An unusual feature was that different rates were assessed against owned, mortgaged, and rented land. Furthermore, there was a separate charge per family, so that every family in the village paid something, even families who had no land. The non-landholding families usually paid nothing toward the village operations financed from crop-money.

The assessment made in 1928, soon after the Nationalist forces took Peking, was by far the largest of the seven collections. In fact, it was only a little less than the total of the other six.

The 1928 rates were 55 cents a mu for owned land, 45 cents for mortgaged land, and 25 cents for rented land. For the first 1929 assessment the rates were 60 coppers per mu on owned land, 40 coppers on mortgaged land, and 20 coppers on rented land. For the second collection they were 35 cents, 25 cents, and 15 cents, respectively. The rates were the same for all four assessments levied in 1930—16 coppers, 10 coppers, and 6 coppers, respectively. Four coppers were equal to approximately one cent silver.

Every family in the village was charged 100 coppers, about 25 cents, for each of the two assessments made in 1929 and 20 coppers for each of the four in 1930. The 1929 books showed 9 of the 64 families as having no land. Five of them made a token contribution. Two paid 200 coppers each; three gave one tou of kaoliang.

The total assessment in 1928 was $494.37½. The actual collection was $494.50. There was no explanation as to why four families paid more than the amount due, one by as much as $1.10, nor why one family underpaid its bill of $17.75 by $1.90.

Only once did the assessment books show 100 per cent of the families paying something. For the other six levies there were from one to 4 families who paid nothing.

XIV: VILLAGE G

THE 1928 LANDBOOKS of Village G, in the Peiping district, gave a variety of information on the number, residence, and landholdings of the families registered, the crop-money charged, a special village assessment, and the delinquencies in both crop-money and assessment payments.

The village had 2, 154.5 mu in its "green circle." This land was registered by 140 different families, and 79 of these families, 56.5 per cent, were living in the village. The other 61 families lived in nine neighboring villages; of the 61 families, 22 came from one of the two nearest villages and 20 from the other. Three villages were represented by only one family each.

SIZE OF HOLDINGS

The landholdings of the 140 families, resident and nonresident, ranged from one to 80 mu. There were 65 families, 46.4 per cent, holding fewer than 10 mu; they held 17.5 per cent of the land. Seventy-six per cent of the families had fewer than 20 mu. Seven families, 5 per cent, had more than 50 mu each. Their total holdings were 19.9 per cent of the farm area.

Resident families registered 1,437.5 mu, two thirds of the total farm area. Their average holding was 18.2 mu. For the nonresident families the average was 11.8 mu. For the different villages in which the nonresident landholders lived the average holding of the families registered with Village G ranged from 4.0 to 17.1 mu per family. The difference between the resident and nonresident averages would be expected. Extravillage holdings were secondary for at least most of the families.

Women, probably widows, held title to the farmland of 5 families —at least, it was registered in their names on the village assessment books. These women probably were the heads of their families. All 5 farms were small, the largest having only 7 mu.

FAMILY NAMES REPRESENTED

The 79 resident landholding families in Village G had 25 different family names. There were 24 different names among the 61 nonresident families. Nine of the 24 names were included in the list for Village G, so there was a total of 40 different names in the total group of 140 families. The largest name group had 28 families. Seventy-two families, a little more than half the total, were included in the three largest name groups. Twenty-seven names, 16 of them in Village G, were listed for only one family. The high proportion of single-family names in Village G, 16 out of 25, suggests that there was a considerable amount of population movement in the Peiping area, with new families coming into the village and some branches of the old families leaving. The semisuburban character of the area and the confusion during 1928 and previous years could well account for this.

SPECIAL ASSESSMENT

In the summer of 1928 Village G levied a special assessment of one tiao, 1,000 cash (about 12.5 cents), per mu to raise money demanded by the armed forces. Collection began on the twenty-fourth day of the sixth month, possibly June 24, or about a month later if the village books followed the lunar calendar. Sixty-five families paid on the first day. By the fifteenth day of the seventh month 90 families had paid all of their assessment and 9 had paid part. But the total collected during the three-week period was 1,590.5 tiao, only 73.8 per cent of the total. In the fall 469.6 tiao, 21.8 per cent, was paid by 43 families when they paid their crop-money.

DELINQUENCIES

When the fall collection ended, there were 11 families, 7.9 per cent, who were delinquent in whole or in part on their assessment payments. Four had paid part of the amount due. Seven had paid nothing. One of the four was short only one tenth of a tiao. The amount unpaid was 93.4 tiao, 4.3 per cent of the total amount assessed. One family overpaid its assessment of 53 tiao by 16.6 tiao; possibly the family was paying up on an earlier delinquency.

From the dates of the collections it seems probable that the village elders had to borrow or advance the money needed to meet military demands and then collect it from the landowners when they had cash after the spring or fall harvest. As has been mentioned previously, the Manchurian army left Peking in May and the Nationalist army arrived in June.

CROP-MONEY RATES

To obtain the funds needed to meet its local expenses Village G made a crop-money charge of 20 cents a mu in the ninth month. Payments began on the tenth day of the month and were completed by the seventeenth, except for one family that paid on the twenty-third day of the tenth month. On the first day 118 families paid. Six families were delinquent: one paid all but 25 cents on an assessment of $1; the others paid nothing. Their farms had from 3 to 22 mu. The total amount delinquent was $10.45, only 1.8 per cent of the total due.

Thirteen families, 9.2 per cent, were delinquent on either crop-money or their special-assessment payments, or on both. There were 4 families delinquent on both, 7 delinquent on the assessment but not on the crop-money, and 2 delinquent on the crop-money but not on the assessment.

On the basis of the 2,154.5 mu assessed for the sixth-month collection, the fall crop-money total would be $430.90. The actual total, however, was $590.90. The difference of $160.00 resulted from the fact that four shops in the village contributed that amount to the village budget by registering, even though they had no land, a total of 800 mu in amounts of 50, 50, 300, and 400 mu. Their contribution was 27 per cent of the crop-money total. They were not assessed for the special summer collection.

XV: VILLAGE H

VILLAGE H had adopted, completely and wholeheartedly, the Nationalist village-organization program—elected village officers, arbitration committee, inspection committee, and finance committee and set up lin and lü, the groups of 5 and 25 families. The village had even gone a step further and started an adult education program. It was a village that, in the past, had been prominent politically as the seat of hsien and chou governments, and economically through its relation to the traffic on the Tientsin–T'ung Chou Canal. By 1933, however, it had lost both its political and its economic position. The government offices had been moved to another location, the canal traffic had disappeared, even the periodic market had been given up. The community had reverted to the status of a simple agricultural village with the local administration as the only political organization. In spite of these losses the field reports stated that Village H led in population, wealth, intelligence, and social and political organization; that it was the first to adopt new ideas and plans; that it was the recognized leader whenever there was need for joint action by the villages of the area.

Village H also was of interest as the home of a large group of related families whose original ancestor came north from Kiangsu Province early in the Ming dynasty. These families maintained a strong clan organization, with an ancestral hall, and they owned 144 mu of clan land. The male members of the clan met two or three times a year for a feast, the care of the family graveyards, and the worship of the spirits of their ancestors.

The village was located about 30 li (10 mi.) south of T'ung Hsien and some 60 li from Peiping. It was on the Peiping-Tientsin highway and was close to the Grand Canal. There had been a direct connection, for small boats, from the canal to the village moat, but it was no longer usable. The passageway had been allowed to silt up and several low bridges had been built across it.

HISTORY

In the early part of the Sung dynasty, during the decade 1021–1030, Village H was made the seat of a hsien government. In 1276, soon after Kublai Khan had moved his capital to the site of the old Yen

Ching and there built a new city, Khanbalig, or *Ta Tu* as it was called by the Chinese, the village was raised in rank and made the center of a chou, several hsien. Its added importance undoubtedly came from its connection with the greatly increased grain traffic on the Tientsin-Peking section of the Grand Canal, made necessary by the rapidly increasing population of the capital. Even before Ta Tu was completed, it had a population of more than 400,000 registered civilians. More than 230,000 tons of grain were transported on the canal in 1329.[1]

In 1372, at the beginning of the Ming dynasty, the village lost its chou status and again became a hsien city, in charge of 180 villages. Some three hundred years later, when the Manchu dynasty came into power, the hsien government was taken away and the village was then simply one of several in T'ung Chou.

In 1695 the chou magistrate, an official in charge of several hsien, stationed one of his assistants in the village to look after the canal traffic and to deal with local crime and disputes. That officer was continued until the revolution of 1911. T'ung Chou then became T'ung Hsien and, since most of the canal traffic had disappeared, no assistant magistrate was appointed to Village H. The district government of the hsien was located in the nearby market town.

Sometime during the six hundred years when the village was a hsien and chou city, a wall and moat were built for its protection. After the hsien government was moved away, little was done to maintain the wall and moat until the 1920's, when repairs were made in order to provide protection from the soldiers and bandits marauding in the countryside.

Trees had grown up around the moat until, from a distance, they completely hid the village wall and buildings. The income from the trees was allocated to the school. This took care of a large part of the school budget.

Contact between the hsien and chou officials and the village leaders was maintained through an appointee of the hsien magistrate, the *pao-cheng* (political agent or "local man"). His connection with the government gave him prestige, power, and wealth. Even after a village head, who ordinarily would handle all dealings with the hsien, was appointed about 1905, the pao-cheng still was able to ask the villagers for contributions after the spring and fall harvests and at the New Year. The villagers resented his requests, but did not feel they could refuse until, in 1922, his excessive exactions were used as the pretext for the organization of a group of villagers and their demand that they be given a part in the village government.

FAMILY COMPOSITION

The village had 375 families: 313 living inside the walls, 53 outside the west gate, and 9 outside the south gate. There were 254 *hu*—the courtyards and buildings reached through a gate opening onto a village street. Some of the hu had as many as five families living in a row of rooms all opening onto the same courtyard. There were 191 families who had their own house and courtyard.

The size of the families ranged from one to 32 persons. The total number of persons was 2,126, an average of 5.7 per family. The median family had 5 members. The size distribution is shown in figure 5 and table 8. Fifty-seven per cent of the families had from one to 5 members, 7.2 per cent had more than 10 members, and 2.4 per cent had more than 15 members.

There were two large family groups in the village. The largest had 69 families. It had a clan organization, an ancestral hall, and a long-continued family history. We have called it Clan X.

Clan X.—Clan X families ranged in size from one to 32 persons, totaling 509 persons.[2] The average family had 7.4 members. The median family had 6 members. For the non-Clan X families the range was from one to 18 persons. The average was 5.3, or 2.1 persons less than the clan families, and the median was 5 persons, or one person less. Forty-six per cent of the clan families had from one to 5 members, 17.1 per cent had more than 10 members, and 8.6 had more than 15 members.

The larger average size of the Clan X families and the fact that 12 of the 26 village families with more than 10 members belonged to Clan X would suggest that a very large proportion of the wealthier families of the village belonged to the clan. Some of our other studies have shown a definite relationship between size of family and size of family income.[3]

LANDHOLDING PATTERN

Since the village had lost its political and economic position, it was natural that agriculture should be the chief occupation of the resident families. The "green circle" or crop area of Village H contained 8,446.5 mu (1,408 acres), according to the land-registration books. Of the 375 village families, 274 were entered as owners or renters. They were farming 7,179 mu of land, an average of 26.2 mu per family. The distribution of the farming families according to the size of their farms is shown in table 5. It will be noted that 36.1 per cent of the families had fewer than 10 mu, 62 per cent had fewer than 20 mu, 74.8 per cent had fewer than 30 mu, and 85.8 per cent had fewer than 50 mu. The largest family holding was 270 mu (45 acres). There were 102 nonresident landowners, representing ten neighboring villages, and they held 1,267.5 mu, an average of 12.4 mu per family.

SHOPS AND MARKETS

There were 43 shops in the village—23 with shop names and 20 small shops. The 16 different types of shops and the number of each are listed in table 34. More than a third of the shops were handling food products.

Periodic markets were held in some of the nearby villages. Village H had succumbed to competition after 1911 and given up its market.

VILLAGE ORGANIZATION

The presence or absence of a hsien or chou government seemed to make but little difference in the local affairs of the village, which originally were looked after by an informal organization of village leaders, usually the heads of the leading families. The organization was earlier called the Green Crop Association, but later it was more generally known as the Public Association. The active members of the association were called heads or association heads. They were a self-perpetuating group. The heads of the five or six most influential families of the village ordinarily served as association heads from generation to generation although, technically, each new representative had to be invited to serve by the surviving association heads. New leaders representing other families were sometimes invited to serve, but their invitation came from those who already were members of the association.

About 1905 the form of organization was changed. The village association was required, by the higher government, to appoint or elect one of its members as village head and another as assistant head. The man chosen as village head at that time kept the position for nearly twenty years, until ill health forced him to retire in 1924. His son succeeded him. The fact that this family had more land and prestige than any other in the village undoubtedly helped persuade the association heads to elect the son to succeed the father, although at the time he was only some thirty years of age, much younger than the other village leaders. Even nine years later, in 1933, there was only one younger man holding a village office. After his appointment as village head in 1924, he held the office for the next nine years except for one year. It seems probable that sickness necessitated the appointment of a substitute for that year. He was still in office when our study ended in 1933, and there was no sign of his giving up his position even though he had to be reëlected annually.

Village H had three assistant heads, as permitted by the Nationalist government's regulations for villages with more than 300 families.

Before 1920 there were five association members. In that year a sixth was added. He was described as a private-school teacher and a writer of judicial papers. His help was needed at that time, for the village was competing with the nearby market town for the district higher primary school.

Until 1929 the representatives of only six families controlled the village association. They were the village head, the three assistant heads, the schoolteacher and a "silent member." Three of the six were members of Clan X. Three had succeeded to their position on the death of a member of their immediate family. Two succeeded their fathers. One succeeded an elder brother who had succeeded his grandfather.

In 1922 some of the village families joined together in an effort to force the association to increase the number of its members. They used the excessive charges of the "local man" as the pretext for their organization and action. They threatened to take the matter to court, but were dissuaded by a compromise which provided that additional association members would be appointed six months later.

Ju I Hui.—Disappointed by the compromise, a small segment of the opposition formed an independent organization, the *Ju I Hui* ("Everything-Satisfactory-to-Their-Will Association"). The first meeting, to celebrate the formation of the new organization, was held on the twenty-ninth day of the sixth month. The group sought to establish themselves as an independent group that would collect crop-money from the farmers and use it for local expenses under their direction. They did not, however, dare call themselves the Public Association or Village Association.

In a counterattack the village authorities sued three of the Ju I Hui members, charging that they had refused to obey the orders of the head of the local self-defense organization. The court papers also stated that the defendants had joined the Ju I Hui. The disobedience pretext was not pushed, but the hsien government did order the dissolution of the Ju I Hui.

The activities of the Ju I Hui gave the village leaders an excuse for disregarding their earlier compromise agreement, and no change was made in the village administration until the arrival of the Nationalist forces six years later, in 1928. Then the cry of the people's rights was heard everywhere. One of the village assistants, who wanted to get rid of the self-defense chief, joined forces with one of the leaders of the group opposed to the village administration and was able to exert enough pressure to force the association heads to yield to the demands of the people's representatives. Six new families were invited to take part in the affairs of the Public Association. Most of the new representatives were appointed as lü chang, heads of administrative units of 25 families each.

1929 elections.—In 1929 the Nationalist government issued its new regulations requiring that village heads and assistant heads be elected by the entire village. Village H followed the new orders, but the old leaders—the village head and his assistants—were able to manipulate the elections so that they all retained their posts. The other leaders were elected to the three-man inspection committee or the four-man finance committee. The schoolteacher and the "silent member," who were the nonofficeholding association members for the years 1920–1929, did not survive the 1929 election. The teacher had become the principal of one of the village schools, but it was the principal of the other school who was elected to the inspection committee. Seven of the ten chief village officers were members of Clan X.

Besides the ten men—village head, three assistant heads, and six committee members—who made up the central political organization of the village, there were fourteen lü chang who, as heads of units of 25 families each, participated in the village council and other activities. Two of the men in the central political organization were also lü chang, so there were actually twenty-two men with a more or less active part in the village administration.

Besides the election of village officers, another revolutionary change was the keeping of minutes and records of meetings, completely changing the old, informal way of carrying on local business.

Most of the village leaders were middle-aged and fairly well-to-do. The average age for the ten chief officeholders was 46.6 years. The average age of the lü chang was 50 years. The landholding of the chief officers averaged 103.7 mu. For the lü chang the average was 65.7 mu.

CROP-WATCHING

Crop-watching was the principal function of the village administration. Four watchmen customarily were employed for the spring season and eight for the fall season. Originally the crop area had been divided into four sections and the watchmen were to be responsible for any thefts occurring in their particular sections. Sometime between 1920 and 1933 the crop-watching and other protective functions of the village administration were combined. The four-section division of the crop area was eliminated, and the area was treated as a single unit.

At first "crop-money" was a proper term for the funds collected by the association, since the funds used only for the crop-watching expenses. Later other village services were financed by increasing the crop-money charge. The leaders of Village H evidently recognized the dual usage of the crop-money, and, since it was used to pay for services other than crop-watching that would in no way benefit the nonresident cultivators, they established two rates, one for residents of the village, the other for nonresidents who cultivated land within the village's "green circle." The nonresidents were charged only half the rate for residents and were exempt from special contributions and assessments. This differentiation in crop-money rates between resident and nonresident cultivators was very unusual. In fact, Village H was the only place where we found it. Ordinarily the villages charged all cultivators, resident and nonresident, the same rate per mu.

We were not allowed to see the account books, so are unable to give any figures on the income of the village or any details of its expenditure.

The spring crop-watching season was generally for one month; the fall season lasted for approximately two months. In 1932 the protection of the wheat crop started on the third day of the fifth month and ended on the second day of the sixth month. The fall season began on the fourteenth day of the seventh month and ended 52 days later, on the eighth day of the ninth month. The land was registered at the beginning of the season. The crop-money was paid at the end of the harvest.

It was said that the wheatfields needed almost no watching during the daytime, as the grain was not tall enough for anyone to hide in the field. During the fall season the fields required constant watching because of the height of the crops. The kaoliang was often more than eight feet tall.

Sometimes at night women would crawl along the ground and try to pick off ears of grain. If they heard the steps of the watchman, they would lie down and pretend to be asleep until he had gone. The gleaners needed special watching just before and during the harvest, especially during the wheat harvesting, which usually was begun about midnight and finished by noon of the next day.

Gleaning problems.—Gleaning the grain dropped during the har-

vest was a generally accepted activity, but it was closely connected
with crop losses, for it gave the gleaners an excuse to be in the fields.
One experienced watchman said that every cultivator had some loss
and that there was some stealing by every gleaner. Even though
every gleaner was a possible thief, there were dozens of gleaners and
only eight watchmen, whose time therefore was best used to keep
track of the "big hands," the known professional crop-stealers who
depended largely on stealing for their living. Many of these were so
ferocious that the watchmen were afraid to do anything to them.
Many villages had to hire the "big hands" as crop-watchmen to keep
them from stealing. Village H, however, was fortunate in having
very few of these professionals, and the villagers had few large losses.
Twenty losses were registered with the village authorities for the
fall season of 1932. Nine of the twenty were reported by Clan X
families. Even the village head was not exempt. Proportionately four
times as many Clan X families reported a loss as did non-Clan X
families.

There were nine losses of corn, five of beans, four of kaoliang, one
of peanuts, and one unspecified. The total amounts were 601 ears
of corn, 150 bean plants, 879 stalks of kaoliang, and a half-mu of
peanuts. The maximum single losses were 160 ears of corn, 54 bean
plants, and 380 stalks of kaoliang.

Fines.—According to common but uncodified practice, a crop-
thief, if he were caught, was liable to a penalty of ten times the
value of the stolen crops. About 1923, however, Village H was sued
before the magistrate for levying unnecessarily heavy fines. As a
result it had to take a middle course—fines which were not too
heavy to make it liable to criticism by the hsien government, but
heavy enough to deter the thieves. Usually the fine was a few dollars. One case was reported where it was $40. In that case the thief
was a "big hand" who earlier had broken into the granary of the
village head. He was suspected of theft because he was selling beans
in the market and it was known that he had not planted any. He was
followed to the fields at night and was caught taking beans and corn.
The village officers, to whom the case was reported, assessed a fine
of $40 and would not release the thief until he had secured five
guarantors who would be responsible for his good behavior.

In 1932 a widow was deprived of her right to glean at harvesttime
as punishment for an earlier theft from the fields.

Regulations promulgated by the hsien government in 1931 provided that, of the fines collected from crop-thieves, 10 per cent
should go to the cultivator to pay him for his loss, 20 per cent to
reward the watchman who caught the thief, and 70 per cent to the

village educational fund. In Village H, however, it was customary to omit the cultivator and give half of the fine to the person who caught the thief and half to the village administration. Sometimes the watchmen who were not involved in catching the thief shared in the half given to the apprehender.

Night watch.—The village maintained the customary night watch, but instead of employing night watchmen, the villagers kept watch on a volunteer basis. There were 120 men, divided into six groups of 20 men each, who took their turn every six days. Five men were assigned to each of the four village gates. Between tours they were quartered in a small house near the gate. At six o'clock in the evening each group was given five keng-p'ai, small wooden identification boards with Chinese characters burned into them. The gong, lo, and the rattle, pang, were sounded at the customary hours of nine, eleven, one, three, and five, when one of the watchmen made a tour of his group's quarter of the village. The number of strokes on the gong told the time according to the number of the watch. As each man finished his tour he sent his keng-p'ai to the village office to show that he had made his rounds at his allotted hour. Usually the night watch was maintained only during two or three winter months.

UNITED GUARD PROGRAM

An expanded local program for the protection of life and property was started by the village in 1920. That year a sort of collective training was set up, in which about sixty persons took part. Every family that had either modern or old-fashioned Chinese weapons sent representatives. Other villages followed the example of Village H and started similar training programs. Village H was elected their leader in organizing a federated protection program. Every night a number of volunteers went out to patrol the villages. It was noted that sometimes the volunteers were allowed to practice shooting. This was a special privilege, as ammunition was scarce and expensive.

In 1921 a united guard was organized by several villages under the leadership of Village H. Five armed guards were employed to patrol the united area.

District guard.—In 1922 the district government of the hsien organized a district guard and required the villages to contribute to its support. The united guard program had to be given up, even though the district guard contributed but little to the safety of the individual villages. The area to be covered was so large and the force was so small that the district guards either arrived too late to prevent trouble or were too few to handle the situation. Though the united guard was disbanded, the individual villages continued their own self-protection work, which generally was adequate to handle any petty thievery and to do preventive and detective work.

By 1933 the guard program and the crop-watching work had been combined and were handled by one group. The village employed four guards for ordinary months and eight for the bad months. The bad months were the fall-crop time. From the ninth to the twelfth month the guards were paid $4 a month. They received $5 a month for the first four months of the year and $6 a month for the four summer months. The yearly total was $60, to which were added tips at festival time and any rewards for catching or discovering thieves. The watchmen were expected to make good any losses caused by unapprehended thieves.

Volunteer guard.—Besides the regular hired watchmen, the village had a supplementary volunteer guard. Every family that had a rifle was required to send a representative for patrol duty. There were thirty volunteer guards, divided into six groups of five men each. During ordinary times they were on duty once every six nights. If conditions were tense, two groups turned out, and during times of crisis and possible disturbance by soldiers or bandits the entire guard kept watch every night.

EDUCATION

The education of the village children, the other main function of the village besides crop-watching and the protection of life and property, was carried on by one small private school of the old type and by the First and Second Village Schools. The First School had the first and third grades of the lower primary school program and the Second School the second and fourth grades, so that there was actually one school with two sections. Each school had one teacher. Ninety-three students were registered for the spring term in 1933. This was 4.4 per cent of the village population.

Teachers' salaries were $175 a year. This was considerably higher than the amounts paid to teachers in the neighboring villages.

Besides its lower primary schools, the village had started an adult education program with four departments—newspapers, books, lectures, and training.

The united higher primary school of the district was located in Village H, but was an entirely separate organization and was managed by a board made up of representatives of the villages served by the school. Village H was, of course, represented on the board.

A neighboring town was the headquarters of the district government and had a periodic market, and when the higher primary school was first organized, this town tried hard to get the school for itself, but failed when Village H offered to allocate the property of the Confucian temple—land, buildings, and trees—to the school and give a special subtsidy of $100. The needed repairs on the temple were made with labor contributed by the villagers.

TEMPLES

There were seven temples and also a monastery and a nunnery in the village area. The City Temple was dedicated to the local tutelary deities. There were additional temples dedicated to Confucius, to the dragon god, to the god of medicine, and to Kuan Ti, the god of war. Yüeh Fei (1103–1141), a faithful general of the Sung dynasty in their fight with the Nüchen Tartars, also had a temple. Yüeh Fei was long held in high esteem, but his deification was not completed until the time of Yüan Shih-kai (1859–1916). Finally, the god of literature had a temple and tower. The number and size of the temples pointed to the earlier wealth and position of the village. The large Confucian temple undoubtedly was a relic of the time when Village H was a hsien city.

CLAN X AND ITS ORGANIZATION

The homes of the Clan X families were largely centered around their ancestral hall, but some of its families were living in all sections of the village inside the wall and in the communities outside the south and west gates. Students from Fukien told us that in most of the villages in that province the ancestral hall was in the front of the village and the expansion of the dwellings of the different branches of the family was allowed only behind the hall.

Ancestral hall.—The ancestral hall of Clan X was a gray brick-and-tile building built around a court. It had some nine chien. In front of the hall was a courtyard surrounded by a fence. On the posts of the gate opening into the front courtyard were paper posters on which were printed couplets suggesting the idea that reverence for the ancestors helped one to gain felicity. The caretaker, a member of the clan, lived in the front rooms.

The ancestral tablet of the clan's first ancestor was in the center room of the rear part of the hall. It stood in a big shrine some eight feet square. Inscribed on the table itself were thirteen characters that read "Here is the spiritual seat of ***, our first ancestor, and ***, his wife." Before the shrine was a square table set with sacrificial utensils, an incense burner, two incense jars, and a pair of candlesticks.

The annual family feast was held in the room to the right of the shrine. The family heads often gathered to discuss clan affairs in the room to the left.

The documents belonging to the ancestral hall were:

The *chia-p'u*, a two-volume family history
Three volumes of memoirs of the past glories of the family and lessons
    for future generations
Twenty volumes of rent accounts of the ancestral land
Twenty volumes of accounts for the ancestral hall
The inventory of the equipment and furnishings of the ancestral hall

The account books of 1930 listed the following utensils in the ancestral hall:

5 square tables	1 wooden bell	1 porcelain teapot
2 painted tables	2 small trestles	4 porcelain teacups
18 benches	1 painted trestle	39 black bowls
3 lamps	1 blanket	19 dishes of various sizes
1 iron lamp	1 bronze pot	

In 1931 there were added:

5 square tables	2 chairs	1 wooden board
15 benches	1 sieve	1 cutting board for meat

The two-volume family history of Clan X told how the house of a family living in the Wu District of Kiangsu Province was destroyed and the family scattered during the devastation connected with the overthrow of the Yuan dynasty. In 1368 the sixth son of the family joined the army of the new Ming emperor and became a member of the expeditionary force sent north to the Peking area. After the fighting was over, he was allowed to register as a resident of Yen Chou, and he settled down in a small village some four li from Village H. He married a local girl and by her had three sons. They and their descendants continued to live in the area. It was the twenty-first generation that we met in 1933.

Clan X may have looked on Kiangsu Province as the original family home, but the immigrant soldier was regarded as the ancestor of the clan in North China and given all the honor and respect that went with that position. He was buried at the top of the first family graveyard, and it was his ancestral tablet that stood in the place of honor in the family's ancestral hall.

A member of the fourth generation of the clan passed the provincial literary examination and was appointed to official position. The family history stated that since then many descendants had been sent to study in the "halls of learning," while others were content to work in the fields.

One of the seventh-generation descendants of the oldest son of the original ancestor became a high official, and at that time the several branches of the family attained the peak of their prosperity. The official moved his family and many of his nearest relatives from the small village where the family had lived for seven generations to the nearby hsien city, which in 1933 was Village H. (In 1933 there were three Clan X families still living in the village where their original ancestor settled after coming north with the Ming army.) Being descended in a direct line from the oldest son of the founder of the family, the official was entitled to hold the family's ancestral tablets. He built an ancestral hall to house the tablets and to honor his original ancestor. He also decreed that the family memorial rites should be performed at least three times a year.

FAMILY HISTORY

From many scattered sources the official brought together and recorded the family history and its moral and ceremonial rules and regulations. The original work was completed in 1576. Eminent literary men of the clan were supposed to add to the family history every decade or so in order to carry on the story of the development and fortunes of the clan. Unfortunately, the last revisions of the Clan X history, made before 1933, were not well done and the record was incomplete.

The Table of Contents of the family history was as follows:

1. Origin of the family name
2. Family lineage
3. Village residential addresses
4. Choice of vocations
5. Official ranks
6. Literary degrees and honorary p'ailous—gateways—erected to honor members of the family
7. Honors conferred on official's parents and wives
8. Famous conduct (good officials)
9. Inherited portraits
10. Dates of birth and death
11. Virtuous mothers

12. Family teachings
13. Location of ancestral tombs
14. System of burial
15. Orders of sacrifices
16. Sacrificial prayers for different seasons

In his preface the original compiler of the family history says in part:

When I was in my childhood, with tufts of hair upon my head, I often asked, during the family gatherings, about the conduct of previous generations. At that time one of my great-granduncles of the fourth generation, who knew the family lineage very well, told me about some of the ancestral virtues so that I was often greatly moved and no small amount of tears were shed.

The chapter on family teachings is one of the most interesting in the history, as it crystallizes morals and personal relationships as of 1576. Translated, it reads:

1. REVERENCE FOR ANCESTORS.[4] All things are derived from the universe. Human beings are descended from their ancestors. Our ancestors have had the merit of giving us protection and the good sense to plan for our welfare. How can we remember them without reverence? If we take care of a spring, its flow is continuous. If we cultivate the roots of a tree, the branches and leaves will flourish. In the same way the rites of "tracing back" to our ancestors had their origin. A kind man and a filial son cannot bear the thought of unrequited favors. We descendants should wholeheartedly cherish this idea, so that the ancestral tombs shall be swept throughout all the seasons, sacrifices offered during the festivals, and worship given on the birth and death anniversaries of our ancestors. All these must be done in a sincere and humble way, paying respect to the ancestors as though they were living. That is the real reverence for ancestors.

2. FILIAL PIETY TOWARD PARENTS. Our body, including our hair and skin, is inherited from our parents. The connection is so close that the affection of parents toward their children and of children toward their parents is almost instinctive. An ancient proverb says, "One who does not live harmoniously with his parents is ashamed to be a man, one who does not obey his parents is ashamed to be a son." Another proverb continues: "One who loves others but not his parents is a man without virtue." Judging from these sayings, the first principle of being a man is to be filial to one's parents. This is the reason why, in other books, the sages record filial piety as the most significant virtue and the emperors commend it as the most important feature of human behavior. We

descendants should strictly follow this illustrious lesson, so that we can enjoy happiness during prosperity and be complacent if poverty is our lot. In the time of moral tranquility we must do our best to make our parents joyful and cheerful. In the time of moral disorder we must give them our best advice in order to keep them from falling into sin. From the humblest to the greatest, by obedience to the commands of our parents we shall reflect glory on them. At all times our conduct should be never failing in virtue. If, from one generation to the next, the rules and rites that have been hitherto established are reënforced over and over again, happiness and cheerfulness will be preserved forever.

3. CHOICE OF VOCATIONS. People in this world almost always choose some sort of vocation. In spite of occupational differences their aim is much the same, to work in order to live. The first and highest profession is that of the scholar. Next in order are the farmers, artisans, and merchants. All these men are industriously working toward the goal of success. Chü Hui-yen, without considering himself a scholar, says: "Those who engage themselves in studying will be famous in the halls of learning; those who engage themselves in agriculture will possess much grain; those who engage in manual labor will be skillful in handiwork; those who engage themselves in business or exchange will acquire much money and goods. Since all of them divide their work and interests, they will live their lives peacefully and happily in coöperation. Otherwise an unemployed man may become an outlaw, respecting neither virtue nor law." If it should happen that one of us remains without a vocation, it would be a serious disgrace for our ancestors. Let us take this as a lesson! Let us take this as a lesson!

4. HONOR GIVEN TO ELDER BROTHERS. Tradition says: "No human relation is more intimate than that of brothers, owing to the fact that they are derived, bone and meat, from the same parents." To love and honour our elder brothers is instinctive. It is a rule which can be applied to the four corners of the world. When brothers live together after marriage, they often misunderstand each other in trivial matters. Bit by bit, because they cannot but put deep confidence in their wives, open conflict results. Believing that love between brothers is instinctive and has a physical relationship just like that of "hand and feet," how can we let it be broken by intimacy with women taken in marriage from other clans, bearing different surnames? Is this not a valuable lesson which all of us should take to heart? If anyone unfortunately becomes involved in unfriendliness, his brothers, in order to preserve the moral obligations of kinship, should forgive him by recalling their gratitude to their parents instead of listening to the murmurs of their wives.

5. CONCORD AMONG KINSMEN. I greatly admire the record which states that Emperor Yao harmonized nine clans as the basis of a peaceful cul-

ture, but I wonder whether this condition has ever existed since then. It is a fact that the greater the increase of population within the clan, the more diversity of personality and character there will be and the greater the difference of conduct and behavior. Some of the people who cling firmly to the sense of egotism will struggle, with might and main, to have power over others. Some of the ignorant and dull will treat their kinsmen as travelers or strangers and without sympathy. Since the ancient patriarchal association has been abandoned, the clan can seldom be harmonious! Ch'eng Ming-tao, a prominent scholar of the Sung dynasty, wished to preserve the ancient association and advanced the argument that during the happy and joyful occasions, such as birth, marriage, the ceremony of capping,[5] the worship of ancestors, etc., and in the time of misfortune, such as death and mourning, the kinsmen should mutually associate with each other in order to keep the relation of "bone and meat" within the clan. I hope that our descendants will follow this valuable teaching, respecting our elders when they associate with them, loving their kinsmen when thinking with gratitude of our progenitor. In this way we will find concord among our kinsmen and our patriarchal line will stretch downward forever without end.

6. CONFIDENCE IN THE VILLAGERS. The villagers who live near us are our neighbors. We can see each other daily in and out of our homes. We know each other very well. Owing to the intimacy of our relationships, friendliness, confidence, and mutual respect should be the observed rules. Men in higher position should not be allowed to mistreat those beneath them, nor the noble be permitted to lord it over the low, the rich over the poor, the strong over the weak, and, last, but not least, the intelligent over the ignorant. Confucius, faithfully confiding in his fellow villagers, is a worthy example. Looking at his trusted action, should we not tread in his steps?

7. PROPER EDUCATION OF CHILDREN. A proverb says: "The transmission of glory from one generation to another depends upon the offspring of the line." Since the children, who succeed to the family worship and inherit the ancestral property, have the responsibility of reflecting luster on their forefathers and enriching their offspring, their education becomes a matter of vital significance. Education does not mean that each child is expected to attain to literary rank or high officialdom, but rather that instruction should be given to each according to his nature. Those who are sufficiently intelligent should be encouraged in the "halls of learning," hoping that they can be useful to both the family and the nation. The less intelligent ones should be instructed to embark on various occupations, agriculture, manufacturing, and commerce. Each should specialize in one vocation, doing it properly and in accord with the stipulated rules. Moreover, each one should associate with the right persons to prevent

his indulging in profligacy. When education is not proper, the vicious nature of the child, like that of a running horse without a bridle, will freely expand, so that he will be doomed to failure.

8. ASSIDUITY AND FRUGALITY. The prosperity of one's family is hard to maintain. Our sages often say: "To tread on the road of success is more difficult than to climb up to heaven, but to upset one's fortune is easier than to burn a hair." I say that laziness and extravagence are the cause of failure, assiduity and frugality the roots of family prosperity. The diligence and frugality of our great sage Yü, from whom his posterity received great good fortune, may serve as an excellent example. The prodigality and lavishness of Mr. Ma, of Honan, who died of starvation and without burial, should be an object lesson to us all. We descendants should toil early and late, exerting our energy with might and main, in order to secure a livelihood. We should expend our resources with care, in order to preserve them. If we keep this in mind, from beginning to end, we can emerge from starvation, obscurity, poverty, and misfortune and attain the state of sufficiency, enrichment, happiness, and renown.

9. DIVISION OF LABOR BETWEEN HUSBAND AND WIFE. Our late princes have instructed us how to live harmoniously in a family. The husband should deal with external matters, the wife with the management of affairs within the family. This is why the division of labor is based on the principle of sexual differences and familial obligations. In ancient times, when the family tradition was solemn and calm, and order strict and stern, peace reigned. Nowadays the family traditions are upset. The wife may have the louder voice and her husband may surrender to her will. This will become an object of adverse criticism. Can it last long? On this account, we descendants should practice moral duties in order to set an example of dignified manners. Orders should be given that no indolence is to be allowed and that family justice is to be upheld. In the end, when husband and wife fulfill their respective duties, an illustrious family will be the result.

10. MARRIAGE TO BE MADE AFTER CAREFUL SELECTION. As a general rule, both men and women, when they reach the stage of maturity, wish to have a family. Marriage, according to the Chinese principle, is contracted for the sake of a beneficial combination between two surnames, or at least between two "greater families." In many cases, however, when consultations are initiated in regard to marriage, both of the contracting parties consider the property of the other rather than their education, but marriage for money only is not to be allowed. In point of fact, the more greedy the expectation, the greater will be the possibility of disagreement or a feeling of animosity. Nay, more, and without exaggeration, a person without education will be a bad blot on the family's reputation. One of our former sages says: "In taking a wife one should see that her family

is inferior, and in promising a daughter in marriage, one should see that her future husband's family is superior." What he means is that such an arrangement will enable a woman to walk in the path of female morality. I want to say, however, that our daughters will be given only to suitable sons-in-law. No suitor will be accepted if he is physically unfit, even if he is rich in property. When choosing a wife, we should select her from a family where education is practiced, even though her family may not be rich. Matrimony based only on property will be like the behavior of savages among whom marriage is by capture or purchase. I do hope that our descendants will take this to heart.

11. CHARITY TO WIDOWERS, WIDOWS, AND ORPHANS. Governmental care is extended first to those who are widowers, widows, and orphans. A kind man will, first and foremost, do good to his kindred. During the Sung dynasty Fan Wen-cheng set up "righteous farms" to support his kinsmen, who, even to this day, enjoy and respect his righteousness. The population of our clan has steadily increased. There are some widowers, widows, and orphans without any support. Remembering that we are descended from the same ancestor, we should, with deep sympathy, extend charity to them, according to our condition and ability. During the cold of winter or the heat of summer their needs should be helped. At times of marriage or burial our assistance is needed. Although we cannot eternally plan for our kinsmen, as did Mr. Fan, we can at least help them in time of emergency. When this is done, our ancestors in heaven will smile at last.

12. GRATITUDE TO SERVANTS. Generally speaking, a man of fortune wishes to employ servants, but it is very difficult to treat properly a person of low degree. If you treat them without gratitude, they can seldom serve you loyally. Mr. Chü of the Sung dynasty, who was quoted above, advised his son, when he sent a servant to accompany him, "The servant is also the son of a man; you must treat him well." As a matter of fact, employers will first take notice of their servants' hunger and obscurity, then spare their energy, and, last, but not least, treat them with grace in order to make them peaceful. They should be encouraged in their daily work-time and again in order to stimulate their assiduity. When an act of deception is discovered, a clear announcement of the matter should be made and a light punishment given in order to make them repent. In this way the enforcement of authority over them will not result in resentment and murmuring. In addition, they will serve willingly. On the other hand, if one treats them cruelly and without gratitude, no loyalty and faithfulness can be expected.

13. AVOIDANCE OF LITIGATION. Litigation, when unavoidable, is unfortunate. When a case is taken to court, one cannot be easily excused before the law. I have seen many a man, who started litigation on a host of

trumped-up charges, lose face before the court, spend all his property, and at last be taken to prison. If he could have forborne his rage for a moment, would he have come to such a terrible end? We descendants of the same family should endure to the very last in case any trouble arises between us and our family. Being a man, I prefer forgiving others to being forgiven by them. If those who are troublesome come to annoy us, we should treat them as though they were mad. In this way our munificence and benevolence will be rewarded by good fortune forever.

14. SEIZURE OF PROPERTY NOT ALLOWED. We have learned time and time again that a kind man feels very much concerned about gain acquired without labor and ashamed of unexpected good fortune. How dare we occupy the things that belong to others? I have often seen many a man plotting to get possession of the fields near his farm and seizing houses near his dwelling place. Then, no sooner was his death announced than all the property was taken back by the former owners, leaving only his bad name behind. As a matter of fact, the property of others is just like our own. How do we feel and react when our property is being taken? Should we be selfish? Even when property must be sold under unavoidable circumstances, a right balance or measurement is required in order to maintain justice. It is not fair for us to speculate at the time of our neighbor's misfortune and emergency. Thus, when justice is upheld, our property will be inherited and last a long time.

15. CAUTIONS TO BE OBSERVED AGAINST LASCIVIOUSNESS. Husband and wife consummate marriage for the purpose of begetting offspring who will inherit the family property and observe the family worship. The system of monogamy has generally been practiced by the common people, but many a wanton takes as many concubines as possible. As a result, suspicion and animosity are engendered on the one hand and shortness of life on the other. In addition, lasciviousness gives rise to adverse and shameful criticism. We descendants should take this as a lesson! If we have no heir and are certain that it will preponderately benefit us to take concubines, we should keep the relationships between our wife and our concubines in proper order in accordance with the family regulations. No favoritism is to be permitted that might break the moral obligation of the family.

16. CAUTION IN REGARD TO SECOND MARRIAGE. To marry a second time is not what a man wishes, but, after his wife's death, it is requisite that he marry again in order to beget offspring. He who is in his prime will mate with a younger woman. He who has grown older will take a worthy woman of about the same age. Do not unite in wedlock a fully grown man with a fresh and young woman, lest she cause great trouble after his death. Moreover, a woman of a specially subtle nature may be made even worse by marriage. She may become a very jealous woman. If a

man marries such a woman, he will unconsciously become biased in her favor and an open conflict between "bone and meat" will result. If anyone of our clan has a case like this, the head of his branch of the family should, according to the judgment of the family history, initiate a trial against him and he will be condemned.

17. HUMILITY AND FORBEARANCE. Pride or arrogance is the greatest among all the vices of human nature, rage or fury the severest among the seven emotions. Thousands of types of sin, hundreds of kinds of wounds, have arisen from both pride and rage. For this reason humility should take the place of arrogance, forbearance the place of fury. As a matter of fact, when one lives in a meek and humble way, forbearance will be observed in associating with others and success will be assured. Chou Kung was polite to the common people. Lü Shih-ta, of the T'ang dynasty, said that when one spits in your face, let the spittle dry without wiping it away. From these examples we can see how liberal and broad-minded these two great men were. We descendants should observe these two words, humility and forbearance. Then no disaster will come to us.

18. ENCOURAGEMENT OF REPUTATION AND CHASTITY. When the virtue of chastity was encouraged during the Eastern Han dynasty, a group of famous scholars appeared. In the time of Tsin the people turned to vain talk and the younger generation, learning from their elders, became extravagant. Persons of good reputation and chastity are primarily formed by their environment. Having been an official in various places, I have seen many an illustrious family or great clan that observed strict family regulations and maintained an ancestral hall in which the virtues of reputation and chastity were encouraged from the highest to the lowest, from the noble to the mean. Greedy officials were not allowed to enter the ancestral hall, even though they might be of the fourth rank or above. Those who broke the clan morality were kept out. We saw only the famous and honorable kinsmen, not the extravagant or the adulterous. I greatly admire such an illustrious family and great clan, so I make this record in order to admonish our descendants forever.

CH'ING MING ASSOCIATION

Clan affairs and the clan hall were looked after by the family's Ch'ing Ming Association, which, in 1933, consisted of fifteen family heads, chosen from the different branches of the family so that every branch had a voice in the clan affairs. Some fifty years earlier there were only nine members in the ancestral hall organization. The increase from nine to fifteen members was brought about by the increase in the clan and the greater diversity of family lines.

The fifteen family heads were divided into five groups of three each. Each group, in rotation, took charge of the clan affairs for one year and so served every five years. The term of office of each group was from the day after the Ch'ing Ming spring festival to Ch'ing Ming the next year. The names of the heads and the time of their service were shown on a list that hung on the wall beside the shrine. In 1933 there were three new names on the list. Two were replacements for deceased members and one for a member who had retired.

The rotation of the groups meant that the clan accounts would be scrutinized by each group as they took over the responsibility for the coming year. It also gave the clan an opportunity for training its leaders.

The worship of the clan ancestors before the ancestral tablet in the hall and at the tombs was the primary function of the Ch'ing Ming Association, but it also undertook social, civic, and educational matters. About 1923 the clan organized a school for the clan children. It was held in the ancestral hall and was supported by the income from the clan lands. The salary of the teacher was reported as $120 a year. The incidental expenses were some $20. Three supervisors were appointed by the clan leaders to look after the school. It was carried on for about five years and then given up when the village school was organized.

Through the years land had been acquired by the clan, usually by gift from wealthy members. The land book for 1932 showed 37 different pieces, with a total of 144 mu. The individual pieces varied in size from one to 10 mu. Almost half were not more than 3 mu (half an acre) and only five were more than 6 mu. The total rent amounted to $316.58, an average of $2.20 per mu. The rent of the individual pieces was from 80 cents to $4 a mu. Four families rented two pieces and one had three. Twelve pieces totaling 55 mu were rented to non-clan families. There were seven pieces, 35.5 mu, on which 10 per cent interest was charged. The total interest was $10. No reason was given for the charge.

Ordinary affairs of the ancestral hall and the clan were handled by the three heads of the Ch'ing Ming Association, but assemblies of the clan could be called at any time. They were loosely organized meetings for discussion, but, it was reported, all resolutions had to be passed unanimously. The carrying out of the resolutions was the responsibility of the current heads of the Ch'ing Ming Association.

The record of an assembly in 1931 showed the adoption of three resolutions:

The utensils of the ancestral hall were for the exclusive use of members of the clan. They could not be loaned to families with a different surname. Clan members could borrow them to use for weddings and funerals.

The Ch'ing Ming feast at the tombs was to be abolished, beginning in 1932.

Rent for the ancestral lands was to be collected during the Ch'ing Ming festival.

Ancestor worship.—The worship of the ancestors in the ancestral hall and at the tombs was the chief function of the Ch'ing Ming Association. There were three seasons for sacrifice and worship: Ch'ing Ming, which came in April, 106 days after the winter solstice; the Spirit Festival,. the fifteenth day of the seventh month; and Han Chieh, the Cold Festival, the first day of the tenth month.

In the clan history it was written:

The rites of cleaning the tombs have their root in the feeling of filial piety. Spring and fall are the seasons which stimulate our feeling of gratitude. Sacrifice in the spring should be performed no later than Ch'ing Ming, and that in the fall should be made no later than the first day of the tenth month. This regulation must be enforced and no negligence allowed.

In 1933 the sacrifices for the Spirit Festival and the Cold Festival were offered by only a few of the family heads. Paper money was burned for the Spirit Festival and paper clothes were burned for the Cold Festival. It was thought that the spirits of the ancestors would be cold if the clothes were not sent. The paper clothes were burned at the tombs of the later ancestors, not at the three oldest graveyards. Evidently the older ancestors were thought to have a complete wardrobe.

Ch'ing Ming activities.—The Ch'ing Ming services and activities lasted for two days; on the day before Ch'ing Ming an offering of food was set out on the table before the main shrine in the ancestral hall. Every family sent at least one man to the meeting. All those attending the services were expected to make obeisance before the shrine of the oldest ancestor, but it was reported that the practice was only loosely observed and that more and more of the participants were omitting this part of the program.

After dining together, the group went to the family graveyard to clean off the weeds and thorns that had grown over the tombs and to repair any damage that had occurred during the year.

On Ch'ing Ming itself the men and boys of the clan gathered for a feast at the ancestral hall and then set out for the family grave-

yards. They went in a long line of carts, about a score of them. No
women or girls took part in the services. At the graveyard the boys
ran about and played with their cousins while their elders set out the
feast they had brought for the ancestors. It included a pig, five bowls
of delicacies, and four bowls of bread.

The service at the grave began with the shooting off of firecrackers. Incense was lighted and paper money was burnt. The paper
money was of three kinds: in the shape of gold and silver ingots, in
sheets printed with the image of Buddha, and in sheets perforated
to resemble strings of cash. The first two kinds were burned, and
a sheet of the perforated cash paper was put on the top of each tomb.
This showed the family's pride in its ancestors and told all passers-by
that sacrifices had been offered.

During the service it was customary to burn a written paper
prayer before the tomb, but in some cases, instead of burning the
written prayer, some of the older men prayed orally to the ancestors,
asking them to grant security and prosperity.

Ordinarily the sacrifices to the ancestors followed the order of
succession or descent. The clan record stated:

Sacrifice should first be offered in the graveyard of the oldest ancestors
and then performed in the order of succession, because a son should not
enjoy the sacrifice before his father. On this account no one is allowed
to offer a sacrifice to parents before making the offering to the remote
ancestors. If any one does not follow this rule, although he offers delicacies, it is deemed unfilial. Not only will our ancestors refuse to enjoy the
sacrifices, but punishment or misfortune will be the result.

Although theoretically this was a sound rule, it was often disregarded by the country people. In 1933 the order of sacrifices in
the three oldest family graveyards was reversed, services for the
oldest ancestors coming last rather than first. This probably was
done because the oldest tombs were located farthest from the village, rather than from any willful disregard of the regulations set
forth in the family record.

The oldest graveyard was some five li from Village H and one li
from the small village where the family's original ancestor had settled. It contained his tomb and 70 others. The second graveyard was
started with the grave of a member of the third generation and contained 70 tombs. The third was started by the seventh generation
and contained 85 tombs.

It was noted that the ceremonies in the three oldest family graveyards were identical and that the same pig, delicacies, and bread were

offered to the three different groups of ancestors. When the services were over, each boy under twelve years of age was given two pieces of bread.

The joint family worship took place only in the three oldest graveyards. The tombs in the later graveyards, of which there were several, were cleaned and repaired by separate groups from the families more closely related to those ancestors.

The feasts for the ancestors and for their living descendants and the other expenses of the Ch'ing Ming celebration cost about $150 and took about half of the income from the ancestral land.

An incident connected with the 1933 Ch'ing Ming celebration showed that the family connection continued for any sons who might have been adopted by other families. During the celebration a man and his son, who lived in a neighboring village, came to the ancestral hall and stated that they were members of the clan. The man gave a different surname and was not known to any of the clan leaders, but his answers to questions about his ancestors for five generations showed that his grandfather had been born a member of Clan X and been adopted by another family. The man and his son were welcomed to the Ch'ing Ming feast and were recognized as kinsmen of the entire group. Adopted sons were not accepted as members of Clan X.

VILLAGE FUNERAL CUSTOMS

The family history of Clan X stated: "Sacrificial ritual is, of all the ceremonies, of the utmost significance. Mourning and burial rites should be performed in solemnity and with care, for they are the foundation of ancestral worship."

In 1933 the funeral customs generally observed in Village H provided that when a well-loved father or a respected kinsman breathed his last, his nearest relatives, wife, sons, daughters, daughters-in-law, and grandchildren, should be present at his deathbed. Just before he died he should be moved from the family k'ang to a wooden bed, for it was thought to be most unpropitious for a man to die on the k'ang. He also should be dressed in his graveclothes, for it was believed that the soul which had left an undressed body would suffer from the cold in the nether world. The graveclothes, "longevity garments," should be prepared before death, but sometimes there was no time to sew the clothes properly and they must be pasted together in the roughest manner. The burial clothes for the upper classes were the long official or ceremonial garment, coat, trousers, boots, and hat. A woman's attire included a long embroidered gown and skirt.

For the lower classes a common long coat and *ma-kua* (jacket), trousers, shoes, and hat were used. At the time of a man's last breath, a piece of silver and several tea leaves were put into his mouth. He should not depart with an empty mouth.

Immediately after death a loud wail was started by the members of the family, especially by the women, who also stamped their feet. The stamping was a ceremonial observance practiced by all families, with or without bitter lamentation.

In the midst of the wailing the body and the wooden bed were moved to a central room where a "soul table" was set up at the end of the bed. A censer, a lamp, and a bowl of millet were arranged on the table. The censer was for burning incense; the lamp, an iron stand filled with oil, was to lead the soul without bewilderment, to furnish light for the family members who watched over the corpse, and to ignite the paper money that, when burned, would delight the soul hovering near the corpse; the bowl of millet was to provide "food for the dead." Seven sticks made of flour were inserted in the millet and seven flour cakes were arranged by the side of the bowl. The sticks were "rods for beating dogs," the cakes were called "cakes for feeding the dogs." It was believed that when the soul came to the "village of ferocious dogs" it could not get by if it did not have sticks to beat the dogs and cakes to feed them. The rods and the cakes were put in the sleeves of the graveclothes after the corpse had been put into its coffin.

Immediately after death the oldest son of the deceased burned a paper cart at the door to provide transportation for the soul of the departed, while a near relative went to Wu Tao shrine in the City Temple to "report to the temple," offer sacrifices, and pray that the gods would protect the soul of the deceased.

The day after death the news was reported, by messenger, to the nearest relatives, to other members of the clan, and to intimate friends. A son, even though living far off, was expected to return home to perform his filial ceremonies, lest he be severely criticized by his kinsmen and neighbors.

OBITUARY NOTICE

The obituary notice, which was printed and circulated, showed the five grades of relations and indicated their mourning garments. The notice usually read as follows:

The crimes and sins of the unfilial (eldest son) and his fellow mourners have been many and serious, but, instead of killing and destroying the perpetrators thereof, the disaster engendered thereby has fallen upon our deceased father (or mother) (his name and an enumeration of his rank and titles or those of her husband). Alas, in the year . . . . . ., the month of . . . . . ., on the . . . . . . day and the . . . . . . hour, his (her) life was cut short by disease in the principal (for women, inner) chamber. He (she) was born in the year . . . . . ., the month of . . . . . ., on the . . . . . . day and the . . . . . . hour, and thus reached the age of . . . . . . years. The unfilial (oldest son) and his fellow mourners have personally attended to the placing of the articles in the mouth of the dead and to the dressing of the body. They have beaten their breasts and stamped their feet, have wailed and cried, and, in obedience to the rescripts, have assumed their full mourning dress on the following day. Wailingly they herewith give notice thereof to those who are related to them as family members, as colleagues, as friends, as fellow villagers.

The mourning male orphans (names of all sons) weep tears of blood in concert and bow their heads to the floor.

One-year trimmed-mourning grandsons (names) weep tears and bow their head to the ground.

One-year mourning-without-staff brothers (names),

Ta-kung cousins and nephews (names),

Hsiao-kung cousins and nephews (names),

Ssu-ma cousins, nephews, and grandnephews (names) all wipe away their tears and bow their heads to the ground.

The family situation was shown on the death notice. If a son signed as "mourning and orphan," both his parents were dead. If only his father had died, he was "orphan"; if only his mother, he was "mourning."

The regular practice had been for the death notice to show only the males of direct patrilineal descent, omitting all female relatives, sister's sons, and sons-in-law. With the growing emancipation of women, however, the names of female descendants were more and more being listed on death notices, especially in the cities.

MOURNING GARMENTS

All the relatives within the five grades of family relationship were to put on mourning. The basic garments were hat, trousers, gown, and shoes all made of coarse unbleached cotton cloth. The roughness of the cloth and different symbols that were worn depended on an individual's relationship to the deceased. As there were five grades of relationship, there were five grades of mourning.

Untrimmed mourning (*chou-shuai*), with the garments made of the coarsest cloth, was worn by widows, sons, and unmarried daughters and by parents for their eldest son or for the eldest son of their deceased eldest son. The figure of a red bat was sewn on the shoulder of the gown as a symbol of future happiness in spite of present grief.

Trimmed mourning (*chi-shuai*), with the garments made of finer cloth than those for untrimmed mourning and with three copper cash and a bit of cotton wool sewn on the front part of the hat to symbolize the closing of the eyes and ears of the wearer during the mourning period, was worn for grandfathers, wives, brothers, and uncles, and by sons for their father's concubine.

Sons and grandsons carried white staves made of kaoliang stalks wrapped with white paper when they walked during the funeral ceremonies.

Ta-kung mourning was worn for grandchildren, cousins, sisters, aunts, and daughters-in-law, and by concubines for their married daughters and own grandsons.

Hsiao-kung mourning was worn for paternal great-uncles, unmarried great-aunts, for married and unmarried daughters, for wives of brothers, and by children for maternal uncles, aunts, and grandparents.

Ssu-ma mourning was worn for parents of wives, for great great-uncles, for cousins twice removed, and for others more distantly related to the deceased than those included in the hsiao-kung group.

Tan-mien mourning, a white strip of cloth around the waist, was worn by those outside the five grades of family relationship. At one time it had included a bare left arm and a hat without a crown.

The length of the official period of mourning depended upon the type of mourning and the relationship to the deceased. It was three years for untrimmed mourning, from three months to one year for trimmed mourning, nine months for ta-kung mourning, five months for hsiao-kung mourning, three months for ssu-ma mourning, and only during the time of the funeral for tan-mien mourning.

Mourning garments for women were similar to those for men, except for a difference in hats. Widows and daughters-in-law wrapped their hair in white cloth. Daughters, nieces and granddaughters, married and unmarried, put on a white fillet on which were sewn three white flowers. It must be remembered that in the villages most of the women wore trousers, so only in the wealthier families would skirts be worn. The duration of mourning was the same for both men and women.

Mourning garments were being worn less and less after the funeral. All relations outside the direct line took theirs off after the burial. Sons, daughters, daughters-in-law, and grandchildren did not wear full mourning after the interment. Sometimes the only mark of mourning was white shoes, or a white button on the cap. The so-called three-years' mourning was usually observed for not more than twenty-four months.

PREPARATIONS FOR THE FUNERAL

For the wealthier families a mat shed usually was erected over the courtyard inside the gate for the days preceding the funeral. Relatives, friends, and acquaintances who came to offer their sympathy to the family were first received there. Gifts of funeral scrolls were hung on the four walls. Things made of paper—horse and mule carts, figures of servants, trunks, rolls of cloth, gold and silver ingots and other kinds of spirit money—were placed round the room and in front of the main gate for exhibition until the time of sacrifice, when they would be burned and, through burning, be turned into utensils, attendants, and money to serve the departed spirit in the world of darkness.

Coffining usually took place on the evening of the day after death or on the third day. The hour was fixed by the geomancer, who could forsee good and evil by his calculations. The coffin was first lined with paper and then oiled. A mattress was spread across the bottom. Various kinds of paper money known as "coffin paper" were put in the four corners. The near relatives each spread a small bundle of hempen threads in the coffin. They also dropped in a few cash, "the money for filling up the back," and several grains of cereal. Then the body was placed in the coffin. Under its head was a "cock pillow," both ends of which were sewn in the shape of cock heads.

When the lid was put on the coffin and nailed down, all the mourners wailed.

CHIEH-SAN CEREMONY

The *chieh-san* ceremony took place on the evening of the third day after death. The male members of the family usually went to the City Temple or to another local shrine to "call the soul home after coffining." The Chinese generally believed that the soul after death went to the temple to register with the local gods. It was also believed that resurrection was impossible after three days, so the family went to the temple to recall the soul to its home for the last time.

Several Buddhist or Taoist priests were usually called on for the service.

In the van of the procession came a boy bearing a lantern that shed its dim and shadowy rays along the way. Immediately following came the priests and then the mourning sons. The eldest son or principal mourner pulled after him a *tiao-chin*, a sheet of paper shaped like a broom, on which the soul was to be carried back home after the temple ceremony. Another son bore a paper tablet on which were written the name and official titles of the deceased.

Following this group came a band of five or six professional musicians. They were called "the hands who use the drum and wind instruments." They played the drum, cymbals, clarinet, gong, flute, and a reed instrument. Besides the music, they sent forth, from time to time, dismal ghost-frightening sounds. In the rear of the procession came other male kinsmen and friends. Each held three incense sticks in both hands and lamented all the way.

The City Temple of Village H, the home of the city god, had been destroyed except for a small hall for the T'u Ti, the local divinity, and the Wu Tao. In this hall the priests performed their services. Incense and candles were lighted. The sons and grandsons all knelt down before the image and bowed their heads to the ground. One son, carrying a strip of white paper, went about trying to paste it on the images of the attendants of the local god. At the same time he kept calling out "Father (Mother), come and take this money." When he finally put the paper on the shoulder of the image of one of the god's attendants, he cried out, "I embrace it," as if he were clasping the soul. Then the strip of paper was transferred to the tiao-chin. A shot signaled the end of the temple ceremonies.

The tiao-chin and the attached paper, to which the soul was believed to adhere, were pulled by the sons of the deceased. As they returned home, they called out, "Father (Mother), come back and take this money for your trip."

At home a sacrifice was prepared outside the gate to the house. A table was set with fruit, cakes, and several vegetarian dishes. The women of the family waited beside the gate to receive the tiao-chin and the spirit tablet. One of them took the tablet, combed it, washed it with a cloth, showed it a mirror. She spoke to it: "Father (Mother), I comb your hair. I wash your face. I show you the mirror. I hope you will enjoy the sacrifice."

When all this was done the tiao-chin and the paper tablet were put into a paper cart which was then set on fire and quickly reduced to ashes. The sacrifice was completed by burning a large pile of paper money.

FANG-YEN-K'OU

After the recall of the soul the rite of pacifying the coffin (*fang-yen-k'ou*) was performed by a group of priests. They sat in front of the coffin and recited prayers that would redeem souls from hell and send them up to heaven. During the prayers they struck a bell, a wooden "fish-head," and a copper gong.

One or more tables containing a sacrificial meal for the soul of the dead were set out before the coffin. The mourners approached the coffin, burned incense, wailed, and kowtowed, bowing their heads to the ground three times. They were encouraging the soul to eat and drink of the sacrifice. Paper money was burned as part of the ceremony. At the end the chief priest scattered cash on the ground to "disperse money for the spirit."

RITE OF CROSSING OVER THE BRIDGE

At midnight some families performed the rite of "crossing over the bridge." A wooden bridge ten feet long, three and a half feet wide, and three and a half feet high was set up in the street outside the family residence. The floor and sides of the bridge were covered with white mourning cloth and a white awning was erected over it. The five grades of mourning relatives knelt at the end of the bridge. The head priest used a white cloth streamer to lead the chief mourner across the bridge. He carried a paper tablet with the name, degrees, and honors of the deceased, and walked with short steps in time with the music played by the priests and professional musicians. The rite was meant to help the soul cross the bridge to the underworld without being thrown into the water by the malevolent spirits.

Prayers for the salvation of the soul were said by Buddhist and Taoist priests. Well-to-do families often had both groups for two or three days. The prayers were sometimes repeated on the seventh day after death, again on the third seventh day, and again on the fifth seventh day.

Family sacrifices were offered morning and evening. Fresh candles were lighted and a meal was set out on the table before the coffin. All the mourners knelt around the coffin and bowed their heads to the floor. The chief mourner held three lighted pieces of incense in his hands as he bowed three times before the coffin. The incense was then placed in the incense burner on the table at the head of the coffin.

DAY OF PUBLIC CONDOLENCE

Relatives, close friends, and neighbors visited the bereaved family as soon as they heard the news of the death. On the day of public condolence there was a large gathering of acquaintances, friends, neighbors, and relatives. Visitors usually knelt in front of the coffin and wailed with the mourners. The chief mourner and others of the family kowtowed three times to the visitor to express the thanks of the family for his having come to share their grief. Visitors usually gave a present to the family—a pair of funeral scrolls, spirit money, fruit, cakes, or sometimes money to help with the funeral expenses. This was practicing filial piety in the Confucian sense. The Master said, "Serving the dead as they were served when alive, and those who have passed away as if they were still abiding among us—that is the height of filial conduct." Often a secretary was invited to list the visitors and their gifts so that later a card of thanks could be sent. A feast was prepared for all the visitors.

TAKING LEAVE OF THE SOUL

A family sacrifice, "taking leave of the soul," was performed at midnight preceding interment. A master of ceremonies, usually an educated kinsman, was appointed. A threefold offering of wine was presented to the deceased. Paper money was burned and finally a written prayer was read and then set on fire by the chief mourner.

TIEN-CHU

Tien-chu—dotting the tablet—was another ceremony that usually was part of the funeral rites. The name and titles of the deceased were written on the wooden tablet that later would be one of the ancestral tablets, but a dot was omitted from the main character, chu. On the morning of the day of interment an official or a man of high position was invited to come and "dot the tablet," putting a dot on the main character and thus completing the spirit tablet. The ceremony was accompanied by music. After the dotting, the master of ceremonies led the chief mourner before the writer of the dot, to whom he kowtowed to express the family's thanks for his services. The tablet was then removed by the chief mourner to the "eastern hall," his bedroom. There a sacrifice was offered to "pacify the tablet."

Occasionally well-to-do families invited a military man to "dig the soil" at the site of the grave. After the dotting of the tablet, he rode a horse out to the burial ground and dug up one shovelful of earth. It was believed that the vigorous strength of the soldier would frighten the malevolent spirits and keep them from disturbing the feng-shui surrounding the grave.

FUNERAL PROCESSION

As the coffin was carried from the house, three sets of firecrackers were set off and the chief mourner broke an earthen dish that had been standing at the end of the coffin, to signify that the sons could no longer serve their father (mother). All the mourners, dressed in their different grades of mourning garments, knelt down and wailed loudly as the coffin left.

The funeral procession was led by a paper-scatterer who threw into the air handfuls of round white pieces of paper with a square hole in the center to make them look like cash. They were believed to pacify any nearby malevolent spirits. The paper-scatterer was followed by many pairs of decorative streamers, "soul banners," and lanterns.

There were two flags at the head of the second division of the funeral. One had a flying dragon on it; the other, a flying tiger. They were followed by a red umbrella of state. Then came two pairs of square boards with long handles. The first pair read "Be respectful and keep silent"; the second, "Run away and flee." For well-to-do families there was next a "pavilion for the portrait," which in the old days was a "pavilion for dignities conferred."

The third division was a band of professional musicians.

Buddhist and Taoist priests constituted the fourth group. They performed services in the mat sheds that were erected by the side of the road by relatives or friends in order to offer a farewell sacrifice of food, incense, and spirit money to the dead. The coffin was stopped in front of the mat shed, while the priests offered prayers and the sons knelt and kowtowed in thanks.

The fifth division was the male mourners, including friends and acquaintances as well as the family. The grandsons and sons of the dead were last in the group. They immediately preceded the coffin. The oldest son, the chief mourner, carried in his hand a white staff with a white streamer. This was the "soul-conducting streamer." The second son carried a white paper tablet. The third son had a bowl of millet, "the food of the dead," in his hands.

The coffin was the sixth part of the funeral procession. The cata-falque was borne by a group of bearers who might number anywhere from sixteen to forty-eight. All of the bearers in the funeral procession were dressed in green robes.

The final division was the mourning women who, with their babies, rode in mule carts. Custom prescribed that they utter loud lamentations, regardless of their actual grief.

The geomancer determined the auspicious position of the grave and fixed it with his compass. He also set the best time for interment. When the coffin had been lowered to the bottom of the grave and properly aligned with the compass, the sons put the paper tablet and the "food for the dead" at its head. The chief mourner threw the first handful of earth on the coffin and was followed by other members of the family, both male and female. Many of the women also put a handful of the soil into their pockets, for it was said that if soil from the grave were brought home it would help enrich the family.

Laborers filled the grave and banked the excess earth into a pointed cone. A bowl and a pair of chopsticks were buried near the top of the cone. All the mourning staffs and paper streamers were burned except the "soul-conducting streamer" carried by the eldest son. His staff was thrust into the top of the grave mound.

CEREMONIES AFTER INTERMENT

The day after interment the sons of the family went from door to door to thank those who had helped with the funeral, especially those who had "dotted the tablet" and "dug the soil." Gifts and cards of thanks were also presented.

Three days after interment all the close mourners, men and women, young and old, went together to offer a sacrifice at the tomb. Incense, paper money, food, and fruit were brought as offerings to the dead. The buried bowl and chopsticks were taken out and given to the children as a sign of long life. The "soul-conducting streamer" was taken down and burned. The mound of earth over the tomb was rounded and smoothed with a shovel. The whole service was known as "rounding the tomb."

After that service no sacrifices were offered at the tomb except at Ch'ing Ming and on the first day of the tenth month, and for some years on the anniversary of death.

CHAO MU BURIAL SYSTEM

According to the old Chinese system, the tombs in the graveyard and the tablets in the ancestral hall were arranged according to the *Chao Mu* system. The Clan X history says:

It is the ancient system that the tombs of the dead be arranged according to the order of Chao Mu. Our two graveyards have strictly followed this rule. The rule is this, graves on the left, the even generations, are called Chao; those on the right, the odd generations, are called Mu.[6] We have kept this system for more than two hundred years. I hope our posterity will not break it. If anyone in authority oppresses those who are low, if the strong cheat the weak, if the many take advantage of the few, or if anyone, believing the words of the geomancer, seeks to benefit his own feng-shui by breaking the burial system, they are all unfilial and should be punished by the clan leaders according to the family law. If this fails, they should be brought to trial in the courts according to civil law. Those who seek to hide such cases are also unfilial. Our ancestors in heaven will punish them so that they will perish soon. Should we not take this to heart? Should we not take this to heart?

It may be said that this passage shows how systematic the Chinese mind is, putting everything in its place, the high and the low, the young and the old, the noble and the mean. Not only are the rooms in the family house arranged according to a definite plan—old and young, parents and children, uncles and brothers, all have their appointed places—but even the location of the graves and the spirit tablets follows a definite system.

XVI: VILLAGE I

VILLAGE I, one of the political communities of the third district of Shu-lu Hsien, was situated east of Shih-chia Chuang and some 150 miles southwest of Peiping. It was in the cotton-growing area of Hopei Province, and cotton dominated its agricultural and economic life. Some 60 per cent of the village land was planted to cotton, and almost every family was raising some. Our field reports noted that cotton was the only cash crop of the area, with the result that a bad cotton year brought financial difficulties and distress to the village.

Because of the limited rainfall of western Hopei, irrigation was usually needed for cotton cultivation. Village I had some 150 wells, each of which ordinarily could irrigate from 20 to 30 mu. If evenly distributed, these wells could give a fairly complete coverage for the some 4,500 mu included in the village area. Only about a third of the farm-operating families owned water wheels, however, and the reports did not indicate whether any rental or borrowing system was available to the nonowners.

Fifty-seven families owned 70 water wheels used for lifting the water from the wells. Ten families had two wheels each, two had three wheels, while two families owned one wheel together. An accurate count of the water wheels was possible, as they were under the supervision of a hired watchman. Up until 1932 this was a private enterprise. In 1930 and 1931 the watchman was paid $2 per wheel per year. If any parts of the wheels were stolen, the watchman was expected to indemnify the owner for his loss. In 1932 the watching of the water wheels was taken over by the village and added to the activities of the local guard. The annual charge was then increased to $3 per wheel per year, and the income was used to help meet the expenses of the guard.

FAMILY COMPOSITION

There were 180 families living in Village I in 1932. The number of individual residents was not reported, but, judging from the averages found in other villages, it probably was about 1,000 persons. The families lived along a central street running east and west. Most of them lived on the south side. Only a few families, at the east end of the village, lived on the north side. The village was large enough so that there was a distinct rivalry between the east and west ends. There was a small central district that was related partly to both ends.

All but seven of the families owned some farmland. No report was made of the nonfarming occupations of the village families, but they undoubtedly included a considerable amount of spinning and weaving of the locally grown cotton.

From the village land registration books it seems clear that the number of families had been increasing during the period under review. A very complete record of the number of landowning families and the amount of land each one owned was available, for each year in the spring they were required to register their land and pay an assessment based on the amount of land they owned both in Village I and in neighboring villages. The assessment rate per mu was fixed by the village authorities and was changed from year to year, depending on the needs of the village and the amount of income received from other sources. Judging from the 1931 figures, the nonlandowning families would not represent more than 4 per cent of the village. Shops and other businesses presumably made no direct contribution to the village finances.

LAND REGISTRATION

In 1910 the number of families registering land with the village authorities was 134 (see table 35). It was the same in 1917 and in 1919, but for some unknown reason was 144 in 1918. There was relatively little change in the amount of land registered. After 1920 the number of families was more than 140. The maximum was 177 in 1928. In 1931 the number was 173. Our field investigators remarked particularly that these were all resident families. They said that Village I did not have a definite area of land controlled by the local administration. The residents registered all the land they owned, even if part of it was located at some distance from the village. This system was unlike that of the assessment of resident and nonresident owners which has been described often for other villages.

Changes in landownership and minor delinquencies in registration accounted for marked fluctuation in the amount of land registered year by year. For no two years was the amount the same. The differences ranged from one to 237 mu. In both 1913 and 1914 more than 200 mu were added to the village total. In 1920 100 mu were added, and in 1923 the increase was 199 mu. The totals ranged from 3,590 mu in 1908 to 4,512 mu in 1926 (table 35). The registration for 1931 was 4,322 mu. The increase in the number of families more than offset the increase in the land registration, however, and the average amount of land per registering family dropped from 31.7 mu in 1917 to 25.0 mu in 1931.

The 1931 area was equivalent to one and one-eighth square miles. The population density, therefore, was approximately 900 persons per square mile of farmland. The large amount of irrigated land and the consequent larger-than-average return undoubtedly was partly responsible for the high population density. The amount of unfarmed land included in roads, the village, and wasteland is not known, so we cannot accurately determine the population density for the total area. It probably was more than 750 persons per square mile.

DISTRIBUTION OF LANDOWNERSHIP

From the land registration books it has been possible to study the distribution of families and of land according to the amount of land registered by each family. Since the number of families and the amount of land varied from year to year, the figures are given in percentages. The distribution of the families is based on an exact count, but for the land the figures are computed on the probable average-sized holding for each of the landowning groups. The figures varied from year to year, influenced by the economic experience of the area, but the distribution in 1931 was very similar to that of 1910. The families with fewer than 5 mu were 14 per cent of the group in 1910, 26.5 per cent from 1920 to 1922, and 15 per cent in 1931. The families with from 5.0 to 9.9 mu were 23.0 per cent in 1912 and 23.1 per cent in 1931, but in 1919 they were only 12 per cent of the group. (See table 36.)

Families with from 10.0 to 19.9 mu generally were approximately one quarter of the group. In 1931 they were 24.2 per cent. The variation was from 19.4 per cent to 28.6 per cent. Those with from 20.0 to 49.9 mu included almost another quarter of the group, 23.2 per cent in 1931, with a variation from 29.5 per cent in 1914 to 17.9 per cent in 1922. The next group, with from 50.0 to 99.9 mu, showed the widest proportional variation, dropping from 9.7 per cent in 1910 to 2.6 per cent in 1923 and then increasing to 11 per cent in 1931. Families with from 100 to 299 mu were 9.7 per cent of the group in 1919 and 1923, but were 5.2 per cent in 1910 and 3.5 per cent in 1931. No family had as many as 300 mu (50 acres). After 1925 there was only one family with more than 200 mu.

A slightly different grouping shows that 38 per cent of the families had fewer than 10 mu; just under 25 per cent had from 10 to 19 mu; about the same proportion had from 20 to 40 mu; and 15 per cent had 50 mu or more.

In 1931 the 15 per cent of the families who had fewer than 5 mu per family owned only 1.5 per cent of the land. The 38 per cent with fewer than 10 mu per family owned 8.3 per cent. At the other end of the scale, the 11 per cent of the families with from 50 to 99 mu owned 29.4 per cent, and the 3.5 per cent with 100 or more mu owned 20.9 per cent. (See table 37.)

Although the proportion of land held by the different groups remained fairly constant in the lower brackets, there was wide variation in the upper groups. From 1910 to 1923 the proportion for the group holding 50 to 99 mu dropped from 24.2 per cent to 5.8 per cent. During the same time the proportion owned by the families with 100 or more mu almost doubled, increasing from 28.4 per cent to 52.1 per cent. This increase was largely at the expense of the groups of families with 20 to 49 mu and 50 to 99 mu. After 1923 these trends were reversed. By 1926 the amount owned by the group holding 50 to 99 mu had increased to 20.7 per cent and that of the families with 100 or more mu had declined to 20.9 per cent.

If the two top groups are combined, the families with 50 or more mu owned 52.2 per cent of the land in 1910 and 50.3 per cent in 1922.

The outstanding events in Hopei Province from 1910 to 1931 were the revolution in 1911, a flood in 1917, drought in 1920, and fighting from 1924 on. We have tried to trace the effect of these events on the land registration in Village I, but cannot find any changes that seem to be direct and recognizable results. The changes seem to have been cyclical in nature rather than caused by specific events.

It must be remembered that the figures given above represent ownership of land. The records do not give any indication of the amounts of landlordism or tenancy, since it was the custom for the landowners to pay the local assessment on the land.

With only some 4 per cent of the families having no land, the percentage of complete tenancy could not be large, and the proportion of part tenancy probably was not high.

THE PUBLIC ASSOCIATION

The organization handling the financial and political affairs of Village I was called the Public Association. It lacked the worship feature usually found in the Green Crop Associations, and the name itself had more of an official and formal atmosphere than the Green

Crop Associations and Public Welfare Associations found in other villages. In the association type of organization, a number of village leaders usually formed a sort of village council to work with and control the village head and his assistant. It was reported that in the Public Association of Village I this group of leaders was missing and that instead there were a number of subordinate leaders, each of whom was the head of a group of 10 families. The village head would call these men together to discuss important issues, but their position, in both theory and practice, was inferior to that of the village head, even though they served as representatives of the people in the election of the village head and his assistant.

Changes beginning in 1928.—This system was changed in 1928 when the Nationalist government came to North China. The emphasis that the Nationalists placed on the authority of the people brought popular elections instead of the old representative elective system. The first popular election was held at the end of 1928. It was carefully supervised by representatives of the hsien and district governments. There was no contest for the position of village head. The incumbent was well liked and was voted for by everybody. Competition centered around the position of assistant head, and candidates were put forward by the east and west sections of the village. Some 210 persons voted. The east candidate won by a margin of 10 votes. Although the women were entitled to vote, our investigators reported that they would not take part in the election.

In 1929 the village head and assistant were both reëlected, but in 1930 the assistant was promoted to be village head. The new assistant was a young man whose father had been village head some years before.

Beginning in 1928, the voters also elected members of the three committees, for the management of village finances, the settlement of village disputes, and the inspection of village affairs.

Instead of the old groups of 10 families, the village was divided into lin and lü, groups of 5 and 25 families. The heads of these groups were at first appointed by the village head and the assistant head, but in 1932 the heads of the lü groups were elected by the families they represented.

Local affairs were managed by the village head and his assistant, but the lü heads and the committee members formed a sort of village council and were consulted concerning important matters. In the group the qualities of position and leadership undoubtedly had a great deal of influence.

On the fifth day of the first month of the new year the elected head of Village I, his assistant, the members of the committee for the inspection of village affairs, and the heads of all the lü met together to appoint the schoolteacher and the policeman, to complete the accounts of the past year, and to post the statement of the accounts. This was an informal meeting without strict organization, procedure, or minutes. Decisions were made after discussion and argument, and were accepted by general agreement rather than by definite voting. The decisions reached were carried out by the village head, his assistant, and the local employees.

The accounts showed no salaries for the village head or the assistant or for the heads of the lin and lü groups. Those officials all served without pay. When they were on village business, however, their expenses were met from local funds. The regular paid personnel of the village administration included the *ti-chia* or political agent, the clerk, the night watchman, and the schoolteacher. The ti-chia and the village clerk carried on the routine work of administration. The term *ti-chia* evidently was a combination of two older terms, *ti-pao* and *pao-chia*. The title was changed to *hsiang-ting* in 1932.

VILLAGE FINANCES

The records and accounts covering the twenty-five years from 1907 through 1931 are the basis of the story told here of the finances of Village I—how the village raised money for its local activities, how much was forthcoming from various sources, and what expenditures were included in the village budget. Hsien taxes and expenditures were not included in our study.

Along with the picture of the financial transactions of the village, we get glimpses of the life of the lowest unit of government in China. It was primarily an association of all those living in a given area, but it did have official functions that were recognized by the central government. Because the village was in an agricultural area, many of its activities and most of its finances naturally were related to the land. Local security, self-protection, and education had a large place in the budget. Occasionally recreation and religion were included through the giving of theatrical plays financed by a special assessment on all the landholders in the village.

In studying the finances we have been faced with the problem of the use of two different money-units. The accounts were kept from 1907 through 1923 in terms of cash, the unit for the copper coinage, and after 1925 in terms of dollars, a silver unit. The figures for 1924 and 1925 were given partly in cash and partly in dollars. To convert from one currency to the other it has been necessary to use a variable exchange rate. In 1907 and 1908 the rate was 2,200 cash per dollar. It was 3,000 for the four years from 1917 through 1920, but it was 4,000 in 1924, and 6,200 in 1925. (See fig. 12.) In only two of the years studied was there any decline in the exchange rate. In 1912 the rate was 2,700. In 1913 it was 2,600. In 1916 it was 2,950 cash, 150 less than the 1915 rate of 3,100.

We have compared these exchange rates with those for Peiping. The rate in Village I was generally about twice that in the city. Changes came at the same time and in about the same proportion. The two-to-one difference between the rates is undoubtedly accounted for by a difference in the size of the tiao, the bookkeeping unit for the copper coins.

Like Village E, Village I evidently used a tiao of 500 cash rather than the tiao of 1,000 cash that was used in the city. This is borne out by the field report that gave the price of the official mortgage forms sold by the village as 200 cash or 10 coppers. The 10-cash copper coins were usually known as "coppers." The 20-cash coins were "double coppers." It seems clear, therefore, that a payment of 100 cash in coin settled a charge of 200 cash. This two-to-one factor was, of course, compensated for in the silver-copper exchange rate. We have not known of any such factor being used when the accounts were kept in dollars.

Because of the increase of the exchange rate and the consequent depreciation in the silver value of the copper coins, the copper and silver figures for the earlier years give quite a different picture of village finance. Often the silver value decreased in spite of an increase in the copper value. Since the only possible picture for the entire period is that given by the silver values, they have been used throughout.

The increasing amounts of cash paid for continuing services, such as salaries of village employees, show the depreciation of the copper currency. In 1910 the annual wage of the ti-chia was 40,000 cash. He was paid 74,270 cash in 1917, 100,000 cash in 1923, and 236,630 cash in 1925. The wage of the village clerk did not increase so rapidly, but it rose from 24,000 cash in 1910 to 114,000 cash in 1925. The village schoolteacher received 80,000 cash in 1910 and 583,500 cash in 1925. The ratios of increase during the fifteen years were approximately six, five, and seven times the 1910 rates.

That there also was a depreciation in the value of the dollar is shown by the increasing amounts of dollar value paid for these continuing services. The dollar equivalent of the yearly salary of the ti-chia went up from $15.10 in 1910 to $38.17 in 1925. The silver wage was fixed at $42 in 1926 and remained constant through 1931. The increase in terms of silver, from 1910 to 1926, was 178

per cent. In Peiping the silver wages of a skilled workman rose
173 per cent between 1910 and 1927.[1] The schoolteacher's salary
increased 220 per cent between 1910 and 1926 and more than 400
per cent between 1910 and 1931, but it is quite evident that part
of the increase was given in order to obtain better and more
adequately trained teachers.

The detailed reports for 1910 and 1930 are given as examples of
the village accounts and as illustrative of items included in the
reports for the twenty-five years. (See tables 40 and 41.) The year-
by-year income and expenses are given in tables 38 and 39.

Income.—The total annual income ranged from $127.20 in 1907
and $126.30 in 1917 to $1,300.35 in 1926 and $1,355.40 in 1931. Be-
fore 1910 it was less than $150 per year. From 1910 to 1922 it ordi-
narily varied between $215 and $368. For two years, 1913 and 1914,
it was higher because of unusually large amounts received in connection with land transfers. In 1917, a year of widespread floods, it
dropped to $126, as there was no land assessment. After 1922 the
amount collected rose rapidly. The 1923 total was almost four times
and the 1925 total was five times the amount for 1922. From 1925
on, the income was regularly more than $1,000 a year, and for two
years it was more than $1,300.

Expenditures.—The total annual expenditure followed practically
the same pattern as the income. It was between $120 and $147
before 1910 and usually between $200 and $320 from 1910 to 1922.
In 1918 it was low, only $194, because the school was suspended that
year—another result of the flood losses of the year before. Beginning with 1924 the total expense was regularly more than $1,000
per year. The maximum was $1,469 in 1931, an amount just over
ten times the total for 1907.

For the twenty-five years from 1907 through 1931 the total expense was $13,043. This represents an average of $522.00 per year
and $2.90 per family per year. For the last eight years, 1924–1931,
the average total was $1,049.00 per year and the average amount per
family was $6.08 per year.

Surplus funds.—Thirteen years there was a surplus varying from
$18.78 to $385.57; twelve years there was a deficit of from $1.27
to $135.64. A comparison of the income and expense totals shows
that through the twenty-five years the village collected $566.71
more than it expended for its current activities. Some of difference
was represented in an increased cash balance. In 1910 the balance
carried forward was $2.15. In 1930 it was $207.72. Part of the surplus income may have been represented by increased loans and deposits. Unfortunately, the accounts did not give the total amounts

outstanding. In 1910 the loans and deposits were increased by $126.97. In 1930 they were decreased by $82.34. Part of the surplus was absorbed by losses on exchange resulting from the depreciation of the copper currency.

From the accounts it is evident that any surplus in the village funds usually was not held by the village authorities, but was turned over to certain residents either as a demand loan without interest or as a term loan with interest. We can only wonder how it was decided who was to receive the funds available for loan, especially when the loans carried no interest. Possibly borrowing was one of the perquisites of the village leaders, or at least of the wealthier families, especially as the borrower had to be ready and able to return the money on call.

In 1913 and 1914 the village received unusually large amounts of money, almost 1,500,000 cash in 1913 and more than 1,000,000 cash in 1914. In 1913 the village used 980,000 cash to purchase six mortgages ranging in amount from 60,000 to 500,000 cash. In 1914 three more mortgages were purchased for a total of 160,000 cash. The total mortgage investment of 1,140,000 cash was equivalent to $434.06. In 1922 one mortgage was increased by 6,000 cash, or $1.90. At the end of 1918 a payment of 20 per cent was made on all the mortgages. One was entirely paid off in 1919 and the rest in 1922. The depreciation of the value of the copper coinage reduced the silver value of the mortgage investment by $86.80, or some 20 per cent, during the ten years it was outstanding.

Ordinarily the mortgagee took over the property and operated it during the life of the mortgage. The village, however, instead of taking over the property, collected interest at the rate of 15 per cent per annum.

It is interesting to note that eight of the nine mortgagors had the same family name. We cannot say, however, that this denotes special favoritism, for we do not know how large a proportion of the families in the village had the same name. In some villages all the families had the same name.

SOURCES OF VILLAGE INCOME

The village income was received largely from four sources: the land-money assessment levied on the land owned by the residents of the village, the charges on the transfer and mortgaging of land, the fees for the measurement of land sold, and the school tuition fees. Other sources of revenue provided a relatively small part of the total income, ordinarily less than 15 per cent. (See table 38.)

Land-money.—Every year, in the spring, the families living in the village were required to register their land and pay an assessment determined by the amount of land owned and the rate per mu established by the village. This assessment was over and above any land tax levied by the hsien government. It was accepted as a purely local financial item. The amount of the levy depended upon the size of the village budget and the income received from other sources. Ordinarily the assessment was paid in two installments, spring and fall; but additional payments could be required in case of special need. (Some villages collected as many as nine assessments in one year.) From 1907 to 1923 the rate per mu varied from nothing to 100 cash per year (see table 35). The average was 47 cash per mu per year. In terms of silver, the assessment was usually from 1.5 to 2.0 cents per mu; the maximum was 4.0 cents. The average for the period was 1.7 cents per mu per year. At these rates the total land assessment was less than $100 per year, except for 1908 and 1910. In 1910, when the assessment rate was 100 cash per mu, the total was 367,852 cash, $147.14. An extra amount was needed that year to pay 180,000 cash, $72, rent for the village schoolhouse. The yearly rent was 30,000 cash, but it was paid in advance for six years. In the other high year, 1908, the accounts did not give the detailed expenditures, so we could not discover the reason for the unusually high assessment of 80 cash per mu.

In 1917 there was no land assessment. It seems that there was no spring collection that year and then the widespread floods of the fall caused so much damage that all taxes and assessments were remitted. There were, however, two assessments in 1918, one of 8 cash per mu for 1917 and one of 30 cash per mu for 1918. Three hundred cash of land-money was received in 1917, but this was a delayed payment for 1916. In 1913 the assessment was only 10 cash per mu, the village having received unusually large amounts of income from land transfers. In 1922 only 10 cash per mu was charged, the payment of eight mortgages held by the village having brought in 838,000 cash, $246.47; also the village had a surplus of 328,188 cash, $102.56, at the beginning of the year.

In 1924 the land-money was put on a silver basis at a rate of 15 cents per mu—fifteen times the equivalent of the previous year's rate. This big increase was necessary for obtaining funds to pay for a new school building which cost 2,493,136 cash, $541.98. From 1924 through 1931 the rate ranged from 12 to 23 cents per mu. The average was 17 cents. The minimum was paid in 1927, the maximum in 1928. The accounts do not show the reason for the increase of almost 100 per cent in 1928, but probably the fighting that began in 1924 and the expense of equipping and maintaining a home guard were factors. The year-by-year changes in the land-money rates are shown in figure 13.

Transfer fees on land sold and mortgaged.—Whenever land was sold or mortgaged, the village collected a transfer fee. The field report gives the rate as 3 per cent on a mortgage and one per cent on a sale. In the middle of 1910 the mortgage assessment was reduced to 2 per cent, though in a few cases the rate was not strictly followed. The village levies on mortgages and transfers were both discontinued after 1920. The two items together produced income varying from 3 cents to $193.08 a year. The only years when the amount was more than $100 were 1910 and 1913; in 1914 and 1916 it was more than $95. For the twelve years from 1909 to 1920 the average was $86.03. The year of the largest income was 1913, when the village bought the six mortgages for almost one million cash. In 1914, another large income year, the village purchased the three additional mortgages. Evidently there was an unusually large amount of land mortgaged or sold those two years; we may wonder whether the financial situation was so serious following the revolution of 1911 that many of the villagers had to borrow on their land. Because of the large income from the mortgage and transfer fees, the village was able to reduce the land assessment for 1913 to only 10 cash per mu. It was 60 cash in 1914. There were no outstanding political events that might account for the large income from land transfers in 1910.

From 1915 through 1920 the accounts separated the amounts received from land transfers and mortgages. For these six years, income from land sales was only one fifth of the amount received from mortgages. No land-transfer fees were reported in 1917, but the mortgage fees amounted to $56.10. Possibly the taxes and fees remitted because of the flood included the transfer fees as well as the hsien land-tax and the village land-assessment.

The village fees on land transfers and mortgages were discontinued in 1921, but in 1926 a new charge was made in connection with mortgages. Forty cents was charged for attaching the village seal to the official mortgage documents. These evidently were issued by the village authorities. The charge was divided between the mortgagor and the mortgagee, 30 cents and 10 cents. The fee was raised to $1 in 1932 and was then collected only from the mortgagor. Beginning in 1930, tax stamps were required on mortgages. The amount of income received from these sources ranged from $1.20 to $36.86.

A small fee was charged for the official forms used for mortgages.

In 1910, when the charge per sheet was 200 cash, 8 cents, the income was $5.50. In 1930 it brought in $5. At other times this income was included in miscellaneous receipts.

Fee for land measurement.—Beginning in 1912, the village made a charge for measuring land that had been sold and was being transferred to a new owner.[2] This was in addition to the fees on sales and mortgages. The hsien authorities appointed persons in various parts of the hsien as official measurers and gave each a standard measure. For an appointment as land measurer, or rather for the use of the official measure, a small fee was paid to the hsien government. It was the duty of this functionary to measure land at the time of transfer. For this service he was entitled to charge a fee. His measurement was accepted as official by the buyer and the seller, for the entries on the village and hsien land books, and for taxes and assessments. The buyer was particularly anxious to get the official measurement, since this would protect him from future trouble concerning boundaries, etc.

Although an individual held the official measure, in 1912 the village took over the measuring of land as a source of income, collecting 106,644 cash, $39.50. Just how the official measurer was persuaded to perform his service when the village collected the fee is not clear. In any case, the accounts for 1912 do not show a payment to him for his services. Possibly he was able to collect additional fees from the landowners.

In 1913 the village collected 584,318 cash, $224.74, for land measurement. That year a compromise may have been arranged with the official measurer, for he was paid 15,000 cash as wages and 8,000 cash as subsidy, a total of $8.50. He was also paid 15,000 cash in 1914 and 1915. He must have felt that his share was too small a part of the amount received and demanded more, for an argument developed with the village officials and was taken to court. Five villages in the area for which the official measurer had obtained appointment from the hsien government joined in the lawsuit.[3] It was not settled until 1915. Evidently the villages won their suit and eliminated the measurer, for thereafter his name did not appear in the accounts. For Village I the expenses of the lawsuit were 37,234 cash, $12.40. The village had to pay a small sum (the exact amount not reported) to the hsien government for permission to act as official measurer. The measuring then was done by the ti-chia and the official records were kept by the village clerk.

Receipts for land measurement fluctuated widely, with extremes of $3.55 in 1918 and $299.46 in 1923. From 1921 on, the amount was regularly more than $100 per year, the average being $162.

The field report stated that the measurement fee was to be collected from the buyer when land was sold and that the charge should be 2 per cent. Measurement was not required when land was mortgaged, for there was no change in ownership. The mortgagee took over the property during the life of the mortgage, but when it was paid, the owner recovered the property.

From the report it would seem that there should be a close correlation between the amount received for land measurement and from the land-transfer fee. The actual figures, however, show no relationship whatever between either the measurement and the transfer amounts or the measurement and the transfer and mortgage fees. There must have been some other unreported factor involved. For example, the measurement fees jumped from $3.55 in 1918 to $118.55 in 1919. The transfer fees in those years were $4.45 and $25.42, and the mortgage fees, $64.17 and $58.68.

Tuition and fees for village school.—Part of the expenses of the village school were met by tuition and other fees paid by the pupils. When the school was opened in 1910, the annual tuition fees were set at 3,000, 4,000, and 5,000 cash, or $1.20, $1.60, and $2.00 per pupil. The amount paid depended upon the amount of land owned by the family. Those with fewer than 15 mu paid 3,000 cash, those with from 15 to 40 mu paid 4,000 cash, and those with more than 40 mu paid 5,000 cash. In 1912 a fourth class was added for families with more than 60 mu; the fee was 6,000 cash. In 1919 a fifth class was added, for families with from 50 to 60 mu, whose fee was set at 5,500 cash; this class was discontinued after two years.

The school opened in 1910 with 12 pupils. All of them were children of families with fewer than 40 mu. We do not know why the wealthier families were not represented. Two years later, 60 per cent of the students came from families with more than 40 mu. By 1914 there were 20 or more pupils enrolled. In 1922 the number jumped from 29 to 37. Because of the flood in the fall of 1917, there was no local school in 1918. The schoolwork, however, was not discontinued, as the former village head supported the school and personally paid that part of the teacher's salary and other expenses not covered by the tuition fees.

In 1923 the tuition fee was made payable in dollars instead of cash. The rates were $1.00 for families with fewer than 15 mu, $1.50 for those with from 15 to 40 mu, and $2.00 for those with more than 40 mu. This was a 28 per cent increase for the 40-to-60-mu families, but only 7 per cent for the families with fewer than 15 mu or more than 60 mu. At the same time the enrollment dropped from 37 to 16 pupils, a loss of 57 per cent. The increase in tuition fees could hardly have been the cause, as most of the loss was in the wealthier groups, where the number of pupils dropped from 22 to 4. The 1924 enrollment was 31 pupils, almost double that of 1923. Most of the increase came from families with the lowest incomes.

Tuition fees were increased again in 1925, to $3.00, $3.50, and $4.00 for the three groups. This increase did not affect the enrollment, which was 33 pupils, two more than in 1924. There were 40 pupils in 1926, 45 in 1930, and 42 in 1931. The enrollment probably did not represent more than one out of five of the children of school age.

We have been interested to note that 45 per cent of the students in 1931 came from families with fewer than 15 mu and 24 per cent from families with more than 40 mu. Of the village families, 52 per cent had fewer than 15 mu and 20 per cent had 40 mu or more. Figures from other sources show that the wealthier families were regularly larger in number and were apt, therefore, to have a larger number of children per family than the poorer families. Consequently, it would seem that the different groups of families were sending about the same proportion of their children to the village school, though one would expect a larger proportion from the wealthier families.

Beginning in 1919, there was a small charge per student for water supplied by the school. It was 600 cash, 20 cents, in 1919, 400 cash from 1920 through 1922, and 600 cash, 15 cents, in 1923. The increase in the exchange rate from 1919 to 1923 was responsible for the decrease of the silver equivalent of 600 cash. For the next two years the charge was 10 cents per student. It was raised to 20 cents in 1926 and continued at that rate through 1931. The income from this source was less than $9.00 per year and from 1919 to 1925 ranged from $2.40 to $4.87.

The total school income ranged from $14.80 in 1910 to $154.44 in 1929. Only once before 1925 was the total more than $50. From 1926 on, it was more than $131. The average for twenty-one years was $68 per year, or a little more than one third of the average expense. (See table 38.)

Interest on mortgages.—Interest on the mortgages held by the village was a sizable item from 1913 through 1921. When the full amount of 1,140,000 cash was outstanding, the 15 per cent amounted to 171,000 cash, or from $57.00 to $61.07 depending on the rate of exchange. As the mortgages were paid off, the interest was reduced until for 1922 it was 125,700 cash, $36.97.

The figures in table 38 show the actual amounts received. About one fifth of the 1915 interest was paid in 1916. Only half of the 1917 interest was collected that year. The other half was received in 1918. The 1918 interest presumably was forgiven because of the flood the previous year, but the 1919 interest was received in 1918. Very good crops in 1918 evidently made possible this advance payment. The interest continued to be paid largely in advance for the next three years. As a result, no interest was collected in 1922 when the mortgages were paid off. Some unpaid interest amounting to 13,200 cash, $3.30, was received in 1923.

Miscellaneous income.—Miscellaneous items of income totaled from $7.66 to $206.70. For only four years out of twenty-five was the amount more than $70. Usually it was less than 15 per cent of total income. The field reports did not give a complete list of the items included under miscellaneous receipts, but the records did show interest on loans, interest on a government bond, the sale of trees belonging to the village, the sale of special official forms and stamps, contributions for the purchase of coal for the school, profit on a play given by the village, and payments by the army for services rendered by the village. In 1923 the village received 460,000 cash, $115, from the sale of trees. The same year there was $42.34 left over from the special assessment for the village play.

VILLAGE EXPENDITURES

The total village expenses followed practically the same pattern as the total income. The minimum was $120.27 in 1909; the maximum, $1,469.16 in 1931. From 1907 through 1909 the total was below $150. From 1910 to 1922 the amount generally was between $200 and $300. In 1923 it jumped to $534.19 and in 1924 to $1,013.18. After 1924 it averaged $1,095. (See fig. 16 and table 39.)

Wages of village employees.—There were only three ti-chia in twenty-two years. One man held the office for the first three years. His successor served for thirteen years, and when he retired his son was appointed to the post. One man held the village clerkship for the first fourteen years, his successor for the last eight.

The wages of the ti-chia during the twenty-two years ranged from $14.52 to $42.00. The rate of payment was changed ten times, partly to adjust for the depreciation of the copper coinage, partly to give an increase in terms of silver. There were two decreases, one of 5,940 cash in 1913, when the new incumbent was appointed, the other of 4,270 cash in 1921. The yearly wage was below $20 until 1916. It was not more than $25.00 until 1924, when it was $31.87. The rate was set at $42 in 1926 and was not changed for the next five years. The increase over the twenty-two years was 178 per cent. From 1910 to 1924 the increase was 110 per cent. The cost-of-living index in Peking rose during the same time only 40 per cent.[4]

The wages of the village clerk ranged from $6.25 to $20.00. There were seven changes in the rate. In 1921 it was decreased from 43,000 cash, $14.33, to 25,000 cash, $7.81, or some 45 per cent. The wages of the ti-chia were reduced the same year, but only by about six per cent. The accounts do not give any reason for the reduction. When a new clerk was appointed in 1924, the wages rose from 25,000 cash, $6.25, to 82,170 cash, $17.86. The rate was set at $20 in 1926. Over the twenty-two years the increase was 108 per cent. Evidently both the ti-chia and the village clerk worked on a part-time basis.

Occasional payments were made by the village to middlemen, or agents, in connection with the sale of land. The field report stated that a commission of from one to 2 per cent was regularly paid on land sales and that this had been taken over by the village in 1909 as a source of revenue. Two years later the village worked out a compromise with those who previously had been receiving this commission and for the next ten years paid them a part of the amount received. The payment to the agents was discontinued after 1920, when the village gave up its charge on the transfer of land. The payments to the agents were usually small amounts. The average total was only $22.31 a year. For more than half the years from 1911 to 1920 the amount was less than $20 per year. It was $48.92 in 1931 and $42.00 in 1919, when the village received especially large amounts from land transfers. The records do not show that the village paid the middlemen a definite proportion of its land-transfer income.

Village school.—The expenses of the village school were from $78.81 to $754.93 per year. From 1910 through 1915 the amount was approximately $100 per year if the $72 paid in 1910 for six years' rent is prorated. From 1916 through 1921 the cost was between $125 and $155. Although the school was closed in 1918 because of the floods in 1917, the village had to pay $15 rent for the schoolhouse. From 1926 through 1931 the school expense was more than $215 every year, and for two years it was more than $320.

The years from 1922 through 1925 were atypical. In 1922 and 1923 the village paid 1,100,000 cash, $293.82, for a site for a school building; in 1924 it paid 2,493,136 cash, $542.00, for a new building; new equipment costing 320,950 cash, $51.77, was purchased in 1925.

The yearly rent for the school building was 30,000 cash, $12, from 1910 through 1915, and then 45,000 cash, $15, from 1916 through 1922. In 1913 $9.82 was paid for the repair of the rented school buildings.

The salary of the teacher ranged from $32 in 1910 to $180 in 1930. It was $165 in 1931. The report showed that there were twelve different head teachers in twenty-two years. Part-time teachers were engaged for three years, 1912, 1913, and 1915, but the school was usually a one-teacher school. Because of the many changes of personnel and the decrease in the value of the cash, the teacher's salary was changed almost every year. There were sixteen changes out of a possible twenty. Five of the changes were reductions.

In 1931 Village I reëngaged the same teacher it had employed in 1916–1919. His 1916 salary was 180,320 cash, $61.12, but in 1931 it was $165.00, an increase of 170 per cent. During the same period wholesale prices in North China increased 65.2 per cent.[5]

There were many miscellaneous school expenses, of such variety and number that no attempt was made to study them. The one miscellaneous item for which we have detailed figures was the amount paid the water carrier for bringing water to the school building. In 1921 this was 15,980 cash, $5. It was $10 in 1924, and $13 in 1929 and 1930. About two thirds of this item was met by the water fee charged the pupils in addition to their tuition. In 1925 the charge was 10 cents. It was doubled in 1926. The annual total spent for miscellaneous school expenditures ranged from $29.20 in 1910 to $189.40 in 1928.

If the rental or purchase cost of the school building is omitted, the other school expenses show three distinct periods: from 1910 through 1915, when the expense was below $90 a year and the average was $79; from 1916 through 1922, when the average was $115; and from 1923 through 1931, when the expenditure was more than $200 a year and the average was $265. The peak years were 1927 and 1928, when the costs rose to $324.74 and $349.40.

Crop-watching.—Crop-watching was not regularly one of the functions of the local administration of Village I. Our investigators reported that because the cotton crop had to be carefully watched by the individual families, the village did not attempt a common watch program. In 1918, however, when the village had a very large harvest following the floods of 1917, four watchmen were engaged at a wage of 13,000 cash, $4.35 each, for the spring season, and in the fall the same watchmen were paid 24,000 cash, $8.00 each. Crop-watchmen were not engaged again until 1929. Then six men were paid $3.95 each to help protect the crops in the fields. According to the regulations adopted in 1932, the protection of the village crops was to be one of the functions of the village guard, but it seems that the guards were not made responsible for any losses.

Night watch.—The night watch had long been a function of the village administration, and men were employed to patrol the village and, with gong and rattle, to warn both thieves and villagers. Usually the watch was maintained during the last three months of the Chinese calendar year, but in some years it was continued for two more months in the early spring. Village I ordinarily hired three watchmen, one for each of the three sections of the village, east, middle, and west. In 1911, the time of the revolution, seven watchmen were employed. Four were paid 4,800 cash each and three received 3,200 cash each, a total of 28,800 cash, $11.08. The next year the total was $12 for each section of the village. For the next ten years the amount was 45,000 cash per year. Because of the decrease in the value of the cash, the silver equivalent dropped from $17.31 to $12.23. In 1923 and 1924 the total was again $12, or $4 for each section. The next year the rate was set at $15 for each section, an increase of 275 per cent, but only one man, the watchman for the middle section, received that amount. The other two men were paid $14 each, making the total $43.

In 1926 the total was $76.36, almost double that for the previous year. The rates for the winter watching remained the same, $15 for the middle section and $14 for each of the others. The total was increased because the watch was continued for two months in the spring. For that time the wage was $10.85 per man for the east and middle sections and $11.60 for the west section.

The spring watching was continued in 1927 and 1928, when $10.00 was paid for one section and $9.32 for the others, a decrease of some 14 per cent. The winter rate remained the same, $15 per section. In 1928 three men were paid $11 each for the spring season and four were paid $12 each for the winter season. In 1929 the night watch was combined with the other duties of the local guard. In 1931, however, two men were engaged for a short time to do additional watching; they were paid a total of $5.

From 1910 to 1928 the amount spent for the winter night-watching increased 290 per cent. All of the increase came after 1924, for the total in that year was $12, or 40 cents less than in 1910. In 1928 the total for the winter season was $48.

Village guard.—In 1926 the old system of village guards, long used during times of disturbance and emergency, was revived by order of the central government. The village guard was under the supervision of the hsien government, but the village head was also head of the village guard and the expenses were met from village funds. In six years the total expenditure for the guard was $1,115.32. The maximum for one year was $280.23 in 1929. This included the amount for wages, arms, uniforms, and supplies. In 1929 the duties of the village guard and the night watch were combined. That year six men were engaged to patrol the village day and night. Their wages were $12 each, the same as that for the night watchmen the year before. The field report states that the guards were expected to serve not for the whole year, but only for the winter months "when there was need for armed protection." The next year the men were paid $16 each. In 1931 they received $20 each. In 1929 the village spent $202.24 for arms and uniforms. In 1931 the amount for supplies and general expenses was $154.42.

In 1932, the year after our study of the accounts ended, the village evidently felt the need for additional services from the village guard and additional funds to finance them. Earlier the village had taken over the agents' commission on land sales and the fees for land measuring. This time it took over the watching of the water wheels, which had been in private hands. The income thus obtained was applied to the expenses of the village guard. In return the guards were made responsible for the protection of the water wheels and the payment for any losses through theft. At a charge of $3 per wheel, the added income amounted to $210 per year. The records, unfortunately, do not show what, if any, adjustment the village made with the person who had been watching the water wheels. The following are the regulations adopted by the village on the first day of the second month of 1932:

1. The finances of the association (Branch Association of the Local Guards) are to be obtained from the special fund received for the protection of the water wheels. The Village Public Association is to pay the expenses of night watching. If too much loss indemnity is to be paid, the village will have to provide the funds.

2. The association employs four guards.

3. The wage of each guard is $7 per month. The one who also keeps the accounts of the association receives $8. The guards have to pay for both their light and their food when they are on duty. The association, however, will give them a food subsidy of $2 a month.

4. Anyone who desires to become a guard must furnish a guarantor who will be responsible in case the guard loses his rifle and for payment of indemnity for losses.

5. The guards of the association are paid at the end of each month. There will be no advance or delay in the payment of their wages.

6. The owner of each water wheel pays $3 for the service of protec-

tion. One dollar will be paid for the loss of one water dipper, $4 for one water winnow (?). If other parts are lost, the compensation will be decided by the village officers.

7. If offenders are fined, the sum received will be divided equally between the guards and the association. The guards will have to share with the association any loss owing to the theft of water wheels or equipment.

8. All the water wheels which were protected last year must be under the joint protection this year. If the owner deceives the association by demanding more than the real loss, he will be fined from one to ten times the original demand.

9. The water wheel protection money is paid in two installments, half to be paid between the first and the fifteenth day of the third month and half between the first and fifteenth day of the eighth month.

10. The responsibilities of the guards are to protect water wheels, to protect green crops, to patrol the village road, and to be responsible for the peace and safety of the village.

11. The guards must obey the regulations of the association. They must not squeeze public money, gamble, drink, or sleep outside at night. Leave of absence must be procured from the head of the association. Anyone who violates the above rules will be punished accordingly.

12. A bonus of 50 cents each will be given to the guards at the end of each month if they have performed their duties well.

13. The village head is at the same time the chief of the local guards.

Military expenses.—Expenditures for supplies and services for the army did not amount to any large sum in the accounts of Village I until 1924. Before that time there had been some small expenditures connected with the enlistment of men for the army. The total was $3.38 in 1921 and $13.38 in 1922. In 1924, when Wu P'ei-fu and Chang Tso-lin started fighting, the armies called on the countryside for men, supplies, transportation, and money. Their demands usually were transmitted by the hsien government to the villages. The cost of the village quota was met from village funds, but we are not sure that the army always paid full value for goods and services. As there was more or less fighting in the Peiping area through 1930, the military demands continued and Village I contributed every year except 1927. The amount ranged from $116.22 in 1924 to $797.54 in 1931. The military item was 63 per cent of the year's expenditure in 1925 and 54 per cent in 1931.

The combined expenses for the village guard and the armed forces during the years from 1924 to 1931 ranged from 30 to 73 per cent of the year's expenditure. A heavy burden was put on the people of the countryside when there was fighting in or near their area. In 1931 the cost to Village I was $4.40 per family.

Occasionally the army paid for some of the services or supplies given by the village, but usually there was little return. In 1930 the army paid $12.60 rent for wagons, but other demands cost the village $442.49. And it must be remembered that the village expenditure may not have been the entire cost to the community. The village people may well have had individual loss and expense when there was fighting in the immediate area or the armies were moving to or from the battlefield, as in 1925 and 1931.

Miscellaneous expenses.—Miscellaneous expenses, in the village accounts, ordinarily included a considerable list of items, but the individual amounts usually were small and did not appear with sufficient regularity to make it worth while to attempt an analysis. The yearly total for all of them together ranged from $3.06 to $285.55. In nine years it was more than $100 and in four years was more than $200.

Village plays.—The village play is an item of special interest. Four times during the twenty-five years—in 1910, 1914, 1922, and 1923—the village raised money by special subscription or assessment, hired a troupe of actors, and gave a series of plays to thank the gods for their help and to entertain the villagers after the farm work was finished for the year. The 1923 accounts gave the dates as the last days of the ninth month, about the end of October. We were not able to discover the reasons why the plays were given in those four special years. The residents of neighboring villages evidently came for the celebration. The account books for one of the plays listed the names of six nearby villages and noted that "all came to pay homage." Those villages may have taken turns in giving plays other years, but this is not certain.

The account books showed that the funds for the plays were raised by general assessment on the landowning families in the same way that the land assessment was raised every year. The regular spring registration books were not used. Special ones were made up for the play. The number of families and the amount of land registered for the plays differed slightly from the figures given by the regular registration books. In 1910 five fewer families registered for the play than for the land assessment. The amount of land was 83 mu less than the 1910 total, but 7 mu more than the 1911 total. In 1923 there were two more families, but 9 less mu.

The assessments for the play were 60 cash per mu in 1910, 140 cash in 1922, and 200 cash in 1923. The rate for 1914 is not known, as the play account books were missing. If there was a surplus, it was kept by the Public Association; if there was a deficit, it was met from other village funds. In 1910 and in 1923 there was a surplus—$15.37 in 1910 and $42.34 in 1923. These have been entered as miscellaneous income in table 38. The deficits were $95.61 in 1914 and $29.22 in 1922. They are part of the miscellaneous expense for those years (see table 39). Since the plays were a special project financed by special assessments, only the net surplus or deficit was entered in the regular accounts.

In 1922 the actors were paid 347,200 cash, $102.12. Another 358,588 cash, $105.44, spent for the other expenses of the plays, made the total 705.785 cash or $207.56. The next year the total expense was almost the same, 739,314 cash, $184.83; although slightly higher in cash, it was less in dollars as the exchange rate had gone up from 3,400 to 4,000 cash per dollar. The actors were paid 300,000 cash, $75. The 1923 accounts listed sixty items of expense, mostly for food for the players and the village leaders who were responsible for the details; a small amount was for miscellaneous expenses such as the erection of a platform, the invitation of the players, etc.

The income account for the 1923 plays gave the names of all of the village leaders who helped with the celebration by giving free service or by advancing money.

Knowing something of the financial problems that the village families faced, we find it striking that usually all of them paid the special assessment for the play. The 1923 accounts showed receipts that corresponded exactly with the number of mu registered and the charge of 200 cash per mu. The 1910 receipt book showed an overpayment by two families and an underpayment of 300 cash by one family. The total receipts were 400 cash more than the expected amount. The regular land assessment also seems to have been paid in full. The 1910 land accounts showed the payment of 100 per cent of the land money due for that year and 5.8 per cent of the amount due for 1909 (see table 40). In 1930 the reported collection of land money was 100 per cent of the amount due (see table 41). "Face" and official and social pressure probably combined to produce a situation wherein all the families paid their land assessments. We were not able to determine what action the village could take in case of continued nonpayment of land assessments. A Chinese, when asked what the guilds did to men who refused to join, said, "But, you see, they always join." Perhaps the same can be said of the payment of the village land-assessment.

XVII: VILLAGE J

VILLAGE J was situated about eight miles from the city of T'un-liu Hsien in Shansi Province. The history of the village was not known in detail, but it was said that the first family to settle there did so during the T'ang dynasty (618–906). Families descended from the first settlers had resided in the village for more than a thousand years, through 35 generations or more, and there were 13 families in this group.

The village area was one li, a third of a mile, in length and half a li in width. There were 8 wells inside the village and 50 wells for irrigation outside. All but two of the wells were privately owned.

FAMILY COMPOSITION

A population survey made some years before our study found 103 families and 620 persons. Our figures showed 110 families, but only 560 persons, an average of 5.1 persons per family. There were nine different family-names represented in the village. The largest name group included 50 families who were subdivided into nine different lines of descent. Other large name groups had 18, 14, and 13 families. The remaining groups had from one to 5 families.

Although the largest group had 50 families and the oldest had 13, the most influential group had 14 families. Of the latter families, only three had unusual political power. The reasons given for their influence were: they were rich; they were honest and just; and they were well educated. One family member held an *en-keng* degree; another was a village schoolteacher. Still another was the local doctor of Chinese medicine. These three families not only had strong political power; they were also greatly respected by their fellow villagers.

The land area totaled some 2,200 mu, or an average of 20 mu per resident family. The agricultural products included millet, corn, wheat, kaoliang, other grain, reeds, and garlic. There were some fruit trees—peaches, apricots, and crab apples—but the villagers paid little attention to them and did not make any attempt to protect their crops. Poplars and elms were the most important trees for lumber.

Most of the 110 families were farmers. In 100 families the making of reed mats was carried on as a home industry. About 200 persons worked at mat making. The mat market was about two miles from the village. It was reported that approximately 50 per cent of the mat sellers in the market came from Village J and that the village output was about 20,000 mats per year.

VILLAGE SCHOOL

The school was directly supervised by the village head and was supported by local funds. Part of its support came from the interest paid to the two village granaries for the use, until harvesttime, of the stored grain. The school's annual expenses were about $100, of which $70 went to the teacher and the rest for all the other expenses. It was held in the Great Buddha Temple and the temple-keeper acted as janitor, but without cost to the school. The courses were said to be modern, but not strictly in accord with the regulations of the Ministry of Education.

The school vacations were fifteen days for the wheat harvest, thirty days for the autumn harvest, and forty days at the New Year. There were one-day holidays for the fifth day of the fifth month and for the winter solstice, and unscheduled holidays whenever there were theatrical performances in the area.

In the village there were five higher-primary graduates; six middle-school graduates, five of whom were of families in one name group; three college graduates, all of whom were of another name group, not that of the middle-school graduates; two holders of the *kung sheng* classical degree; and two holders of the *hsiu ts'ai* degree.

Besides the village school, there was a private school with 15 students, some of whom came from other villages and lived in Village J during the school term.

TEMPLES

There were six temples in the village:

The Great Buddha Temple, with 30 or more rooms
The Temple of the Master, Ts'u Shih, with 17 large rooms
The temple of Kuan Ti, with 11 large rooms
The White Clothes Temple of the goddess of mercy, with three large rooms
The temple of the god of earth, with three small rooms
The temple of Yü Huang, with three small rooms

Kuan Ti was the most worshiped deity. Next was the god of earth. The Wu Tao deities were on the west altar of the Kuan Ti Miao.

Besides the regular festival times, the villagers went to the temples to burn incense on the first and the fifteenth days of each month. Special service times for the different temples were the fifteenth day of the first month at the Kuan Yin Miao, the temple of the goddess of mercy; the second day of the second month at the T'u Ti Miao, the temple of the god of earth, which housed the god of the locality; and the eleventh day of the first month and thirteenth day of the fifth month at the Kuan Ti Miao.

Special occasions for individual offerings were on the birth of a child and one month thereafter, at the Kuan Yin Miao; before setting out to look for a job, at the Kuan Ti Miao; and requesting a child, at the Lao Nai Nai Miao ("Old Grandmother Temple") which was outside the village.

There were theatrical stages at the temples of the Great Buddha and Kuan Ti.

A temple-keeper lived in the Great Buddha Temple. For his services he received his room and the rent-free use of 10 mu of temple land.

VILLAGE GRANARIES

There were three granaries in the village: the Old Granary, which held more than 1,000 tou of grain; the East Granary, holding more than 400 tou; and the Granary for Construction, holding more than 500 tou. The first two granaries were under the control of the eight village leaders; the third was managed by the most influential family in the village.

The grain was lent to needy people, most often during the sixth and seventh months when their last year's crops were exhausted. In normal years the village granaries lent grain to needy people in neighboring villages as well as in Village J. They were to return the grain, with interest, after the harvest. The interest was paid in grain. The surplus of the village-owned granaries was used for the support of the village school.

The grain lent from the family-run granary was regularly returned with 30 per cent interest, which was used to repair temples and bridges. It was explained that while an interest charge of 30 per cent for the loan of grain for a three- or four-month period seemed high, the price of the returned grain and the interest was usually less than the price of the grain lent four months earlier.

In poor years grain was expensive and was lent only to Village J residents. They were to return the loan after the harvest, sometimes with interest and sometimes without, depending upon the decision of the village elders. In years of very good harvest the grain was lent to Village J residents only and they returned it without interest.

When a village granary was established or when the grain had become depleted, a supply was collected by assessing all the farming families an amount that was proportionate to the size of their land-holdings. Such an assessment was usually made after a very good year when grain was cheap. Sometimes wealthy families donated grain.

VILLAGE ADMINISTRATION

Before 1913 all local affairs were managed by the village she, an indigenous autonomous association. In 1913, on orders from the provincial government, Village J adopted the village-head-and-assistant-head type of organization as its official form of administration, but the she still continued to function. It dealt with the internal affairs of the village, while the official administration under the village head and assistant head dealt with matters of concern to the district, hsien, and provincial authorities.

The village had had only one head for twenty years. He belonged, naturally, to the most influential family. He had tried to resign his post several times, but was not allowed to do so. The assistant head was always a member of the largest family in the village.

By 1933 the village was following the election rules adopted by the Nationalist government and was electing its village head and assistant annually. The election, held in the Great Buddha Temple, was supervised by an officer sent by the district government, but the result was always the same—the old head was reëlected. At the time of our study the hsien magistrate had issued a new regulation which made three years the maximum time a village head could hold office. The rule had been adopted because it had been found that in many villages bribery had been used to influence the election. This was not true in Village J. We may wonder whether, under the new regulation, its village head was forced to retire.

The village head and his assistant appointed the heads of the lin and lü. Village J had four lü and twenty lin heads. The lin heads had but little to do. The lü heads coöperated with the village head and assistant head in handling local affairs.

There was a large tablet, inscribed "Village Self-Government," which stood sometimes in front of the gate of the Kuan Ti Miao and sometimes in front of the Ts'u Shih Miao, as there was no official village headquarters. All meetings of the village officers were held in the home of the village head.

On the eve of Chinese New Year's the village head appointed two public servants, the *hsiang-yo* and the *ti-fang*.[1] In many ways they corresponded to modern police officers. They were appointed by having their names posted in a public place and generally without their previous consent. They were to serve for one year and without pay. It was said that there was no record of any appointee having refused to serve; in fact, they could not refuse. Although many of the responsibilities of the two officers were very similar, the hsiang-yo was a slightly higher officer and usually came from a slightly higher economic level. Under the Ch'ing dynasty both appointees had to be below the rank of a hsiu ts'ai.

The hsiang-yo was to act as an informal arbitrator and hear all suits before they went to the higher authorities; he was to see to it that the accused did not avoid the issue by leaving the area; and he was to be a witness when land divisions were established by possession.

In the case of robbery or theft both the hsiang-yo and the ti-fang were notified.

Rotation of leaders.—The village she had eight leaders who served for a term of one year. For the selection of the leaders the village was divided into eight approximately equal groups of families. Each group selected one of its family heads to serve as its representative in the she. It was customary to select the leaders in rotation from the different families, so that the head of each of the 110 families living in the village would serve as a she leader for one year every thirteen years.

The new leaders were chosen after the completion of the sacrifices on the twenty-third day of the twelfth month, the day on which the kitchen god was burned so he could go up and make his annual report to his celestial superior. On New Year's Day they met with the old leaders to discuss the transfer of the village business, especially the money and the accounts. The last business meeting of the old group was ordinarily held on the first day of the tenth month, as there was little business after the harvest.

The man who was appointed to keep the village accounts was usually the most influential man in the group and automatically was the leader of the she for the year that he held office.

Religious ceremonies.—The she leaders arranged for the regular religious sacrifices held on the eleventh day of the first month, the second day of the second month, the third day of the third month, the thirteenth day of the fifth month, the sixth day of the sixth month, the first day of the seventh month, the harvest thanksgiving in the eighth month, the ninth day of the ninth month, the first day of the tenth month, and the twenty-third day of the twelfth month. After the services were over, the offerings of food that had been placed before the altars were divided among the she leaders. On the eleventh day of the first month, however, when special offerings were made to Kuan Ti, and on the sixth day of the sixth month, when offerings were presented to the dragon god, and also on the thanksgiving day in the eighth month, all the villagers shared in the distribution. In Village J the special thanksgiving offering was in the form of a Chinese house, with three rooms, made from flour boiled in fat.

The field report said that by custom there were performances of plays on the thanksgiving day and that plays were performed occasionally on the days honoring Kuan Ti and the dragon god.

Crop-watching.—The she leaders arranged for the protection of the spring wheat crop and the fall crops. They hired only one crop-watcher. He was paid by the she and received $3 for the spring season and about $5 for the fall season, which ran from the first of the seventh month to the end of the harvest, about the end of the ninth month. Besides his pay, the watchman was also given food that was prepared for him by the farming families. In the spring season families with fewer than 50 mu did not give any food, those with from 50 to 100 mu gave food for one day, those with 100 mu or more gave food for two days.

In the fall season those with fewer than 30 mu were exempt from the food contribution, those with from 30 to 60 mu gave one day's food, those with from 60 to 90 mu gave two days' food, and so on in steps of 30 mu. The head of the she arranged the order in which the families were to supply the food and sent a slip of paper to the first family on the list. After they contributed their share, they were to send the slip on to the family next in line. If they failed to do so, they were responsible for an extra day's food.

If the crops were especially good and the one employed watchman was unable to protect the crops properly, the farmers assisted him, usually going out in turn in groups of five. Again the slip was passed from one group to the next. The groups were arranged by the she leader, and the number of times a family had to provide a volunteer was determined by the number of mu the family was farming.

The garlic and reed crops also needed watching, but the necessary arrangements were made by the farmers concerned with those crops, not by the she. The period for the garlic-watching was from the fifth to the seventh month and for the reeds from the eighth to the tenth month. The arrangements for the pay and food for the watchers of these crops were similar to those for the watchers of the spring and fall crops.

If the crop watchmen caught anyone who had harmed the crops, the temple bell was rung to summon the she leaders to discuss and determine the punishment—usually beatings for the poor and fines for the well-to-do. If the watchman caught a thief or trespasser during the daytime, he was to receive half of the fine. If he caught any at night he was supposed to receive the whole fine. Fines paid to the she were used to buy oil, lanterns, chairs, and tools.

Night watch.—The village night watch was carried on from the first day of the tenth month to the second day of the second month. Only one watchman was employed. He was paid $2 per month, but, unlike the crop-watchers, was not provided with food by the various families. He regularly made the rounds of the village for the second, third, and fourth watches. He rang the number of the watch on a metal gong, but did not use the wooden pang usually carried by the night watch in other villages. During the third watch he knocked on the door of every house in order to keep the occupants alert and vigilant.

In the eleventh and twelfth months, from seven to eight volunteers shared the work with the hired watchman. Again the order of service for the volunteers was worked out by the head of the she and the families were notified of their turn when they received the slip passed on to them by the preceding family. Although no cooked food was furnished, the hired watchman and the volunteers were each given half a catty of flour for every night's work.

According to regulations, all males between the ages of eighteen and thirty-five years were required to serve in the self-protection organization of the village, but the organization was purely on paper, as no one joined it. Again, according to regulations, one out of every three brothers should join the village militia or guard, but that organization, too, existed only on paper.

Funds for public affairs.—Funds for public affairs were collected from the farming families. The she charged a total of 30 or 35 cents a mu, and the village self-government assessment was 10 cents a mu. The she collections were made by its leaders three times a year, when the principal sacrifices were offered and dramatic performances were sometimes presented—on the eleventh day of the first month, the sixth day of the sixth month, and the thanksgiving day in the eighth month. Before 1912 the amounts collected usually were 8 cash per mu in the first month, 12 cash in the sixth month, and 24 cash in the eighth month. The rates in the 1930's were 5 cents per mu for the first collection, 10 cents for the second, and 15 or 20 cents for the third.

Dramatic performances were sometimes given on two special occasions: in thanksgiving for protection from sickness and in praying for rain during a time of drought. Expenses for the first were met by a per capita assessment on rich and poor alike. For the second type the cost was met partly by an assessment per mu of land and partly by subsidy from the Old Granary.

Administration of the land tax.—For assessing and collecting the land tax, the hsien was divided into 22 *li*. Each li was further divided into 10 *chia*, or neighborhoods. Depending on the size of the villages, a chia might include several villages or a village might include more than one chia. Village J was a single chia.

Each li had a li elder and a secretary. The elder was to follow up those who had not paid their taxes; the secretary was to determine the amount of tax to be paid by the individual families, changing it as their landholdings changed.

Every chia had a *t'an-tou*—the keeper of the official tou measure—who also was responsible for endeavoring to collect any unpaid taxes due from the chia landowners. For that service he was paid by the village she the sum of 1,000 coppers per year, about $2.50 in 1932.

The established hsien land-tax for Village J was 130 taels. It was said that the tax had been fixed nominally at one tael for every 20 mu, but that underregistration usually made it one tael for considerably more than 20 mu. This would not work out on the basis of the 2,200 mu reported as the "green circle" of Village J, but that might be expected, as the tax was collected on the basis of the residence of the owner rather than the location of the land. Taxes on any land that residents of Village J owned in other villages were assessed to Village J rather than to the village where the land was situated; similarly the nonresident owners of Village J land were assessed where they resided.

Although the amount of the tax was quoted in taels, the amount to be collected was determined by the tael-dollar exchange rate. The official rate was about $1.39 per tael, but in 1932 the collections were made at the rate of $2.50 per tael[2] for hsien and provincial taxes and an additional $2.00 per tael for district expenses, police, schools, etc. The two together made the tax bill for Village J some $585 per year.

Other assessments.—Besides the taxes, the village had to pay for the entertainment of officials traveling through and the support of troops stationed in the area. The entertainment expenses were relatively minor, but the military assessments were heavy, as the troops expected the area to provide their support, except for their ammunition. Money for the military was to be collected by the t'an-tou on orders from the li elder. The t'an-tou consulted with the village head, who then ordered the lü-chang to assist in the collection of the money.

The assessments were made on two bases, depending on whether the funds were for transport or for food, clothing, and fuel. For transport expenses the basis was the number of animals owned by the family. A mule and a horse each counted as one unit, oxen and asses as a half unit. For other military expenses the assessment basis was the number of mu owned. Assessments for military food and clothing ordinarily were collected by the she leaders on a village-wide basis, whereas those for transport usually were gathered by the lü-chang from the 25 families in his lü.

NAN YÜ SHAN SHE

Besides the she that looked after much of the village business, Village J had another totally independent she known as the Nan Yü Shan She ("South Jade Mountain she"). It had funds that it used for religious sacrifices and for accumulating the utensils and vessels regularly needed for funerals and weddings. Residents of Village J and the neighboring villages were allowed to use the equipment upon the payment of a small rental fee. The income of the she came from the profit derived from the mutual pooling of funds to be used for loans. The she differed from other moneylenders only in that its profit was used for philanthropic purposes.

XVIII: VILLAGE K

VILLAGE K is our sample village in Shantung. It was situated about three miles from the city of Taian. A census made shortly before our study gave the population as 380 families and 1,875 persons, an average of 4.9 persons per family. The land registered with and controlled by the village was 830 local mu, or 2,490 of the mu used in the Peiping area, one half instead of one sixth of an acre. The average farm was only 2.2 big mu or 6.6 small mu. Judging from this very low average, only a small proportion of the families were engaged in purely agricultural work. Nearness to the city undoubtedly made it possible for many families to earn their livelihood in nonagricultural activities.

POLITICAL ORGANIZATION

On the political side, the collective activities of the village were, in the latter years of the Ch'ing dynasty, taken care of by the heads of two large and prominent clans. By 1912, when we could get definite, dated historical material, the number of village elders had been increased to five, all of whom were large landowners. They divided the village activities among the different members of the group; some kept accounts, some managed the crop-watching, and some took care of miscellaneous matters.

In 1912 the number of village elders was increased to ten. One of the group was called the association head, and the others were known as assistants. Not until 1921 was the association head given the title of village head. At that time the function of crop-protection was the most important work of the village, and the "Association for the Protection of the Crops" was the controlling agency in the village.

Kung K'an I Po ("Watch the Crops Together") was a slogan still to be seen in 1933 on the walls of the temple. It either referred to an earlier period when the people came out in turn to watch the crops, or was part of an attempt to develop coöperative action among the farming families to replace the nine hired crop-watchers.

Changes in 1926.—In 1926 there was a fundamental change in the village organization. The man who had been village head for many years became tired of his responsibilities and of giving a large part of his time to community activities. During the preceding years the military had made many demands on the village, and it had been the responsibility of the village head to see that these demands were met and to work out the program for meeting them. The army became irritated with him, as they felt that he did not follow their orders closely and that he was dilatory. The villagers also objected to his administration; they felt that he spent too freely, and, of course, he was the one who called on them for the money. Unable to satisfy either group, he resigned.

After his resignation nobody dared to accept the position of village head—it involved too much work and too much responsibility. The village, therefore, was divided into six sections, each of which elected a section head and an assistant. When the whole village was involved in any problem, the six heads and their assistants met and made decisions that each of the six section leaders was to carry out in his particular area. As there was no over-all leader among the six section heads, a temporary chairman was selected to preside in an informal way whenever the group of section heads met. Even when the Nationalist government ordered the village to elect a head, the section heads simply asked the political agent to act in that capacity. For local affairs the six section heads and their assistants were the only ones to act.

In 1930 the village adopted a series of formal regulations outlining (1) the organization of the village assembly and its powers and responsibilities as the legislative body; (2) the organization and powers of the village administration as the executive body; (3) rules and regulations for the qualification and election of the village head, assistant head, and six section heads; and (4) a series of regulations governing the villagers' actions, especially those that were forbidden, and setting forth the punishment that would be meted out to those who violated the prohibitions.

These regulations were adopted in line with the new legislation enacted by the Nationalist government and also as a means of giving more power to the individual citizens and restricting the power of the village officials.

The full text of the regulations is given below. In general, the village assembly, made up of those more than twenty years of age, was to meet once a year to elect the village head, the assistant head, and the section heads and to pass on the proposed budget for village income and expense.

The village administration, which was to be elected annually, was to carry out orders of the higher government, all decisions of the village assembly, and all other village activities that needed their attention, and to appoint those who would be in charge of finance, education, and the local guard.

The age qualification for membership in the village administration was "more than twenty-five years of age."

It will be noted that the regulations called for the election by the assembly of two sets of village heads and assistants, with the hsien magistrate making the final selection. The hsien government was also to issue election certificates to the six section heads when it was notified of their election.

The punishment for trespass in the fields, theft of crops, and violation of other village regulations was to be kneeling before the temple altar for the time it took to burn one stick of incense and fines of from 10 cents to $15. Serious cases of those refusing to accept the decision of the village authorities were to be sent to the district or the hsien government.

The field reports commented that the rules and regulations adopted by the village assembly were not always meticulously observed.

REGULATIONS FOR THE VILLAGE ASSEMBLY, VILLAGE K

1. Any village resident more than twenty years of age can be a member of the village assembly (the customary family-unit system is to be followed). The following, however, are not allowed to join the assembly:

> Anyone guilty of bad behavior and corrupt action
> Opium sellers
> Gamblers
> Thieves
> Anyone suffering from mental disease
> Anyone undergoing criminal punishment
> Anyone barred by the village assembly

2. The functions of the village assembly shall be:

> The election of the village head, the assistant head, and the section heads
> Such functions as are delegated to it by the higher governmental organizations
> Adoption and modification of the village regulations
> To act on proposals made by the section heads
> To act on proposals made by the village head and assistant head
> To adopt other beneficial actions

To act on any measures proposed by twenty members of the
assembly.
The assembly shall hold two kinds of meetings:
A regular annual meeting
Special meetings called in case of emergency by the village head
A majority of the citizens must be present before the meeting is begun
These regulations shall be effective from the day they are adopted and
promulgated.

[Adopted, June 28, 1930]

VILLAGE COUNCIL REGULATIONS,
VILLAGE K

1. The village council is the executive organ for village affairs. It shall
consist of the following eight persons: the village head, the assistant
head, and the six section heads.
2. The activities of the village council shall consist of the following:
Those ordered by a higher government authority
Those delegated to it by the village assembly
Other matters beneficial to the village
Reporting on the condition of village affairs and on any special
business
3. Decisions of the village council shall be made by a majority of its
members.
4. Within one month after the spring festival the village council shall
appoint officers who shall be in charge of the village finances, the village
school, and the village guard.
5. Important business shall be referred to the village assembly for its
decision and before it is executed by the village council.
6. A record shall be kept of all village activities and a list of all those
participating in those activities.
7. The expenses of the village council must be approved by the village
assembly.
8. These regulations shall be effective from the day they are promulgated.

REGULATIONS FOR THE ELECTION OF VILLAGE
OFFICERS, VILLAGE K

1. Any citizen more than twenty-five years of age, who is not a teacher
and whose work is not outside the village, is qualified to be a candidate
for the office of village head or assistant head, provided he participates

in the village assembly and is honest and sincere and has some literary knowledge.

2. Two sets of village heads and assistant heads must be elected by the village assembly and submitted to the hsien government for its selection. The head of the district or his assistant shall be present to supervise the village election.

3. The village head and the assistant head shall be elected for a term of one year. The election shall be held within one month after the spring festival. If reëlected, the officials shall continue their services.

4. If new officials are elected, the old village head and assistant head must be prepared to hand over their offices to the new incumbents within three days after they have received their certificates of appointment from the hsien government. If the village head is reëlected, he shall report to the higher authorities, district and hsien, the dates of his new term.

5. The section heads shall be elected by the residents of each section within ten days after the new village head takes office. The names of the new heads shall be reported to the higher governments, and certificates of election shall be issued to each new officer.

6. These regulations shall be effective from the day they are promulgated.

REGULATIONS CONCERNING VILLAGE RESIDENTS, VILLAGE K

1. The regulations must be adopted by the village assembly.
2. These regulations prohibit the following:
    Opium smoking
    Gambling and prostitution
    Damage to the trees
    Trespassing in the fields

3. Any violations of these regulations shall be punished by a fine of from 10 cents to $15 and/or by customary punishment, such as kneeling before the temple altar for the period of the burning of a stick of incense. The old punishment of beating is not allowed.

4. Punishment for any infractions shall be determined by the village council, i.e., the village head, the assistant head, and the six section heads. Any member of the council who is related to the accused shall not sit with the council when the case is heard.

5. Those guilty of serious offenses must be sent to the hsien government. If an offender does not obey the orders of the village administration, he shall be sent to the district government or to the hsien government.

6. These regulations shall be effective from the day they are promulgated.

EDUCATION

The activities of the village organization were largely limited to education and the protection of the crops. Originally there were five private schools conducted as money-making activities by individuals. After the establishment of the republic a public or village school was started by the village leaders. In 1929, after the Nationalist government gained control of North China, the village school was reorganized under the supervision of and by order of the hsien bureau of education. In 1933 the school had 2 teachers and 72 pupils. One of the teachers was appointed by the hsien bureau of education, the other by the village school trustees. The combined salaries of the two teachers amounted to $160 a year, part of which was met by the tuition fees paid by the pupils. The rest came from the 2 per cent commission the village collected from the buyers of local land.

CROP-WATCHING

The protection of the crops was entrusted to nine watchmen responsible for eight sections. Two men were assigned to the hilly section in the northwest part of the village land. This was said to be a difficult area, but the second watchman for that section was the head watchman and rarely went out to the fields; instead, he spent much of his time in the village temple helping with the administration of village affairs.

Every watchman was expected to be physically strong and was usually poor and in need of employment. Applicants for the job had to be guaranteed by two residents of the village. An employment contract was signed by the watchman, the village head, and the watchman's two guarantors. One such contract read as follows:

I, ..., am willing to take charge of one section of village land and will protect the crops in that area. If damage is caused in that area by trespass, by the grazing of animals, or by crop-thieves, it will be my responsibility to find the owner of the animals or the thief. After I have found the persons responsible, I will report them to the damaged landowner so that he may take further action. If I cannot find the cul-

prit, I will be responsible for the damage done and will compensate the
owner for it. This is a written copy of what I have orally promised.

[*Signed*] .... Watchman
.... Village Head
.... Guarantor
.... Guarantor

It will be noted that the agreement says nothing about the rights
of the watchman, his term of employment, or his wages. Ordinarily
he could continue to hold the job as long as he wanted to, subject,
of course, to his good behavior.

In Village K the watchmen were usually paid in wheat for the
spring season, in millet for the fall season, and in money for the
winter. The rates paid by the landowners were reported to be four
catties of wheat per mu for the flat land and three catties per mu for
the hilly land. The millet rates were six catties per mu for the flat
land and four for the hilly land. The winter assessment was given as
10 cash per mu. Where payment was in kind it seems probable that
the assessment and payment rates, uninfluenced by any monetary
changes, had been approximately the same over a long period of
time.

The eight regular watchmen were said to get about 270 catties of
wheat, 460 catties of millet, and 10,000 cash apiece, with the head
watchman receiving an additional 10 per cent. In 1932 the cash payment amounted to about $2.50. The reported grain-assessment rates
would provide approximately the amount of grain received by the
watchmen, but it would require 10 coppers, 100 cash, rather than
10 cash per mu, to approximate the money received by the watchmen. Since 10 coppers were worth only 2.5 cents, that seems to be a
more logical rate. It must also be remembered that the rates quoted
were for the big mu used in Village K, which was three times the
size of the mu of the Peiping area.

The collection for crop-protection had no connection with the
financing of other village activities. A different form of assessment
was used to obtain the funds needed for those projects. The unit of
land taxation fixed by the hsien was ordinarily the basis of assessment
for such other village income.

CASES OF TRESPASS AND THEFT

In spite of the number of crop-watchers and their patrolling of the
fields, there were nearly always some minor cases of trespass and
theft. Usually they were so minor that neither the cultivators nor the

village authorities took them very seriously. Only two major cases were reported by the village. In one the head watchman caught a professional thief carrying a large load of millet. The watchman accused him of theft, but there was no proof that the grain was stolen and the accused refused to admit his guilt. The watchman and the thief got into a fight over the matter and both were injured. The other watchmen came to the help of their leader and arrested the accused. Later on, the head watchman gave him a thorough beating before bringing him before the village authorities. Finally the authorities ordered the thief to apologize to the landowner and that closed the case.

The second major theft occurred in 1919 when a group of thieves organized a secret society for the express purpose of stealing. Anyone, rich or poor, could join the organization, but the number of members was limited to twenty. There was to be a chief to manage the organization, an accountant to keep the records, and two managers to buy weapons and sell the stolen crops. Every member was to contribute $1 for the purchase of weapons. Fifteen men joined the society. Most of them came from poor families, but there were also some from well-to-do families.

After they had elected their leader, obtained their weapons, and made their business connections, the chief and ten members made their first foray at eleven o'clock on the night of the twentieth day of the sixth month. They captured the watchman and tied and gagged him. Then they cut a field of millet as rapidly as they could. Before daybreak they had finished 2 mu (one acre) and taken the grain to a predetermined location where they sold it to a group of bullies from other villages nearby. The money was paid over after a few days.

The thieves painted their faces and disguised their voices so that they were not recognized. But a man who had risen very early that morning and seen what was going on was convinced that they were local people. Acting on his information, the watchmen carefully searched the village. After several days' work they were able to report to the village officials both the existence of the secret society and the names of its members. The entire group was arrested and fined. After they took an oath that they would never again take part in any such activity, they were released.

HUNG CH'IANG HUI

The Red Spear Society (*Hung Ch'iang Hui*) was organized in Village K in 1925 when the "Honan Teacher," a religious leader, came to the village. Many people, including the village head, joined the society. The Teacher appointed the village head president of the local branch. The society became practically one of the village activities, with the village head leading it, with most of the villagers enrolled as members, and with the organized group giving protection against soldiers and bandits.

The organization of the society included two sections, a civil section for the control of finances and the keeping of records and other documents, and a military section for training the members in fighting and magic. The Honan Teacher had the supreme authority in the training of the members. The village head, as president of the branch, had considerable authority over the finances and organization.

Red spears were the only weapons used by the society. By means of magic and the wearing of a special talisman the members were supposedly made immune to bullets if they also refrained from sexual intercourse, from eating meat or other food from animals, and from all immoral actions. The expenses of the society were relatively small, as they included only the purchase of the red spears and other simple equipment and the support of the Honan Teacher. It was reported that each member was expected to contribute according to his financial ability, that ability generally being measured by the number of mu of land he owned.

The local village societies were all united under a Grand Teacher and a General President who had their headquarters in a village not far from Village K. The united organization had so much power that the small bandit groups were unable to operate. In fact, it was said that they "ran away like rabbits." The pressure on the bandits was such that to avoid starvation they decided to join forces and attempt to destroy the Red Spears. Some six hundred men were brought together and armed with rifles, knives, and other weapons.

The bandit group decided that they would act on the twentieth day of the third month of 1926. The plot was discovered and some two thousand members of the Red Spear Society were gathered to repel the attack. The temple headquarters of the society were left empty, but members were hidden all around the area. When the bandits reached the temple, they were attacked by the Red Spear men, who, because of their strong belief that they were immune to bullets, were very brave even when they faced rifle fire.

The two hundred bandits who came to Village K were defeated. They lost twenty-nine killed and another twenty-nine captured; many others were wounded, but were able to get away. The losses of the local Red Spear Society were five killed and twenty-nine wounded. The explanation of the failure of the magical incantations and charms was that someone threw shrimp skins into the village well and so vitiated the magical power of the Honan Teacher.

The Nationalists, when their forces reached Shantung, ordered the Red Spear societies to disband. The promoters of the movement made a show of compliance, but, in general, they simply changed the name and carried on as the Wu Chih Tao, a type of Taoist belief credited with unlimited power. The organization was able to help the Shansi soldiers of Governor Yen Hsi-shan defeat General Ma, one of Chiang K'ai-shek's commanders, during the civil war of 1930. When the fighting was over and Chiang had won, General Ma returned to the area and announced that he was going to punish the villages and level them to the ground. It was only after an apology from the magistrate and the complete dissolution of the Wu Chih Tao that General Ma was persuaded to give up his plan.

DISTRICT GUARD

After becoming firmly established in Shantung, the Nationalist government worked to establish the district guard as an official and legal organization for self-defense. A branch office was located in Village K. All adult males in the age group between twenty and forty years were expected to serve in the guard. In Village K there were 490 men who were eligible.

Every night thirty-two guards came out to keep watch on the four sides of the village. The hsien government gave the village four modern rifles, one for each section of the village. Other equipment included mainly red spears and broad knives. In case of emergency the guard was doubled to sixty-four men and divided into eight groups.

Notes

CHAPTER I: A SUMMARY

1 Chung-li Chang, *The Chinese Gentry* (Seattle: University of Washington Press, 1955), p. 33.
2 Sidney D. Gamble, *Ting Hsien: A North China Rural Community* (New York: Institute of Pacific Relations, 1954), pp. 129–130.
3 In some cases the magistrate might have to confirm the appointment.
4 Gamble, *Ting Hsien*, pp. 125–126.
5 All dollar figures are for Chinese silver dollars.
6 Seattle: University of Washington Press, 1960, pp. 6, 321, 505, 509.

CHAPTER II: VILLAGES—GENERAL DESCRIPTION

1 Gamble, *Ting Hsien*, pp. 143, 460.
2 *Ibid.*, p. 53.
3 See pp. 239–252.
4 Gamble, *Ting Hsien*, p. 49.
5 Sidney D. Gamble, *How Chinese Families Live in Peiping* (New York: Funk and Wagnalls, 1933), p. 124.
6 Gamble, *Ting Hsien*, p. 461.
7 These figures do not make any allowance for ownership of village land by nonresident families, nor do they take into account any land that resident families owned in other villages. In considering the averages we have assumed that these two items balance each other, at least approximately.
8 Gamble, *Ting Hsien*, p. 211.
9 *Ibid.*, p. 225.
10 *Ibid.*, pp. 209, 224.
11 *Ibid.*, pp. 24, 25, 55.
12 Sidney D. Gamble, *Peking: A Social Survey* (New York: George H. Doran Co., 1921), p. 99.
13 Gamble, *Ting Hsien*, p. 33.
14 John Lossing Buck, *Chinese Farm Economy* (Chicago: University of Chicago Press, 1930), pp. 337–338.
15 Gamble, *Ting Hsien*, pp. 41–44.
16 *Ibid.*, p. 21.

CHAPTER III: THE VILLAGE ASSOCIATION

1 *She* is pronounced like "shuh." It is a term that has been used since very early times. With the character *shu*, meaning "registration," it was used in the *Tso Chüan*, about the second century B.C., which told how the dukedom of Ch'i gave 500 shu-she to the dukedom of Wei. Yen Tzu told how Kuan Chung (d. 643 B.C.) was given 500 shu-she by Duke Huang. In the *Shih Chi* it was stated that King Chao of Ch'u contemplated giving Confucius some shu-she. The supplementary notes stated that there was a she for every 25 families in the community.

According to the *Li Chi* (the "Book of Rites"), there were many types of she—the grand she established by the king for the people, the royal she established by the king for himself, the state she established by the lords for the people, the feudal she established by the lords for themselves, and the ordinary she for the lower officers of the common people. The twenty-five-family unit was still the basic she. The Han and the Sui chronicles also spoke about the she and the number of families it should contain.

In the Sung dynasty the scholar Chu Hsi (1130–1200) initiated a system of village granaries called *she-ts'ang*. Ten families were to be organized into a *chia* and five chia into a she led by a *she-chang*, or chief, who took care of the grain stored in the granaries. The same scholar made improvements in the village school. The organization for the school was the same as that for the granary; it was called *she-shou*.

Under the Yuan dynasty the term "she" was used for a village-wide organization that was to oversee local affairs, such as agriculture, water utilization, the destruction of locusts, land colonization, and crop protection. Fifty was the minimum number of families for a she. Places with 100 families had two she. Those with fewer than 50 families were to unite with other villages to become she. The she for the village granary and the village schools were continued with their own managing heads, but under the supervision of the village she.

This form of village organization was not continued under the Ming dynasty. Later the government promoted the independent organization of school and granary she, but they were set up by only an occasional village.

Two she days, festivals, were held every year, in the spring to pray for a good year and in the fall to give thanks for the harvest. The villages celebrated these occasions with plenty of special cakes and wine.

Until 1918 most of the village associations of a religious or economic nature in Shansi were called she. In Honan we found three villages where the term was so used. One had a *Ch'iu Pao She* ("Thanksgiving Association") that was in charge of all sorts of economic and religious activities. Another had four she, each with four elders in charge of its activities; a general manager presided over the four groups. In the third village the association for crop protection was called the *Shou Wang She* ("Watch and Guard Association").

In Li-Ch'eng Hsien, Shantung, one village had a she with 12 elders who held office in rotation, six one year and six the next. In another village in the same hsien were two she, one on the east side and one on the west. In a village of Chang-ch'iu Hsien, Honan, there was one she until 1921, when there were three because of a disagreement and division among the village leaders.

2 For explanation of this change see pp. 38–44.

3 Some of the associations attempted to simplify and put into writing their formal rules and regulations. We found several of these documents during our study. Our Chinese colleagues' comment on them was: "When a written regulation conforms to old customs and traditions, it has no particular value for the people because it adds nothing new to the village association. When it attempts to introduce something new or eradicate something old, it also has no value, either for the villagers or for us, because it is a mere sheet of paper which can command no respect." Though these documents were evidently of doubtful value to the villagers, they give us a record of what the association leaders felt were the basic rules of the organization.

4 The "Second Eighth Month" is an example of the insertion of intercalary months to adjust the Chinese lunar calendar to the solar year. There were seven such months in every 19-year period.

CHAPTER IV: VILLAGE LEADERS

1 Chang, *The Chinese Gentry*, p. 3.

2 Hosea B. Morse, *The International Relations of the Chinese Empire* (London: Longmans, Green & Co., 1910), Vol. I, p. 370 n.

3 Kenneth Scott Latourette, *The Chinese: Their History and Culture* (New York: Macmillan, 1934), Vol. II, p. 43.

4 For details see p. 151.

5 See chap. v, pp. 100–101.

6 Chang, *The Chinese Gentry*, p. 61.

7 In one village a grain shop, which registered 320 mu of land and had a record of 120 years of service, was listed as one of the association heads. It has been omitted from the tables.

8 For a description of the activity of bullies in North China villages see Arthur H. Smith, *Village Life in China: A Study in Sociology* (New York: F. H. Revell Co., 1899), pp. 211–225.

CHAPTER V: CROP WATCHING

1 For their ordinary meetings the village elders used one of the smaller rooms of the temple. The village police used another for their head-quarters.
2 For details see pp. 90–91.
3 For additional data on the exchange rate see pp. 126–128.
4 T'ien-p'ei Meng and Sidney D. Gamble, "Prices, Wages and the Standard of Living in Peking," *Chinese Social and Political Science Review*, special supplement, July, 1926, pp. 69, 72.
5 War lord from Manchuria.
6 This and the following cases were all reported by the same village.
7 Probably an oxidized mercuric sulphate, or an arsenic compound, readily available in the Chinese apothecary shops and used in the villages to control rodents.
8 Leafless parasite plants of genus *Cuscuta*.
9 Illustrative material from nonsample villages.

CHAPTER VI: OTHER VILLAGE FUNCTIONS

1 Gamble, *Ting Hsien*, p. 193.
2 *Ibid.*, p. 198.
3 *Ibid.*, pp. 191, 207.
4 As has been noted previously, this event was celebrated on the sixth day of the sixth month in some villages and on the twenty-fourth day of the sixth month in others.
5 Gamble, *Ting Hsien*, pp. 21, 402.
6 This was 5 fewer families than the 64 living in the village in 1932, but the lawsuit was held in 1915 and the number of families could well have been increased meanwhile by division and possibly by the im-migration of the two families who were unrelated to either of the two family lines resident in the village for almost five hundred years.
7 Our report did not give the Chinese names of the two goddesses of earth, but it seems probable that one was T'u Ti P'o P'o, the female part or wife of T'u Ti, the god of the local earth, and the other Hou T'u, the goddess of the whole earth, whose position was equal to that of heaven. Hou T'u had a fish that held up the world. When the

fish moved, the world shook: Japan's many earthquakes were caused by its location on the fish's tail.

8 Gamble, *Ting Hsien*, pp. 329–334, 344–370.
9 *Ibid.*, p. 405.

CHAPTER VII: MONEY, EXCHANGE, AND VILLAGE FINANCE

1 [Republic of China,] National Tariff Commission, *The Shanghai Market Prices Report* (Shanghai: Oct.–Dec., 1933), p. 47.
2 Figures that may have been collected on exchange rates in Shantung, Honan, and Shansi were not translated and sent on to us before the field notes were lost when the Japanese army invaded Peiping.
3 See note on intercalary months, chap. iii, n. 4.

CHAPTER VIII: VILLAGE A

1 Gamble, *Ting Hsien*, p. 58.
2 Buck, *Chinese Farm Economy*, pp. 337–338.
3 In Village J the exchange rate was given as $2.50.

CHAPTER IX: VILLAGE B

1 Gamble, *Ting Hsien*, p. 22.
2 See p. 41.
3 In 1931 it was down to 6,264 mu.

CHAPTER X: VILLAGE C

1 Gamble, *Ting Hsien*, p. 41.
2 *Lien Hua Lao* was the name of a song said to have been sung by Kuan Yin, the goddess of mercy. Moved by the grief and prayers of a man who had been unable to fulfill his vow that for his mother's recovery from a serious illness he would collect money to repair a bridge in the village, she came down from her lotus throne, changed herself into a beggar woman and, taking two petals from the lotus, went out into the village to gather the funds needed to repair the bridge. The lotus petals turned into two petal-shaped pieces of

bamboo, and the goddess used their clicking as her accompaniment as she sang her *Lien Hua Lao* song.

CHAPTER XI: VILLAGE D

1 See p. 52.
2 For further details see p. 206.

CHAPTER XII: VILLAGE E

1 Meng and Gamble, "Prices, Wages and the Standard of Living in Peking," p. 89.
2 Based on the annual total expenditures as shown in the account books.

CHAPTER XV: VILLAGE H

1 Jung-pang Lo, "The Controversy over Grain Conveyance During the Reign of Qubilai Oagan, 1260–94." *Far Eastern Quarterly*, XIII, No. 3 (May, 1954), pp. 263, 285.
2 See also p. 319, Table 8.
3 Gamble, *How Chinese Families Live in Peiping*, pp. 21, 286, 315, and *Ting Hsien*, pp. 24, 66, 84, 117.
4 Headings have been added by the translator.
5 Capping was a family ceremony held in olden times for a son when he attained the age of twenty years.
6 Right and left of a person looking out from the altar with the ancestral tablets or from the tomb of the first ancestor at the top of the grave-yard.

CHAPTER XVI: VILLAGE I

1 Sidney D. Gamble, *Peking Wages*, Yenching University (Peiping), Department of Sociology and Social Work, Series C, No. 21, Dec., 1929, p. 8.
2 The field report gave 1912 as the year when the village began to collect a fee for land measurement, but the detailed account for 1910 showed $4.33 received for that service.
3 The measurer lived in one village and had a deputy in each of the other four.

4 Meng and Gamble, "Prices, Wages and the Standard of Living in Peking," p. 72.

5 Nankai Institute of Economics, "Economic Indices," *Nankai Quarterly*, IX, No. 2 (1936), p. 537.

CHAPTER XVII: VILLAGE J

1 In 1737, the second year of his reign, Ch'ien Lung established the office of ti-fang. One was to be appointed in every village. The duties at that time were to register land, households, and marriages; to advise and encourage people to pay their taxes; and to arrest criminals.

2 In Village A the exchange rate was given as $2.30.

TABLES

TABLE 1

NUMBER OF FAMILIES IN FOUR GROUPS OF VILLAGES

Number of families in village	Ting[a]		Tsou-p'ing[b]		Wan-p'ing, 4th District		Wan-p'ing, 5th District	
	Number	Per cent	Number	Per cent	Number	Per cent	Number	Per cent
Below 50	90	19.9	108	30.9	20	40.0	12	30.0
50– 99	118	26.1	131	37.3	17	34.0	9	22.5
100–149	71	15.7	70	20.0	7	14.0	9	22.5
150–199	60	13.3	22	6.3	2	4.0	4	10.0
200–249	35	7.7	10	2.9	2	4.0	2	5.0
250–299	36	8.0	4	1.1	...	...	2	5.0
300–349	16	3.5	2	0.6	2	4.0	1	2.5
350–399	10	2.2	2	0.6	...	...	...	...
400–449	6	1.3	1	0.3	...	...	...	...
450–499	4	0.9	...	...	...	...	...	...
500 and above	7	1.4	...	...	...	...	1	2.5
Total	453	100.0	350	100.0	50	100.0	40	100.0
Average	150	...	90	...	...	80	...	125

[a] Data from Sidney D. Gamble, *Ting Hsien: A North China Rural Community* (New York: Institute of Pacific Relations, 1954), p. 55.
[b] Unpublished census, 1932.

TABLE 2

SURNAMES IN 62 TING HSIEN VILLAGES

Number of surnames	Number of villages	Number of surnames	Number of villages
1	1	9	4
2	1	10	5
3	5	11	7
4	6	12	...
5	6	13	1
6	4	14	4
7	7	15 or more	6
8	5		
		Total	62

SOURCE: Franklin C. H. Lee, *Ting Hsien She Hui Kai K'uang Tiao Ch'a*, National Association of the Mass Education Movement, 1933, p. 121.

TABLE 3

LAND AREA IN VILLAGE "GREEN CIRCLE," FIVE GROUPS OF VILLAGES

Area in mu	Wan-p'ing Hsien, 4th District	Wan-p'ing Hsien, 5th District	Ting Hsien, 1st Police District	Ting Hsien, 1st Experimental District	Ting Hsien, all villages[a]
0– 499	2	4	4	1	20
500– 999	7	8	13	6	66
1,000–1,499	5	5	15	8	62
1,500–1,999	4	5	11	5	41
2,000–2,499	6	4	3	6	58
2,500–2,999	12	3	8	1	36
3,000–3,999	3	4	9	12	56
4,000–4,999	1	1	2	8	42
5,000–5,999	1	1	3	4	25
6,000–6,999	3	2	1	3	26
7,000–9,999	5	3	2	6	11
10,000 or more	1	...	...	2	10
Total	50	40	71	62	453
Minimum	200 mu	309 mu	245 mu	260 mu	245 mu
Maximum	11,500 mu	8,791 mu	7,800 mu	10,200 mu	32,500 mu
Average	3,090 mu	2,570 mu	2,200 mu	3,650 mu	3,120 mu

[a] Data from Gamble, *Ting Hsien*, p. 465.

TABLE 4

AVERAGE CROP AREA PER RESIDENT FAMILY, FIVE GROUPS OF VILLAGES

Area in mu	Wan-p'ing Hsien, 4th District	Wan-p'ing Hsien, 5th District	Ting Hsien, 1st Police District	Ting Hsien, 1st Experimental District	Ting Hsien, all villages[a]
0.1– 9.9	...	2	1	...	11
10.0–14.9	...	5	7	1	64
15.0–19.9	3	10	28	16	142
20.0–24.9	6	8	24	23	108
25.0–29.9	3	9	7	11	67
30.0–34.9	5	4	3	7	33
35.0–39.9	10	2	1	3	13
40.0–44.9	6	...	...	...	8
45.0–49.9	6	...	...	...	2
50 or more	11	...	...	1	5
Total	50	40	71	62	453
Minimum	17.4 mu	6.4 mu	9.8 mu	11.4 mu	...
Maximum	87.5 mu	35.1 mu	35.8 mu	50.0 mu	...
Average	38.2 mu	20.7 mu	21.6 mu	22.8 mu	20.4 mu

[a] Data from Gamble, *Ting Hsien*, p. 222.

TABLE 5

FAMILY LANDHOLDINGS IN SEVEN SAMPLE VILLAGES,
PER CENT OF FARMED AREA

Area in mu	A Per cent	B Per cent	C Per cent	F Per cent	F, Res.[a] Per cent	G Per cent	G, Res.[a] Per cent	H, Res.[a] Per cent	I Per cent
0– 4	21.4	7.7	...	14.9	14.6	16.4	19.0	...	15.0
5– 9	30.3	17.0	33.9[b]	38.3	30.9	30.0	19.0	36.1[b]	23.1
10–14	19.6	14.3	...	10.6	16.4	19.3	16.4	...	...
15–19	14.3	10.4	36.2[c]	14.9	12.7	10.7	12.7	25.9[c]	24.2[c]
20–29	3.6	16.4	10.3	11.7	10.9	10.1	13.9	12.8	...
30–39	5.4	8.4	4.9	3.2	9.1	5.0	8.9	6.6	...
40–49	1.8	5.9	3.1	2.1	1.8	3.5	3.7	4.4	23.2[d]
50–59	1.8	4.5	...	...	1.8	2.9	3.8	...	...
60–79	1.8	3.5	...	...	...	1.4	1.3	...	...
80–99	...	2.8	5.8[e]	...	...	0.7	1.3	9.5[e]	11.0[e]
100 or more	...	9.1	5.8	2.2	1.8	...	...	4.7	3.5
No data	...	...	...	2.1	...	...	...	...	...
Total	100.0	100.0	100.0	100.0	100.0	100.0	100.0	100.0	100.0
Under 20 mu	85.6	49.4	70.1	78.7	74.6	76.4	68.1	62.0	62.3
Under 50 mu	96.4	80.1	88.4	95.7	95.4	95.0	93.6	85.8	85.5
Total families	116	317	224	94	55	140	79	274	173

[a] Resident families.
[b] Includes 0–4 mu area.
[c] Includes 10–14 mu area.
[d] Includes 20–39 mu area.
[e] Includes 50–79 mu area.

TABLE 6

RESIDENT AND NONRESIDENT LAND CULTIVATORS
LISTED ON LAND BOOKS OF SEVEN VILLAGES

Village	Resident	Nonresident	Total	Per cent nonresident
A	86	30	116	25.8
B	287	18	325	6.0
D	98	35	133	26.0
F	55	39	94	41.5
G	79	61	140	43.6
H	276	102	376	37.0
L	54	46	100	46.0

TABLE 7

SIZE OF FARM FIELDS, VILLAGE D
AND FOUR TING HSIEN VILLAGES

	Village D			Four Ting Hsien villages[a]	
Area in mu	Number of fields	Per cent of farmed area	Area in mu	Number of fields	Per cent of farmed area
0– 4	72	22.7	0– 4	2,669	70.3
5– 9	149	47.0	5– 9	760	20.0
10–14	62	19.6	10–14	220	5.8
15–19	31	9.8	15–24	88	2.3
20 or more	3	0.9	25 or more	26	0.7
			No data	35	0.9
Total	317	100.0			
			Total	3,798[b]	100.0

[a] Data from Gamble, *Ting Hsien*, p. 225.
[b] There were 1,139 families in the four villages.

TABLE 8

SIZE OF INDIVIDUAL FAMILIES IN FOUR VILLAGES AND ONE CLAN

Number of persons in family	Village A	Village B	Village C	Village H	Total	Clan X (of Village H)
1	4	16	11	26	57	5
2	4	27	25	28	84	4
3	16	57	53	39	165	3
4	13	68	64	60	205	7
5	3	60	40	62	165	13
6	7	21	26	54	108	10
7	7	27	20	35	89	9
8	3	17	14	19	53	2
9	3	7	8	18	36	1
10	2	4	2	8	16	3
11	1	2	4	4	11	2
12	1	...	1	5	7	1
13	...	1	3	3	7	1
14 or more	...	...	5	14	19	8
Total	64	307	276	375	1,022	69
Total persons	312	1,406	1,373	2,126	5,217	509
Persons in average family	4.9	4.6	5.0	5.7	5.1	7.4
Persons in median family	4	4	4	5	5	6

TABLE 9

COMPARATIVE AGE DISTRIBUTION, VILLAGES A AND C, TING HSIEN,
CHIHLI, AND UNITED STATES RURAL FARM POPULATION

(In per cent of total populations)

Age	Village A	Village C	Ting Hsien[a]	Chihli[b]	United States rural farm[c]
Under 15 years:					
Males	30.4	24.3	33.4	36.1	35.0
Females	26.2	26.6	32.8	33.7	37.2
All	28.5	25.4	33.1	34.9	36.0
Under 25 years:					
Males	49.7	45.2	50.8	51.7	54.8
Females	41.1	45.4	49.2	49.6	56.2
All	46.1	45.1	50.0	50.6	55.4
25–49 years:					
Males	31.5	36.0	33.5	32.9	27.4
Females	31.2	33.1	33.0	33.4	29.0
All	31.4	34.6	33.2	33.1	28.0
50 years and older:					
Males	18.8	18.8	15.7	15.4	17.8
Females	27.7	21.5	17.8	17.0	14.8
All	22.5	20.3	16.8	16.3	16.6
Males	171	675	15,780	1,062	—
Females	141	698	14,862	1,104	—
Total persons	312	1,373	30,642	2,166	—

[a] Data from Gamble, *Ting Hsien,* p. 58.

[b] Data from John Lossing Buck, *Chinese Farm Economy* (Chicago: University of Chicago Press, 1930), pp. 337–338.

[c] Data from United States Census, 1930, Vol. II, p. 501.

TABLE 10

Age and Sex Distribution in Five-Year Age-Groups, Villages A and C Combined

Age (years)	Males	Females	Age (years)	Males	Females
0– 4	82	92	45–49	47	55
5– 9	71	68	50–54	45	47
10–14	63	62	55–59	43	44
15–19	98	90	60–64	29	28
20–24	76	61	65–69	17	28
25–29	72	64	70–74	15	22
30–34	63	52	75–79	8	9
35–39	52	54	80–84	1	9
40–44	63	51	85–89	1	3
			Total	846	839

TABLE 11

Age When Married, Village C

Age (years)	Number Males	Number Females	Age (years)	Number Males	Number Females
11	1	2	25	10	4
12	2	1	26	14	6
13	4	2	27	6	5
14	16	16	28	3	1
15	14	16	29	5	2
16	31	71	30	7	2
17	36	13	31	7	...
18	53	125	32	3	...
19	36	27	33	1	...
20	31	79	34	...	1
21	30	13	37	1	...
22	32	26	38	2	...
23	13	5	Unknown	5	3
24	14	14	Total	377	434

TABLE 12

AGE, EDUCATION, AND LANDOWNERSHIP OF ASSOCIATION HEADS,
VILLAGES A AND C

	Village A			Village C		
Member	Age (years)	Years of education	Number of mu owned	Age (years)	Years of education	Number of mu owned
A	62	8	28	40	8	450
B	55	11	36	45	6	250
C	54	5	19	36	8	170
D	45	8	30	42	5	160
E	44	4	18	21	8	350
F	38	5	7	54	6	80
G	28	6	46	48	6	70
H	26	6	39	30	8	150
I	—	—	—	40	8	80
J	—	—	—	45	8	20
K	—	—	—	21	8	100
L	—	—	—	70	8	50
M	—	—	—	54	6	65
N	—	—	—	34	5	100
O	—	—	—	52	4	80
P	—	—	—	54	4	80
Q	—	—	—	43	6	60
R	—	—	—	40	6	60
S	—	—	—	54	6	0
T	—	—	—	50	6	560
Average	44	6.6	27.5	43.6	6.5	146.5

NOTE: Members A–F are members of Village C executive committee.

TABLE 13

VILLAGE ASSOCIATION HEADS: AGE DISTRIBUTION, AGE WHEN APPOINTED,
YEARS OF SERVICE, GENERATIONS OF FAMILY SERVICE

Twelve villages					Five villages	
Years of age	Age	Number appointed when this age	Years of service	Heads	Genera-tions in service	Families represented
15–19	1	13	1– 5	34	1	11
20–24	5	20	6–10	29	2	4
25–29	4	22	11–15	27	3	12
30–34	8	25	16–20	19	4	8
35–39	10	25	21–25	8	5	6
40–44	29	18	26–30	7	6	4
45–49	24	9	31–35	7	7	2
50–54	26	6	36–40	5	8	1
55–59	13	2	41–45	2	...	...
60–64	9	1	46–50	...	...	...
65–69	4	...	51–55	2	...	...
70–74	2	...	56–60	1	...	...
75–79	4	...	...	...	...	...
80–85	2	...	...	...	...	...
Total	141	141		141		48

TABLE 14

Wages and Bonuses of Watchmen in a Village in the Peiping Area, 1909–1924

Year	Annual		Seasonal	
	Tiao	Dollar equivalent[a]	Tiao	Dollar equivalent[a]
1909	60[b]	$46.80[b]	15.0	$11.70
1910	...	...	17.6	13.40
1911	60	46.00	15.0	11.50
1912	...	...	...	...
1913	...	...	...	...
1914	70	53.00	19.5	14.80
1915	70	51.70	19.0	14.00
1916	75	56.00	19.5	14.60
1917	75	60.70	19.5[b]	15.80[b]
1918	75	55.90	20.0	14.90
1919	75	54.40	20.0	14.50
1920	80	56.70	25.0	17.70
1921	75	49.10	20.0	13.10
1922	70	41.00	20.0	11.70
1923	80	41.40	27.0	14.00
1924	110	47.20	30.0	12.90

Real Wages Index Number

	Annual	Seasonal
1924 (1909 = 100)	71	78
1924 (1914 = 100)	66	62

[a] Converted at Peking exchange rates to nearest 10 cents. Exchange figures from T'ien-p'ei Meng and Sidney D. Gamble, "Prices, Wages and the Standard of Living in Peking," *Chinese Social and Political Science Review*, special supplement, July, 1926, p. 89.

[b] Italics: Estimated, not in original record.

TABLE 15

FALL CROP-MONEY RATES OF 21 NEIGHBORING VILLAGES
NEAR PEIPING, 1929–1933
(In cents per mu)

Village	1929	1930	1931	1932	1933	Average	Index numbers[a]
1	70	35	65	50	50	54	71
2	50	40	40	45	45	44	90
3	45	45	40	45	45	44	100
4	40	40	45	45	45	43	112
5	45	35	40	40	45	41	100
6	40	25	35	45	50	39	125
7	30	30	40	45	50	39	167
8	50	40	30	30	35	37	70
9	50	40	30	30	30	36	60
10	30	35	37	34	30	33	100
11	40	30	30	30	30	32	75
12	30	30	30	30	40	32	133
13	40	30	35	30	20	31	50
14	30	20	25	20	60	31	200
15	30	25	25	30	30	28	100
16	35	30	25	20	20	26	57
17	30	25	20	25	25	25	83
18	30	30	10	20	20	22	67
19	20	20	20	20	30	22	150
20	15	18	20	20	30	21	200
21	15	20	15	18	30	20	200
Average	36.4	30.6	31.3	32.0	36.2	33.3	99

[a] Index numbers showing relation of 1933 rate to that of 1929.

TABLE 16

FARMING FAMILIES AND REGISTERED LAND AREAS, VILLAGE A, 1926–1932

Year	Families			Mu		
	Resident	Non-resident	Total	Resident	Non-resident	Total
1926	53	27	80	856	86	942
1927	54	27	81	833	91	924
1928	53	27	80	796	92	888
1929	51	27	78	766	92	858
1930	54	27	81	756	92	848
1931	55	30	85	768	86	854
1932	56	30	86	743	86	829

TABLE 17
Income and Expense, Village A, 1926–1932

INCOME

Year	Crop money	Persimmons	Apricots	Trees	Rent	Military	Misc.	Total	Cumulative surplus
1925									$ 70
1926	$ 252	$ 375	$...	$ 10	$ 15	$ 36	$ 20	$708	275
1927	288	40	30	...	2	29	26	415	290
1928	352	175	29	...	...	19	32	607	156
1929	273	100	22	475	38	51	64	1,023	344
1930	253	110	5	...	...	...	41	409	270
1931	273	220	25	...	25	...	35	578	372
1932	232	270	50	...	20	...	214	786	563
Total	$1,923	$1,290	$161	$485	$100	$135	$432	$4,526	...

EXPENSE

Year	Watch	Guard	Police	Military	Temple	Thanksgiving	School	Misc.	Total
1926	$ 36	$ 5	$ 10	$ 287	$ 95	$ 38	$...	$ 32	$ 503
1927	38	20	35	126	112	30	...	39	400
1928	31	32	6	563	87	...	...	22	741
1929	62	36	6	336	216	60	...	119	835
1930	61	27	...	122	143	41	28	53	475
1931	52	31	10	29	199	46	53	64	484
1932	40	33	17	82	191	43	68	121	595
Total	$320	$184	$ 84	$1,545	$1,043	$258	$149	$450	$4,033

TABLE 18
Miscellaneous Income and Expense, Village A, 1931–1932

INCOME		EXPENSE	
Repayment, land-tax advance	$ 28.37	Roadbuilding	$ 55.08
Land cultivation	4.00	Bridge repair	4.20
Slaughtering tax	1.00	Slaughtering tax	2.30
New Year feast	.40	Travel	2.40
		Rural bank	3.43
		Tax advance	33.00
		Miscellaneous	21.05
Total	$ 33.77	Total	$121.46

TABLE 19

NONAGRICULTURAL OCCUPATIONS OF VILLAGE B RESIDENTS

Work or shop	Number of persons	Work or shop	Number of persons
Awning shop	1	Miller	1
Bean curd maker	9	Native goods shop	6
Camel driver	15	Noodle maker	1
Carpenter	1	Oil press	4
Chairmaker	1	Pea curd maker	2
Charcoal burner	16	Vegetable garden	3
Cook	1	Wooden fork maker	3
Physician, old style	6	Wooden sieve maker	1
Foreign goods shop	3		
Mason	1	Total	75

TABLE 20

CROP-MONEY CHARGES AND RECEIPTS, VILLAGE B, 1923–1932

Year	Charge	Number of mu of land	Due	Paid	Per cent collected
1923	$0.048[a]	...	...	$ 379	...
1924	0.085[a]	...	...	666	...
1925	0.035[a]	...	...	278	...
1926	0.13	8,712.50	$1,133	943	72.5
1927	0.10	8,761.00	876	838	95.5
1928	0.25	8,579.20	2,145	1,865	87.0
1929	0.16	8,674.25	1,488	1,268	85.0
1930	0.08[b]	12,700.38[c]	1,016	965	94.0
1931	0.1035[b]	12,528.30[c]	1,297	1,025	79.0
1932	0.15[a]	...	...	1,783	...

NOTE: The total due, 1926–1931 was $7,955; collected, $6,904 (86.8 per cent).
[a] Approximate.
[b] Actual; half of quoted rate.
[c] Actual; reported on the village books at half of actual.

TABLE 21

INCOME AND EXPENSE, VILLAGE B, 1923–1932

INCOME

Year	Crop-money	Bond	Fines and indemnities	Misc.	Total	Loans
1923	$ 379	$ . . .	$ 15	$ 1	$ 395	$ 222
1924	666	99	13	106	884	136
1925	278	49	31	5	363	174
1926	943	. . .	9	21	973	280
1927	838	. . .	43	15	896	60
1928	1,865	50	6	21	1,942	1,175
1929	1,268	. . .	33	20	1,321	263
1930	965	. . .	61	. . .	1,026	294
1931	1,025	. . .	34	. . .	1,059	319
1932	1,783	7	54	159	2,003	1,003
Total	$10,010	$205	$299	$348	$10,862	$3,926

EXPENSE

Year	Crop-watching	Guard	Police	Military	Collection	Misc.	Total	Loans repaid
1923	$ 99	$ . . .	$ 42	$ 77	$ 40	$ 130	$ 388	$ 372
1924	146	. . .	42	397	55	109	749	186
1925	138	. . .	42	180	58	299	717	15
1926	137	. . .	62	499	43	25	766	399
1927	159	77	63	462	43	136	940	67
1928	213	744	53	688	55	124	1,877	1,287
1929	181	331	41	115	57	154	879	780
1930	202	233	63	144	64	289	995	335
1931	222	292	13	80	72	228	907	456
1932	352	976	124	201	86	461	2,200	1,032
Total	$1,849	$2,653	$545	$2,843	$573	$1,955	$10,418	$4,929

TABLE 22

SCHOOL INCOME AND EXPENSE, VILLAGE B, 1923–1931

Year	Income	Expense	Year	Income	Expense
1923	$ 295	$ 182	1928	$ 351	$ 510
1924	439	365	1929	351	394
1925	440	321	1930	435	420
1926	363	396	1931	429	306
1927	377	376			
			Total	$3,480	$3,270
			Average	$ 387	$ 363

TABLE 23

EXPENDITURE FOR VILLAGE, UNITED, AND DISTRICT GUARDS,
VILLAGE B, 1927–1932

	Village	United	District	Total
1927	$ ...	$ ...	$ 77	$ 77
1928	346	327	71	744
1929	48	270	13	331
1930	219	...	14	233
1931	...	281	11	292
1932	643[a]	296	37	976
Total	$1,256	$1,174	$ 223	$2,653

[a] Includes $292 of village funds that, with $1,000 raised by special subscription, were used for the purchase of arms.

TABLE 24

MISCELLANEOUS EXPENSE ITEMS IN ACCOUNTS, VILLAGE B,
NUMBER OF YEARS REPORTED AND TOTAL AMOUNTS, 1923–1932

Item	Number of years reported	Total amount	Item	Number of years reported	Total amount
Wall repairs	3	$ 400	Tips	7	$ 110
Other repairs	1	12	Buying land	1	13
Girls' school	2	84	Mortgage repayment	1	73
Indemnity	5	21	Loans to hsien	3	128
Litigation	4	200	Loans to individuals	2	38
Servant	7	288	Miscellaneous	10	589
			Total, 1923–1932	...	$1,956

TABLE 25

ORIGIN OF FAMILIES, VILLAGE C

Location	Number of families	Location	Number of families
Shansi	197	Hopei, Ta-ch'eng Hsien	5
Shantung	4	Peiping	4
Hopei, Ch'ang-p'ing Hsien	51	No data	1
Hopei, Wan-p'ing Hsien	14	Total	276

TABLE 26

YEAR DATES WHEN FAMILIES FIRST CAME TO VILLAGE, VILLAGE C

Date	Number of families	Date	Number of families
1483–1512	9	1723–1752	35
1513–1542	32	1753–1782	30
1543–1572	44	1783–1812	22
1573–1602	10	1813–1842	18
1603–1632	5	1842–1872	7
1633–1662	22	1873–1902	10
1663–1692	5	1903–1932	16
1693–1722	11		
		Total	276

TABLE 27

SIZE, TYPE, AND OWNERSHIP OF HOUSES, VILLAGE C

Number of rooms	Houses with earth roof	Houses with tile roof	Total houses	Houses rented[a]
1	4	1	5	4
2	27	3	30	15
3	96	12	108	20
4	18	5	23	4
5	43	3	46	2
6	18	1	19	3
7	6	1	7	...
8	11	...	11	...
9	4	1	5	...
10	4	...	4	...
11–15	9	2	11	...
17 or more	7	...	7	...
Total	247	29	276	48
Total rooms	1,244	122	1,366	138
Average number of rooms per family	5.0	4.2	4.95	2.9
Per cent of total rooms	91.1	8.9	...	10.1
Per cent of total houses	89.5	10.5	...	17.4

[a] Included in totals.

TABLE 28

PERSONS IN NONAGRICULTURAL OCCUPATIONS, VILLAGE C

Type of occupation	Number of persons employed	Type of occupation	Number of persons employed
Industrial	43	Commercial, inside village	22
Woolen cloth	14	Peddling	7
Vermicelli	14	Grocery shop	6
Bean curd	4	Meat shop	4
Mason	6	Undertaker	2
Carpenter	5	Small inn	2
		Teahouse	1
Communications	6	Commercial, outside	
Professional	7	village	120
Public service	4		
Private service	5	Total	207

TABLE 29

LANDOWNERSHIP OF VILLAGE HEADS, VILLAGE D

Village head	Mu owned	Mu cultivated	Mu rented out by head	Mu rented to head
1	30	84	...	54
2	4	23	...	19
3	50	50	...	...
4	17	7	10	...
5	23	10	13	...
6	42	72	...	30
7	109	31	78	...
8	5	5	...	...
9	132	54	78	...
10	102	68	34	...
11	29	15	14	...
12	0	65	...	65
13	21	11	10	...
Average	43.5	38	...	...

TABLE 30

INCOME AND EXPENSE, VILLAGE D, 1931

INCOME

Crop-money	$ 884	Fines for trespass	$ 6
Advance crop-money	60	Military refund	19
Noodle-money	17	Total	$1,022
Tuition fees	36	Loans	615
			$1,637

EXPENSE

Military		$ 419
Cash	$ 272	
Straw	33	
Straw transportation	45	
Indemnity for soldiers' depredations	69	
District		89
Police	38	
Office	31	
Loan	20	
Village		120
Guards	15	
Police	60	
Night watch, winter	45	
Crop-watching		144
Opening meeting	17	
Thanksgiving meeting	23	
Wages	104	
School		133
Teacher	90	
Expenses	43	
Purchases of supplies		44
Tree planting		28
Travel		21
Temple repair		22
Interest on loans		88
Land assessment		5
Debts from previous years		122
Miscellaneous		66
Total		$1,301
Loans repaid		615
		$1,916

TABLE 31

POSSIBLE CROP-MONEY RATES AND CROP AREA, VILLAGE E, 1920–1930

Year	Collection	Cash per mu	Cents per mu	Mu paid
1920	Extra	100	3.58[a]	2,824
	Spring	100	3.50[a]	2,732
	Fall	180	6.00[a]	2,694
1921	Fall	320	10.12[a]	2,779
1922	Fall	540	13.84[a]	2,732
1923	Spring	200	5.00[a]	2,643
	Fall	340	8.42[a]	2,663
1924	Spring	400	8.52[a]	2,736
	Extra	. . .	10.00	2,805
	Fall	900	16.36[a]	2,758
	Extra	. . .	2.00	2,550
1925	Spring	340	5.66[a]	2,684
	Fall	340	5.40[a]	2,664
1926	Spring	. . .	50.00	2,576
	Fall	860	11.62[a]	2,622
1927	Spring	. . .	10.00	2,660
	Fall	. . .	20.00	2,639
1928	Spring and fall	. . .	90.00	2,798
1929	Spring	. . .	20.00	2,842
	Fall	. . .	20.00	2,712
1930	Spring	. . .	40.00	2,823
	Fall	. . .	30.00	2,733

[a] Silver equivalent of copper rate.

TABLE 32

DETAILED INCOME AND EXPENSE, VILLAGE E, 1920–1930

Year	Total income	Total expense	Crop watch	Ferry subsidy	School fund	Village police, self-defense	Office and misc.	Military and political	Construction and repair
1920	$ 359	$ 357	$ 89	$ 12	$ 80	$ 57	$ 19	$ ...	$100
1921	281	267	86	8	80	59	11	23	...
1922	378	376	60	11	198	48	6	40	13
1923	356	379	81	17	120	58	34	57	12
1924	1,016	958	95	11	80	51	227	397	97
1925	296	321	88	14	85	65	30	...	39
1926	1,593	1,482	125	24	132	73	42	1,086	...
1927	794	976	184	23	128	118	13	510	...
1928	2,518	2,428	183	23	90	1,376	103	653	...
1929	1,110	1,296	159	21	90	592	147	258	29
1930	1,949	1,715	176	24	95	1,013	226	181	...
Total	$10,650	$10,555	$1,326	$188	$1,178	$3,510	$858	$3,205	$290
Per cent of total exp.	...	...	12.6	1.8	11.1	33.3	8.1	30.4	2.7

TABLE 33

SIZE OF FARMS REGISTERED WITH VILLAGE ASSOCIATION,
RESIDENT AND NONRESIDENT FAMILIES, VILLAGE F, 1920–1929

Number of mu	1920	1921	1922	1923	1924	1925	1926	1927	1928	1929
0– 4	21	16	14	15	17	14	14	16	14	17
5– 9	23	24	25	26	24	23	23	30	36	27
10–14	16	16	12	13	11	8	14	14	10	17
15–19	14	9	11	8	9	11	10	12	14	13
20–29	7	10	12	13	13	15	12	10	11	12
30–39	7	6	5	7	8	8	4	6	3	3
40–49	. . .	2	2	1	. . .	. . .	2	2	2	2
50–99	3	. . .	1	1	3	3	1	2	. . .	3
100 or more	1	2	2	1	1	1	2	1	2	1
No data	. . .	1	. . .	. . .	2	3	5	5	2	1
Total	92	86	84	85	88	86	87	98	94	96
Per cent, fewer than 15 mu	65.2	65.0	60.7	63.6	59.1	52.5	58.6	61.3	63.8	63.5

TABLE 34

SHOPS IN VILLAGE H

Kind of shop	Number	Kind of shop	Number
Bean curd	7	Oil	2
Miscellaneous	5	Thread	2
Drugs	4	Brewery	1
Meat	4	Matting	1
Awning	3	Reed	1
Bean-curd thread	3	Soda	1
Chair	3	String	1
Clothing	3		
Cake	2	Total	43

TABLE 35

LANDOWNERS, LAND AREA, ASSESSMENTS, AND EXCHANGE RATES,
VILLAGE I, 1907–1931

Year	Land-owners	Land area	Assessment per mu		Exchange rate
			Cash	*Dollars*	
1907	. . .	3,650.5	60	$ .027	2,200
1908	. . .	3,590.5	80	.036	2,200
1909	. . .	3,586.5	30	.013	2,400
1910	134	3,678.5	100	.040	2,500
			60ᵃ	.024	
1911	140	3,752.4	60	.023	2,600
1912	. . .	3,751.4	40	.015	2,700
1913	141	3,988.8	10	.004	2,600
1914	136	4,208.3	60	.021	2,800
			. . .ᵃ		
1915	136	4,263.3	60	.019	3,100
1916	135	4,244.5	50	.017	2,950
1917	134	4,246.5	None	None	3,000
1918	144	4,229.3	8ᵇ	.003ᵇ	3,000
			30	.010	
1919	134	4,221.4	40	.013	3,000
1920	147	4,321.9	20	.007	3,000
1921	153	4,362.0	40	.013	3,200
1922	151	4,295.8	10	.003	3,400
			140ᵃ	.041	
1923	154	4,494.5	40	.010	4,000
			200ᵃ	.050	
1924	155	4,449.1	. . .	.150	4,600
1925	158	4,501.9	. . .	.150	6,200
1926	164	4,512.7	. . .	.200	. . . .
1927	168	4,442.2	. . .	.120	. . . .
1928	177	4,393.4	. . .	.230	. . . .
1929	175	4,381.3	. . .	.150	. . . .
1930	173	4,335.9	. . .	.150	. . . .
1931	173	4,322.7	. . .	.200	. . . .

ᵃ Special assessment for village play, details missing.
ᵇ For 1917 expense.

TABLE 36

DISTRIBUTION OF FAMILIES ACCORDING TO AMOUNT OF LAND OWNED
PER FAMILY, VILLAGE I, 1910–1931
(Per cent)

Amount of land, in mu	190	1914	1917	1919	1921	1923	1926	1931
4.9 or fewer	14.2	16.9	15.7	23.1	25.5	20.1	23.2	15.0
5.0 9.9	23.9	18.3	15.6	11.9	18.3	19.5	14.6	23.1
10.0–19.9	19.4	22.1	26.2	26.2	25.4	28.6	26.2	24.2
20.0–49.9	27.6	29.5	26.8	24.6	19.0	19.5	22.0	23.2
50.0–99.9	9.7	5.1	6.7	4.5	3.3	2.6	7.9	11.0
100 or more	5.2	8.1	9.0	9.7	8.5	9.7	6.1	3.5
Total	100.0	100.0	100.0	100.0	100.0	100.0	100.0	100.0
Number of families	134	136	135	134	151	154	164	17

TABLE 37

DISTRIBUTION OF LAND ACCORDING TO AMOUNT OWNED PER FAMILY,
VILLAGE I, 1910–1931
(Per cent)

Amount of land, in mu	1910	1914	1917	1919	1921	1923	1926	1931
4.9 or fewer	1.3	1.4	1.2	1.9	1.9	1.7	2.2	1.5
5.0– 9.9	6.4	4.5	3.7	2.9	4.7	5.0	4.3	6.8
10.0–19.9	10.3	10.7	12.2	12.4	13.2	14.2	14.8	13.9
20.0–49.9	29.8	30.1	24.3	23.6	20.5	21.2	25.3	27.5
50.0–99.9	23.8	11.8	13.5	9.2	7.8	5.8	20.7	29.4
100 or more	28.4	41.5	45.1	50.0	51.9	52.1	32.7	20.9
Total	100.0	100.0	100.0	100.0	100.0	100.0	100.0	100.0
Total mu	3,678	4,208	4,246	4,221	4,362	4,494	4,512	4,323

TABLE 38

VILLAGE INCOME, VILLAGE I, 1907–1931

Year	Land-money	Land transfer[a]	Land measure	School	Mortgage interest	Misc.	Total
1907	$ 99.56	$ 2.45	$	$	$	$ 25.19	$ 127.20
1908	130.10	.03	....	....	....	16.17	146.30
1909	45.18	67.57	....	....	....	26.30	139.05
1910	147.14	125.44	....	14.80	....	38.48	325.86
1911	86.61	76.90	....	17.88	....	33.49	214.88
1912	55.58	63.47	39.50	18.50	....	37.00	214.05
1913	15.32	193.08	224.74	33.46	56.54	23.11	546.25
1914	91.03	95.34	75.38	35.98	61.07	41.56	400.36
1915	82.52	47.07	35.56	29.03	43.06	22.82	260.06
1916	72.19	95.31	9.32	35.25	70.14	59.04	341.25
1917	.10	56.14	14.25	19.65	28.50	7.66	126.30
1918	53.62	68.62	3.55	....	74.60	29.31	229.70
1919	56.17	84.10	118.85	40.74	40.80	27.33	367.99
1920	28.82	35.22	47.74	47.55	42.70	8.95	210.98
1921	54.82	....	150.84	48.32	34.74	....	288.72
1922	12.82	....	116.60	53.00	....	32.53	214.95
1923	44.94	....	299.46	24.90	3.30	184.54	557.14
1924	674.86	....	107.70	47.55	....	134.08	964.19
1925	675.28	....	128.23	106.50	....	153.80	1,063.81
1926	902.54	3.34	187.38	137.26	....	69.83	1,300.35
1927	533.06	1.20	129.97	138.61	....	9.88	812.72
1928	1,010.48	5.96	97.35	131.40	....	23.28	1,268.47
1929	657.19	16.70	258.43	154.44	....	8.94	1,095.70
1930	650.39	10.79	201.56	153.58	....	21.95	1,038.27
1931	864.54	36.86	107.80	139.50	....	206.70	1,355.40

[a] Land transfer fees were discontinued in 1921; the income from 1926 on is for "seal fees," for attaching the village seal to mortgage documents.

TABLE 39

VILLAGE EXPENSES, VILLAGE I, 1907–1931

Year	Ti-chia	Clerk	School	Night watch	Agent[a]	Military	Misc.	Total
1907	....	....	....	....	....	....	....	$ 144.32
1908	....	....	....	....	....	....	....	147.57
1909	....	....	....	....	....	....	....	120.27
1910	$15.10	$ 9.60	$133.20	$12.40	$	$	$ 30.52	200.82
1911	15.38	11.54	88.22	11.08	9.20	....	100.12	235.54
1912	18.87	11.11	80.78	12.00	18.74	....	29.30	170.80
1913	17.31	15.38	92.39	17.31	48.92	....	44.85	236.16
1914	16.07	14.29	82.11	16.07	24.87	....	226.29	379.70
1915	14.52	12.90	78.81	14.52	10.77	....	110.28	241.80
1916	21.62	16.95	155.63	15.22	19.90	....	50.09	279.41
1917	24.76	14.00	127.83	15.00	14.82	....	52.38	248.79
1918	24.76	14.33	15.00	15.00	7.33	.87	116.80	194.09
1919	24.72	14.33	148.25	15.00	42.00	....	70.85	315.15
1920	24.76	14.33	133.03	15.00	26.58	....	65.11	278.81
1921	21.88	7.81	130.41	14.06	....	3.38	63.90	241.44
1922	20.59	7.35	214.19	13.23	....	13.38	50.30	319.04
1923	25.00	6.25	441.70	12.00	....	....	49.24	534.19
1924	31.87	17.86	754.93	12.00	....	116.22	80.30	1,013.18
1925	38.17	18.39	289.97	43.00	....	677.19	3.06	1,069.78
1926	42.00	20.00	224.65	76.36	34.52	489.80	225.20	1,112.53
1927	42.00	20.00	337.99	73.64	257.70	....	141.80	873.13
1928	42.00	20.00	363.10	81.00	146.78	120.18	109.84	882.90
1929	42.00	20.00	304.16	....	280.23	289.35	225.02	1,160.76
1930	42.00	20.00	282.22	....	121.64	422.49	285.55	1,173.90
1931	42.00	20.00	235.59	5.00	274.42	797.54	94.61	1,469.16

[a] In this column, the amounts from 1926 on are for guard expense.

TABLE 40

Income and Expenses, Village I, 1910

INCOME		EXPENSES	
Land-money	$147.14	Political agent	$ 15.10
Land-money for previous year	2.60	Village clerk	9.60
Commission on land sales		Night watchman	12.40
and mortgages	125.44	Schoolteacher	32.00
Fee for measuring land	4.33	School rent	72.00
Tuition fees	14.80	School, other expenses	29.20
Deed papers	5.50	Mortgage taxes	9.76
Interest on bond	5.22	Deed papers	1.13
Interest on loan	1.72	Miscellaneous	19.61
Sale of trees	1.00		
Surplus from play	15.97	Total	$200.80
Contribution for school coal	1.20	Loan	44.69
Gain on exchange	.92	Deposit	84.00
Total	$325.84		$329.49
Loan repaid	1.72		
	$327.56		

TABLE 41

Income and Expenses, Village I, 1930

INCOME		EXPENSES	
Land-money	$ 650.40	Political agent	$ 42.00
Land measurement	201.56	Clerk	20.00
School fund	153.58	Home guard	121.64
Sealing documents	10.79	Schoolteacher	180.00
Deed papers	5.00	Other school expenses	89.22
Stamps	3.25	Water carrier	13.00
Wagon rent (army)	12.60	Military	422.49
Miscellaneous	1.10	Military bond	51.45
		Poles for electric lines	14.26
Total	$1,038.28	Peoples' bank	15.00
		Miscellaneous	204.83
		Total	$1,173.89

Glossary

(Including village terms, currency, weights, and measures)

BLACK LAND—Land not entered on tax rolls.

BIG HANDS—Bullies; also professional crop-stealers.

CASH—Bronze coins with a square hole in their center; one thousandth (0.001) of a TAEL.

CATTY—One and one-third pounds.

CENT—One hundredth (0.01) of a DOLLAR.

CHAO-MU (昭穆)—"Bright and solemn"; the system for arranging spirit tablets in the family shrine and graves in the family cemetery, even generations on the left, odd generations on the right. Right and left are designated from the standpoint of one looking from the altar or the top of the cemetery.

CHEN (鎮)—Town.

CHIA (甲)—Neighborhood of 10 families, a subdivision of a PAO or a LI; 10 chia equal one pao or one li.

CHIA-CHANG (甲長)—Usually, the head of a 10-family neighborhood; in some places in Shansi, the leader in charge of the political affairs of several villages.

CHIA-P'U (家譜)—Family history.

CHIA-SHOU (家首)—Head of a CHIA.

CHIEN (間)—Space between two roof trusses, usually from 10 to 12 feet square. In small houses a room is one chien.

CHIHLI—The name of Hopei Province before 1928, when Chihli was divided largely into Hopei, Jehol, and Chahar provinces.

CH'ING-CH'UAN (青圈)—"Green circle"; land adjacent to and controlled by a village.

CHING-LI (經理)—Village administrator or manager.

CH'ING-MIAO HUI (青苗會)—Green Crop Association.

CH'ING MING (清明)—Spring tomb festival held in April, 106 days after the winter solstice; Arbor Day.

CHOU (州)—Administrative unit for several HSIEN, discontinued in 1913.

CH'Ü (區)—District; a subdivision of a HSIEN.

CHU-CHIA (主家)—Head of a SHE.

CHUANG (莊)—Village; equivalent of TS'UN.

CHUANG-CHANG (莊長)—Village head; equivalent of TS'UN-CHANG.

COPPER—Copper coin; a single copper equals 10 CASH; a double copper equals 20 CASH.

CROP-MONEY—Funds collected from landowners and operators to finance crop-watching and other village activities.

DOLLAR—Chinese silver coin, YUAN, containing seven mace, two candareens (0.72 Chinese ounces) of silver, 890 fine.

EN-KUNG (恩貢)—One of the literary degrees awarded to scholars successful in special examinations regularly held in Peking every twelve years or sometimes on special occasions. Candidates were chosen by the Commissioner of Education of the province. Also awarded, *honoris causa*, by the emperor.

FA-CH'UAN (法船)—Paper boat burned on the fifteenth day of the seventh month.

FENG-SHUI (風水)—"Wind and water"; the natural influences for good and evil of a locality.

FU (府)—Administrative unit next smaller than a province and larger than a CHOU, discontinued in 1913.

GREEN CIRCLE—Land controlled by a village.

HAN CHIEH (寒節)—The Cold Festival, held on the first day of the tenth month.

HO HUI (合會)—United Association.

HO-CHUANG HUI (合莊會)—United Association.

HSIANG (鄉)—Incorporated village or community, of a minimum of 100 families.

HSIANG-CHANG (鄉長)—Village head.

HSIANG-SHOU (鄉首)—"Incense head," or "head of pilgrims"; also, a community leader. Same as HSIANG-T'OU.

HSIANG-TING (鄉丁)—Village employee; replaced TI-CHIA in 1932.

HSIANG-T'OU (鄉頭)—"Incense head"; sometimes a religious leader, sometimes a village association executive.

HSIANG-YÜEH (鄉約)—Village contract for mutual improvement and support. Also, a village officer in Shansi, appointed by the village head for a one-year term of unpaid service; his work was similar to that of the police; higher rank than TI-FANG.

HSIEN (縣)—Political administrative unit, equivalent to a county.

HSIEN-CHANG (縣長)—Magistrate of a HSIEN.

HU (戶)—Residence unit, area using one gate for access to village street.

HUI (會)—Association.

HUI-SHOU (會首)—Head of a HUI.

HUI-T'OU (會頭)—Head of a HUI.

HUNG-CH'IANG HUI (紅槍會)—"Red Spear Society"; a secret society in Honan and Shantung.

Hung-fan (紅礬)—A common poison.

I-p'o Hui (義坡會)—Public Ground Association.

I-t'ien She (義田社)—Public Field Association.

K'ang (坑)—A raised brick bed, large enough for five or six persons; it was warmed in winter by heat from the stove used for cooking the family's food.

Kaoliang (高梁)—A nonsaccharine sorghum grown for its grain. The leaves are used for stock food and the stalks for construction work.

Keng-fu (更夫)—Night watchman.

Keng-p'ai—(更排)—Wooden identification board carried by night watchman.

Kuan (罐)—One thirty-fourth of a Tou.

Kuan Ti (關帝)—Chinese god of war; also a god of wealth.

Kung-cheng (公正)—"Just and fair," used as a title for a village leader.

Kung-cheng She-shou (公正社首)—Head of a village association.

Kung-i Hui (公義會)—"Righteous Public Association."

Kung-sheng (貢生)—Literary degree; see En-kung. Also granted *honoris causa*.

Land-money—Annual payment to village by landowners in village where there was no crop-watching.

Li (釐)—Administrative unit of 100 families.

Li (釐)—Tax unit subdivision of a Hsien.

Li (里)—One third of a mile.

Li-chang (里長)—Political leader for several villages, appointed by the magistrate.

Li-lao (里老)—Just and able leader assigned to act as arbitrator.

Liang (兩)—A Chinese ounce, one sixteenth of a Catty.

Lin (隣)—Administrative unit of 5 families.

Lin-chang (隣長)—Head of a Lin.

Local Man—A village resident appointed by the magistrate to act as a liaison person between the village administration and the Hsien government. Ti-pao.

Lü (閭)—Administrative unit of 25 families, 5 Lin.

Lü-chang (閭長)—Head of a Lü.

Miao (廟)—Temple.

Mien-ch'ien (麵錢)—Money paid for a meal with noodles.

Mu (畝)—One sixth of an acre.

Noodle-money—Amount paid toward the cost of the meal served to landowners and operators when they paid their crop-money. Noodles were the main dish.

P'ai (牌)—Section of a village, usually 10 families.

P'ai-chang (牌長)—Head of a P'ai.

P'ai-t'ou (牌頭)—Section head, the assistant to a Chuang-chang.

PAN-SHIH JEN（辦事人）—Men who conduct affairs, association heads.

P'ANG SHE-SHOU（幫社首）—Associate village head.

PAO（保）—Village administrative unit of 100 families.

PAO-CHANG（保長）—Village leader appointed by the magistrate, on nomination of the village. Also the head of a PAO, 100 families.

PAO-CHENG（保正）—Same as TI-PAO, a political agent living in a village, appointed by the magistrate.

PAO-CHIA（保甲）—Political organization originated by Wang An-shih of the Sung dynasty for mutual control in ordinary times and mutual assistance in troublous times. (PAO, 100 families; CHIA, 10 families.)

PIEN-TS'UN（編村）—Incorporated village.

RED SPEARS—See HUNG-CH'IANG HUI.

SATELLITE VILLAGE—Separate residence area, part of the political organization of a nearby larger village.

SHE（社）—Village association; also a group of 50 families borrowing grain from a village granary.

SHE-SHOU（社首）—Head of a SHE.

SHE-TS'ANG（社倉）—System of village granaries initiated by Chu Tzu of the Sung dynasty.

SHEN-T'OU（神頭）—"God head"; a village land unit. Thirty mu of land equal one shen-t'ou; 20–30 mu equal one half shen-t'ou.

SHENG（升）—One tenth of a TOU.

SHOU-SHIH（守事）—Head of affairs.

SPIRIT MONEY—Plain paper cut in the shape of coins; silvered paper formed in the shape of silver bullion "shoes." Burned so that the soul could use it in the other world.

TA-HUI（大會）—Big HUI.

TA-SHE（大社）—Big SHE.

TAEL—One Chinese ounce of silver bullion.

TAN（石）—A bag; usually a measure of grain, 10 TOU.

T'AN-TOU（探斗）—Keeper of the official TOU measure.

TI-CHIA（地甲）—Political agent in a village, changed to HSIANG-TING in 1932.

TI-FANG（地方）—Similar to TI-PAO; also, village officer appointed for one-year term of unpaid service.

TI-PAO（地保）—LOCAL MAN; local representative of magistrate.

TIAO（弔）—Money of account, ordinarily equal to 1,000 CASH. Some villages used a 500-cash tiao.

TOU（斗）—Peck measure for grain: 20 catties of millet, 19 catties of wheat, 17 catties of kaoliang.

TS'UN（村）—Village.

TS'UN-CHANG（村長）—Village head. During T'ang dynasty a gatekeeper and sheriff.

Ts'un-fu (村副)—Assistant village head.

Ts'un-shou (村首)—Village head.

Ts'un-t'ou (村頭)—Village head.

Ts'ung Chiu-shou (總區首)—Chief head of village association.

Ts'ung-kuan (總管)—General manager of village affairs.

Ts'ung She-shou (總社首)—Supreme village head.

T'u Ti (土地)—Local god.

Tuan-ch'ing Hui (斷青會)—Green Crop Cutting Association.

United Village—Two or more neighboring residence areas politically joined together.

Village Council—Officers of village elected under terms of Hsien Organization Act of 1929.

Wu-tao (五道)—Local gods to whom deaths are reported. They represent Heaven, Hell, men, animals, and hungry devils.

Yang-ke (秧歌)—Planting songs; name given local village plays.

Yuan (圓)—Silver coin; same as Dollar.

Yüeh-cheng (約正)—Village contract chief.

Yüeh-chiang (約講)—Village contract lecturer.

Yüeh-fu (岳飛)—Assistant contract chief.

Yüeh-shih (約師)—Village contract recorder.

HSIEN IN WHICH
ONE OR MORE VILLAGES
WERE STUDIED

HONAN
Chen-ch'iu
Chi
Hsin-hsiang
Hui
Lin
Yen-shih
Yü-shih

HOPEI
Ch'ang-p'ing
Ku-an
Shen-tse
Shu-lu
Ting
T'ung
Wan-p'ing
Yung-ch'ing

SHANSI
Chao-ch'eng
Chi
Ch'i
Chieh-hsiu
Ch'in
Fen-hsi
Ho-ching
Hsin
Hsing
Hsi-yang
Kuo
Lan
Li-shih
Lin-chin
Ling-ch'iu
Ling-shih
Luan
Lu-ch'eng
Ning-wu
Shen-ch'ih
Ta-t'ung

SHANSI
T'ai-ku
T'ai-yuan
Ting-hsiang
Wen-sh'ui
Wu-chai
Wu-hsiang
Wu-t'ai
Yang-ch'eng
Yang-chü (T'ai-yuan)
Yü-hsiang
Yü-tz'u

SHANTUNG
Chang-ch'iu
Chi-nan
Ch'ing-chou
Li-ch'eng (Chi-nan)
Ling
T'ai-an
Tsou-p'ing

INDEX